Anthropological Approaches to the Study of Ethnomedicine

Anthropological Approaches
to the Study
of Ethnomedicine

Edited by
Mark Nichter

University of Arizona
Tucson, USA

Gordon and Breach Science Publishers

Switzerland USA Australia Belgium France Germany Great Britain India Japan
Malaysia Netherlands Russia Singapore

First published 1992
Second printing 1994

Gordon and Breach Science Publishers

Y-Parc
Chemin de la Sallaz
1400 Yverdon, Switzerland

Christburger Str. 11
10405 Berlin
Germany

820 Town Center Drive
Langhorne, Pennsylvania 19047
United States of America

Post Office Box 90
Reading, Berkshire RG1 8JL
Great Britain

Private Bag 8
Camberwell, Victoria 3124
Australia

3-14-9, Okubo
Shinjuku-ku, Tokyo 169
Japan

12 Cour Saint-Eloi
75012 Paris
France

Emmaplein 5
1075 AW Amsterdam
Netherlands

Some of the essays in this book were first published in Volume 13, Numbers 1–2 of the journal *Medical Anthropology*.

Cover: Possessed priest (pujari) of a Bhuta cult shrine, Tulunad Southwestern India. Patron Bhuta spirits promise fertility, bounty, and protection to the village in return for tribute and fame. Illness incurable by routine forms of treatment is interpreted as a sign of the Bhuta's anger associated with unfulfilled vows and ritual transgressions.

Library of Congress Cataloging-in-Publication Data

Anthropological approaches to the study of ethnomedicine / edited by
  Mark Nichter.
      p.   cm.
    ". . . an expanded collection of essays . . . originally organized for
  a special edition of the journal Medical anthropology, volume 13
  (1–2) 1991"—Pref.
    Includes bibliographical references.
    ISBN 2–88124–530–7.—ISBN 2–88124–529–3 (pbk.)
    1. Folk medicine.   2. Medical anthropology.   I. Nichter, Mark.
  GR880.A8   1990
  615.8'—dc20
                                                                    92–20369
                                                                         CIP

Contents

Preface

This book consists of an expanded collection of essays on ethnomedicine originally organized for a special edition of the journal *Medical Anthropology* [Volume 13 (1–2) 1991]. The collection represents a broad range of research illustrating contemporary trends in the anthropological study of ethnomedicine which span positivist, interpretive and critical theory, as well as postmodern concerns and approaches. The objective of this volume is to broaden appreciation of ethnomedicine as a multidimensional subject of inquiry contributing to and benefiting from contemporary anthropological theory and methods. It is the hope of the contributors that the collection will raise questions which inspire future research endeavors. Each of the research approaches represented has a contribution to make to ethnomedical scholarship. Consideration of the strengths and weaknesses of multiple approaches ensures against theoretical closure and opens the way to productive dialogue.

Introduction

By M. Nichter

Ten essays and a critical commentary highlighting major themes and suggesting avenues of further investigation comprise this collection. The essays draw upon ethnographic research in Central and South America, the Caribbean, South and Southeast Asia, and Africa. Individual essays discuss the importance of systematically collecting data on measures of healing efficacy, the prevalence of folk illnesses, and the distribution of knowledge about illness attributes; the negotiation and instantiation of illness identities; the power of discourse to produce as well as cure affliction; metamedical discourse as moral commentary; linkages between medico-religious institutions, models of self, power, and the state; and the relationship between ethnomedical research and anthropological studies of the body, gender relations, self, and "Other." The essays are divided into four sections focusing on (1) epidemiological approaches to the study of ethnomedicine; (2) discursive practices in the context of healing; (3) the body, state, and production of medico-religious knowledge; and (4) illness as metaphor as well as vehicle for self expression.[1]

Before presenting these ten essays, I would like to address two fundamental issues influencing the current state of ethnomedical scholarship. The first relates to the scope of ethnomedical studies and the second to the construction of "Other" as it influences the presentation of ethnomedical data.[2]

Ethnomedical inquiry is multidimensional and metamedical. It is based on the interpretation of bodily experience as well as the embodiment of ideology, discourse as well as disease, accommodation as well as resistance, and healing as well as curing. Juxtaposed to medical anthropology which often has an applied agenda, ethnomedical inquiry is less guided by pragmatic interests such as the transfer of knowledge or the evaluation of health-related behavior in terms of public health criteria. Ethnomedicine, as the organizing theme for this volume, is broadly conceived. It entails a study of the full range and distribution of health related experience, discourse, knowledge, and practice among different strata of a population; the situated meaning the aforementioned has for peoples at a given historical juncture; transformations in popular health culture and medical systems concordant with social change; and the social relations of health related ideas, behaviors, and practices.

All too often, ethnomedicine is simplistically compartmentalized as a subfield of medical anthropology, delimited to the study of folk illnesses, traditional medical systems, herbal remedies, and healing rituals.[3] While these subjects are central to ethnomedicine, they are points of departure, not the focus of a fixed gaze. Ethnomedicine is not limited to the study of medical traditions. It is more than the rarified or privileged study of the spectacular or the quintessential, be this in the form of exotic healing rituals, surgical procedures, or cultural bound syndromes (Kleinman 1980).4 Ethnomedicine is grounded in the study of everyday life, perceptions of the normal and natural, the desirable and feared, and that form of embodied knowledge known as common sense as it emerges in efforts to establish or reestablish health as one aspect of well-being. Ethnomedical inquiry entails the study of how well-being and suffering are experienced bodily as well as socially, the multivocality of somatic communication, and processes of healing as they are contextualized and directed toward the person, household, community and state, land and cosmos.5 Ethnomedicine also entails a study of the afflicted body as a space where competing ideologies are contested and emergent ideologies are developed through medico-religious practices and institutions which guide the production of knowledge.

Ethnomedical studies commonly address one or more of the following twelve broad and often overlapping forms of inquiry:

1. Descriptive studies of folk, non-biomedical, or biomedical forms of healing inclusive of health beliefs, notions of ethnophysiology, etiology, dietetics, pharmacopeia, technology, and ritual.

2. Historical studies of disease and medical treatment which look at the relationship between disease conceptualizations, systems of healing, and the moral values and social order of civilizations.

3. Ethnographic studies which attempt to discover "authentic" cultural forms of illness and healing in need of documentation before they are "lost" or "corrupted" by contact with the world system inclusive of cosmopolitan market-oriented forms of entrepreneurial medicine.

4. Studies of continuities and discontinuities in medical systems and health cultures inclusive of popular interpretations of expert systems of knowledge and changing perceptions of health.

5. Studies of health care seeking and patterns of resort (e.g., by illness, age, gender) in pluralistic health care arenas which may include multiple forms of traditional and cosmopolitan medicine.

6. Studies of illness classification, the language of illness, and the negotiation of illness identities within therapy management groups. This entails the study of illness taxonomies as well as taskonomies (Nichter 1989); genres for conveying health related knowledge; illness narratives and their moral implications; styles of practitioner-patient discourse; and reasons why affliction (severity, causality, etc.) is and is not spoken about directly and with specificity (e.g., the study of ambiguity, the use of qualifiers, diminutives). These studies range broadly from research inspired by ethnoscience and cultural idealism to social interactional studies paying credence to agency and the social relations underlying the production of illness representations.

7. Research which documents the relationship between illness beliefs and social norms. The role of sickness attribution in maintaining social order is emphasized. Often focused upon are societies having no formal institutions responsible for social control or societies in which the effectiveness of such institutions has waned.

8. Critical studies of medical systems and their transformations which situate them historically in terms of the relations of production and the conditions of political economy they support; domination in the form of medicalization; and health commodification. This includes studies which attend to the ways in which medical traditions and systems serve state apparatuses (be they precapitalist or capitalist), as well as studies which examine the ways and means coexisting ideologies are mediated and accommodated by medico-religious systems responsive to change. It also includes historical studies of disease and those factors favoring alternative interpretations of etiology and searches for knowledge.

9. Studies of positively and negatively valued somatic states which serve as: (a) natural symbols for the social body; (b) a powerful idiom for core cultural meanings and preoccupations; (c) evidence of hegemony and biopower (manipulation of the body concordant with modes of production/consumption and the needs of the state); (d) medical iconography where diagnosis constitutes exegesis rendering the body a social text within which corruption and resistance are visible; and (e) bodily expressions of resistance, distress, and/or fortitude.

10. Comparative studies of cultural illnesses and healing techniques guided by either a search for universalism or cultural relativism.

11. Cross-cultural comparative studies of human physiological processes (e.g., birth, maturation, aging) with culture constituting a mediating or confounding variable.

12. Studies of the efficacy of medicines, healing techniques, and procedures which are contextualized and attend to their content as well as performance, expectations, as well as criteria of assessment.

The contributions of these studies to ethnomedical knowledge are as much a result of the questions they raise as by the data they generate. The variety of contributions makes clear that when one vantage point is advocated to the exclusion of others, theoretical closure is fostered.

Comaroff (1981, 1983) has warned against two general forms of theoretical closure which are worth restating and expanding upon. The first entails "analytical involution," the decontextualization of healing systems and/or illness as a discrete domain of empirical inquiry. Healing systems and illness constructs take on meaning in context, not as bounded sets of activities, imposed categories, or stock responses to objectified forms of misfortune. An analysis of illness and idioms of distress, forms of conflict resolution, and modes of therapeutic transformation demands a multidimensional assessment sensitive to coexisting health ideologies and shifts in social relations associated with modes of production, forms of technology, the availability and distribution of resources, changes in population dynamics, etc. Unreflective empiricism applied to the study of health, illness and healing is ethnocentric, yielding "disembodied classifications of terms, whose meanings remain nominal, telling us nothing of their pragmatic use, their polysemic quality, their cultural significance" (Comaroff 1983: 9).

A second mode of theoretical closure which Comaroff has cautioned against is associated with an objectified, often reified notion of culture wherein health beliefs/healing practices are interpreted in relation to a fixed set of values, ideas, and social relations which underestimates intracultural variability and resistance. Characteristic of the second mode of closure is an ahistorical approach to the study of health cultures and medical systems. One form of this approach poses a distinction between traditional and modern modes of thought.[6] This distinction is based on notions of closed and open systems as these relate to the expansion of one's knowledge base. It is wrongly presumed that traditional systems of ethnomedicine are circular in their reasoning, are consensual and complacent, rely little on experimentation, and entail no critical thinking (Janzen 1981; Trawick 1986). Biomedicine, in contrast, is presented as logical and self-correcting through the deployment of standardized, replicable procedures which test for the falsification of hypotheses. Overlooked is a discussion of the relations of power and production of knowledge crucial to an understanding of any system of ethnomedicine, including biomedicine, and its transformation over time.

Biomedical research is not the "objective other" which it is often made out to be. As Latour (1988) has argued, scientific innovation does not merely gain acceptance through recognition of the merits of scientific proof. The diffusion of scientific innovation is influenced by political and economic contingencies which mobilize allies.[7] "Scientific reasoning" is motivated and as much a product of culture and practical reason as are traditional systems of ethnomedicine.[8] As Karl Popper (1959: 93–95) pointed out long ago, scientific facts are saturated both by theories that purport to account for them and by a host of cultural metaphors and assumptions (Roscoe 1991). Culturally stylized biomedical diseases (menopause: Lock 1982, Martin 1988; PMS: Johnson 1987; hypoglycemia: Hunt, Browner, and Jordan 1989, Singer 1984; chronic fatigue syndrome: Greenberg 1990; obesity: Ritenbaugh 1982; somatization disorders: Kirmayer 1986) and the metaphors which guide biomedical thinking and education (Caster 1983; Davis-Floyd 1990; Martin 1987, 1990, 1991; Millard 1990; Osherson and Amarasingham 1981; Nichter 1990a) reveal the ideologies which pervade contemporary American ethnomedicine.

The ethics of a strictly empirical and unmotivated science has itself been questioned. Toulman (1982), for example, has argued that a modernist science guided strictly by empiricism needs to be replaced by a postmodern paradigm which is ecological in the sense of Bateson's notion of creatura (Bateson 1972; Bateson and Bateson 1988). This postmodern paradigm is based on motivated inductive reasoning inspired by a new appreciation for cosmology and a reconsideration of agency as a means of saving our planet.[9] Basic to this paradigm is a reconceptualization of biomedicine as ethnomedicine and science in general as motivated.

Many medical anthropologists have noted that biomedicine is a form of ethnomedicine, but several go on to treat disease as a universal construct in contrast to illness as an individual's cultural and idiosyncratic experience of socially devalued states of being. This dichotomy leads to muddles regarding the use of the terms illness and disease (Hahn 1984; Shweder 1988). More consistent with an ethnomedical perspective is the notion that disease is a construct created and reproduced by any/all medical systems on the basis of some generally agreed upon criteria which do not necessarily privilege knowledge based upon "visible democratic facts" (Keller and Grontkowski 1983).

The second mode of closure may also be fostered by two other forms of analysis. The first entails the study of health related behavior from an adaptationist vantage which is functionalist and teleological (Alland 1987; Bargatzky 1984; Singer 1989a). This approach examines the survival value of health related acts in terms of the dominant social structure, motivated notions of the natural and normal, and a limited range of physiological and social response. Some forms of cultural behavior have been argued to be "healthy" in only the most circuitous ways. The significance of health/illness related behaviors needs to be assessed in broader terms which pay credence to power relations (domination, discipline, resistance) as they are articulated at the site of the body. The consideration of the extent to which behaviors are transitional, adaptive, or maladaptive over the long or short run requires assessment which attends to several different levels of analysis.

Another form of analysis which leads to theoretical closure assesses medical systems as epiphenomena of a prevailing and reified hegemony which constrains through symbolic domination at the site of the body (Comaroff 1985). Some critiques of biomedicine, for example, leave one with the impression that there is a reified "biomedicine" out there serving the interests of "capitalism" through processes such as commodification and medicalization. While such analyses are insightful, they mask as well as reveal (Morgan 1987). Underappreciated are coexisting ideologies embedded in medical practices and discourse, the role of medico-religious institutions in the mediation of conflicts between competing ideologies, and the heterodox and dynamic nature of medical traditions.[10] Ethnomedical studies may benefit significantly from extending Wolf's examination of the interplay between capitalist and precapitalist social formations to the health care arena. As Wolf has pointed out, the social relations of modes of production "may characterize only part of the total range of interactions in a society; they may comprehend all of a society; or they may transcend particular, historically constituted systems of social interaction" (Wolf 1982: 76–77).[11] Sociopolitical assessments of the ontology and social relations of illness forms, and the popularity of systems of medical treatment require that the researcher take stock of the "discipline" of medicine as well as the means by which medical systems provide spaces for emergent, negotiated forms of resistance at the site of the body.

Many scholars of ethnomedicine have come to recognize the pitfalls of theoretical closure. Some have argued for a broad-based medical anthropology and ethnomedicine (e.g., Fabrega 1990; Kleinman 1988; Morgan 1990), while others have advocated a narrowing of focus either as a means of increasing resolution or as a corrective for vantages which have been underappreciated. Among "critical medical anthropologists," for example, some have directed attention to hegemonic and counterhegemonic forces broadly influencing sickness (e.g., Comaroff 1981b; Frankenberg 1980), while others have focused on political economic factors influencing the distribution and social relations of sickness as well as curative practice (e.g., Singer 1989b, 1990). Another group has redirected attention to biocultural assessments of behavior in an effort to complement, if not place in relief, interpretive and critical studies which address the body but not physiology (e.g., Browner, Montellano, Rubel 1988; McElroy 1990). Members of both groups are presently exploring common ground in studies attentive to broader, multidimensional conceptualizations sensitive to social relations, political economy, and the limitations of models of adaptation (Armelagos, Leatherman, Ryan, and Sibley 1992). Still others have tried to bring ethnomedicine to its senses, placing emphasis on how sound and movement (e.g., Bahr and Hefer 1978; Roseman 1988) as well as smell

(Corbin 1986; Howes 1987; Winter 1976) and taste (Stoller 1989) inspire memory (Ackerman 1990) and become repositories of cosmological, social, and therapeutic power.

A second general issue I would like to raise flows from the forms of closure highlighted above. It involves the motivation underlying accounts of health behavior and healing systems inclusive of voices privileged and vantages assumed. Of concern here is the construction of an "other" as it serves the implicit interests of the researcher. Two vantages inform a great many studies of ethnomedicine: the "nostalgic" and the "paternalistic scientific." Each of these vantages entails coextensive stances.

Rosaldo (1989), in a recent discussion of imperialist nostalgia and colonialism, has noted that nostalgia has a capacity to transform the complicit into innocent bystanders vis-à-vis mystification. This often entails a fair amount of romanticism. Anthropology is implicated for the role it plays in reproducing the ideology of imperialist nostalgia through a search for authentic cultural forms untainted by modernity. Tradition is invented in the sense that flexible customs are transformed into static prescriptions (Ranger 1983) reflecting the motives and purposes of "writers of culture" (Linnekin 1991; Wagner 1975).

Imperialist nostalgia may underlie some studies of ethnomedicine where attention has been drawn away from power relations underscoring health practice to an appreciation of the intricacies of a healing ritual, treatment procedure, or cognitive model. It may also influence studies of healing ritual and traditional medicine which present them as enduring and conservative instead of innovative and responsive to change. Nostalgia is further engaged in by those who have a need to create a non-Western, traditional medicine as a means of calling attention to the alienating, dehumanizing practices of biomedicine.[12] Typically, positive aspects of traditional medicine/health culture are played up, pronounced, or assumed. They are then juxtaposed to negative aspects of biomedicine whereby patients are reified into objects of knowledge and doctors rely on technology to cure. Curing is juxtaposed to healing as meaningful conciliation of sources of suffering.

For example, the communication skills of a traditional practitioner may be praised and adherence to traditional practitioners (their regimens, advice, etc.) presumed, while poor communication, impersonality, and noncompliance are associated with cosmopolitan practitioners. Traditional practitioners are described as sharing with a populace common cultural models without the anthropologist demonstrating consensus or supplying data to confirm that traditional practitioners engage in meaningful communication or a negotiation of an illness identity any more than skillful cosmopolitan practitioners. The clinical space is often described in terms of the power to heal being transformed into the power to control. Broad stereotypes are made such that the medicalization of life problems by traditional practitioners and the cultural sensitivity of doctors are underreported.

This is an issue which Carolyn Nordstrom and I (1989) explored in a study of health care seeking to practitioners of both biomedicine and ayurvedic medicine in Sri Lanka. We identified two patterns which crosscut medical systems. The first pattern involved patients who searched for a medicine which had the power to cure or served as a commodified fix for health. The second pattern involved the search for a practitioner who had the power of the hand to cure one's illness through an affinity to their person. Underlying these two patterns of care seeking are capitalist and precapitalist values having particular cultural salience as well as metamedical uses of illness as means of establishing self identity.

Another form of nostalgia is indulged in by some proponents of a "self styled," postmodern anthropology. Keenly sensitive to the authorial intentions of ethnographers, scholars associated with this movement champion reflexivity and caution against the embedded bias of an authoritative ethnographic voice which privileges order. The movement serves as a corrective for ethnography, inclusive of ethnomedicine. It encourages anthropologists to document and reflect upon the fragmentary nature of the postmodern world, avoid a totalizing narrative voice, and pay credence to emergent dialogue between informants and themselves. Anthropologists are encouraged to engage in collaborative ethnographies wherein the anthropologist becomes a "reader of cultural criticisms discovered ethnographically, rather than an independent intellectual originator of critical insight" (Marcus and Fischer 1986: 133).

Paying credence to the fragmentary aspects of life is important as a complement to ethnographic studies of social structure, power relations, and health ideology which emphasize patterns at the expense of diversity, models at the expense of ambiguity and alienation. However, the privileging of the fragmentary, the reflexive and resistance is itself historically situated, and the product of a strikingly Western postmodernism (Wolfe 1988). Proponents of anthropology as cultural critique who read into ethnographies strategies and intentions of fictionalization are themselves open to charges of countertransference and ethnocentrism (Strathern 1987a, b).

"Postmodern despair" over truth as unknowable constitutes an inversion of Western arrogance by shifting attention to the anthropologist.

In turning inward, making himself, his motives, and his experience the thing to be confronted, the postmodern anthropologist locates the "other" in himself. It is as if, finding the exotic closed off to him, the anthropologist constructs himself as the "exotic." Ethnographers are turned into the natives to be understood and ethnography into a virgin territory to be explored (Mascia-Lees, Sharpe, and Cohen 1989).

Just as the crude application of a political economic analysis leaves one with the sense that it is the same story again and again, many postmodernist accounts leave one with the sense that the experience of decentering and fragmentation is always central.[13] Both paradigms are based on the assumption that culture is epiphenomenal and the proponents of each use a discourse about culture to pursue their own projects. While postmodern concerns are relevant to the study of ethnomedicine (e.g., Trawick, the present volume), ethnomedical inquiry that narrowly focuses on a search for "the other within us" must beware of nostalgia of a different order.[14]

A second means of constructing the other in ethnomedical studies is through the "paternalistic scientific." This approach may take several forms. In each, science represents the moment of the universal under which particulars are subsumed. Science constitutes the universal point of reference. This posture is apparent in studies of ethnomedicine which appear to be relativistic, or pay credence to the emic classification of illness, but minimize (except by lip service) the emic aspects of bioscience. The biomedical is taken as a ubiquitous gold standard against which all other forms of knowledge may be judged.[15] Just as some researchers have been motivated to create an "other" in the form of traditional medicine to reveal the shortcomings of biomedicine, other researchers have been motivated to represent traditional medicine as the vestige of a closed system of thought supplemented by fortuitous practices which have survival value.

Another group of scholars have assumed a paternalistic scientific vantage while sifting through traditional health cultures for practices which make biomedical sense. Among this group there is a tendency to "scientize" culture. An analysis of the survival of cultural practices is based upon biomedical criteria. Trial and error practice motivated by the doctrine of signature and sympathetic magic reasoning is recognized. The assumption is made that cultural practice that has survived must have some "scientific" basis.[16] For example, an Indian colleague once explained to me that the reason Hindu devotees circumambulate a ficus tree as part of a particular ritual performance was because of the ozone given off by the tree. The rejuvenation value of ozone contributed to the survival value of the practice. An educated Brahman priest overhearing the conversation immediately retorted, "This vapor is something our wise *rishis* (sages) did know about. They designed rituals so that this wisdom would not be lost to the people over the ages." I was at once presented with a paternalistic scientific explanation, "Look what the innocents discovered by 'trial and error'," and a Sanskritic nostalgic explanation which emerged with scientism, "Our *rishis* knew everything there was to know and designed life accordingly."[17] Ozone remained ubiquitous as the measure of the ritual's worth.

The example is instructive. The cultural meanings of the ficus tree are as manifold as its branches, from its medicinal properties to the sound of its leaves in the wind, the color of its sap, and the shape of its leaves to the meaning the tree assumes when defining sacred space or providing a "rejuvenating vapor." The construction of history, like an analysis of why people circumambulate the ficus tree, is motivated and prompted by changing measures of legitimacy reflected in discourse. In India, the Sanskritic and the "scientific" are merging in popular culture apparent in emergent representations of ayurveda cloaked in the language of science complete with statistical tests and reference to experimental design (Nichter 1989). These emergent representations and transformations are as much a focus of ethnomedicine as a system of humors or the semiotics of pulse reading.

It is in the best interests of our discipline to remain flexible, pay heed to ways and means of theoretical closure, and retain a sensitivity to our complicity in the construction of "others." Central to the study of ethnomedicine is a study of how "others" and "selves" are constructed in the contexts of affliction and social transition, the role illness constructs play in defining moral worlds, relations of power and perceptions of normality, and the process of provisional closure entailed in healing which Herzfeld (1986) has alluded to.

While we should properly be reluctant to reify the data of our ethnographic analyses, villagers do. When conducting these cures, they provisionally reify disease as means of reducing its inchoateness: this is reductionism of an instrumental kind. The sense of systematic solution is one that they aim to achieve; and it is as comforting and yet as illusionary as the dream of a perfect ethnographic analysis.

Notes

1. My use of the term *epidemiology* extends beyond host-pathogen-environment relations to the approach taken by epidemiologists when studying the sensitivity and specificity of signs associated with diseases and treatment response.

2. I would be hesitant to characterize ethnomedicine as a subdiscipline of medical anthropology. The two interest areas are broadly defined, overlap, and are addressed by different groups of scholars in the US, Europe, and the Third World. Each term carries with it a set of popular associations and stereotypes which serve to bring together interest groups as well as distort the scope of scholarly activity. Ethnomedicine is commonly associated with the ethnography of health and curative/ healing behavior of the "Other," despite the fact that biomedicine is considered a form of ethnomedicine with multiple variants. Medical anthropology is commonly associated with ethnomedicine; biocultural and political studies of health ecology; the evaluation of health and medical related behaviors from both an emic and etic vantage point; health systems analysis and the study of health provider-client interactions; and political economic studies of health ideologies, the distribution of illness, health care resources, and the process of medicalization. In my own work I tend to draw a distinction when I am engaging in problem solving activities where the transfer of biomedical knowledge or technology is entailed in clinical or development contexts. I tend to use the term *anthropology of health and development* when I am attempting to situate health as either an outcome of development–underdevelopment or a factor influencing the development process.

3. For a brief summary of how the term *ethnomedicine* has been used by other anthropologists see Rubel and Hass (1991). My use of the term is more inclusive than definitions offered by Fabrega (1974, 1975) as well as Foster and Anderson (1978).

4. On the issue of misplaced attention given to the exotic in the anthropological literature at the expense of the mundane see Wikan (1989) who summarizes the critiques of Kleinman, Bourdieu, and Rosaldo.

5. The study of ethnomedicine cannot be separated from the anthropological study of the body and human suffering broadly conceived (Hahn 1984; Scheper-Hughes and Lock 1987) nor the study of the body as inscribed surface of events (Foucault 1977).

6. A distinction between traditional and modern modes of thought has been the subject of considerable debate within anthropology, a review of which lies outside the scope of this introduction. For a critical review see Trawick (1986).

7. Both Latour (1988) and Toulman (1972) argue that scientific innovation often involves the translation of older wisdom into new science maintaining a sense of continuity as distinct from constituting paradigm leaps or epistemological ruptures.

8. As Roscoe (1991) has noted, "positivism" and the method of the natural sciences is not objective but subjective and interpretive. "Facts" are interpretations constrained by sense experience. The scientific method in its quest for logical consistency risks "theoretical underdetermination" as a form of closure. There are always an infinite number of theories that will fit any particular set of "facts" more or less adequately. Statistics are often used to justify ideological claims. With regard to the objectivity of quantitative studies, reviews of methods employed in articles found in prestigious medical journals have repeatedly demonstrated that statistical procedures are often manipulated, ignored, or used to mystify in order to demonstrate significance. On the pitfalls of the dogmatic misrepresentation of statistics see Park (1985). For a feminist critique of the biological and biomedical sciences as being "objective" see Bleier (1984), Haraway (1981), Hubbard (1990), and Longino (1990).

9. Toulman's approach needs to be distinguished from more naive attempts to look to the past as a means of regaining control of our social ecological environment such as that espoused by O'Neil (1986). O'Neil tends to romanticize the other (precapitalism) through notions of the anthropomorphic and familial.

10. This includes more subtle and penetrating forms of praxis analysis which incorporate meaning centered analysis. The insights of Raymond Williams (1977) on coexisting ideologies and hegemony as a process as distinct from a reified construct are helpful. I refer to competing ideologies in this book along the lines of Williams (1977) recognizing the limitations of the term ideology posed by Foucault (1980: 117–118). Attention needs to be directed not only to ideologies as motivated stances associated with historically situated struggles for power, but emergent discourse(s) which are more fluid and less consolidated as positions. Helpful is the attention drawn to heteroglossia by the postmodern movement. Attention to multiple voices which reveal the fragmentary nature of peoples lives is useful as a complement (not a substitute) to the study of organizational structures and the internal state apparatus. See Bakhtin's (1981) account of centrifugal and centripetal forces in society.

11. In discussing peasant communities Wolf (1955) argues that they are part-societies and part-cultures. For an illustration of how they are constituted as virtual products of a history of interactions and consequences see Greenberg (1991) and Scott (1985).

12. One might draw an analogy between the way in which money and medicine have been represented by anthropologists fostering either a "discourse of nostalgia" or a "discourse of civilization." As Harris (1989) has pointed out, the first group romanticizes the pristine precapitalist world as more harmonious and less exploitive. It is juxtaposed to the capitalist world where the priority of collective interests is replaced by accumulation and individual gain. It is argued that social and human responsibility toward members of the community declines. Traditional medicine is described as fostering social cohesion as a backdrop against which to criticize biomedicine for destroying the quality of community life even if the quantity of individual life is prolonged. The second group links money (and/or medicine) to civilization as a radical leveler eroding preexisting modes of social stratification. Money and secular medicine are argued to be progressive and liberating.

13. Stephens (1989) argues that a postmodern approach inversely mirrors world systems theory.

14. Cautioned against is entanglement in a hermeneutic knot fostered by solipsistic forms of self-centered postmodernism. I do not wish to imply that postmodern inspired studies of reflexive experiences are not important to ethnomedical inquiry and worthwhile. Understanding of that which is of "compelling significance" to others (Wikan 1991) often requires a lived appreciation of embodied meanings opened up by personal experiences (e.g., Rosaldo 1989). Reflexive accounts of suffering which incorporate the depositioned experience of the ethnographer are also important when they provide an understanding of cultural models known through routinely applied scripts (Nichter 1990b). I use the term *self centered postmodernism* to identify one form of postmodern inspired research which has influenced anthropology. There are several other readings of the postmodern which might inform future anthropological research, if not evoke critical commentary by anthropologists. For example, Baudrillard (1981, 1987) characterizes the postmodern in terms of a proliferation of redundant signs and sign fetishism, a virulence of the code, the promiscuity and obscenity of information and a serialized lifestyle. Baudrillard employs several metamedical metaphors to describe postmodern life and challenges neomarxist writings of the micro-politics of desire which emphasize discipline at the site of the body. This suggests an alternative frame of relevance for ethnomedical studies of Western culture.

15. This position was recently the subject of a heated debate following an article by Browner, de Montellano and Rubel (1988). The authors call for increased cross-cultural ethnomedical research using biomedicine as an external referent in order to avoid the intellectual impoverishment of a meaning-centered medical anthropology which is overly relativistic.

16. I am referring to a form of medical materialism which might, for example, argue that prohibitions against pork eating by the Jews is directly linked to prevention of trichinosis. Juxtaposed to such an approach would be studies which investigate the interaction between the material and symbolic over time (e.g., Laderman 1981).

17. Parry (1985) has described this position in an examination of the Brahmanic tradition in India and the technology of the intellect. He summarizes the position as a belief that Shastra (Sanskritic texts) are a highly developed science which the rishis (sages) incorporated within religion so that wisdom would survive as blind faith in times of degeneration. This position holds that every detail in ritual performance represents scientific principles to be rediscovered by human intellect.

References cited

Ackerman, D.
  1990   A Natural History of the Senses. New York: Random House.
Alland, Alexander Jr.
  1987   Looking Backward: An Autocritique. Medical Anthropology Quarterly (n.s.) 1: 424–431.
Armelagos, George, Thomas Leatherman, Mary Ryan, Lynn Sibley
  1992   Biocultural Synthesis in Medical Anthropology. Medical Anthropology, Volume 14(1): 35–52.
Bahr, D.M. and J.R. Haefer
  1978   Song in Piman Curing. Ethnomusicology 22(1): 89–122.

Bakhtin, Mikhail
  1981 Dialogue Imagination. Michael Holquist, ed. and Caryl Emerson and Michael Holquist, trans. Austin: University of Texas Press.
Bargatzky, T.
  1984 Culture, Environment, and the Ills of Adaptationism. Current Anthropology 25(4): 399–415.
Bateson, Gregory
  1972 Steps to an Ecology of the Mind. New York: Ballantine Books.
Bateson, G. and M. Bateson
  1988 Angels Fear: Toward an Epistemology of the Sacred. New York: Bantam Books.
Baudrillard, Jean
  1981 De la Séduction. Denoel-Gonthier: Paris.
  1987 Forget Foucault. Simiotext: New York.
Bleier, R.
  1984 Science and Gender: A Critique of Biology and its Theories on Women. Pergamon: New York.
Brenneis, Donald
  1987 Performing Passions: Aesthetics and Politics in an Occasionally Egalitarian Community. American Ethnologist 14: 236–50.
Browner, C., B. Ortiz de Montellano, and A. Rubel
  1988 A Methodology for Cross-Cultural Ethnomedical Research. Current Anthropology 29: 681–702.
Caster, J. H.
  1983 Metaphor in Medicine. JAMA 250(14): 1841.
Csordas, Thomas and Arthur Kleinman
  1990 The Therapeutic Process. In Thomas Johnson and Carolyn Sargent, eds. Medical Anthropology: Contemporary Theory and Method. New York: Praeger Publishers.
Comaroff, Jean
  1981 Healing and Cultural Transformation: The Tswana of Southern Africa. Social Science and medicine 15B: 367–378.
  1983 The Defectiveness of Symbols or the Symbols of Defectiveness? On the Cultural Analysis of Medical Systems. Culture, Medicine and Psychiatry 7: 3–20.
  1985 Body of Power, Spirit of Resistance. Chicago: University of Chicago Press.
Corbin, A.
  1986 The Foul and the Fragrant and the French Social Imagination. M. Kochan, R. Porter and C. Prendergast trans. Cambridge: Harvard University Press.
Davis-Floyd, Robbie
  1990 The Role of Obstetrical Rituals in the Resolution of Cultural Anomaly. Social Science and Medicine 31(2): 175–189.
Fabrega, Horatio Jr.
  1974 Diseases and Social Behavior: An Interdisciplinary Perspective. Cambridge: MIT Press.
  1975 The Need for an Ethnomedical Science. Science 189: 969–75.
  1990 A Plea for a Broader Ethnomedicine. Culture, Medicine and Psychiatry 14: 129–132.
Foster, George and Barbara Anderson
  1978 Medical Anthropology. New York: Wiley.
Foucault, Michael
  1977 "Nietzche, Geneology, History," in Language, Counter-Memory, Practice. Ed. Donald Bouchard and trans. Sherry Simon. Ithaca: Cornell University Press.
  1980 Power/Knowledge. Colin Gordon, ed. New York: Pantheon.
Frankenberg, R.
  1980 Medical Anthropology and Development: A Theoretical Perspective. Social Science and Medicine 14B: 197–207.
Greenberg, D. B.
  1990 Chronic Mononucleosis, Chronic Fatigue Syndrome, and Anxiety and Depressive Disorders. Psychosomatics 31(2): 129–137.
Greenberg, James
  1991 Capital, Ritual and Boundaries of the Closed Cooperative Community. Unpublished manuscript.
Hahn, Robert
  1984 Rethinking "Illness" and "Disease." Contributions to Asian Studies 18: 1–23.

Haraway, D.
1981   In the Beginning Was the Word: The Genesis of Biological Theory. Signs 6: 469–481.
Harris, Olivia
1989   The Earth and the State: The Sources and Meanings of Money in Northern Potosi, Bolivia. In J. Parry and M. Bloch, eds. Money and the Morality of Exchange. Cambridge: Cambridge University Press.
Herzfeld, Michael
1986   Closure as Cure: Tropes in the Exploration of Bodily and Social Disorder. Current Anthropology 27(2): 107–120.
Howes, D.
1987   Olfaction and Transition: An Essay on the Ritual Uses of Smell. The Canadian Review of Sociology and Anthropology 24(3): 390–416.
Hubbard, R.
1990   The Politics of Women's Biology. Rutgers, New Jersey: Rutgers University Press.
Hunt, L., Browner, C.H., and B. Jordan
1990   Hypoglycemia: Portrait of an Illness Construct in Everyday Use. Medical Anthropology Quarterly 6: 191–210.
Janzen, John M.
1981   The Need for a Taxonomy of Health in the Study of African Therapeutics. Social Science and Medicine 15B: 185–194.
Johnson, Tom
1987   Premenstrual Syndrome as a Western Culture-Specific Disorder. Culture, Medicine and Psychiatry 11: 337–356.
Keller, E.F., and C.R. Grantkowski
1983   The mind's eye. In S. Harding and M. Hintikka, eds., Discovery reality. Dordrecht, Holland: Reidel Press. Pp. 207–224.
Kirmayer, L.
1986   Somatization and the Social Construction of Illness Experience. In Illness Behavior: A Multidisciplinary Model. S. McHugh and T. Vallis, eds. New York: Plenum Press.
Kleinman, Arthur
1980   Patients and Healers in the Context of Culture. Berkeley: University of California Press.
1986   Social Origins of Distress and Disease: Depression, Neurasthenia, and Pain in Modern China. New Haven: Yale University Press.
1988   Comments on "A Methodology for Cross-Cultural Ethnomedical Research," C.H. Browner, B.R. Ortiz de Montellano and A.J. Rubel. Current Anthropology 29: 681–702.
Latour, Bruno
1988   The Pasteurization of France. Cambridge: Cambridge University Press.
Linnekin, J.
1991   Cultural Invention and the Dilemma of Authenticity. American Anthropologist 93: 446–450.
Lock, Margaret
1982   Models and Practice in Medicine: Menopause as Syndrome on Life Transition. Culture, Medicine and Psychiatry 6(3): 261–280.
Longino, H.
1990   Science as Social Knowledge: Values and Objectivity in Scientific Inquiry. Princeton: Princeton University Press.
Marcus, George E. and Michael M.J. Fischer
1986   Anthropology as Cultural Critique. Chicago: University of Chicago Press.
Martin, Emily
1987   The Woman in the Body. Boston: Beacon Press.
1988   Medical Metaphors of Women's Bodies: Menstruation and Menopause. International Journal of Health Services 18(2): 237–254.
1990   Science and Women's Bodies: Forms of Anthropological Knowledge. In M. Jacobus, E. Fox Keller, and S. Shuttleworth, eds. Body Politics. Routledge: New York and London. 69–82.
1991   The End of the Body? American Ethnologist 12: 121–140.
Mascia-Lees, Frances E., Patricia Sharpe, and Colleen Ballerino Cohen
1989   The Postmodernist Turn in Anthropology: Cautions from a Feminist Perspective. Signs: Journal of Women in Culture and Society 15(1): 7–33.

McElroy, Ann
  1990 Biocultural Models in Studies of Human Health and Adaptation. Medical Anthropology
         Quarterly 4(3): 243–265.
Millard, Ann
  1990 The Place of the Clock in Pediatric Advice: Rationales, Cultural Themes, and Impediments to
         Breastfeeding. Social Science and Medicine 31(2): 211–221.
Morgan, Lynn M.
  1987 Dependency Theory in the Political Economy of Health: An Anthropological Critique. Medi-
         cal Anthropology Quarterly 1(2): 131–154.
  1990 The Medicalization of Anthropology: A Critical Perspective on the Critical-Clinical Debate.
         Social Science and Medicine 30(9): 945–950.
Nichter, Mark
  1989 Anthropology and International Health: South Asian Case Studies. Dordrecht, Netherlands:
         Kluwer Press.
  1990a Vaccinations in South Asia: False Expectations and Commanding Metaphors. In Anthropol-
         ogy and Primary Health Care. J. Coreil and D. Mull, eds. Connecticut: Westwood Press.
  1990b On the Alchemy of Work and the Lessons Gained from the Witnessing of Suffering in Other
         Lifeworlds. American Anthropological Association Annual Meeting, New Orleans.
Nichter, M. and C. Nordstrom
  1989 The Question of Medicine Answering: The Social Relations of Healing in Sri Lanka. Culture,
         Medicine and Psychiatry 13: 367–390.
O'Neil, John
  1985 Five Bodies: The Human Shape of Modern Society. Ithaca: Cornell University Press.
Osherson, S. and L. Amarasingham
  1981 "The Machine Metaphor in Medicine." In Eliot Mishler, L. Amarasingham, Stuart Hauser,
         Ramsey Liem, Samuel Osherson, and Nancy Waxler, eds. Social Contexts of Health, Illness
         and Patient Care. Cambridge University Press. pp. 219–249.
Park, Thomas K.
  1985 Pyrrhonism in Anthropological and Historical Research. History in Africa 12: 225–252.
Parry, Jonathan
  1985 The Brahmanical Tradition and the Technology of the Intellect. In Reason and Morality.
         Joanna Overing, ed. Pp. 200–225. New York: Tavistock Press.
Popper, Karl
  1959 The Logic of Scientific Discovery. New York: Basic Books.
Ranger, Terrance
  1983 The Invention of Tradition in Colonial Africa. In The Invention of Tradition. E. Hobsbawn and
         T. Ranger, eds. Pp. 211–262. Cambridge: Cambridge University Press.
Ritenbaugh, Cheryl
  1982 Obesity as a Culture-bound Syndrome. Culture, Medicine and Psychiatry 6: 347.
Rosaldo, Rosaldo
  1989 Imperialist Nostalgia. Representations 26: 107–122.
Roscoe, P.
  1991 The Perils of "Positivism": A Critique of the Image of "Positivism" in Cultural Anthropology.
         Unpublished manuscript.
Roseman, M.
  1988 The Pragmatics of Aesthetics: The Performance of Healing Among Senoi Temiar. Social Sci-
         ence and Medicine 27: 811–818.
Rubel, Arthur and Michael Hass
  1990 Ethnomedicine. In Thomas Johnson and Carolyn Sargent, eds. Medical Anthropology: Con-
         temporary Theory and Method. New York: Praeger.
Scheper-Hughes, N. and M.M. Lock
  1987 The Mindful Body: A Prolegomenon to Future Work in Medical Anthropology. Medical An-
         thropology Quarterly 1(1): 6–41.
Scott, James
  1985 Weapons of the Weak. Yale University Press: New Haven.
Shweder, Richard
  1988 Suffering in Style. Culture, Medicine and Psychiatry 12: 479–497.
Singer, Merrill
  1984 Hypoglycemia: A Controversial Illness in U.S. Society. Medical Anthropology 8: 1–35.

1989a The Limitations of Medical Ecology: The Concept of Adaptation in the Context of Social Stratification and Social Transformation. Medical Anthropology 10: 223–234.

1989b The Coming of Age of Critical Medical Anthropology. Social Science and Medicine 28(11): 1193–1203.

1990 Reinventing Medical Anthropology: Toward a Critical Realignment. Social Science and Medicine 30: 179–187.

Stephens, S.

1989 The Condition of Postmodern Anthropology. Paper presented at the American Anthropological Association meetings, Washington, D.C., November 1989.

Stoller, Paul

1989 The Taste of Ethnographic Things: The Senses in Anthropology. Philadelphia: University of Pennsylvania Press.

Strathern, M.

1987a An Awkward Relationship: The Case of Feminism and Anthropology. Signs 12(2): 276–292.

1987b Out of Context: The Persuasive Fictions of Anthropology. Current Anthropology 28(3): 251–270.

Toulman, Steven

1972 Human Understanding. Vol. I. Oxford: Clarendon Press.

1982 The Return to Cosmology. Berkeley: University of California Press.

Trawick, Margaret

1986 The Ayurvedic Physician as Scientist. Social Science Medicine 24(12): 1031–1050.

Wagner, R.

1975 The Invention of Culture. Englewood Cliffs: Prentice Hall.

Wikan, Unni

1989 Managing the Heart to Brighten Face and Soul: Emotions in Balinese Morality and Health Care. American Ethnologist 16(2): 294–311.

Williams, Raymond

1977 Marxism and Literature. Oxford: Oxford University Press.

Winter, R.

1976 The Smell Book. Philadelphia: J.B. Lippincott.

Wolf, Eric

1955 Types of Latin American Peasantry: A Preliminary Discussion. American Anthropologist 57: 452–471.

1982 Europe and the People Without History. Berkeley, California: University of California Press.

Wolfe, A.

1988 Suicide and the Japanese Postmodern: A Postnarrative Paradigm? The South Atlantic Quarterly 87(3): 571–589.

The Efficacy of Ethnomedicine: Research Methods in Trouble

Robert Anderson

One of the tasks of medical anthropology is to conduct research to evaluate the efficacy of traditional health care practices. The benefits of health care may be evaluated in numerous ways, but in this article we examine only the problem of how to determine whether a therapeutic intervention changes the pathophysiology of a disease. The randomized controlled trial is acknowledged as an ideal that will rarely be attainable by medical ethnographers. Individual case studies are primarily useful for hypothesis formation. We are left then with observational studies (case series) as a feasible and useful alternative. Those presently in the anthropological literature are examined and each is found to be flawed to some extent. Future investigations can profit from what was learned in these pioneer studies by giving more attention to patient selection, treatment description, and objective measures of outcome.

INTRODUCTION

The purpose of this article is to identify some guidelines for research in one limited area of medical anthropology, namely, the determination of whether or not a given form of traditional healing is beneficial to patients. Within this demarcated area not all ways of measuring benefit will be evaluated in detail, because the article is further limited to the issue of how one can identify benefit in terms of improvements in a patient's post-treatment disease status. In exploring this area of research strategy, we will examine five published projects already undertaken by anthropologists for this purpose. Each of these studies, including one that I carried out myself, is seriously flawed. However, taken together, they serve a useful purpose by alerting us to errors that we can avoid in the future.

Numerous anthropologists agree with the statement that, "There is an interesting void in both the medical and anthropological literature on the efficacy of traditional healing" (Morse, McConnell, and Young 1987: 89; also see Etkin and Ross 1983: 231; Romanucci-Ross, Moerman, and Tancredi 1983: ix; Csordas 1988: 121). Because measures of the clinical effectiveness of traditional forms of healing have nowhere been firmly established in biomedical terms, we find ourselves as anthropologists in an embarrassing position. We speculate about how healing methods may be beneficial in curing disease or may constitute highly meaningful activities in a society, but, with few exceptions, we have not scientifically explored whether the healing systems we document can directly affect the pathophysiology of a disease.

ROBERT ANDERSON, a physician anthropologist, is Director of Manual Medicine at the San Francisco Spine Institute at Seton Medical Center and Professor of Anthropology at Mills College, Oakland, CA 94613. He has published extensively on chiropractic as well as on the etiology, diagnosis and treatment of spinal disorders. Most recently, he carried out an as yet unpublished field study of the treatment of back pain by bonesetters in Katmandu, Nepal.

Although meaningful in some ways, it is not adequate within a scientific discipline to claim efficacy for shamanism, for example, ". . . simply because it *does* work." It is not enough merely to assert that, "the ancient methods of shamanism are already time-tested. . ." (Harner 1982: xiv, xxii, his italics). After all, bleeding and purging as treatment techniques were time-tested in Western medicine for a documented 24 centuries (5th century B.C.E. to 19th century C.E.), yet ultimately proved biomedically useless or harmful in nearly every case (Louis 1836). Similarly, it is not adequate simply to note that the therapy of healers is "often effective," without making any effort to count successes and failures (Prince 1964: 110). Nor is it acceptable to assume that traditional forms of healing produce the beneficial effects of a placebo (Moerman 1983) without testing even that modest but important assumption (see reports of efficacy below).

Will conclusions about biomedical efficacy prove of value to the anthropologist investigating ethnomedicine? The answer is that such knowledge can be essential. As an illustration, I have argued elsewhere that the relationship between medicine and chiropractic can be understood as shaped by caste system dynamics comparable in some ways to those that structure the interaction of Brahmans and untouchables in India (Anderson 1981). Inherent in a caste ideology is the belief (in emic terms) that social rank differences are justified by a true biological or moral inferiority of people of low caste when, in fact, anthropologists can demonstrate (in etic terms) that they are equal in their human endowment. On the basis of several blinded, controlled trials (Greenland et al. 1980; Hadler et al. 1987) and a well designed and executed observational study (Cassidy, Kirkaldy-Willis, and Mc-Gregor 1985; Kirkaldy-Willis and Cassidy 1985; Cassidy, Kirkaldy-Willis, and McGregor, 1988), chiropractors can be shown to be quite effective in the treatment of certain spinal disorders. Their place in health care therefore does, at least to that extent, reflect a caste dynamic. Were chiropractors mere quacks, the dynamic would be thoroughly different.

One anthropologist, concluding that the caste analogy ". . . meets with limited success only. . . .," nonetheless addresses the issue of ranking. "While seeking to better their ranking relative to other health-care professionals, chiropractors assert their ability to act as responsible practitioners, entitled to acceptance as independent healers, worthy of a status approaching that of their medical doctor rivals" (Wiesner 1983: 476). What does this statement mean if chiropractors offer no more than the benefits of a placebo or if their treatments cause harm? Is it not greatly different if they offer an effective treatment not offered by medical doctors? The answer, of course, is that it makes an enormous difference.

Investigation into the biomedical efficacy of traditional methods of curing is so essential and yet so neglected that one anthropologist was prompted to ". . . present the complex issue of how we evaluate therapeutic efficacy as *the* central problem in the cross-cultural study of healing" (Kleinman 1980: 312, his italics). Others, noting that, "We have not yet directly addressed the crucial issue of the comparative efficacy of cures. . . .," conclude that issues of efficacy ". . . should become the next major thrust of medical anthropology inquiry in the decades ahead" (Moore et al. 1987: 221).

My own position is somewhat restrained. Among many areas of inquiry that medical anthropologists need to address at this time, certainly one of great importance is to identify the benefits that may accrue to individuals and societies from the practice of one form or another of ethnomedicine (ethnotherapy). Different investigators may chose to evaluate benefits in diverse and mutually unrelated ways. The very question of benefits is itself a confusing ethnocentric compôt of emic and etic thinking (Kleinman 1975: 115). Yet one task of necessity is to investigate efficacy in terms of health improvement as measured in biomedical terms.

MEASURING PATIENT SATISFACTION

One may circumvent the issue of whether or not a mode of treatment changes the natural history of the disease by asking, not whether pathophysiology is affected, but whether patients are satisfied with treatment outcomes. It is certainly valid and useful to argue that anthropologists need to identify the benefits of medical beliefs and practices not in biomedical terms but in terms of whether curing procedures address "instrumental and moral imperatives." It has been argued that ". . . an established cure is *always able to work* in the sense that it meets the *expectations* of the sick person and his kin, and that it produces certain results in a predictable way" (Young 1976: 7, his italics; see also Ahern 1979; van der Geest and Whyte 1989).

Efficacy thus defined can be documented in terms of patient satisfaction or societal benefits. One can, for example, quantify the extent to which patients indicate that they feel better after treatment or feel that the treatment was worth the time and expense. It should be recognized, of course, that self-evaluation by former patients provides a very limited measure of success, even when a large number of responses is examined, if one's concern is with biomedical evaluation of changes in the disease process.

To illustrate, in a field investigation of the prevalence of back pain in a randomized, stratified sample of ordinary working people who were members of a transit union in California (N = 195), I found that many had experienced musculoskeletal pain for which they had sought care. Of those who had gone to a physician, only 50.0 percent reported that they felt improved as a result of treatment. In contrast, of union members who had sought care from chiropractors, 81.8 percent recalled that treatment made them feel better. Chiropractors fared much better than did physicians by this measure, but although quantified, it does not demonstrate that chiropractors are biomedically more effective than physicians.

As concerns efficacy, all that one can conclude from these findings is that these subjects felt better about their chiropractors than about their physicians. It should be noted that in a study carried out in Utah, it was determined that treatment results were approximately the same whether the spinal patient saw a physician or a chiropractor; but while physical outcomes were the same, the patients of chiropractors were significantly more satisfied with treatment. The investigators concluded that ". . . it appears that the chiropractor may be more attuned to the total needs of the patient than is his medical counterpart" (Kane et al. 1974; cf. Coulehan 1985; Deyo and Diehl 1986).

Reports of patient satisfaction are very useful. They provide information about how patients retain their personal dignity and emotional stability during an illness, but they cannot be interpreted as measures of clinical cure of the underlying disease. If this were not so, research in Taiwan would justify a program to replace Western medical practitioners with Chinese shamans. In three series of 25 patients who had sought care from medical doctors, only 30 to 35 percent evaluated their care as satisfactory. This response to physicians was distinctly inferior to the response of 21 patients who sought out shamans for care. Patient satisfaction with shamanic healing reached an enviable 85 percent (Kleinman 1980: 291).

LABORATORY RESEARCH

In this article, we limit our concern with efficacy to the issue of how one can measure the ability of some form of traditional healing to change the natural history of a disease for the better. One can approach this task of biomedical evaluation in various indirect ways. One often well-exploited possibility is to undertake bio-chemical assays, and by this method to identify physiologic responses to treatments, such as to identify increases in blood endorphin levels subsequent to treatment with acupuncture needles (Skoler 1984; for a flawed study, see Krieger 1979).

Animal models can be exploited in many cases. To illustrate from a single study, guinea pigs with full-thickness burns were found to heal better after treatment with *aloe vera*, a folk remedy, than after the application of silver sulfadiazine, a phar-maceutical substance (Rodriguez-Bigas, Cruz, and Suarez 1988).

Very useful inferences as to the efficacy of indigenous medications can be made on the basis of chemical analysis to identify physiologically active substances (Etkin and Ross 1983; Moerman 1989). As an example, this type of research has demonstrated that many of the medicinal plants of the ancient Aztecs (Ortiz de Montellano 1975; Davidson and Ortiz de Montellano 1983; Browner, Ortiz de Montellano and Rubel 1988) as well as those used in an indigenous community in southern Mexico contain chemicals ". . . which would appear to enable them to accomplish their intended effects. . ." (Ortiz de Montellano and Browner 1985: 57).

These approaches are highly valuable and useful, particularly when more direct investigations cannot be carried out. At the same time it must be recognized that such approaches are not completely adequate in themselves. One can easily err, for example, if ". . . it is assumed," as some have done, "that if the proper chemical substance is present, the dosage prescribed would be adequate to produce the desired result" (Ortiz de Montellano 1975: 216; for failure to dose adequately, see Brun and Schumacher 1987; Estes 1979). It requires a leap of faith to extrapolate from laboratory analyses and animal experiments to the assumption that healing methods actually work in human patients (Etkin 1988; Romanucci-Ross and Moer-man 1988).

CASE STUDIES

Case studies commend themselves to anthropologists as a way to carry out direct biomedical evaluations of the response of patients to the treatment of diseases when the investigator has little control over events (Yin 1989: 13). When it is not feasible to implement a more thorough research design, it is nonetheless useful to report even a single case study.

A psychiatrist, for example, provides a case study of an individual diagnosed as suffering from schizophrenia. The patient was treated by shamans and by psychiatrists. He failed to respond adequately to either kind of treatment (Nishimura 1987). In this case, shamanic treatment failed as treatment for a major psychosis, as did psychiatry. As limited as it is, this case study at the least demonstrates one possible outcome of healer intervention.

In my own work, while doing the history and physical of a hospital patient admitted for possible spinal surgery, I recorded that she had earlier suffered a medically documented sciatica. To avoid spine surgery she flew to the Philippines where she was "operated" on by psychic surgeons utilizing shamanic methods rather than actual surgery. In all, she underwent 44 "surgeries" of pure *legerdemain*. Although it would seem unlikely from the perspective of biomedicine that her disease would respond to this kind of procedure, her incapacitating low back pain was in fact cured by Filipino shamans. She was well for the next seven years until re-injury, whereupon she returned to a medical orthopedic ward. This constitutes a retrospective case study of an indigenous healing approach that worked. It cannot be taken as a demonstration that psychic surgery offers a predictable cure in the treatment of sciatica, but it does demonstrate the possibility of a successful outcome.

Case studies are valuable, more so if they are prospective, but on a single case basis they are merely suggestive, with no identifiable external validity. A single case history cannot be used to decide whether or not a particular approach to healing is more beneficial than self-limiting or placebo effects or mere chance (e. g., Goldberg 1989: 118–120). On the basis of a single case, one cannot say that Japanese shamans are not able to treat schizophrenia successfully, and one cannot say from a single case example that psychic surgeons treat vertebral disc disease with success.

Nevertheless, in spite of limitations, the case study is useful. Methodologically, it has additional potential. It has been suggested that, "the time-series descriptive study is often the best available compromise between the demands of science and the limitations (and opportunities) of clinical practice" (Lowden, Keating, and Meeker 1986: 267). A time-series descriptive case study of a cervical pain case treated with chiropractic manipulation illustrates the utility of this approach. In this case, 13 clinical variables were measured before, during and after treatment. All but one of the outcome variables changed in the expected direction of clinical improvement during the first three weeks of treatment. This documentation was improved by measuring multiple outcome variables repeatedly, but it still leaves untouched the issue of how one can generalize from a single case study.

It should be noted that intra-subject experimental designs have been suggested as providing ways to improve the usefulness of the case study method (Keating et al. 1985). A reversal (withdrawal) design, for example, can clearly reveal the effects of the intervention if symptoms improve during a first treatment phase, revert towards baseline levels when treatment is interrupted, and again demonstrate improvement when treatment is reinstated. The efficacy of psychotropic herbs in moderating psychotic behavior, for example, could be evaluated in this manner if it were ethically acceptable and logistically practical to organize (Leitenberg 1973).

Experimental designs, however, will rarely be acceptable to indigenous practitioners nor feasible for anthropological field workers. The simple pre- and post-treatment case documentation recommends itself precisely ". . . when the relevant behaviors cannot be manipulated" (Yin 1989: 19).

Case studies are therefore where anthropological investigations will probably have to begin, and useful work can be carried out at this level. By working with case studies, we can set standards for providing complete descriptions of the disorder and of the treatment. We can work towards developing objective outcome measures. We can, perhaps, develop intra-subject experimental designs. Importantly, a series of well executed case studies can approach the validity of an observational study if enough cases are documented (see below on random selection and sample size). Finally, good case studies can provide a basis for designing more extensive formal studies.

CONTROLLED BLINDED TRIALS

Laboratory research and case studies appeal to anthropologists who are so constrained by the difficulties of field ethnography that more rigorous research designs are impossible to implement. However, there is a more ideal research strategy that could be pursued were we not constrained by field conditions. The "gold standard" for establishing the biomedical efficacy of medications or treatment protocols is the randomized, blinded, controlled trial.

For many reasons, anthropologists are unlikely to carry out clinical trials that meet this gold standard. In particular, when working with native practitioners, it will rarely be possible to include two aspects of method that lie at the heart of the prospective clinical trial: 1), the random assignment of some patients to a control group and 2), the enforcement of blinding procedures as concerns the nature of the treatment and the recording of outcome measures.

Controls

In a full trial, the treatment population should be randomly divided into two or more separate groups. The most convincing results in terms of statistical measures of significance derive from trials in which patients are randomized in part into a treatment group and in part into a control group that either receives a different form of treatment, receives no treatment, or is subjected to a sham treatment that cannot be distinguished from the treatment under investigation.

Comparisons with a control of no treatment or a placebo permit the effectiveness of the treatment to be measured against healing that may take place as a consequence of the natural history of the disease (the self-limiting effect), or healing that can result simply from the psychological benefits of being treated (the placebo).

Comparison to a control in which some other form of treatment is provided is easier to organize, since all participants receive some appropriate form of treatment. It is less satisfactory as a scientific measure, however, because it tells the researcher only the benefits that derive from one form of treatment as opposed to another. If outcomes are significantly different, one has learned something useful. If they are the same, one has also learned something useful. In either case the researcher cannot know if the treatment was superior to a placebo or to no treatment at all.

Within anthropology, virtually no investigation of an indigenous form of treatment has utilized a control. A prospective study of the accuracy of iridologists in diagnosing kidney disease by identifying colors and shapes in the iris of the eye, although a trial of diagnostic acumen rather than of the efficacy of treatment, constitutes a rare example of the use of controls in investigating a non-mainstream form of clinical practice. Iridology diagnosis was shown to be no more accurate than mere guessing (Simon, Worthen, and Mitas 1979). A study of the effectiveness of spiritualist healers in Mexico refers to controls, but the controls were utilized to establish a baseline for evaluating questionnaire responses obtained from temple clients. No controls were utilized in that study for the evaluation of treatment response as such (Finkler 1985).

Blinding

Clinical trials can be subtly but powerfully distorted if they are not blinded as well as controlled. At the least, in single blind trials, the clinician who evaluates the patients for signs of improvement should not be aware of whether the patient under examination received the experimental treatment or the control procedure. In a double blind trial, the patient also should be unaware of which treatment was received, so that reported changes in symptoms are not biased by attitudes the patient may have toward the treatment under study. The iridology study cited above was successfully blinded (Simon, Worthen, and Mitas 1979). To my knowledge, no prospective clinical trial of indigenous healing has been even single blinded.

In major medical centers, under the very best of circumstances, to conduct controlled, blinded trials is complex, time-consuming, frustrating, and very expensive (Buerger 1977; Greenland et al. 1980; Hawthorne 1985; Fletcher 1989). Further, to design, administer and fund such trials is becoming increasingly difficult (Antman, Schnipper, and Frei III 1988; Marwick 1988). Within medicine, investigators show a growing willingness to compromise methodological rigor in the face of practical realities. "We cannot afford to conduct randomized controlled trials for every test, procedure, or medication in use. . ." one medical critic has observed. "Alternative designs for studies of effectiveness are therefore urgently needed" (Greenfield 1989; cf. Rudicel and Esdaille 1985; Hurst 1989).

Anthropologists working under field conditions have additional, more compelling reasons to search for alternative designs, since they exert far less control over the treatment situation than do institution-based researchers, and large-scale funding is also less available. For these reasons, anthropologists need to consider the advisability of undertaking observational studies as a productive alternative. Observational studies can produce information superior in validity to that of individual case studies even though they fall short of the credibility of findings that derive from controlled, blinded clinical trials.

OBSERVATIONAL STUDIES

In this article I will argue that an alternative design that might be feasible for use by anthropologists is the longitudinal observational study, or case series. Medical researchers would seem to agree (Greenfield 1989; Moses 1984). "Whereas many experts demand randomized trials to determine the value of a specific form of treatment," one medical editorial notes". . . observational studies are also useful in arriving at a conclusion regarding the value of a specific type of treatment" (Hurst 1989).

In this type of study one measures the response of patients to treatment. Observational studies differ from clinical trials in that comparisons are not made to a control group and blinding is not attempted. They differ from case studies in that treatment effects are documented for a substantial sample of patients, thus establishing a basis for estimating the predictability of outcomes. Aside from the need to screen carefully for bias in the absence of blinding procedures, the major shortcoming, and one of admitted importance, is that it is usually not possible to distinguish improvement that may result simply from the placebo effect or from the natural remission of symptoms.

Previous Observational Studies

In the current anthropological literature, five observational studies have been published which will now be examined. For convenience, I will refer to these anthropological investigations as follows: *Salish* designates a study of native American shamanism practiced in the context of periodic ritual dances (Jilek 1982); *Taiwan* refers to the practice of Chinese temple shamans (Kleinman 1980); *Mexico* refers to spiritualist temple healing rituals (Finkler 1985); *Cree* will identify the treatment of psoriasis by an Indian healer (Morse, McConnell, and Young 1987; Morse, Young et al. 1987; Young et al. 1987); and *Juarez* stands for the practice of a bonesetter in Cd. Juarez, Mexico (Anderson 1987).

Reports of Efficacy

Each of the five anthropological studies appears to support conclusions about the efficacy of the treatments under investigation. The *Salish* study reported that of 11 subjects characterized by depression, anxiety, and psychosomatic somatization, three became free of symptoms, seven demonstrated improvement, and one showed no change. Of 13 others characterized by aggressive and antisocial tendencies with or without substance abuse, seven were rehabilitated, four were improved, one was unchanged, and one got worse.

The *Taiwan* study reported that 10 of 12 subjects were at least partially improved, of which five were completely cured. Two were treatment failures. These findings are less sharply delineated than the figures would imply, since, as Kleinman carefully points out, it is possible that some of those who reported that they were improved may in fact have experienced no change in symptoms or have gotten worse. The shaman, in contrast, regarded all of these cases as partially or fully cured (Kleinman 1980; 320, 328–330).

After six months, six subjects in the *Cree* study were greatly improved, four were unchanged, and one had dropped out (Morse, Young, et al. 1987: 37).

Of 11 clients of the bonesetter in the *Juarez* study, two were found to have obtained excellent results, four were described as obtaining good results, four reported or demonstrated slight improvement, and one was unchanged.

In contrast to the above studies, of the 66 patients in the *Mexico* study, 38 experienced failure while 28 experienced success. Since the anthropological literature on the whole seems to reflect an unconscious bias in favor of identifying treatment success, at least on the level of placebo benefits, this finding in *Mexico* serves as a valuable reminder that when objectively followed, patients may be found to end up unchanged or even worse (see also Simpson 1989), and that a placebo benefit does not always occur.

What can one make of these figures, including those from my own study (*Juarez*)? The answer is that each of these treatments was found to be beneficial for some patients, but that outcome measures have uncertain predictive value because all five of these studies are flawed, as will be discussed below.

PATIENT SELECTION

Sample Size

In what follows, a number of design requirements will be examined. While error in any of these dimensions can seriously compromise the validity of reported findings, none has been a problem more consistently in anthropological and medical research than that of sample size. The number of patients evaluated constitutes a critical dimension of clinical research (Cohen 1977; Laupacis, Sackett, and Roberts 1988). Four of these studies relied upon samples so small that chance alone could determine outcome findings (*Salish*, N = 24; *Taiwan*, N = 19, of which 7 were lost to follow-up, leaving an effective sample of 12; *Cree*, N = 13; *Juarez*, N = 11). Although the *Mexico* study obtained data on over a thousand individuals, the actual clinical trial subjects were relatively few. The trial began with 108 subjects, of which 21 must be disregarded because they sought concomitant medical treatment and another 21 either did not comply with the treatment regimen or were lost to follow-up, leaving an effective sample of 66 as well as considerable doubt about remaining randomness of selection when one-third of the sample fell out of the study.

In recent years, it has become increasingly clear that failure to achieve appropriate sample size determination through statistical power analysis has flawed many medical trials of efficacy (Arkin and Wachtel 1990; Colton 1990). Anthropologists also need to be wary of limiting their studies in this manner (Pelto and Pelto 1978: 163). When only small samples are available, efficacy can only be identified if the effect of the treatment is very strong and clear-cut (Schweizer and Lang 1989). None of the five anthropological studies provides a rationale or statistical power evaluation to justify the choice of sample size. With the possible exception of the *Mexico* study, none appears to have enrolled a sample large enough to eliminate the possibility of errors due to small sample size. The smallness of sample sizes reduces these, in effect, to case series of uncertain validity (Cohen 1977).

RANDOM SELECTION

Patient assignment must be random to avoid bias, conscious or unconscious, in deciding which individuals will be examined for treatment response. It is essential that bias not eliminate individuals whose inclusion might change the ultimate findings. Three of the anthropological studies selected randomly by admitting subjects to the trial on the basis of successive appearance (*Taiwan, Juarez*) or every fifth appearance (*Mexico*) to attend the ritual or treatment. Not every subject selected in this random way was admitted to the study in the *Mexico* investigation, but exclusion criteria were clearly stated. Individuals who came with a problem of living rather than an illness were excluded; thus, randomness was initially achieved, although it was not clearly preserved in the post-treatment period (see sample size above). Admission to the *Salish* and *Cree* studies was not by random selection.

Accurate Diagnosis

In the selection of a study sample, size and randomness are not the only important issues. It is critical that the inclusion and exclusion criteria be consistent with an accurate diagnosis, and that the study be limited to a single disease or a discrete disease category. In the herbal repertoire of European folk medicine, foxglove (the folk source for digitalis) was highly effective in the treatment of congestive heart failure (dropsy), but not in the treatment of many other disorders for which it was used. In 19th century medical practice, the herb fell out of favor for decades because it was ineffective in so many cases for which it was prescribed (Estes 1979). Were one to evaluate the efficacy of foxglove, it would be essential that only true dropsy patients be selected.

The failure to select in terms of an accurate diagnosis constitutes a major flaw in most anthropological studies. The *Cree* study stands apart as exemplary by virtue of objectively identifying a single skin disease, psoriasis, and in accurately measuring severity of the lesions. None of the remaining four anthropological studies satisfies this requirement. The *Salish* study limited itself to two psychiatric syndromes, but they were vaguely defined (11 subjects diagnosed with depression, anxiety and psychogenic somatization and 13 subjects with aggressive and antisocial tendencies, usually complicated by ethanol or other substance abuse). The *Juarez* study examined musculoskeletal disorders, which comprises a very broad, unmanageable cluster of quite diverse complaints, while patients described in the *Taiwan* and *Mexico* findings represented a completely open spectrum of diseases.

Stratification

In addition to sample size, randomness and accurate diagnosis, the evaluation of treatment results in many cases, but not in all, can be more meaningful if the sample is stratified, usually for age, sex, occupation, education, marital status, race, ethnicity and class. Which criteria are significant will depend, of course, on the nature of the study, and unstratified samples are not necessarily compromised in every case. Of the five anthropological investigations, the *Cree* study recorded the age, sex and ethnicity of patients, but could draw no statistical inferences from these variables. It probably did not matter as concerns the treatment of psoriasis. The *Salish* population was noted to include approximately half males and half females, as well as primarily young adults. The difference between the range of psychiatric problems of young men and those of young women could be great, but the sample size was too small to permit evaluation of this variable. The *Mexico* study stratified for a number of variables, but salience was not explored. The *Taiwan* and *Juarez* studies failed to stratify, and thus give no basis for judging treatment response, as this may vary within a population.

DESCRIBING TREATMENT

Identification of Treatment Protocol

Having carefully selected a study population in terms of sample size, randomness, accuracy of diagnosis and stratification, it then becomes essential that the treatment be clearly described and consistently applied. This is the one area in which all of the anthropological studies offer adequate information. It should be noted that in the *Cree* study, the healing ritual was not conducted in a Cree setting and the patients were English-speaking non-Indians. Thus, "a major tenet of naturalistic research was violated. . .," and relevance to Cree medical culture was obscured (Morse, McConnell, and Young 1987: 91).

Hypothesis Formation

Whereas all of the studies adequately describe the treatment, none clearly defines the purpose of the study in terms of hypothesis testing. Consistent with the anthropological style of writing and the openness of the anthropological method, none of the studies were that formal. It is simply implicit in all of these investigations that the purpose is to see if the treatment works. Future research will expectably meet research standards more explicitly by incorporating this formal requirement (Hawthorne 1985).

Number of Practitioners

Related to the identification of treatment protocol, an often neglected aspect of clinical trials in those circumstances in which physician skill is a factor is to insist that several practitioners be employed. This can be necessary in order to be sure that the treatment effect is a product of the type of practice rather than of the skills of a particular practitioner. It was a feature of the iridology research described above (Simon, Worthen, and Mitas 1979). It was also true of the *Salish* and *Mexico* studies, as well as of the *Taiwan* research, which added to the primary study a report of follow-ups on six patients ministered to by a different shaman. The *Cree* and *Juarez* studies each report on a single healer. Would findings in these two studies have been the same if several practitioners were observed? Do findings reflect the skills of one individual alone, or are they characteristic of a category of healer? In these two studies one cannot know.

MEASURING OUTCOME

Objective Versus Subjective Evaluation

Many clinical studies are published in which doctors evaluate their own results in reporting on series of cases they have treated, citing successes and failures (e.g., Tollison, Kriegel, and Satterthwaite 1989; Goldenberg 1987; Rasmussen 1985). Whether the measures are subjective or objective, however, one must acknowledge a distortive bias in evaluations if the treater is also the evaluator. One tends to exaggerate treatment effects in one's own patients. Is the anthropologist free of unconscious bias in doing evaluations? Probably not. However, the fact that one does not attempt to blind assessments in an observational study does not imply that one abandons all hope of remaining free of bias in evaluation outcome. On the contrary, even without blinding, considerable objectivity can be maintained. Measures of disease and cure, such as blood tests or x-rays, can sometimes be used. They are less subject to bias than are subjective measures such as descriptions of pain. Again, the *Cree* study is exemplary. The sizes of psoriatic lesions were objectively measured by non-treating physicians who used tape measures and followed predetermined protocols. The remaining four studies relied upon the subjective evaluations of either the patients or the examiners. It should be noted, however, that the use of questionnaires in the *Taiwan* and *Mexico* studies reduced the likelihood of unconscious bias. Well designed questionnaires can substitute for objective clinical measures or add to them.

Prospective Versus Retrospective Designs

Identifying results is better done if the trial is prospective, since recall of the original disease state and process of treatment can be of uncertain validity. The *Mexico*, *Cree*, and *Juarez* investigations met this criterion while the *Salish* and *Taiwan* trials did not.

Timing Post-Treatment Evaluations

Identifying results is also better done if post-treatment effects are measured after the passage of some period of time subsequent to the treatment. The longer the period of follow-up, the less likely that a placebo is involved, since placebos are by definition of temporary duration. A weakness of the *Juarez* study is that it recorded only immediate post-treatment changes. The evaluations were carried out in the presence of the practitioner just after the treatments were finished. Follow-ups under those conditions influence patients to report benefits, even if they are minimal or non-existent. The other four studies included good follow-up periods: *Salish* after a minimum of four years; *Taiwan* at two months post-treatment; *Cree* at weeks 1, 2, 4 and 22 after the commencement of treatment; and *Mexico* at 7 to 13 days post-treatment. In the latter case, an additional follow-up took place at 30 to 45 days, but it elicited subjective evaluations of patient responses, which offer less secure findings than the earlier pre- and post-treatment administration of the Cornell Medical Index as a measure of illness.

CONCLUSION

Anthropologists often accept anecdotal evidence for the efficacy of indigenous forms of healing, but the rigor of our investigations would be enormously increased if we would document the biomedical efficacy of diverse forms of traditional medicine as objectively as is possible. The ideal assessment of efficacy would be the randomized clinical trial, but it seems unlikely that field anthropologists will be able to design workable trials that are both controlled and blinded. Case studies can be carried out, but the generalizability of findings is so weak that they, too, are usually no more than anecdotal. Observational studies provide a desirable and feasible alternative. Five such anthropological studies were examined in this article. Each was flawed in one way or another, a testimony to how difficult this kind of field work can be. Yet, these efforts support the conclusion that efficacy can be determined by this means if proper attention is given to patient selection, treatment description, and objective outcome measures.

Where adequate observational trials are not possible, case studies should be undertaken as an alternative still vastly superior to the reporting of unstructured impressions. Laboratory studies, although highly valuable as measures of potential efficacy, cannot substitute for field trials and case studies as measures of what traditional healers actually achieve. Explorations of patient satisfaction have enormous value, but they are not measures of biomedical efficacy.

As anthropologists concerned with efficacy research, we are in trouble methodologically, but we are not alone, and we are not without prospects. Within academic medicine, too, efficacy research faces difficulties. We can shift to other paradigms just as researchers in medicine are shifting. To evaluate therapeutic efficacy ought to be an important part of what we do as medical anthropologists. Reflecting on the problems of testing efficacy, the experienced *Cree* researchers observe that, "this type of research becomes a compromise between feasibility and validity; between doing, or not doing, the research." In addition, "the methodological, political and legal barriers to conducting such research may be insurmountable" (Morse, McConnell, and Young 1987: 89). Conducting observational studies is not for the faint-of-heart.

As we attempt to give an anthropological perspective to traditional healing, it makes a difference in our overall interpretation of cultural dynamics whether or not a given treatment exerts a beneficial effect upon the natural course of the disease. As medical anthropologists, it should be our business wherever possible to include in our documentation of ethnomedicine some measure of benefit as assessed in biomedical terms.

ACKNOWELDGMENTS

I want to express my heartfelt gratitude to Lawrence S. Greene, Editor-in-Chief of *Medical Anthropology*, and four anonymous reviewers for utilizing the peer review process in a positive way as a means to provide supportive, constructive criticism that helped enormously in reorganizing and rewriting the original draft of this paper. I profited also from first draft comments by Edna Mitchell and William Meeker, and from reference assistance by Janice Perlman-Stites.

REFERENCES CITED

Ahern, E.
    1979   The Problem of Efficacy: Strong and Weak Illocutionary Acts. Man 14(1): 1–17.
Anderson, R.
    1981   Medicine, Chiropractic and Caste. Anthropological Quarterly 54(3): 157–165.
    1987   The Treatment of Musculoskeletal Disorders by a Mexican Bonesetter (*Sobador*). Social Science and Medicine 24(1): 43–46.
Antman, K., L. E. Schnipper, and E. Frei III
    1988   The Crisis in Clinical Cancer Research. The New England Journal of Medicine 319(1): 46–48.
Arkin, C.F., and M. S. Wachtel
    1990   How Many Patients Are Necessary to Assess Test Performance? Journal of the American Medical Association 263(2): 275–278.
Browner, C. H., B. Ortiz de Montellano, and A. J. Rubel
    1988   A Methodology for Cross-Cultural Ethnomedical Research. Current Anthropology 20(5): 681–702.
Brun, V., and T. Schumacher
    1987   Traditional Herbal Medicine in Northern Thailand. Berkeley: University of California Press.
Buerger, A. A.
    1977   Clinical Trials of Manipulation Therapy. In Approaches to the Validation of Manipulation Therapy. A. A. Buerger and J. S. Tobis, eds. Pp. 313–319. Springfield, IL: Charles C. Thomas.
Cassidy, J. D., W. H. Kirkaldy-Willis, and M. McGregor
    1985   Spinal Manipulation for the Treatment of Chronic Low-Back and Leg Pain: An Observational Study. In Empirical Approaches to the Validation of Spinal Manipulation. A. A. Buerger and P. E. Greenman, eds. Pp. 119–148. Springfield, IL: Charles C. Thomas.
    1988   Manipulation. In Managing Low Back Pain. 2nd ed., W. H. Kirkaldy-Willis, ed. Pp. 287–296 . New York: Churchill Livingstone.
Cohen, J.
    1977   Statistical Power Analysis for the Behavioral Sciences. Revised Edition. New York: Academic Press.
Colton, T.
    1990   The Power of Sound Statistics. Journal of the American Medical Association 263(2): 281.
Coulehan, J. L.
    1985   Chiropractic and the Clinical Art. Social Science and Medicine 21(4): 383–390.
Csordas, T. J.
    1988   Elements of Charismatic Persuasion and Healing. Medical Anthropology Quarterly n.s. 2(2): 112–142.
Davidson, J. R., and B. Ortiz de Montellano
    1983   The Antibacterial Properties of an Aztec Wound Remedy. Journal of Ethnopharmacology 8: 149–161.

Deyo, R. A., and A. K. Diehl
    1986   Patient Satisfaction with Medical Care for Low-Back Pain. Spine 11(1): 28–30.
Estes, J. W.
    1979   Hall Jackson and the Purple Foxglove: Medical Practice and Research in Revolutionary America, 1760–1820. Hanover, NH: University Press of New England.
Etkin, N. L.
    1988   Ethnopharmacology: Biobehavioral Approaches in the Anthropological Study of Indigenous Medicines. Annual Review of Anthropology 17: 23–42.
Etkin, N. L., and P. J. Ross
    1983   Malaria, Medicine, and Meals: Plant Use among the Hausa and Its Impact on Disease. *In* The Anthropology of Medicine: From Culture to Method. L. Romanucci-Ross, D. E. Moerman, and L. R. Tancredi, eds. Pp. 231–259. South Hadley, MA: Bergin & Garvey.
Finkler, K.
    1985   Spiritualist Healers in Mexico: Successes and Failures of Alternative Therapeutics. Praeger Special Studies. South Hadley, MA: Bergin & Garvey.
Fletcher, R. H.
    1989   The Costs of Clinical Trials. Journal of the American Medical Association 262(13): 1842.
Goldberg, J.
    1989   Anatomy of a Scientific Discovery. New York: Bantam.
Goldenberg, D. L.
    1987   Fibromyalgia Syndrome: An Emerging but Controversial Condition. Journal of the American Medical Association 257(20): 2782–2787.
Greenfield, S.
    1989   The State of Outcome Research: Are We on Target? The New England Journal of Medicine 320(17): 1142–1143.
Greenland, S., L. S. Reisbord, S. Haldeman, and A. A. Buerger
    1980   Controlled Clinical Trials of Manipulation: A Review and a Proposal. Journal of Occupational Medicine 22(10): 670–676.
Hadler, N. M., P. Curtis, D. B. Gillings, and S. Stinnett
    1987   A Benefit of Spinal Manipulation as Adjunctive Therapy for Acute Low-Back Pain: A Stratified Controlled Trial. Spine 12(7): 703–706.
Harner, M.
    1982   The Way of the Shaman: A Guide to Power and Healing. New York: Bantam.
Hawthorne, V. M.
    1985   The Randomized Controlled Trial and Low Back Pain: An Introduction. *In* Empirical Approaches to the Validation of Spinal Manipulation. A. A. Buerger and P. E. Greenman, eds. Pp 151–163. Springfield, IL: Charles C. Thomas.
Hurst, J. W.
    1989   The Value of Coronary Bypass Surgery Compared with Medical Therapy. Journal of the American Medical Association 261(14): 2118.
Jilek, W. G.
    1982   Indian Healing: Shamanic Ceremonialism in the Pacific Northwest Today. Cultures in Review Series. Surrey, BC, Canada: Hancock House Publishers.
Kane, R. L., et al.
    1974   Manipulating the Patient: A Comparison of the Effectiveness of Physician and Chiropractor Care. Lancet 1333–1336.
Keating, J. C., Jr., J. Seville, W. C. Meeker, R. S. Lonczak, L. A. Quitoriano, M. Dydo, and D. L. Leibel
    1985   Intrasubject Experimental Designs in Osteopathic Medicine: Applications in Clinical Practice. Journal of the American Osteopathic Association 85(3): 192–203.
Kirkaldy-Willis, W. H., and J. D. Cassidy
    1985   Spinal Manipulation in the Treatment of Low-Back Pain. Canadian Family Physician 31: 536–540.
Kleinman, A. M.
    1975   The Symbolic Context of Chinese Medicine: A Comparative Approach to the Study of Traditional Medical and Psychiatric Forms of Care in Chinese Culture. American Journal of Chinese Medicine 3(2): 103–124.

1980   Patients and Healers in the Context of Culture. Berkeley: University of California Press.
Krieger, D.
   1979   The Therapeutic Touch: How to Use your Hands to Help or Heal. Englewood Cliffs, NJ: Prentice-Hall.
Laupacis, A., D. L. Sackett, and R. S. Roberts
   1988   An Assessment of Clinically Useful Measures of the Consequences of Treatment. The New England Journal of Medicine 318(26): 1728–1733.
Leitenberg, H.
   1973   The Use of Single-Case Methodology in Psychotherapy Research. Journal of Abnormal Psychology 82: 87–101.
Louis, P. C. A.
   1836   Researches on the Effects of Bloodletting in Some Inflammatory Diseases, and on the Influence of Tartarized Antimony and Vesication in Pneumonia. Boston: Hilliard Gray.
Lowden, T. A., J. C. Keating, and W. C. Meeker
   1986   A Multivariate Time-Series Descriptive Case Study of Chiropractic Care in the Treatment of Cervical Pain. Journal of Manipulative and Physiological Therapeutics 9(4): 267–277.
Marwick, C.
   1988   Philosophy on Trial: Examining Ethics of Clinical Investigations. Journal of the American Medical Association 260(6): 749–751.
Moerman, D. E.
   1983   Physiology and Symbols: The Anthropological Implications of the Placebo Effect. In The Anthropology of Medicine: From Culture to Method. L. Romanucci-Ross, D. E. Moerman, and L. R. Tancredi, eds. Pp. 156–167. South Hadley, MA: Bergin & Garvey.
   1989   Poisoned Apples and Honeysuckles: The Medicinal Plants of Native America. Medical Anthropology Quarterly n.s. 3(1): 52–61.
Moore, L. G., P. W. Van Arsdale, J. E. Glittenberg, and R. A. Aldrich
   1987   The Bicultural Basis of Health: Expanding Views of Medical Anthropology. Prospect Heights, IL: Waveland Press.
Morse, J. M., R. McConnell, and D. E. Young
   1987   Documenting the Practice of a Traditional Healer: Methodological Problems and Issues. In Health Care Issues in the Canadian North. D. E. Young, ed. Pp. 89–94. University of Alberta Occasional Publication No. 26. Edmonton, Alberta: The Boreal Institute for Northern Studies.
Morse, J. M., D. E. Young, L. Swartz, and R. McConnell
   1987   A Cree Indian Treatment for Psoriasis: A Longitudinal Study. Culture VII(2): 31–41.
Moses, L. E.
   1984   The Series of Consecutive Cases as a Device for Assessing Outcomes of Intervention. New England Journal of Medicine 311(11): 705–710.
Nishimura, K.
   1987   Shamanism and Medical Cures. Current Anthropology 28(4): S59–64.
Ortiz de Montellano, B.
   1975   Empirical Aztec Medicine. Science 188: 215–220.
Ortiz de Montellano, B., and C. H. Browner
   1985   Chemical Bases for Medicinal Plant Use in Oaxaca, Mexico. Journal of Ethnopharmacology 13:57–88.
Pelto, P. J., and G. H. Pelto
   1978   Anthropological Research: The Structure of Inquiry. Cambridge: Cambridge University Press.
Prince, R.
   1964   Indigenous Yoruba Psychiatry. In Magic, Faith, and Healing: Studies in Primitive Psychiatry Today. A. Kiev, ed. Pp. 84–120. Glencoe, IL: The Free Press.
Rasmussen, G.
   1985   A Randomized Clinical Trial of Manipulation: Diagnostic Criteria and Treatment Techniques. In Empirical Approaches to the Validation of Spinal Manipulation. A. A. Buerger and P. E. Greenman, eds. Pp. 179–184. Springfield, IL: Charles C. Thomas.
Rodriguez-Bigas, M., N. I. Cruz, and A. Suarez
   1988   Comparative Evaluation of Aloe Vera in the Management of Burn Wounds in Guinea Pigs. Plastic and Reconstructive Surgery 81: 386–389.

Romanucci-Ross, L., and D. E. Moerman
   1988   The Extraneous Factor in Western Medicine. Ethos 16(2): 146–166.
Romanucci-Ross, L., D. E. Moerman, and L. R. Tancredi
   1983   The Anthropology of Medicine: From Culture to Method. South Hadley, MA: Bergin & Garvey.
Rudicel, S., and J. Esdaille
   1985   The Randomized Clinical Trial in Orthopedics: Obligation or Option. Journal of Bone and Joint Surgery 67A: 1284–1293.
Schweizer, T., and H. Lang
   1989   Sample Size and Research Strategy in Cultural Anthropology. Current Anthropology 30(4): 514–517.
Simon, A., D. Worthen, and A. Mitas
   1979   An Evaluation of Iridology. Journal of the American Medical Association 242: 1385–1389.
Simpson, W. F.
   1989   Comparative Longevity in a College Cohort of Christian Scientists. Journal of the American Medical Association 262(12): 1657–1658.
Skoler, M. J.
   1984   Acupuncture: An Old Art Coming of Age in America? Medical World News May: 50–61.
Tollison, C. D., M. L. Kriegel, and J. R. Satterthwaite
   1989   Comprehensive Treatment of Acute and Chronic Low Back Pain: A Clinical Outcome Comparison. Orthopaedic Review XVIII(1): 59–64.
van der Geest, S., and S. R. Whyte
   1989   The Charm of Medicines: Metaphors and Metonyms. Medical Anthropology Quarterly 3(4): 345–367.
Wiesner, D.
   1983   A Caste and Outcaste System in Medicine. Social Science and Medicine 17(8): 475–479.
Yin, R. K.
   1989   Case Study Research: Design and Methods. 2nd ed. Applied Social Research Methods Series, vol. 5. Newbury Park, CA: Sage Publications.
Young, A.
   1976   Some Implications of Medical Beliefs and Practices for Social Anthropology. American Anthropologist 78(1): 5–24.
Young, D. E., J. M. Morse, L. Swartz, and G. Ingram
   1987   The Psoriasis Research Project: An Overview. In Health Care Issues in the Canadian North. D. E. Young, ed. Pp. 76–88. University of Alberta Occasional Publication No. 26. Edmonton, Alberta: The Boreal Institute for Northern Studies.

An Epidemiological Description of a Folk Illness: A Study of *Empacho* in Guatemala

Susan C. Weller, Trenton K. Ruebush II, and Robert E. Klein

Although anthropologists have provided descriptions of many folk illnesses, few have systematically evaluated their prevalence and determined who is at greatest risk for acquiring them. This report attempts to provide a systematic description of the folk illness *empacho* including the symptoms that define it. Illness prevalence was estimated and subpopulations at greatest risk were identified from illness histories collected from a random sample of households in rural Guatemala. *Empacho* was found to constitute a distinct cluster of symptoms: diarrhea, vomiting, headache, and lack of appetite. It differed from other gastrointestinal illnesses in that headaches were more likely and stomachaches were less likely to be reported. *Empacho* was highly prevalent and occurred in adults and children. Further, results showed that although *empacho* was frequently diagnosed by residents, folk healers were rarely consulted for any illness. Nevertheless, a strong association exists between a household diagnosis of *empacho* and the use of folk healers by those households (p < .001).

When an illness is only recognized within a culture and not between cultures, it is considered to be "culture-bound." Such illnesses, also called "folk" illnesses, are a continuing thread through much of the medical anthropological literature. These syndromes have received considerable attention, partly because of their exotic nature and partly because they are presumed to reflect issues of importance within the culture in which they occur. While anthropologists have provided descriptive reports of many of these conditions, few have systematically evaluated the prevalence of folk illnesses and determined who is at greatest risk for acquiring them. A logical next step, therefore, is an "epidemiological" description of folk illnesses. It is with this aim in mind that this report attempts to provide an epidemiological description of the folk illness *empacho*.

While many folk illnesses are considered to be psychosocial in origin (Simons and Hughes 1985), some may be linked to organic disease. *Susto, mollera caida,* and *empacho* are syndromes commonly reported in Latin America. *Susto* has been widely discussed, usually within the context of culturally-bound, psychogenic illnesses. It is a "fright sickness" where a frightening experience causes the "spirit" to become detached from the body. Insomnia and malaise are the principal symp-

SUSAN C. WELLER *is Associate Professor of Preventive Medicine and Community Health at the University of Texas Medical Branch, Galveston, TX 77550. She is a medical anthropologist interested in health beliefs and utilization of health-care services. For the past several years she has been collaborating with Ruebush and Klein on projects related to health-seeking behavior associated with malaria.*

TRENTON K. RUEBUSH II *is a physician-epidemiologist with the Centers for Disease Control. He lived in Guatemala for six years while studying various aspects of malaria.*

ROBERT E. KLEIN *is a psychologist jointly affiliated with the Medical Entomology Research and Training Unit of the Centers for Disease Control and with the Universidad del Valle in Guatemala City.*

toms. *Susto* may be treated by religious rituals or by administering herbal teas (Trotter 1982). Individuals reporting *susto* also may experience more social stress, organic disease, and a higher mortality rate than those without *susto* (Rubel, O'Nell, and Collado-Ardon 1984).

Mollera caida and *empacho*, in contrast, have attracted attention because they have been linked with diarrheal diseases in infants and children (Kendall, Foote, and Martorell 1983). These diagnoses may be folk labels for underlying physical illness(es). *Mollera caida* refers to the "fallen" fontanel (soft-spot) on an infant's head. It is believed to be caused by a fall or by sudden withdrawal of the breast during breast-feeding. The most common treatment is to push up on the infant's palate (Trotter, Ortiz de Montellano, and Logan 1989). In Western medicine, a sunken fontanel is considered to be a sign of dehydration and is treated by rehydrating the infant. *Empacho* is a gastrointestinal illness where food gets stuck in the stomach or intestinal tract and must be dislodged in order to effect a cure (Trotter 1985a). It is thought to be caused by eating too much or too little or by specific foods. Also the treatment of *empacho* has been implicated in cases of lead poisoning (Trotter 1985b).

Since folk illnesses do not translate well into biomedical categories, folk illnesses are often thought to be best treated by folk healers. Folk healers are lay practitioners who cure with herbs, massage, spiritual powers, and/or witchcraft. Several types of folk healers can be found in Latin America: *herbalistas, curanderos, espiritistas, brujos, sobadores,* and *comadronas. Herbalistas* specialize in the selection and preparation of herbal remedies. *Curanderos* (curers) and *espiritistas* cure physical and spiritual maladies with herbs, prayers, rituals and touch. *Brujos* (witches) also use herbs and rituals but their intention is generally thought to be malevolent. *Sobadores* (masseurs) use massage or rubbing as their major form of therapy, with or without other remedies. *Comadronas* (midwives) specialize in birthing, but also may be consulted about other maternal and infant health matters. Most folk healers are not considered to practice Western-style medicine, with the possible exception of the midwife who also may give injections.

With few exceptions, reports from the anthropological literature tend to be case reports or descriptions of a series of cases. Reports usually describe individuals with a folk illness or individuals treated by a folk healer. Unfortunately, neither the distinguishing features of the illness nor the place of that illness within the entire system of illnesses can be determined from a "case series." In order to identify the distinguishing characteristics of a syndrome, it must be contrasted with other illnesses. Without such a comparison, symptoms belonging to an entire class of illnesses may be mistakenly attributed to a single illness. Similarly, a series of cases of folk healer consultations cannot provide information about the type of individuals or cases seen by folk healers. A group of non-folk diagnoses or non-folk healer consultations is needed for comparison, in order to determine the distinguishing characteristics associated with folk diagnoses or characteristics of those using folk healers (Browner, Ortiz de Montellano, and Rubel 1988). Also, the "place" of folk illness within the overall illness system, that is, the prevalence of disease or the disease burden, can only be estimated from a random sample or census of all illness cases. Without either a representative sample of illnesses or a proper comparison group, the nature and role of folk illness within a culture is neither complete nor necessarily accurate.

In this paper we focus on a common folk diagnosis, *empacho*, and attempt to address the following questions: First, what is its place within the overall burden of diseases? Specifically, what is the prevalence of *empacho*? Second, who is at-risk for acquiring the condition? Third, does *empacho* comprise a distinct symptom complex? Is there a set of signs and symptoms that differentiates it from other diagnoses? Finally, how are folk illnesses, and *empacho* in particular, cured? Are folk illnesses treated by folk healers?

METHOD

Procedure

The data for this report come from a larger study on health-seeking behavior conducted on the Pacific Coast of Guatemala. Most of the residents on the Pacific coastal plain and all of the individuals interviewed in this case study were of mixed European-Mayan Indian descent (Ladinos). Illness cases were collected from a *random* sample of households in rural communities. A census was taken in six villages and a random sample of 25 households was selected in each (150 households). Communities were selected in pairs on the basis of their size, population distribution, and access to health care. Two villages were larger (population of > 1400) with a pharmacy, government health post, and stores, and were located more than 15 km. from a city and a physician. The four smaller villages (population 500–800) did not have a physician, pharmacy or health post, but were approximately 5 km away from all three.

Families were visited in June 1986 and asked about all the illnesses that had occurred in their household since Easter (three months). Easter was chosen as a point of reference because it is a major holiday in Guatemala and marking the recall period with an important event improves the quality of recall data (Jabine et al. 1984). For each reported illness, a detailed series of standardized questions was asked, including symptoms and treatment. Specifically, informants were asked about any symptoms they might have had since Easter ("¿*Que malestares ha tenido?*") and what illness they though they had ("¿*Que enfermedad tenía?*") Multiple steps in seeking treatment were recorded. In order to be considered a new step, treatments had to be separated by at least one half day. Open-ended interviews also were conducted exploring *empacho*, its symptoms and cures.

Analysis

Prevalence of *empacho* and determination of subpopulations at greatest risk were estimated from the self-reported illnesses. Prevalence and incidence can be used to estimate the actual disease frequency within the study area. Prevalence is a measure of existing disease cases, either at a single point in time (point prevalence) or over a specified time period (period prevalence). Incidence is a measure of the rate of new cases in disease-free individuals over a specified time period. The main difference between prevalence and incidence is in regard to chronically ill cases: prevalence counts all cases regardless of when the illness began, while incidence counts only those cases occurring in individuals who were disease-free at the beginning of the time period. Thus, in a community where the disease burden consists principally of acute, transient illnesses, period prevalence and incidence may be equivalent. Further, these indices can be expressed as the probability of any person acquiring the disease (case counts represent individuals) or as the number of disease cases to be expected (case counts include all cases and may involve double-counting of individuals) (Mausner and Kramer 1985).

Symptoms that define and distinguish *empacho* were determined by contrasting *empacho* with other illnesses. Chi square tests were used to test for symptoms that differentiated a diagnosis of *empacho* from a non-*empacho* diagnosis. A Bonferroni corrected significance level was used to take into account the use of multiple significance tests (Kirk 1968). Since 30 symptoms were tested, a .05 probability level was adjusted with a Bonferroni correction (.05/30) and a .0017 significance level was used. A discriminant analysis was used to see how well characteristic symptoms and demographic variables together were predictive of *empacho*. Finally, treatment strategies were compared between folk and non-folk diagnoses. Prevalence of folk healer consultations was estimated. Use of a folk healer (yes/no) was then compared to use of a folk diagnosis (yes/no) to see if individuals with folk diagnoses are more likely to seek folk treatment. Actual remedies used by informants are also reported.

RESULTS

Prevalence

Of the 150 households selected for interviewing, 119 households reported at least one illness and a total of 279 illness cases were reported. The 150 households included 607 individuals. Across the 279 reported illness cases, some illness labels appeared both as an "illness" and as a "symptom." This overlap was concordant with the "complexity" of the illness. For example, if an individual had one "symptom," e.g., a headache or stomachache, then that symptom was usually reported as the "illness" as well. An illness with multiple symptoms could be labeled by the most salient symptom or be given a new and distinct label. Also, because the illness cases are self-reported, they are essentially self-diagnoses. Cases of folk illnesses included 26 cases of *empacho* (23 as initial diagnoses and 3 subsequent diagnoses). The raw case count in Table I (diagnoses mentioned by three or more individuals) indicates that *empacho* has a prominent position among common acute illnesses.[1] In fact, *empacho* is about as common as the "flu."

Disease burden can be estimated from the total number of cases of *empacho* divided by the number of individuals in the sample households. Since reported illnesses covered a three-month period in our study, this ratio (26/607) can be multiplied by four to estimate the number of cases per year (assuming that there are no dramatic seasonal fluctuations). This can be further broken down by age ("adults" 15 or more years of age and "children" less than 15 years) and gender by

TABLE I. Most frequently reported illnesses
on the Pacific coastal plain of Guatemala.

English Gloss	Spanish	Cases
Common cold	*Catarro*	41
"Malaria"/Fever	*Paludismo*	31
Worms (*Ascariasis*)*	*Lombrices**	31
"Flu"	*Gripe*	29
Empacho*	*Empacho**	23
Headache	*Dolor de cabeza*	13
Boils	*Granos*	9
Cough	*Tos*	8
Diarrhea*	*Asientos**	7
Chicken Pox	*Varicela*	6
Bronchitis	*Bronquitis*	5
Nervousness	*Nervios*	5
Muscle/joint pain	*Dolor de cuerpo*	5
Temperature/Fever	*Calentura*	4
Wounds	*Heridas*	4
Difficulty Breathing	*Fatiga*	4
Bruise/Wound	*Golpe*	4
Pregnancy problems	*Problema con el embarazo*	3
Fungal infection	*Hongos*	3
Kidney problems	*Problema con los rinones*	3
Gastroenteritis*	*Inflamacíon intestinal**	3
Stomachache*	*Dolor de estómago**	3
Intestinal parasites/ "Diarrhea"*	*Amebas**	3

*Gastrointestinal illnesses

examining those sub-groups separately. Table II displays the proportion of each of those groups expected to have *empacho* during one year. Based on actual age and sex distributions these proportions can be re-expressed in terms of village size. In a village of 1000 individuals, 171 cases of *empacho* would be expected per year: 92 per 557 adults and 79 per 443 children; 105 per 530 males, and 66 per 470 females; 66 per 297 male adults, 26 per 260 female adults; 40 per 234 male children, and 40 per 209 female children. (Approximately half of the population (44%) is less than 15 years old.) These data indicate that on the Pacific Coast of Guatemala, *empacho* occurs in both adults and children.

TABLE II. Incidence of *empacho* by age and gender.

	Expected proportion of population per year:		
Age	Gender		
	Male	Female	Total
Children	.169	.189	.142
Adults	.222	.101	.166
Total	.199	.140	.171

Symptoms

Open-ended interviews with an independent, convenience sample of 19 informants provided descriptions of *empacho* symptoms similar to those reported in previous research: lack of appetite, temperature, diarrhea, headache, stomachache, vomiting, and abdominal distension. *Empacho* is thought to be caused by eating too much or too little, from not eating on time, or from not eating at all. It can also be caused by eating food that is too dry, too hot, or by specific food items (e.g., raw *platano*).

The 26 case histories of *empacho* obtained as part of the large survey contained similar symptoms. An examination of those cases revealed that the most frequently mentioned symptoms are diarrhea, lack of appetite, headache, vomiting and stomachache (Table III). However, a more important question concerns the identification of symptoms that differentiate *empacho* from other illnesses. To do this, symptoms were tested to see which ones maximally discriminated between (1) *empacho* and all other illness labels, (2) gastrointestinal illnesses and non-gastrointestinal illnesses, and (3) *empacho* and other gastrointestinal illnesses. *Empacho* (n = 26) can be distinguished from other illnesses (n = 253) by the lack of appetite (p $\leq$ .0000045), and the presence of diarrhea (p $\leq$ .0000077) and vomiting (p = .0026). Seventy-seven (77/279) of all cases reported a gastrointestinal (GI) illness (i.e., *lombrices, asientos, empacho, gastritis, disenteria, inflamación intestinal, dolor de estómago,* or *amebas*) at sometime during their infirmity. Gastrointestinal illnesses (n = 77) can be differentiated from non-GI illnesses (n = 202) by the *presence* of vomiting (p $\leq$ .00001), diarrhea (p $\leq$ .000004), stomachache (p $\leq$ .000004), and abdominal distension (p $\leq$ .00012); and the *absence* of fever (p $\leq$ .00004), headache (p = .0018), muscle joint pain (p $\leq$ .000025), sneezing (p = .00156), and runny nose (p < .00004). *Empacho* (n = 26) tended to be different (although not statistically significant at p < .0017) from other GI illnesses (n = 51) in the presence of a headache (p = .0094), lack of appetite (p = .0089), and the absence of a stomachache (p = .0037). Thus, of the

TABLE III. Symptoms reported
in 26 cases of *empacho*.

Symptoms	Number of Cases
Diarrhea	12
Lack of appetite	9
Headache	7
Vomiting	5
Stomachache	5
Abdominal distension	3
Fever	2
Nausea	2
Chills	1
Tiredness	1
Toothache	1
Cough	1
Difficulty breathing	1

symptoms associated with *empacho*, some are indicative of a GI illness in general (vomiting and diarrhea) and others (lack of appetite, headache, no stomachache) are indicative specifically of *empacho*.

The comparison of symptoms and characteristics of individuals reporting *empacho* with those reporting another GI illness, shows that those with *empacho* have a significantly different profile (Table IV). They have more headaches (27 vs. 4%), lack an appetite (35 vs. 8%), have fewer stomachaches (19 vs. 57%), take more "steps" during a curative treatment (2.2 vs. 1.7 steps), and tend to be male (62 vs. 39%). Both groups have similar ages (22.0 vs. 16.8 years) and rates of fever (8 vs. 10%), vomiting (19 vs. 12%), diarrhea (46 vs. 51%), and perceived severity of illness episode (10 vs. 8% responding severe). Households also had comparable levels of income (Q180.64 vs. Q141.01) and educational level for head of household (1.3 vs. 1.7 years).

Together, headache, lack of appetite, stomachache, number of steps and gender discriminate *empacho* from other GI ailments fairly well (r = .59, p < .001, n = 77). Predictions based on these five variables, however, show that the model is better at predicting the absence of *empacho* than it is at predicting the presence of *empacho*: 44/51 of those without *empacho* were correctly identified, while only 13/26 of those with *empacho* were correctly identified. This means that if a woman has a stomachache and diarrhea, but no loss of appetite or headache, a diagnosis of *empacho* can be ruled out. On the other hand, a man with a headache, lack of appetite, and no stomachache may or may not have *empacho*.

TABLE IV. Symptoms and personal characteristics associated with *empacho* and other illness categories.

Symptoms	Empacho (N = 26)	GI Illnesses[a] (N = 51)	Non-GI Illnesses[b] (N = 202)
Lack of Appetite	35%	8%	5%
Headache	27%	4%	30%
Abdominal distention	12%	8%	1%
Vomiting	19%	12%	2%
Diarrhea	46%	51%	2%
Stomachache	19%	57%	3%
Fever	8%	10%	43%
Muscle/joint pain	0%	4%	20%
Sneezing	0%	0%	12%
Runny nose	0%	0%	22%
Other Variables			
Male	62%	39%	46%
Age (mean years)	22.0	16.8	24.6
Steps in seeking cure	2.2	1.7	1.7
Monthly income	180.64Q	141.01Q	149.12Q
Per capita income	33.07Q	27.88Q	29.32Q
Education (years)	1.3	1.7	1.5
Literacy	58%	63%	55%

[a]Gastointestinal illnesses excluding *empacho*.
[b]Upper respiratory illnesses, skin conditions, and malaria.

Few individuals changed their assessment of their diagnosis (9/279). Of those who did, most changes occurred within the GI category. Of the GI illness cases, seven individuals changed their diagnosis during the course of the illness and four of the changes involved *empacho*. The similarity of *empacho* to other illnesses can be seen in the switching of diagnoses. The changes involving *empacho* were: from "worms" (*lombrices*) to *empacho*; from *empacho* to "worms"; from "malaria" to *empacho*; and from "malaria" to "worms" to *empacho*. An initial diagnosis of malaria may be due to the presence of a fever. If the fever subsides or if GI symptoms become more prominent, the diagnosis may be changed to a GI illness.

Treatment

Although folk diagnoses are quite common, folk healer consultations are not (Table V). Only seven of the 279 initial actions involved a folk healer and six additional cases consulted a folk healer at a later stage of treatment (the 13 cases are detailed in Table VI). Five began with a folk healer (*sobador* or *curandero*) and consulted no one else; two began with a folk healer (*sobador*) and continued with self-treatment (home, store, pharmacy); four began with self-treatment and ended with a folk healer (*sobador*); one went to a government health post and then to a folk healer (*curandero*); and one began with self-treatment, consulted a folk healer (*curandero*), and then went to a pharmacy.

These data indicate that folk healers are not widely used. Quite notably, the most frequent source of care was self-treatment, without consultation with anyone outside the household. When individuals did seek advice/care outside the home, the majority of actions involved Western-style care. Folk healers were infrequently consulted, and were consulted about as often as physicians. Furthermore, folk healers were not necessarily "last resort" choices: five cases consulted only a folk healer, five cases began with one form of treatment and ended with a folk healer, and three cases sought other treatment after consulting a folk healer. Nevertheless, a comparison of those who reported a folk illness (*empacho*) during their illness with those who did not, shows a strong relationship between the presence of a folk illness and use of a folk healer (odds = 67.65:1, Q = .97, p < .00005, n = 279)[2]. (Refer to Table VII.) This relationship, however, could be inflated by the large number of illnesses that were self-treated. Since the only reported folk illness is gastrointestinal (*empacho*), we examined the GI illnesses separately. Even with a dramatic drop in the number of self-treated non-folk illnesses, the relationship remains (odds = 76.42:1, Q = .97, p < .00005, n = 77). Thus, there is an extremely strong preference to consult a folk healer for *empacho* even though the predominant source of care for any illness is self-treatment.

An individual with *empacho* is approximately 76 times more likely to seek folk treatment than an individual with another GI ailment. The association is dramatic, but asymmetric. If an individual consulted a folk healer (for A GI illness), we can predict 38% better than chance that "he" had *empacho* (lambda = .38)[3]. However, if someone has *empacho* we cannot predict whether that person will actually seek folk treatment (lambda = .09)! This is because half of those with *empacho* seek folk treatment and half do not.

TABLE V. Treatment source choices for 279 illness histories.

Treatment Source	Initial Action
Self-treatment	202
Friend or relative	22
Store/pharmacy	15
Health Post	10
Community Malaria Worker	8
Physician	8
Folk healer	7
"Empiric doctor"*	4
Hospital	3
	279

*Lay person or nurse practicing Western-style medicine.

Remedies used for *empacho* were quite similar to those used for other gastrointestinal illness. The most frequently mentioned treatment for a GI illness, including *empacho*, was an antacid containing sodium bicarbonate, for example, Alka Seltzer®. *Empacho* was most often treated with Alka Seltzer® or sodium bicarbonate, along with a stomach massage, and possibly a purgative. (A detailed listing of *empacho* remedies appears in Table VIII.) Non-*empacho* GI illness remedies included Alka Seltzer®, anti-worm medications (Padrax®, Lombrisaca®), and antibiotics (tetracycline). Non-GI illnesses were treated principally with aspirin-containing compounds (Mejoral®, Neomelumbrina®).

DISCUSSION

When *empacho* is compared to other gastrointestinal illnesses, it has a distinctly different profile. Both unstructured interviews and systematically collected illness

TABLE VI. Illness episodes in which a "folk" healer was consulted.

Illness	No. of Cases	Successive Sources of Health Care			
		First	Second	Third	Fourth
Empacho	4	*Sobador*			
Empacho	1	*Sobador*	Pharmacy		
Empacho	1	*Sobador*	Store	Medicine*	
Empacho	2	Store	*Sobador*		
Lombrices/ Empacho	1	Herbs	*Sobador*		
Empacho	1	Pharmacy	Store	Pharmacy	*Sobador*
Empacho	1	Health Post	*Curandero*	*Curandero*	
Granos	1	*Curandero* (Naturalist)			
Paludismo	1	Store	Herbs	*Curandero*	Pharmacy

*Medicine at home that previously had been purchased in a store or pharmacy.

TABLE VII. Association between folk illness and seeking care from a folk healer.

Diagnosis	Folk Healer	Other Actions	
For all 279 illness cases:			
Empacho	11	20	31
Other	2	246	248
	13	266	279
For gastrointestinal illnesses only:			
Empacho	11	15	26
Other GI	0	51	51
	11	66	77

TABLE VIII. Treatments for *empacho*.

No. of Cases	
21	Antacids containing sodium bicarbonate (Alka Seltzer®, Sal Andrews®, sodium bicarbonate)
9	Lemon juice
8	Antimicrobials Antibiotics: tetracycline and/or chloromphenicol Sulfa drugs: sulfadiazine
6	Herbal remedies *pericon* *yerba buena* *hoja de zer (lavado)* *tripa de pollo (lavado)* *apazote* *salavia sija* *yervena (lavado)*
5	Milk of Magnesia® (magnesium hydroxide)
4	Olive oil/cod liver oil
4	Aspirin-containing compounds/acetominophen
4	Salt, sugar, and/or cinnamon
4	Anti-parasitic drugs Antihelminthics: Padrax®, Combatrin® Antiamebics: Diiodohydroxyquin-containing compound
3	*Sal Inglesa* (Worcestershire sauce)
3	Mineral water
2	*Brazas apagadas* (hot coals immersed in water; drink water)
2	*Sulfato de soda*
1	Vitamins
1	Burnt tortilla
1	Alcohol rub (with aspirin and lemon juice)
1	*Suero* (intraveneous fluids)

cases characterized *empacho* with symptoms of diarrhea, vomiting, headache, and lack of appetite. However, the presence of a headache, the lack of appetite, and the absence of a stomachache differentiates the diagnosis *empacho* from other GI diagnoses. The reported diagnosis of *empacho* is also quite common, occurring in 17% of the population per year. It is, in fact, for Guatemalans living on the Pacific Coastal Plain, as common as the "flu" (*gripe*) and occurs in both adults and children.

Other reports have indicated that individuals at greater risk for *empacho* are infants and children (Trotter 1985a, 1985b; Rivera 1988). However, previous reports were not based on random sampling and therefore it is difficult to know if they are biased and reflect the fact that *most* illnesses occur in infants and children or if *empacho* affects a different sub-population of Mexican-Americans than Guatemalans. Even studies based on random samples need to take care that estimates of illness prevalence use the proper denominator. Rivera (1988) reported that 20 out of 128 (15.6%) randomly selected Hispanic women in Colorado reported having had *empacho* at sometime in the past (note that this is not true prevalence) and that 29 children also had had *empacho*. If "29 children" indicates the number of households reporting *empacho* in children, then 22.7% (29/128) of households may have had *empacho* in children. However, if 29 children, that is, individuals had *empacho* and each household had an average of four children, then approximately 5.7% (29/512) of children may have had *empacho* at sometime in the past.

The principal treatment for *empacho* in Guatemala is an antacid containing sodium bicarbonate and a stomach massage. Other remedies for *empacho* include herbal teas, and antimicrobial and antiparasitic drugs. Descriptions of *empacho* remedies from Mexico (Baer et al. 1989; Baer and Ackerman 1988) and from Mexicans living in the Southwestern United States (Trotter 1985b) have included lead-containing compounds of *greta, azarcon,* and *albayalde.* Such home remedies have been implicated in cases of lead poisoning (Ackerman *et al.* 1982; Bose et al. 1983). In Guatemala, no lead-containing compounds were reported.

Empacho is also more likely than other illnesses to be treated by a folk healer. Specifically, those who had *empacho* and consulted a folk healer, consulted a *sobador* (masseur). Although folk healer consultations are infrequent, there exists an association between folk diagnoses and folk healer consultations; e.g., even though the predominant source of care is self-treatment, there exists a strong preference for folk healers to treat *empacho*. The association, however, is asymmetric. Individuals that went to a folk healer, tended to report a folk diagnosis (*empacho*). Individuals with a folk diagnosis, however, were equally likely to chose folk or non-folk therapy.

Although *empacho* was highly prevalent in the study area, other folk illnesses were not. This could mean that other folk diagnoses do not exist in the study area or that they occur at a rate less frequent than our sample size could detect (less than 1/607 individuals over a three-month period). It is also possible that respondents were reluctant to report folk diagnoses, but the high prevalence of *empacho* makes this unlikely.

Some have criticized the anthropological literature for failing to give an accurate representation of the relative position of folk illnesses within the context of all health problems (Trotter 1983). The design of our study facilitated an epidemiological description of the folk illness *empacho*. Random sampling of households allowed for a representative description of village health and an estimation of the relative disease burden from various illnesses. In this study, we found that *empacho* is a very common illness; it is the fifth most common diagnosis.

ACKNOWLEDGMENTS

An earlier version of this article was presented at the Annual Meeting of the Society for Applied Anthropology in Santa Fe, NM in April 1989. We would like to thank Drs. Alfredo Mendez-Dominguez and Hector A. Godoy for their help during the course of this study. We would also like to thank Lee Pachter, Arthur Rubel, Roberta Baer, and two anonymous reviewers for comments on an earlier draft. The interviews were conducted by Sheila Gongora and Vidalina Ramos. This work was begun while S. C. Weller was at the University of Pennsylvania. This investigation received financial support from the Social and Economic Research component of the UNDP/World Bank/WHO Special Programme for Research and Training in Tropical Diseases and from the University of Pennsylvania Research Fund.

NOTES

1. Translation of diagnostic terms is approximate. *Paladismo* is translated as "malaria," but it does not necessarily mean that the organic condition malaria is present. Similarly, *amebas* is translated as "intestinal parasites." Both conditions are prevalent enough on the Pacific Coast of Guatemala that residents are familiar with the signs and symptoms of each, but the "organic" condition may or may not be present. There were also five cases of *nervios* (four women and one man) glossed here as nervousness. *Nervios* appears to be a much milder and less frequent condition than is found in other areas (Low 1985).
2. A continuity correction (adding .5 to each cell frequency) was implemented prior to calculating measures of association. The cross-products ratio is a measure of the size of an association expressed as "odds." Thus, those with a folk illness were 67.65 times more likely than those not reporting a folk illness to consult a folk healer. Yule's Q is an odds ratio based correlation coefficient, re-expressing the odds ratio on a scale (-1 to $+1$) similar to the Pearson correlation coefficient.
3. The asymmetric measure lambda tells how much better than chance individuals can be classified as: (1) having *empacho* if we *know* that a folk healer was consulted or (2) consulting a folk healer if we *know* an individual has *empacho*. "Better than chance" refers to how much better we can predict what an individual will do, as compared to simply flipping a coin.

REFERENCES CITED

Ackerman, A., E. Cronin, D. Rodman, et al.
    1982   Lead Poisoning from Lead Tetroxide Used as a Folk Remedy. Morbidity and Mortality Weekly Report 30(52): 647–648.
Baer, R., and A. Ackerman
    1988   Toxic Mexican Folk Remedies for the Treatment of *Empacho*: The Case of Azarcon, Greta, and Albayalde. Journal of Ethnopharmacology 24: 31–39.
Baer, R. D., J. Garcia de Alba, L. M. Cueto, A. Ackerman, and S. Davison
    1989   Lead Based Remedies for *Empacho*: Patterns and Consequences. Social Science and Medicine 29(12): 1373–1379.
Bose, A., et al.
    1983   Azarcon *por Empacho*. Another Cause of Lead Toxicity. Pediatrics 72: 106–108.
Browner, C. H., B. R. Ortiz de Montellano, and A. J. Rubel
    1988   A Methodology for Cross-Cultural Ethnomedical Research. Current Anthropology 29(5): 681–702.

Jabine, T. B., M. L. Straf, J. M. Tanur, and R. Tourangeau, eds.
  1984 Cognitive Aspects of Survey Methodology: Building a Bridge Between Disciplines. Washington, DC: National Academy Press.
Kendall, C., D. Foote, and R. Martorell
  1983 Anthropology, Communications, and Health: The Mass Media and Health Practices Program in Honduras. Human Organization 42(4): 353–360.
Kirk, R. E.
  1968 Experimental Designs: Procedures for the Behavioral Sciences. Belmont: Brooks/Cole.
Low, S. M.
  1985 Culturally Interpreted Symptoms or Culture-Bound Syndromes: A Cross-Cultural Review of Nerves. Social Science and Medicine 21: 187–196.
Mausner, J. S., and S. Kramer
  1985 Epidemiology: An Introductory Text. Philadelphia: W. B. Saunders.
Rivera, G., Jr.
  1988 Hispanic Folk Medicine Utilization in Urban Colorado. Sociology and Social Research 72(4): 237–241.
Rubel, A. J., C. W. O'Nell, and R. Collado-Ardon
  1984 *Susto*, A Folk Illness. Berkeley: University of California Press.
Simons, R. C., and C. C. Hughes, eds.
  1985 The Culture-Bound Syndromes. Dordrecht, Holland: D. Reidel.
Trotter, R. T.
  1982 *Susto*: The Context of Community Morbidity Patterns. Ethnology XXI(3): 215–226.
  1983 Morbidity Patterns and Mexican American Folk Illnesses: A Comparative Methodology. Medical Anthropology 7(1): 33–44.
  1985a Folk Medicine in the Southwest, Myths and Medical Facts. Postgraduate Medicine 78(8): 167–179.
  1985b Greta and Azarcon: A Survey of Episodic Lead Poisoning from a Folk Remedy. Human Organization 44(1): 64–72.
Trotter, R. T., B. R. Ortiz de Montellano, and M. H. Logan
  1989 Fallen Fontanel in the American Southwest: Its Origin, Epidemiology and Possible Organic Causes. Medical Anthropology 10(4): 207–217.

Discourse, *Daño*, and Healing in North Coastal Peru

Bonnie Glass-Coffin

This paper argues that discourse is culturally recognized as powerful and dangerous, significantly informing both the illness experience known as *daño* (magical aggression) and its traditional cure in North-coastal Peru. Words are viewed as a type of symbolic currency which negotiate and "transact" identity in an economic, social, and psychological environment in which self-esteem is generally viewed as a scarce commodity and tied to the opinions of others. In the case presented, gossip is a verbal mode of *daño* that is perceived as a threat to the victim's constructed identity: the physical and emotional symptoms of *daño* directly relate to the anxiety about what people will say (*que dirán*). I examine the symbolism of the *mesa* or traditional healing ceremony in terms of this "economy" of discourse to illustrate how the patient's personal experience is linked to a culturally powerful metaphor and then transformed in order to effect the cure.

INTRODUCTION

In this article I discuss an idea which owes its theoretical genesis to the work of G. H. Mead and which has recently received attention through anthropological forays into literary criticism, social-psychology, phenomenology, hermeneutics, and socio-linguistics. This idea is the "constructive" nature of personal identity.[1] Personal identity is constructed, we are told, as it is "displayed (enacted, expressed, or performed) both to other aspects of itself and to others through language, gesture and appearance, at a particular time and in a socially organized context" (Weigert, Teitge, and Teitge 1986: 49). Discourse, as language usage or performance—shaped by the agendas of human intent (Ricoeur 1971)—must be integral to identity construction.[2] Discourse also shares an intimate relationship with threatened identity and the experience of illness.[3] Detached from the conversational context in which it occurs, it can be extracted and appropriated. When abstracted, it reports the speech of others and can be used, negotiated, and controlled as a manifestation of social power to threaten or restore identity. Discourse, in short, has the power to wound and to heal.

The importance of discourse to the transformative or healing power of ritual has

BONNIE GLASS-COFFIN, *a doctoral candidate in anthropology at UCLA, is completing her dissertation on "Women as Magical-Religious Specialists in North Coastal Peru." Her research interests are in the areas of medical anthropology, psychological anthropology, and shamanism, and she has carried out fieldwork in Trujillo and Chiclayo, Peru.*

often been suggested.[4] But to understand how words can transform identity in the context of a healing ritual, we must first have a sense of how these are embodied and where their wounding power lies. In the discussion that follows, I suggest that words are not only the instruments of illness, but also the symbolic currency with which patients, healers, and families alike "transact" and negotiate the illness experience. The economic metaphor here is apt. Discourse—whether formal (healer/patient communication), or informal (recounting of illness stories/daily events), situated or entextualized[5] (gossip/hearsay), is inevitably an exchange. One must seek out the "economy" that governs the ebb and flow of what Bourdieu calls "symbolic capital."[6] Although symbolic capital is governed by different rules than the accumulation and loss of material wealth, Bourdieu suggests that it, like money, is calculated as a means to the same end—that of acquiring *worth*. And symbolic capital, or self-worth, is intimately linked to the construction of personal identity.

This article suggests a way to view the "economy of symbolic capital" on the North coast of Peru as it relates to the traditional ritual healing system (for which the region is famous) and to the culture-specific illnesses that result from the various forms of magical aggression known as *daño*. It explores the roles that discourse, with its regulating metaphor of 'exchange,' plays in this illness-healing system. I believe that the merit of this discussion lies in the 'grounded' or empirical unravelling of these concepts within a specific cultural context—not according to their theoretical importance to contemporary social theory—but as culturally significant semantic networks.

In the discussion that follows, I analyze the relationship between the symbolic economy of discourse, the negotiation of self-worth, and the experience of illness as expressed in the ritual language and symbolic interpretation of the healing ceremony of one very articulate ritual healer, or *curandero*, on Peru's North coast. I examine the impact of the symbolism of his ceremony on the illness experience of one young woman who was interviewed before and after her participation in the healing ceremony. To begin, I offer some background, gathered during various opportunities ranging over 41 months from 1975 to 1989, on the economic, social, and psychological environment as I observed and experienced it and which underscore the relationships between discourse, identity management, and the experience of illness in and around the city of Trujillo.

BACKGROUND AND SETTING

Economic Environment

Trujillo is a coastal city of approximately 500,000 people situated in the middle of the Moche River valley 400 km. north of Lima, Peru. Beyond the city periphery the lush green of the irrigated sugar cane softens the otherwise unrelenting landscape that, squeezed between the Andes to the East and the Pacific Ocean, has the reputation for being one of the driest deserts in the world. The regional economy depends heavily on a post-hacienda style sugar industry. In the city itself, small and medium-sized industries developed, flourished, and stagnated between the 1950s and late 1970s.

Commercial and service sectors employ far more people than industry but wages are low and competition is stiff for available jobs. According to the 1981 census, 46.6% of economically active men and 25% of the economically active women in Trujillo and the surrounding countryside classify themselves as "independent" workers (Forsberg and Francke 1987: 235). Further, almost one third of the income for households surveyed in coastal Peru comes from these "independent" economic activities (INE 1989: 228). As de Soto (1989) contends, the state-level mercantilism[7] endemic to Peru drives people from participation in the formal economic system. As "independents," job security is absent and most economic activities are practiced outside the law. Consequently, economic activities involving the least risk— such as those where invested capital can be easily liquidated—are favored in these tenuous and threatening circumstances.

Here, *redistributive* rather than *productive* economic activities abound—commodities of every type are bought and sold informally. When interviewing patients of *curanderos* living in and around Trujillo, *comerciante* (merchant) was how many of the respondents described their occupations (Glass-Coffin 1985; Vásquez 1988: 90). Even when listing another occupation, rare was the existence of a household whose members were not also involved in some kind of petty commerce to supplement the household income. Common examples of informal business ventures include: retailing heavily-taxed home appliances and electronics after smuggling these across the Ecuador-Peruvian border, turning a personal automobile for a few hours a day into an informal taxi, travelling from the coast to the mountains or the tropical forest in order to trade commodities between regions at a small profit, maintaining a small in-home *bodega* as a slightly higher priced alternative to buying foodstuffs, household and office supplies, or personal accessories in the centralized market.

Like so many other "developing" economies, little upward mobility and endemic un- and under-employment have combined with hyper-inflation[8] to decrease buying power over the last several decades. In the absence of a sufficiently developed productive economy, one of the few means available for capitalizing on run-away inflation is to hoard commodities, selling these slowly, as prices rise. Shortly before each announced price increase, staples such as cooking oil, sugar, bread and milk "disappear" from the markets—hidden by merchants who wait out the public outcry until the appearance of the higher price before they sell.

In the atmosphere of resource scarcity described above the individual must maintain a network of informal (usually family) resources to ensure survival. When hospitalized, for instance, it is the family who provides the bed-sheets, the meals, and, due to recent monetary shortages in the Ministry of Health and Social Security systems, even the cotton gauze, surgical thread and other materials necessary for the most basic medical interventions. Any bureaucratic hassle, from application for a driver's license to obligatory military service is simplified because of "who you know." This dependence on others limits options for overtly expressing the aggression and hostility engendered in this economically competitive and highly frustrating setting. In the absence of overt mechanisms, magical aggression by means of sorcery (*daño*) is a culturally relevant illness which, according to Peruvian scholars

(Chiappe 1979; Chiappe, Limlij, and Millones 1985; Rotondo 1970) can best be described as a projective mechanism for this unexpressible hostility.

Social and Psychological Environment

Not surprisingly, socialization techniques and family relationships reflect the stress of this economically competitive and frustrating environment. My first intimations of the "exchange" value of discourse for negotiating symbolic capital and construct-ing and protecting personal identity paralleled my own socialization into the cultural rules of urban, North-coastal Peru. In 1975, before I had studied anthro-pological methods, I lived as a "daughter" among a middle-class, *mestizo* family and studied as "classmate" at a large public school in Trujillo for 11 months as part of a high-school exchange program. The family had migrated to the coast from a town of about 30,000 inhabitants located in the northern *sierra* five years before my arrival. It was a large family: the husband and wife shared their home with seven of their 11 children, the husband's mother and a domestic servant. They had built their six bedroom house of *material noble* (brick and cement) with the help of their oldest son, who had recently completed his university education as a civil engineer at a prestigious university in Lima. They owned an automobile and a black and white television, and supported themselves on the single salary of the father who worked as an office manager at a savings and loan association in the town center.

Their children's education was a high priority for the family. One of the main reasons they moved to Trujillo was its reputable university and they built their house just across from the university campus. Quite apart from their formal studies, enculturation into the etiquette demanded of educated, middle-class chil-dren was also emphasized in the household. The children were taught obedience and respect to elders, loyalty to family, and duty to society. Most importantly, they were taught to bring honor to the family, through their actions and their words. Upholding the behavioral as well as the moral ideals expected of them was the best way to do this, of course—whether remaining virgins until marriage (for the daughters), maintaining family solidarity and harmony, or sharing their wealth and good fortune with visitors.

When ideals could not, for whatever reason, be upheld—when one daughter became pregnant before her wedding, when an illicit love affair between first cousins shredded family harmony, when animosity between mother and daughter generated complaints that food was being distributed among household members unequally—the children were socialized to project the appearance that all was well, and to keep knowledge of these moral and behavioral deficits within the household through careful management of information shared with outsiders. When guests arrived, no matter how tight the budget, no matter how tense the atmosphere between family members, the best tablecloth was laid and special foods were bought in honor of the occasion. In the name of hospitality, feelings were masked and harmony prevailed—at least until the guests departed.

Through the months of my residence in the household, I slowly gained command of the language and became more proficient at sorting out how it was used by the household members to interact with one another, to command attention, and to manage this presentation of family-image. At social gatherings, story-telling domi-nated the conversation, communicating events and action in which the narrator had participated. These stories were carefully constructed to be entertaining while managing the images that were projected, presenting what was appropriate and steering inquiry away from what was unfit to share.

Within the informal discourse shared among family members, this image-management was also practiced. Personal stories recounted in response to the query: *¿Qué te cuentas?* (What do you have to say for yourself?) selectively presented aspects of identity that reconfirmed that which had already been presented, rectified that which had been "spoiled" and defended that which had been chal-lenged (cf. Goffman 1959). In this narrative environment I learned that identity is not only constructive[9] but also interactive and negotiated—the object of the negotia-tion being how much influence each "narrator" gets to exert on the construction of his or her "truth." As Weigert notes, "one or another identity may be presented by self or imposed by others as each negotiates for control of the situation" (1986: 46). In short, we are not affected only by what we say but by what is said about us.

In the effort to manage the images presented to outsiders, my adoptive family taught me that what other people will say (*qué dirán*) is much more likely to be antagonistic than supportive because the world is full of envy. *No confíes en nadie* (don't trust anybody) was an admonishment I commonly heard. Because even the best of friends, out of envy, would be looking for information which could be embellished and misconstrued in order to discredit me, I would be wise to give no ammunition for misrepresentation.

Once, when I was overwrought with grief over a personal loss and received no support from anyone in the household I looked to friends outside the family for comfort. I was later admonished by one of the siblings for my impropriety—I had unmasked a gap between ideal and real in which the family could be perceived as being disloyal to their "adopted" daughter and sister. I had opened them to the danger of gossip and the "fear of ridicule or rejection by those upon whose opinion one's self-esteem depends" (Deigh 1983: 243).

Rotondo (1970) found that this anxiety was a prevalent concern among the urban Peruvians whom he used as part of his culture and personality studies two decades ago. He maintained that, for his sample, positive interpersonal relationships with significant others (family and friends) were more important to an individual's sense of well being than internally generated mechanisms. He suggested that self-esteem was most easily threatened when one perceived disapproval or antagonism in these relationships. Just as children are taught from a very early age the importance of others for their economic survival, he argued, so are they taught about the impor-tance of others for their emotional survival. I suggest that antagonistic discourse like gossip and ridicule are the discursive objects of this emotional anxiety.

In an attempt to apply some of these concepts to the impressions about discourse that I describe above, I asked 15 women to verbalize their "most desired characteris-tics in a friend." The term most frequently used by these women was *sincera* (sincere). *De doble cara* (two-faced), *hipócrita* (hypocrite), and especially *chismosa* (gossiper) were the terms used to describe least desired characteristics. Their anxiety about *qué dirán* translated, as Unni Wikan (1984) has suggested, not as "how they will evaluate and judge" but as "how they will condemn and distort."

Daño and Dependence

The human environment in urban, North-coastal Peru is best characterized by dependence. By and large, individuals depend for their economic capital on the (steadily-diminishing) profit-margins they can achieve by redistributing goods and services. Individuals depend for their symbolic capital upon others as well, competing also for scarce honor and self-worth.[10] It is an environment where control over one's "capital" is practically non-existent and highly-prized. It is an environment where manipulating another's "capital" comes to substitute for positive control over one's own. Enter *daño*.

Daño, in its many forms, is always a purposeful attack on another individual's physical, economic, or social health. *Daño*, in its most dangerous aspect, involves the evil intent of a human enemy (at least an acquaintance of the victim and often a family member) who, because of jealousy, envy, or revenge contacts a wizard (*brujo*) in order to intentionally hurt or kill the chosen victim. Through magical means involving the use of spirit familiars, the *brujo* effects the *daño* through capture of the victim's spirit or shadow. Rather than maintain custody of the patient's spirit, he turns it over to the dominion of a powerful spirit force in whose custody the patient's spirit, and hence the patient will suffer. Where the victim's spirit is to be turned over (*entregado*) to an *anima* (spirit) of a deceased person for example, the *brujo* may prepare a potion which the victim will unwittingly drink that contains the bones of the dead. He may also invoke the victim's name—easier to accomplish if he has in his possession an appurtenance such as the victim's fingernails or clothing— then send the *daño* back to the victim with an evil air (*aire*) in which the ground up bones are magically blown (*soplado*). He may also have the ground up bones placed in the victim's path so that they will be stepped on and absorbed into his body. He will commonly form a likeness of the victim with some personal possession (a *muñeco* or *paquete*) and bury it in the cemetery with the deceased.

Because of the anti-social character of this kind of magic, the actual ceremony where the *daño* is effected is almost never witnessed. Rather, it is suspected and attributed as the cause of many resultant illnesses. Accusations of *daño* are applied to illness which is experienced in much broader terms than the purely somatic. Economic difficulties such as those engendered by the unexpected destruction of an income generating asset, gradual loss of clients to a neighboring merchant, unexpected wash-out of a cash-crop, or a disappeared farm-animal are often attributed to *daño*. It is not uncommon for patients to bring their taxi-cabs, transport vehicles, farm animals or even a sample of their store merchandise to the healer for a ritual cleansing, curing, and protection from suspected *daño*. Interpersonal difficulties such as marital infidelity, promiscuity, domestic violence, incest, stressful in-law relationships leading to conjugal separation, or adolescent-disobedience/ rebellion are often attributed to *daño*. Somatic complaints that don't respond well to bio-medical intervention are also suspect—rashes, infected wounds, numbness, dizziness, head-ache pain, even paralysis (cf. Vásquez 1988).

In North-coastal Peru, the most common motivation for suspecting or accusing someone of effecting *daño* is envy (Sharon 1978:23–29). Given the situation described above, this is not surprising. With the limited economic base that an emphasis on redistribution fosters, resource scarcity is perceived as absolute shortage and envy is endemic. It is, as Foster suggested (1972), the expected attitude towards disproportionate possession of a limited good.

Significantly, the anxiety of being envied is directed against the most intimate members of one's social network rather than against outsiders. In my experience, the overt solidarity between persons with close social ties—friends, business associates, lovers, and kin (especially afines) often masks a profound economic-interest in the relationship. The popular saying, *"no hay amor sin interés"* (there is no love without interest) often reflects the economic meaning of the term and is used to describe this conflict between social responsibility to one's kin and the desire to be economically independent.

In the transaction-oriented economy described above, competition for profit tends to emphasize individual initiative. It isolates and atomizes, undercutting more traditional values of family cooperation and reciprocity.[11] In a setting where social relationships are dysfunctionally rigid—where the endemic frustrations to economic limitations are denied most other forms of expression—it is not surprising that most accusations of *daño* are levied against the most intimate members of one's social network. The combination of dependence and frustration, a combination that is growing daily in Peruvian cities, is a fertile breeding ground for *daño*.

The following case illustrates both the social and economic imperatives at work on one patient's "symbolic capital" and the intricate connections between *daño*, discourse, and the experience of illness which I have outlined above. It was recorded as part of a patient-focused study designed and directed by Douglas Sharon (Director of the San Diego Museum of Man) and Donald Joralemon (Smith College) in which I participated for nine months as an assistant in the collection of field data between April 1988 and September 1989.[12]

CASE STUDY

The First Interview

Mari was interviewed in May of 1988 on her first visit to the healer, don Nilo, who conducted his all night healing ceremonies or, *mesas*,[13] on Tuesday and Friday nights at the edge of a cornfield on the outskirts of Trujillo. Most patients gathered at his home in a small fishing village, several miles to the south of the field. Just before 10 p.m. they would squeeze into jalopies commissioned to be 'taxis' just for the trip to the ritual-site. After the all-night ceremony, they would again be ferried from the cornfield to the main highway to Trujillo, where they would wait for transportation to take them home, or, more frequently, straight to work after the sleepless night spent with don Nilo and those family members or friends who had accompanied them in their pursuit of a cure for their illnesses.

Mari lived near the healer in a large, all-wood house just off the main square and she knew of him although she had never before participated in his *mesa*. She was a slender young woman, 27 years of age, married and the mother of an 18-month-old daughter. The night she was interviewed her husband accompanied her. Before the ceremony she described her problem as follows:[14]

Interviewer: Please briefly describe why you came to the *curandero*. What is the problem which you are experiencing?

Mari: I feel bad, a lot of kidney pain, my ovaries hurt, I have a burning sensation when urinating . . . nothing that I eat agrees with me . . . nothing. That's why I came. I have gone to see three doctors, none cured me . . . No, one told me that what I had was vaginitis, he gave me medicine, he cured me of the burning, in other words he allowed me to urinate all right but then the kidney problems began. Another told me that this was an infection of the urinary tract . . . so he cured one kidney and the pain started in the left kidney together with the left ovary . . . I go to another doctor and he told me that it was an inflammation, he cured me of this and then the stomach [began]. I would eat, then throw-up, eat, then throw-up, I didn't want anything. I drank a little milk and I threw it up. I could get nothing, nothing down. I also went—perhaps you have heard of the congregation of Mahi Kari[15]—I have also gone there . . . Well, that (Mahi Kari) did cure me a little but it takes time and my pain is so great that, for this, I have come to the *curandero*. I have gone to see the cards[16] and I have been told that I have *daño*.

I: Uhmhum. Let's see. And is this the first time that you have come to the *curandero*?

M: . . . No, I went before, the first time for my husband and the second time for my daughter in San Pedro de Lloc.[17]

I: To another ·*curandero* over there?

M: Yes to different ones. Well, my husband . . . he almost died, they left him almost an invalid. I mean, he had an accident, nothing more than that he went to swim at the beach and he fell head-first and he was left paralyzed for about three months. They made him see doctors, they couldn't find the answer, they said he was dying. So they finally took him to be cured and it was *daño* that he had. . .

I: And why didn't you return to the healer in San Pedro [for the current problem]?

M: In San Pedro? . . . Because I, I don't want to go back there, because that is where they have done the *daño* on me . . . . It began from one minute to the next, I wasn't suffering from anything, from one minute to the next it came upon me—the *mal* [bad, evil, illness] . . . In other words, they tell me that they did it to me, just like that! The same symptoms that I have told you . . . . . so that, in other words, I would shrivel-up little by little, little by little, they were going to . . . they are going to put me in the hospital, in other words they cut me, they operate. [Because of the operation] things get messed-up and I die.

I: I see. And, did they tell you that it was the *curandero* who did it to you . . .

M: . . . no, no, no

I: It was somebody else?

M: It was someone else . . . another woman [who had contracted the *curandero*].

The Ceremony

To begin his ceremony, don Nilo laid out the *mesa* and began, accompanied by his ceremonial rattle or *chungana*, to invoke the *cuentas* or accounts of every power-object on his *mesa*. Like "account," (its closest English cognate), the Spanish word, *cuenta*, most often refers to a report or statement about numbers and more specifically about money. It is managed, exchanged, tallied and distributed in accordance with the wishes of the signator. But it can also be understood as a record of events and the action of "recounting" these. Like the linguistically related term *cuento* (gossip), it is managed, measured, manipulated and "transacted" as it is verbalized. For don Nilo, each of the helping-spirits who assist him in the all-night ritual to seek out and destroy the *daño* and to recover the patient's soul are physically present on his *mesa* in the swords, staffs, rocks, shells, and other objects which he has inherited or bought or found. The history of his relationship with these spiritual beings as well as their inherent powers are contained in their *cuentas*. He calls the spirit of each of these into his service as he activates its *cuenta*. Their power becomes his as he verbalizes it. Each *cuenta* is chanted or sung; the words and melody together form a magical song that don Nilo calls *tarjo*.[18]

After singing the *tarjos* which activate the *cuentas* of all of the objects on his *mesa* and of the *San Pedro* which gives vision and the *tabaco*,[19] don Nilo, empowered by their spirits, began the diagnostic portion of the ceremony, called *rastreo* in which he would determine the cause of Mari's suffering and the origin of her *daño*. As he stared into her eyes and concentrated on the sights, sounds, and smells which were spiritual manifestations of her suffering, he suddenly asked her if she heard the screeching of a nearby *lechuza*[20] or barn owl. She commented that she did and he asked her if she knew what that sound was. He told her that it was *chisme* or gossip and that the barn owl began screeching because her mother-in-law was gossiping about her.[21] Don Nilo asserted that she was suffering from *daño*, that her spirit had been captured by a spiritist, and *enterrado* (buried with the spirit of a corpse in a cemetery). She would have to travel to Medio Mundo to see a spiritist who was also a specialist in *sacando entierros*[22] in order to be completely free of the *daño*. He described the woman responsible, indicating that she was very close to Mari's husband. Mari instantly recognized the description as that of her mother-in-law.

After the *rastreo*,[23] Don Nilo began the *jalada del espíritu* in which he called Mari's spirit to the *mesa* through an accounting of her personal *cuenta*. He had learned that Mari's spirit had been *contado* or accounted by the enemy sorcerer who, once gaining power over it, was able to bind it to the spirit of a corpse. Don Nilo would have to unbind her spirit by undoing the *cuenta* in order to rescue it.

During the *jalada del espíritu* (call to the spirit) the *tarjo* Mari heard, roughly translated[24] was this:

"... *Why do you forsake one another, angry and bitter . . . lovely lady with your husband, totally despondent, totally forlorn . . . you only cry, and sigh and worry . . . don't cry my lovely lady . . . I know what the matter is, I know what is wrong. . .*

. . . With my lovely, healing herb, my San Pedro I am flying among the mountains, among the ancient tombs, the enchanted cities, among the cemeteries. . .

. . . I am asking and seeking, calling and imploring by your name and by your shadow, Mari Flores de García . . . in the cemetery he finds you, my wise San Cipriano and he gives you his hand, he carries you away from the skeletons who hold you. . .

. . . You fly by the stars, through the atmosphere and the clouds, enchanted you come as a wind, as the air, they bring you in. . .

. . . Come in, come in, come in, your shadow and your spirit, your lovely name into my garden, I give your spirit to your body. . .

. . . Here you are unbinding, here you are untangling, throwing off the shackles you stand clear and free and tall while I tell it from the place of a hundred glories where I begin to sing. . .

. . . How lovely they account for you my healing herbs and potions with the dawning, with the morning, here in my fields and gardens, you are well named and accounted for.

. . . Up with your name, your shadow and your fortune and down with adversity and down with the desertion of your husband's love.

. . . With the morning and the new day, entrusted to my lovely, living herbs, well commended and remembered they walk together with the herbs of verb and the word, your words well received, your words well cherished. . . ."

This *tarjo*, which was sung approximately five hours after he began the all-night ritual, had an obvious impact on Mari. Standing before the don Nilo's *mesa* and listening to its poetry, she began to cry. Before she left in the morning, she indicated that she felt better and that her pain had subsided during the night. We said goodbye, and I reminded her that we would like to interview her in a few months, to discuss the outcome of her treatment with don Nilo.

The Second Interview

I interviewed Mari in her home, three months later, on August 5, 1988. Her husband was not present at the time of the second interview. She seemed much freer talking with me, perhaps because I had shared in her experience at don Nilo's *mesa*—she used the "tu" form when addressing me. Her husband's absence must also have influenced the ease with which she spoke about the marital problems that they had shared, and about the role she felt her mother-in-law had played in their distress, and in her *daño*.

After they had married, they had lived in San Pedro, with his parents, but his mother had never accepted the competition for her son's emotional and economic resources that their marriage represented. He was often in-and-out of work, and finances were difficult. Soon before she became ill, they had moved to Trujillo to live with her parents because her father had been able to get him a job at a local ice-making factory but he had become unhappy with the job and had been threatening to quit at the time they first went to see don Nilo. To her family, he seemed irresponsible and they often complained about her choice in husbands. She commented that she had not been able to care for her husband and child as she should—she could not keep up with the cooking and cleaning expected of her, had little interest in sex and often had to turn child-care responsibilities over to her mother. As her illness worsened, he began visiting his mother more frequently without leaving her any money to buy food for their daughter. She was forced to ask for help from her family since her illness prevented her from working to contribute to the family income as she had when she and her husband were first married.

Interviewer: Well, Mari. Tell me, since the treatment with don Nilo, do you feel better or not?

Mari: I felt good, I was really fine, but since I left off going to the *mesa* because of not having enough money, the situation has gotten worse. He told me that I had to go to Medio Mundo to *sacar mi muñeco* but because of not having the money I haven't gone down there and now I have problems with my husband. He left and he doesn't send me money. It's the same, just the same as when I first started going to don Nilo, but don Nilo brought him back again. Everything was fine, it was just wonderful when I went to the *mesa*. But now, since I quit going everything is like before, everything just like before. My husband has gone, he doesn't send money, he left me. No money, not even for my child, nor for me. My daughter is sick, I am also sick, everything is bad, everything is going bad. . .

I: And tell me, what did don Nilo tell you about your sickness, is it *daño* or. . .

M: It's *daño*. What I had was *daño*. They did *daño* on me. But, I mean, I had to go to get those *muñecos* in order to be completely cured and like I told you, I haven't gone yet to Medio Mundo . . . I mean, he can lift me up but I'll fall back down, that's what he told me . . . it's not up to him. . . .

I: And tell me, do you have any idea who did the *daño* to you and why?

M: Yes, it was in San Pedro . . . I have the idea that it could be my mother-in-law . . . together with another girl that she has up there in San Pedro . . . I mean, ever since we've been married, it seems that before marrying they had done *daño* on us because then . . . I mean, we . . . our marriage has always gone like this: down, down, down, problems, arguments, no money, everything, everything goes wrong, we haven't had any luck since we've been married. It seems like we were united . . . two complete opposites. . . .

I: How long has it been since you heard from. . .

M: From my husband? It's been about 15 days. But he comes, I mean he comes to see the baby, he doesn't bring money, and he goes. When he comes, I speak-out but . . . he says he doesn't have any, any, any! He leaves me with debts, he says that I incurred them so I have to find the way to pay them . . . I say, if it's necessary I can look for someone else to take care of me, no? But he doesn't care. For example, he came now about 15 days ago and he left us without a cent, me telling him that my daughter didn't have milk. Nothing! He doesn't care about anything! Whether she eats or doesn't, whether or not the baby lives, no? I called him on the telephone to tell him that the baby has a lump here, of some kind, a really ugly one, they told me that it's goiter. I called to tell him and nothing. He hasn't worried himself at all!

I: And tell me, what was your experience like during the first night (at don Nilo's ceremony)? . . . What did you feel?

M: I got really emotional in seeing how beautifully don Nilo works, it was very lovely, I didn't think it would be like that, he put a lot of effort in my case, a lot! Maybe out of friendship or, maybe it's the way he works. He is a very easy person to talk to, he knows how to talk to his patients. It was a very lovely experience that I had. . .

I: And what things did he do to cure you, to help you that night?

M: He sang, and when he sang he cleansed me and everything, he made it go away from me. I mean, as he was cleansing me, he was telling me what it was that I had and he even made me cry, he even made me cry. . . . Yes, he sang very lovely, he worked very beautifully. I can't complain except to say that it's my fault, I can't go because of the money. If I could maybe it would be different.

The emotional response to don Nilo's singing was probably heightened as she was provided with a language in which to express and define her pain. As others have suggested (Dow 1986; Lévi-Strauss 1950), perhaps it was don Nilo's ability to first link her personal experience to the culturally mythic and then manipulate this that engaged her emotions. I suggest that the link to be examined between Mari's personal experience and the culturally mythic is that of the *cuenta*. As a metaphor for the exchange value of discourse, it symbolized, for don Nilo, the culturally recognized power of words to "transact" symbolic, as well as material, capital.

I have already discussed the importance of protecting appearances and the fear of what people will say (*que dirán*) as an example of the power of discourse to wrench away the power of identity-management in North coastal Peru. In the symbolic context of the ritual, Mari suffered the effects of *daño* because her mother-in-law, with the aid of the sorcerer, *amarró* or bound up her spirit in the *cuenta*. The sorcerer who had accounted Mari's spirit had power over it because he had captured and possessed it through invoking his own *cuentas*.[25] Just as in everyday life—in the symbolism of his ritual—narration was possession and possession was power. Just as she might regain her image by unbinding it from the narrative told by a gossiping mother-in-law, it was a symbolic unbinding through which don Nilo released her spirit from the sorcerer and freed her from the *daño*. Don Nilo made the correspondence between the social and symbolic danger of narrative clear to Mari during his *rastreo* as he equated the sound of the *lechuza* with the evil powers of narrative as manifested in gossip. But it was during the *jalada del espíritu* that this link between her personal illness experience and the culturally perceived power of discourse was expressed most clearly of all:

". . . *With the morning and the new day, entrusted to my lovely, living herbs, well-commended and remembered they walk together with the herbs of verb and the word, your words well-received, your words well-cherished.* . . ."

I suggest that it was here that the *cuenta* became imbued with affective power for Mari. An example of what Munn (1973) calls "iconicity," it represented the feelings and emotions which affected her self-worth in concrete form.

Mari probably did not experience this correspondence between her personal experience of *daño* and the metaphorical importance of the *cuenta* at a conscious level. Her description of her feelings about the ritual would not indicate otherwise. She did indicate that her symptoms abated, her husband became more attentive and her life improved during the months in which she attended his *mesas* and she does not blame him for the 'relapse' which she was experiencing at the time of her second interview. I suggest that don Nilo's diagnosis of *daño* not only gave her an explanation for her physical symptoms but it also gave her a justification for not living up to the role of ideal wife and mother. It gave her a new narrative which allowed her to short circuit the shame and embarrassment (*vergüenza*) she might feel at the thought of being unable to keep her husband from straying back to his mother. When her situation deteriorated and he began to stray once more, she attributed the relapse to her inability to complete the recommended treatment.

It would require a detailed analysis of the interrelatedness of mind and body states well beyond the scope of this article to draw any conclusions about Mari's recovery and later relapse. Here, I have limited myself to examination of the culturally recognized power of discourse to threaten identity and to shape illness experience in one cultural setting. What remains to be explored is: how the symbolism of the *mesa* is grounded in the political economy of the region; the correlation between economic, social and psychological relationships as expressed through discourse and accusations of *daño*; and how the healing ceremony symbolically rebalances that which is dysfunctional in these relationships. It is to this discussion which I will now turn.

DISCUSSION

Following de Soto's hypothesis that state-level Peruvian economy is dysfunctional to the degree that redistributive activities proliferate in the absence of production (1989), it could be said that Peruvian economics are out-of-balance. Where redistributive activities predominate, economic well-being fluctuates with one's ability to turn a profit through the exchange of commodities. In this environment, economic gain does not depend on man's ability to dominate the forces of nature but on the ability to dominate the wits of other men. Not surprisingly, anxiety is directed towards other humans, whose actions and motivations are inherently mistrusted. Socialization techniques emphasize the adversarial relationships between humans. Deceitful teasing, like the father who encouraged his child to jump into his arms from a low stone wall only to step away and let the child fall, teach mistrust and suspicion.[26] The world is transformed into a malevolent realm (Westen 1985).

I have suggested that, in this environment, discourse is also perceived as a type of symbolic capital and that emotional well-being fluctuates with one's ability to control the terms in which that part of one's identity—projected through discourse—is tallied, measured, and valued. Anxiety is other-directed—*lo que dirán* is always suspect. At the same time, psychological dependence is such that self-esteem depends, as Rotondo has suggested, on the opinions of others.

I have argued that this "externalization of personality" is culturally constituted and grounded in the political economy described above. I believe that, just as what is dysfunctional about this economic environment is made manifest socially through envy and accusations of *daño*, what is dysfunctional is made manifest psychologically through the damning power of discourse.

If, as others have suggested,[27] the healing ceremony is a culturally adaptive mechanism for rebalancing these manifestations of life out-of-balance, how does this occur in the case presented? To answer this, we must return to the symbolism of the *mesa*.

Mesa Symbolism

Sharon has documented the roots of the healing tradition in which don Nilo participates in the pre-Columbian dialectic of Andean cosmology (1978: 73–100). He suggests that the opposite forces represented on the healer's *mesa* represent traditional dualities of Andean tradition which are mediated and transcended through the ritual itself to restore health. Dialectically, the *mesa* rebalances the life-giving and life-taking forces, rebalances good and evil. Discussing this dialectic, Joralemon noted that the healer's central role is to balance the opposing forces concretized in the opposing sides of the *mesa* (1984:10).

Don Nilo's ceremony reflects the dualism found in the ritual cures of other healers in the area.[28] His *mesa* is divided into two fields or *campos*. The left side of the *mesa*, like that of many other healers is called the *campo ganadero*. On don Nilo's *mesa*, just as on the *mesas* of many other healers in the area, the *campo ganadero* is associated with the "evil" or "life-taking" powers which must be invoked to *voltear* (turn around), *botar* (throw away), or, additionally for don Nilo, to undo or *descontar* the *cuenta*. Based on what we know of North-coastal healing, the sorcerer who had worked his evil on Mari had invariably used the powers of the left side of his *mesa*, very likely referred to—just as don Nilo's *mesa*—as the *campo ganadero*.

The origin of the term is sometimes associated with the Spanish verb *ganar* (to win) referring to the "winning of souls" which sorcerers undertake with the help of their *compactos* (pacts) with evil spirit forces—especially with Satan. An alternate hypothesis, suggested by reading Quispe (1969: 80), is that *ganadero* refers, quite literally, to *la persona que comercia con ganado* or one who buys and sells livestock. In Quispe's description of the *herranza* rituals of two communities in the central highlands of Ayacucho, he documents *mesas* identical in many ways to the *mesas* on the coast.[29] Absent from the *mesa* Quispe documents, which are dedicated to animal husbandry and livestock management rather than agricultural enterprise, are the jars of herbs called *seguros* or *madregueras* which are invariably found on the right side of don Nilo's *mesa*.

Don Nilo, like other healers documented, often refers to the right of his *mesa* as the *campo yerbatero* or field of herbs. This right side of North-coastal *mesas*, according to Sharon (1978, 1989) and Joralemon (1983, 1984, 1985) is associated with "good" or "life-giving" powers. In the symbolism of don Nilo's *mesa*, it is the power of the right field of the *mesa* that was invoked as he created a new *cuenta* for Mari. As expressed in the *tarjo*, he placed this new *cuenta* within the gardens and fields of the right side of the *mesa*. It was in these gardens that Mari was "well named and accounted for."

What I am suggesting here is that the "good" or "life-giving" and "evil" or "life-taking" properties of the right and left sides of don Nilo's *mesa* have economic referents as well. The right hand *yerbatera* part of the *mesa*, as don Nilo describes it in his *tarjo*, is symbolically associated with the economic activity of gardening or farming while the left hand *ganadero* part of the *mesa* is symbolically associated with the economic activity of buying and selling livestock.

Quispe has suggested that agriculture and livestock management are two economic strategies expressing opposite, but complementary, elements of highland life. Why, as a general rule, are these two complementary opposites: the *ganadero* and the *yerbatero* associated with "life-taking" and "life-giving" powers respectively on the coastal *mesas*? As a possible explanation, I suggest that it is the symbolic association of these two economic activities with redistribution and production[30] that governs their placement on the *mesa*.

I do not mean to suggest that these activities *as they are practiced* are only or even largely productive or redistributive—only that this is the way in which they are symbolized on the *mesa*. All opposite forces represented in concrete form upon the *mesa* are distilled and absolute: good-evil, white-black, God-Satan. Just so, it would appear, *ganadero* and *yerbatero* and their symbolic meanings are presented.

The association of life-taking forces with the buying and selling associated with the *ganadero* is evidenced in don Nilo's use of discourse and *cuenta*. When I asked him about the origin of this term, he explained that a *cuenta* was like a debt and that *descontando* was like paying off the debt. Clearly, the *cuenta* is a symbolic commodity which can be transacted and controlled like any other limited resource. As a debt, the *cuenta* is realized through a series of contracts (*compactos*) between the sorcerer and evil spirits (especially Satan) in which the victim's soul is sold to the devil.[31] Symbolically, Satan—the winner of souls—is the *ganadero*. Using the cattle-broker symbolism suggested above, he is also the cattle-master to whom the debt is owed, and the *cuenta* is bound. During the course of the cure don Nilo is able to unbind (*desatar, desamarrar*) the *cuenta* through the power of his *tarjos*.

Just as the *cuenta* is a type of symbolic capital, the *tarjos* are symbolically used to stand for it and pay it off. Evidence for this comes from Bachmann's early ethnography as quoted in Giese (1987: 319). Giese suggests that *tarjo* as the word for the power-songs used by healers like don Nilo derives from *tarja* which was the payment received by each worker for his day's work on North-coast *haciendas* at the turn of the twentieth century. Similarly, Quispe (1969: 44) notes that the tool used to tally the livestock which were to be turned over to the *cargo* of the next year's keepers was called the *taja*.[32]

Remember that after Mari's *cuenta* was unbound from the clutches of the sorcerer who had captured it, don Nilo placed her spirit symbolically within the gardens of his *mesa* where she would be "well named and accounted for." This process was implemented using elements from the right side, or *yerbatera* side, of the *mesa* like the jars of herbs called *seguros* and was accompanied by *tarjos* to *levantar* (raise-up) and *florecer*, or cause her spirit to flower.

This process involved a symbolic shifting from left side to right side of the *mesa*, and, I suggest, from the symbolic meanings associated with redistributive to productive economic activities. I further suggest that the shift from left to right, from the symbolism associated with exchange and transaction to that associated with growth and flowering, reflects a symbolic realization of the need to rebalance the dysfunctional social and psychological relationships, including the "externaliz-ation of personality" created by an economy which is too completely "redistribu-tive." Being bound on the left side it seems is symbolically associated with negative dependence upon others—with being a *amarrado* or bound-up as a slave. The right side represents freedom precisely because it gives you back your generative powers, your power to blossom, or *florecer*.

Don Nilo's manipulation of the *cuenta*, transferring it from the left to the right, from the redistributive to the productive, was an attempt to diminish Mari's anxiety about the discrediting gossip spread by her mother-in-law, and, more generally, to diminish her anxiety in general about what people will say or *qué dirán*. I suggest that the healing transformation of the ritual ultimately depends on transforming the perception of oneself from that of emotionally dependent to emotionally inde-pendent. This transformation occurs with internal growth and flowering—with the recognition that self-esteem depends not upon what others may say or think but upon internally generated mechanisms which, like the healing herbs of the *mesa*, are gifts from the gods. These sustain and give life to the human community, even while refusing to be bounded by it. In this sense, discourse is also a link between what is culturally shared and intensely private. As a template which shapes experience, and which negotiates between public and private arenas of persuasion, it is a powerful and dangerous means of traversing the fundamental boundaries of self and other, individual and social, and public and private realms of experience in North-coastal Peru.

CONCLUSIONS

Admittedly, the correlations suggested here are tentative. They are based on im-pressions gathered over time and unfolded slowly, always at the periphery rather than at the center of the intended topic of investigation—but then, this is one of the hazards and the joys of traditional anthropological research. Here, they are sub-stantiated by a single case-study as well as analysis of the healing ritual of a single healer. Comparative research among other healers as well as carefully structured measures which elicit attitudes about discourse as it relates to identity-manage-ment must be undertaken before the ideas presented here can be substantiated. Still, they suggest that narrative discourse may be recognized as a powerful identity-shaping tool in a cultural setting very different than our own. The ideas presented here also challenge us to be mindful and to explore relationships between discourse, identity-management, and the experience of illness in other cultures as we continue to strive for a meaning-centered, medical anthropology.

ACKNOWLEDGMENTS

Earlier versions of this paper were presented at the II Congreso Internacional de Medicinas Tradicionales in Lima, Peru, June 1988 and at the 88th Annual Meeting of the American Anthropological Association, Washington D.C., November 15–19, 1989. The draft from the Lima presentation was published under the title "El daño, el cuento y el chisme: el poder de la palabra en la medicina tradicional de la costa norte del

Perú" in MASA 1988: 3(2): 48–51 and in Actas del II Congreso Internacional de Medicinas Tradicionales. Lima, 1989. I am especially grateful to Rosario Bazán Cabellos, Rafael Vásquez Guerrero, Eliana Novoa de Vásquez and Robert R. Desjarlais, Douglas Sharon, Donald Joralemon, Carole Browner, Lawrence S. Greene, and the four anonymous reviewers for their helpful comments on earlier drafts of this paper. Thanks also to Daniel R. Coffin, for editorial assistance. Interpretations and errors are, of course, of my own doing and I accept full responsibility for these.

NOTES

1. After some deliberation, I have decided to use the term "identity" instead of "self" or "person" in spite of the trend recent in anthropological literature (cf. Gredys Harris 1989; Carrithers, Collins, and Lukes 1985; Elster 1985; White and Kirkpatrick 1985; Marsella 1985; Shweder and Levine 1984) because I am interested here specifically in the self as it becomes, evaluates, communicates, interacts, and negotiates. This focus on process, with its social psychological heritage (cf. James 1952; Mead 1934; Goffman 1959, 1963; Berger and Luckmann 1966; Blumer 1969; Bateson 1972) is at the core of the "identity" concept. This view argues that—far from the mainly psychobiological, or historically bounded notion that Erikson first delineated (1946, 1956, 1959)—identity is the concept which best describes this constructionist view of the emergent self. Identity thus defined intersects and ties together the concepts of "person," "self" and "individual" because it focuses on the expression through which subject/object, self/other, private/public aspects of these are mediated. Language (Gredys Harris 1989) is a key mechanism through which this mediation occurs, both to others and to oneself (Weigert 1986: 50). Identity, as defined here, denies the existence of a "true self" which exists at the base of and underlies the roles or masks which humans don (cf. Mauss 1985), suggesting rather that the self "becomes" only as it reflects (including self-reflection) and is enacted (Weigert 1986). Achieving personhood—with the jural and moral rights and responsibilities that this implies (Gredys Harris 1989; Poole 1982)—requires validation. This process is also incorporated into the identity concept, as suggested above. For reviews of the identity concept see especially Weigert, Teitge, and Teitge 1986; Fogelson 1979; Robbins 1973.
2. See Jerome Bruner (1987), J. Walkup (1987), McAdams and Ochberg (1988), and Shotter and Gergen (1989).
3. See Kapferer (1979, 1983), Marsella (1985), Boddy (1988) and most recently in a panel devoted to "Person, Self, and Illness" at the 88th Annual Meeting of the American Anthropological Association in Washington, D.C., November 15–19, 1989.
4. Fernandez (1974, 1986), Levi-Strauss (1950), Tambiah (1968), Taussig (1987).
5. Abstracted and decontextualized from its immediate situation of utterance . . . detaching it from whatever meanings prevailed at the time of its original utterance, and redefining it in a new context (Kuipers 1989: 110).
6. Bourdieu argues that we "extend economic calculation to all the goods, material and symbolic, without distinction, that present themselves as rare and worthy of being sought after in a particular social formation—which may be 'fair words' or smiles, handshakes or shrugs, compliments or attention, challenges or insults, honour or honours, powers or pleasures, gossip or scientific information, distinction or distinctions, etc. . . . (Bourdieu 1977: 178–179).
7. According to Mario Vargas Llosa's prologue to *The Other Path*, Hernando de Soto defines mercantilism as the "bureaucratized and law-ridden state that regards the redistribution of national wealth as more important than the production of wealth. . . . 'redistribution,' as used here, means the concession of monopolies or favored status to a small elite that depends on the state and on which the state itself is dependent" (1989: xvi). He argues that it is this "system" rather than market economics which informs the political economy of Peru. Mercantilism has engendered an elite entrepreneurial class who benefit from laws dedicated to obtaining monopolies rather than encouraging free competition and rewarding creativity. There is a closed circle of benefactors who, instead of favoring the production of new wealth, discourage this in favor of recirculating an ever-diminishing amount of capital. The kinds of activities which proliferate are elephantine bureaucracies which create maze-like entanglements in order to discourage the creation of business and industry. For example, "in order to register a small-scale factory, a citizen has to fight for ten months through eleven different

ministerial and municipal departments and, just to keep things moving, bribe at least two people" (1989: xvii).

8. As an example of the 'run-away' nature of Peruvian inflation, note that the yearly variation of consumer prices figured between 1988 and 1989 from January to January was 2280%, from February to February 2933%, from March to March 3414%, from April to April 4329% and from May to May 5150%. (Indice de Precios . . . 1989). From April 1987 to July 1990, the national currency has suffered a devaluation of 428,000% against the US dollar.

9. In this view, it is through the stories that we tell about our lives that we select, craft and script ourselves. More than just reflect the way we think about ourselves, our narratives "construct" who we are. As Bruner notes, "the self-telling of life narratives achieve(s) the power to structure perceptual experience, to organize memory, to segment and purpose-build the very 'events' of a life. In the end, we become the autobiographical narratives by which we 'tell about' our lives" (1987: 15). A review of the exhaustive literature supporting this concept is beyond the scope of this paper. Early statements of this idea range from Peirce's theory of signs "the word or sign which man uses is the man himself" (Wiener 1958: 71) in semiotics, to the Sapir-Whorf hypothesis in linguistic anthropology (see Hymes 1972, 1983; Gumperz 1982a, 1982b). In literary criticism, one main premise of post-structuralism is that "language is constitutive of reality rather than merely reflective of it" (quoted in Tompkins 1980: 226). The persuasive aspects of language (Burke 1969) as well as a concern for the resulting relations between discourse and power (Foucault 1972; Fowler 1985) are but a few expressions of the relationship of personal narrative to identity formation and negotiation that I am developing here. For more recent development of these ideas in anthropology and psychology, see Berger and Luckmann (1966), Myerhoff (1982, 1986), Van Dijk (1985), Abrahams (1986), Bruner (1986), Bruner (1987), Walkup (1987), McAdams and Ochberg (1988).

10. The underlying ethos engendered by these economic relationships is not unlike Foster's concept of "limited good" (1965). In Foster's discussion, he argued that in peasant societies "all of the desired things in life such as land, wealth, health, friendship and love, manliness and honor, respect and status, power and influence, security and safety, exist in finite quantity and are always in short supply" (p. 296). He suggested that this cognitive orientation occurs in economies *which are not productive* (emphasis mine, see p. 297). Although Foster advanced this concept to describe peasant communities, the emphasis on redistribution rather than production in both state-level economics and in the economic activities of informals might, just as Foster asserted for peasant economies, help explain why envy, accusations of witchcraft, suspicion and mistrust of the intentions of others also prevail in North-coastal Peru.

11. Taussig (1980, 1982) has discussed the shift from perception of the Self as socially constituted to atomized and isolated that occurs with the advance of market organization in post-hacienda, wage-labor economics of Colombia. The conflict between family-level reciprocity and the individual initiative and competition that is characteristic of the advance of market organization in North-coastal Peru can be illustrated by the following example from my field experience. Seven siblings invested capital into land and materials for an export crop, which was to be managed by one of the siblings. When harvest-time came, the manager was greeted by the sad news that the selling price for the crop was being maintained artificially low by a competing corporation that had much larger capital investments in the same export crop. One of the employees of this large corporation was the manager's sister. In a conversation with her husband, another employee of the corporation, he asserted to me that driving down prices in order to run the small producer out of business was part of the corporate strategy. When confronted with the disparity between corporate policy and her own family's probable loss of their investment, she was nonplussed. As a salaried employee of the corporation, she stood to gain much more by the take-over mentality of her employer than she would lose as an investor in the family venture.

12. The research was supported by a grant from the National Institute of Mental Health (IRO1 MH38685-01A1). My thanks to Drs. Joralemon and Sharon for their permission to publish case material for which they hold copyright with the San Diego Museum of Man. They are in no way responsible for my interpretations. I have elected to use a pseudonym for the patient at Dr. Joralemon's suggestion.

13. The *mesa* refers to the all-night ceremony as well as the ritual altar upon which the healer's power-objects (saint's images and crucifixes, pre-Colombian artifacts of ceramic, metal, and stone, sea-shells, crystals, staffs, swords, rattles, the hallucinogenic *Trichocereus pachanoi*, macerated black or

white tobacco, jars of herbs macerated in sacred water collected from specific mountain lakes, perfumed water, honey and lime-juice and sometimes containing mercury, photographs, seeds) are spread. It is the core element of the healing tradition practiced on the North-coast and in the Northern highlands of Peru. Excellent descriptions of the *mesa* and more general descriptions of the tradition of which it is a part can be found in Sharon (1976, 1978), Joralemon (1984, 1985), Polia (1988), Giese (1987).

14. Translation of the taped transcript is mine.

15. A Japanese-inspired, highly hierarchical healing congregation in which energy is transferred to the patient through a laying-on of hands. Mahi-Kari was introduced into Peru in the early 1980s from Japan and has gained widespread popularity. For an analysis of this sect see Miyananga (1983).

16. Divinitory card readings conducted by specialists and often used as diagnostic technique for magically caused illnesses.

17. A small town about an hour's bus ride North of Trujillo where her husband's parents live.

18. Strictly speaking, the *cuenta*, according to Giese (1987: 219, 319–320) refers to the invocations which are chanted or sung while the melody or tune is called the *tarjo*. "*Los cánticos de la ceremonia se llaman cuentas. Y los tonos son los tarjos. Cada cuenta tiene su tarjo*" (Giese 1987: 320). Translation: The songs of the ceremony are called *cuentas* and the tunes are the *tarjos*.

19. *San Pedro* is the local name given to *Trichocereus pachanoi*, the mescaline-bearing succulent whose spirit-power is recognized as the source of the healer's psychic vision. Only by receiving the spirit of *San Pedro* can he communicate with the spirit world and combat the sorcerer who has inflicted the *daño* on his patients. *Tabaco* refers to a liquid mixture in which black tobacco leaves are macerated together with cane alcohol or the more expensive grape distilled *Pisco* as well as various colognes and scented waters which "acts as an auxiliary catalyst in support of the visionary function of *San Pedro* (Sharon 1978: 37).

20. The *lechuza* or barn owl provokes powerful response when it is heard screeching through the night. It is culturally recognized as an evil omen and harbinger of death. In the symbolism of other ritual healers in the area, the *lechuza* heralds the presence of an evil spiritist. It is always associated with cemeteries.

21. Ridicule and verbal argument, as verbal forms of aggression are also embodied by animal sounds in don Nilo's ritual symbolism. *Chisme*, or gossip, manifests itself through the screeching sound of the *lechuza*, or barn owl. *Burla*, or ridicule, manifests through the rasping sound of the *grillo*, or cricket, and *pleito*, or verbal argument, manifests through the barking sound of nearby dogs.

22. Don Nilo often sent clients to this young man who lived six hours south of Trujillo, near Lima. With the help of an *anima* or spirit of a deceased person (embodied in a skull which he kept in his possession), this young man would call upon the *anima* to deliver the *entierro* (which could be in the form of a doll made of a piece of the patient's clothing, a picture of the patient, a letter in his hand-writing or other appurtenance) from where it had been buried by an enemy spiritist. This deliverance would release the patient's soul from the clutches of the spirit of the corpse inhabiting the spot where the packet had been buried.

23. See Sharon (1989: 170–174) for a detailed description of the ritual sequence of the *mesa*.

24. In order to retain something of the rhythm and poetry of the *tarjo*, the translation is necessarily "rough."

25. When I asked him about the power of the *cuenta*, don Nilo emphasized the importance of the verbalizing and the complicated natures of the orations themselves for defense from other sorcerers. He said that the oration is his protection. A very complicated *cuenta* is a means of escape from the enemy sorcerer because it keeps him from "focusing" on the healer—which he must do in order to capture the healer's spirit as he tries to release that of the patient from the clutches of the enemy sorcerer. The healer told me, "*no me pueden agarrar porque soy la lanza, soy la espada, soy el remedio, soy el San Pedro, soy el cerro, soy la plata, soy el raiz, soy la corteza, soy el arbol crecido . . . por eso la oración es bién grande* (trans. "he can't grab me because I am the lance, I am the sword, I am the remedy, I am the San Pedro, I am the mountain, I am the silver, I am the bark, I am the tree grown up . . . this is why the oration is so large").

26. This incident was recounted to me by a Peruvian friend when discussing socialization techniques that had been used in her immediate family.

27. See Sharon (1978, 1989), Joralemon (1984), Myerhoff (1976).

28. I am basing my summary of documented *mesas* in the paragraphs that follow on the work of Sharon (1978), Joralemon (1983, 1984, 1985), Polia (1988) and most especially on a preliminary reading of a work by Sharon (1989) in which he has undertaken the monumental task of analyzing the dialectics of North-coast shamanism through documentation and comparison of 10 North-coast healers, one of whom is don Nilo.

29. These ritual ceremonies serve to brand and establish ownership of the herd and ensure fertility while symbolically bonding the religious, the social and the economic into an integrated whole.

30. Livestock management, encarnated in the commercial activity of the *ganadero*, Quispe notes *no es de consumo, sino de cambio. Los comuneros exportan en pequeña escala . . . mediante los negociantes ganaderos"* (1969: 12). It is not a subsistance activity, but one of exchange. It is, in the *herranza* associated with the human community as symbolized by human mimicking of animal behavior and vice versa. As an exchange or redistributive activity it depends on ownership—a type of human control. The *yerbas* (herbs) associated with the right side of coastal *mesas* are healing herbs with an uncultivated rather than domesticated origin, originating on sacred mountains nourished by the waters of sacred lagoons which are earthly representations of the life-giving powers of Divine sources (see Polia 1988). As is clearly seen in don Nilo's *tarjo*, the right hand side of his *mesa*, is also associated with gardening or farming—symbolizing, I believe a kind of wealth which emphasizes the generative or productive, rather than the redistributive aspects of economic life.

31. Furthermore, as Joralemon has noted in a recent paper (1990), *contando* (accounting for) and *nombrando* (naming) appeared to be linked in that they relate to the accounting of sins on Judgment Day in the Catholic tradition, where every person's sins are recorded in the Book of Life. In Peruvian folk Catholicism, Satan is often depicted as the record keeper. "In ritual processions, for example, a costumed performer representing Satan carries an open book in which he writes the names of sinners. To be 'accounted,' then, is to have lost one's soul to Satan." My thanks to Dr. Joralemon for this insight.

32. See Ramirez (1966: 36–39) for a detailed description of the *tarja* as an accounting tool. The origin of the term *tarja* may be related to the name of an early Spanish coin, valued at about one-fourth of a Real. I am grateful to Douglas Sharon for pointing out the relationship between the *tarjo* and the *cuenta* to me, as well as for these insights.

33. Viewed in these terms, gossip is a type of discourse which is redistributive rather than productive. The gossip mongerer manages the redistribution of a limited resource rather than creating a new product. Gossip is a form of commerce. This type of discourse possesses, controls and selectively redistributes information to enhance one's own position. It does not surprise me that it is so prevalent in a society where frustrated industry and failing production has created a situation where only the merchant—who redistributes rather than produces—amasses wealth. As a Peruvian friend recently commented, it is moral as well as economic bankruptcy that plagues Peruvian social relations.

REFERENCES CITED

Abrahams, R.
    1986   Ordinary and Extraordinary Experience. *In* The Anthropology of Experience. V. W. Turner and
        E. M. Bruner, eds. Pp. 45–72. Urbana: University of Illinois Press.
Bateson, G.
    1972   Steps to an Ecology of Mind. Philadelphia: Intext.
Berger, P., and T. Luckmann
    1966   The Social Construction of Reality. Garden City, NY: Doubleday.
Blumer H.
    1969   Symbolic Interactionism: Perspective and Method. Englewood Cliffs, NJ: Prentice-Hall.
Bourdieu, P.
    1977   Outline of a Theory of Practice. Cambridge: Cambridge University Press.

Boddy, J.
   1988   Spirits and Selves in Northern Sudan: The Cultural Therapeutics of Possession and Trance. American Ethnologist 15(1): 4–27.
Bruner, E.
   1986   Experience and its Expressions. *In* The Anthropology of Experience. V. W. Turner and E. M. Bruner, eds. Pp. 3–30. Urbana: University of Illinois Press.
Bruner, J.
   1987   Life as Narrative. Social Research 54(1): 11–33.
Burke, K.
   1969   A Rhetoric of Motives. Berkeley: University of California Press.
Carrithers, M., S. Collins, and S. Lukes, eds.
   1985   The Category of the Person: Anthropology, Philosophy, History. Cambridge: Cambridge University Press.
Chiappe, M.
   1968   Psiquiatría folkórica peruana: El curanderismo en la costa norte del Perú. Anales del Servicio de Psiquiatría 11(1–2).
   1979   Nosografía curanderil. *In* Psiquiatría folklórica. C. A. Seguín, ed. Pp. 76–93. Lima: Proyección Cristiana.
Chiappe, M., M. Limlij, and L. Millones
   1985   Alucinógenos y shamanismo en el Perú contemporaneo. Lima: Editor El Virrey.
Deigh, J.
   1983   Shame and Self-Esteem: A Critique. Ethics 93: 225–245.
Desjarlais, R.
   1989   Healing Through Images: The Magical Flight and Healing Geography of Nepali Shamans. Ethos 17: 289–307.
De Soto, H.
   1989   The Other Path: The Invisible Revolution in the Third World. New York: Harper and Row.
Dow, J.
   1986   Universal Aspects of Symbolic Healing: A Theoretical Synthesis. American Anthropologist 88(1): 56–69.
Elster, J., ed.
   1985   The Multiple Self. Cambridge: Cambridge University Press.
Erikson, E.
   1946   Ego Development and Historical Change. Psychoanalytic Study of the Child 2: 359–396.
   1956   The Problem of Ego Identity. Journal of the American Psychoanalytic Association 4: 56–121.
   1959   Identity and the Life Cycle: Selected Papers by E. H. Erikson. Psychological Issues, vol. 1. New York: International Universities Press.
Fernandez, J.
   1974   The Mission of Metaphor in Expressive Culture. Current Anthropology 15(2): 119–145.
   1986   The Argument of Images and the Experience of the Return to the Whole. *In* The Anthropology of Experience. V. W. Turner and E. M. Bruner, eds. Pp. 159–187. Urbana: University of Illinois Press.
Fogelson, R.
   1979   Person, Self, and Identity: Some Anthropological Retrospects, Circumspects, and Prospects. *In* Psychosocial Theories of the Self. B. Lee, ed. Pp. 67–109. New York: Plenum Press.
Forsberg, M., and M. Francke
   1987   Situación socio-económica de la mujer costeña. *In* La costa peruana: Realidad poblacional. C. Peñaherrera et al., eds. Pp. 225–248. Lima: Ediciones AMIDEP.
Foster, G.
   1965   Peasant Society and the Image of Limited Good. American Anthropologist 67: 293–315.
   1972   The Anatomy of Envy: A Study in Symbolic Behavior. Current Anthropology 13: 165–202.
Foucault, M.
   1972   The Archaeology of Knowledge and the Discourse on Language. New York: Pantheon Books.
Fowler, R.
   1985   Power. *In* Handbook of Discourse Analysis: Discourse Analysis in Society. T. Van Dijk, ed. Pp. 61–82. London: Academic Press.

Geertz, C.
1973 The Interpretation of Cultures. New York: Basic Books.

Giese, C. C.
1987 "Curanderos," Traditionelle Heiler in Nord-Peru (Küste und Hochland). Berlin: Free University, Ph.D. dissertation.

Glass-Coffin, B.
1985 Health Care Decision-Making Among an Urban Middle Class Population, Trujillo, Peru. Los Angeles: UCLA, Department of Anthropology, Master's thesis.

Goffman, I.
1959 The Presentation of Self in Everyday Life. Garden City, NY: Anchor Books.
1963 Stigma: Notes on the Management of Spoiled Identity. Englewood Cliffs, NJ: Prentice Hall.

Good, B., and M. J. Delvecchio Good
1980 The Meaning of Symptoms: A Cultural Hermeneutic Model for Clinical Practice. *In* The Relevance of Social Science for Medicine. L. Eisenberg and A. Kleinman, eds. Pp. 165–196. D. Reidel.

Gredys Harris, G.
1989 Concepts of Individual, Self, and Person in Description and Analysis. American Anthropologist 91(3): 599–612.

Gumperz, J.
1982a Discourse Strategies: Studies in Interactional Linguistics. Cambridge: Cambridge University Press.
1982b Language and Social Identity. Cambridge: Cambridge University Press.

Herrnstein-Smith, B.
1980 Afterthoughts on Narrative: Narrative Versions, Narrative Theories. Critical Inquiry 213–236.

Hymes, D.
1972 Models of Interaction of Language and Social Life. *In* Directions in Sociolinguistics: The Ethnography of Communication. New York: Holt-Rinehart, and Winston.
1983 The Linguistic Method in Ethnography: Its Development in the United States. *In* Essays in the History of Linguistic Anthropology. Amsterdam/Philadelphia: John Benjamin's Publishing.

Indice de Precios al Consumidor de Lima Metropolitana y Variación Porcentual
1989 Analysis Laboral, XIII (144): 11.

Instituto Nacional de Estadística (INE)
1989 Perú: Compendio estadístico, 1988. Lima.

James, W.
1952 (1890) The Principles of Psychology. Chicago: Encyclopedia Britannica.

Joralemon, D.
1983 The Symbolism and Physiology of Ritual Healing in a Peruvian Coastal Community. Los Angeles: UCLA, Department of Anthropology, Ph.D. dissertation.
1984 Symbolic Space and Ritual Time in a Peruvian Healing Ceremony. San Diego Museum of Man Ethnic Technical Notes 19: 1–20.
1985 Altar Symbolism in Peruvian Ritual Healing. Journal of Latin American Lore 11: 3–29.
1990 Cleansing the Body: Metaphors of Healing in Peruvian *Curanderismo*. Paper presented at the Annual Meeting of the American Ethnological Society, Atlanta, GA.

Kapferer, B.
1979 Mind, Self, and Other in Demonic Illness: The Negation and Reconstruction of Self. American Ethnologist 6(1): 110–133.
1983 A Celebration of Demons: Exorcism and the Aesthetics of Healing in Sri Lanka. Bloomington, IN: University of Indiana Press.

Kleinman, A.
1980 Patients and Healers in the Context of Culture: An Exploration of the Borderland Between Anthropology, Medicine, and Psychiatry. Berkeley: University of California Press.

Kuipers, J. C.
1989 "Medical Discourse" *In* Anthropological Context: Views of Language and Power. Medical Anthropology Quarterly 3(2): 99–123.

Lévi-Strauss, C.
1950 The Effectiveness of Symbols. Structural Anthropology. New York: Basic Books.

Marsella, A. J.
  1985   Culture, Self and Mental Disorder. *In* Culture and Self: Asian and Western Perspectives. A. Marsella, G. DeVos, and F. L. K. Hsu, eds. Pp. 281–307. New York: Tavistock.
Mauss, M.
  1985   [1938] A Category of the Human Mind: The Notion of Person; the Notion of Self. *In* The Category of the Person: Anthropology, Philosophy, and History. M. C. S. Collins, and S. Lukes, eds. Pp. 1–25. Cambridge: Cambridge University Press.
McAdams, D. P., and R. L. Ochberg, eds.
  1988   Psychobiography and Life Narratives. Durham: Duke University Press.
Mead, G. H.
  1934   Mind, Self, and Society. Chicago: University of Chicago Press.
Miyananga, K.
  1983   Social Reproduction and Transcendence: An Analysis of the Sekai Mahikari Bunmei Kyodan: A Heterodox Religious Movement in Contemporary Japan. Vancouver, BC, University of British Columbia, Ph.D. dissertation.
Munn, N. D.
  1973   Symbolism in a Ritual Context: Aspects of Symbolic Action. *In* Handbook of Social and Cultural Anthropology. J. J. Honigmann, ed. Pp. 579–612. Chicago: Rand McNally.
Myerhoff, B.
  1976   Shamanic Equilibrium: Balance and Mediation in Known and Unknown Worlds. *In* American Folk Medicine. W. D. Hand, ed. Pp. 99–108. Berkeley: University of California Press.
  1982   Life History Among the Elderly: Performance, Visibility, and Re-Membering. *In* A Crack in the Mirror: Reflexive Perspectives in Anthropology. J. Ruby, ed. Pp. 99–120. Philadelphia: University of Pennsylvania Press.
  1986   Life Not Death in Venice: Its Second Life. *In* The Anthropology of Experience. V. W. Turner and E. M. Bruner, eds. Pp. 261–288. Urbana: University of Illinois Press.
Polia Meconi, M.
  1988   Las lagunas de los encantos: Medicina tradicional del Perú septentrional. Lima: Gráfica Bellido.
Poole, F. J. P.
  1982   The Ritual Forging of Identity: Aspects of Person and Self in Bimin-Kuskusmin Male Initiation. *In* Rituals of Manhood. G. Herdt, ed. Pp. 99–154. Berkeley: University of California Press.
Quispe, M. U.
  1969   La herranza en choque Huarcaya y Huancasancos, Ayachucho. Lima: Imprenta Gráfica Industrial.
Ramirez, M. J.
  1966   Huancabamba: su historia, su geografía, su folklore. Lima: Imprenta del Ministerio de Hacienda y Comercio.
Rappaport, R.
  1974   Obvious Aspects of Ritual. Cambridge Anthropology 2(1): 3–69.
Ricoeur, P.
  1971   The Model of the Text: Meaningful Action Considered as Text. Social Research 38(3):
Robbins, R. H.
  1973   Identity, Culture, and Behavior. *In* Handbook of Social and Cultural Anthropology. J. J. Honigmann, ed. Pp. 1199–1222. Chicago: Rand McNally.
Rotondo, H.
  1970   Estudios sobre la familia en su relación con la salud. Lima: UNM San Marcos.
Rubel, A., C. O'Nell, and R. Collado-Ardón
  1984   Susto, A Folk Illness. Berkeley: University of California Press.
Sarbin, T. R., ed.
  1986   Narrative Psychology: The Storied Nature of Human Conduct. New York: Praeger.
Seguin, C. A.
  1979   Introducción a la psiquiatría folklórica. *In* Psiquiatría folklórica. C. A. Seguin, ed. Pp. 13–66. Lima: Centro de Proyección Cristiana.
Sharon, D.
  1976   Distribution of the *Mesa* in Latin America. Journal of Latin American Lore 2(1): 71–95.

1978 Wizard of the Four Winds: A Shaman's Story. New York: Free Press.

1989 The Dialectics of North Peruvian Shamanism. Unpublished manuscript.

Shotter, J., and K. L. Gergen, eds.

1989 Texts of Identity. Newbury Park, CA: Sage Publications.

Shweder, R., and R. LeVine

1984 Culture Theory: Essays on Mind, Self, and Emotion. Cambridge: Cambridge University Press.

Tambiah, S. J.

1968 The Magical Power of Words. Man 3: 175–208.

Taussig, M.

1980 The Devil and Commodity Fetishism in South America. Chapel Hill: University of North Carolina Press.

1982 El curanderismo popular y la estructura de la conquista en el suroeste de Colombia. América Indígena 42(4): 559–614.

1987 Shamanism, Colonialism and the Wild Man: A Study in Terror and Healing. Chicago: University of Chicago Press.

Tomkins, J.

1980 The Reader in History: The Changing Shape of Literary Response. *In* Reader Response Criticism: From Formalism to Post-Structuralism. Baltimore: Johns Hopkins University Press.

Van Dijk, T. A.

1985 Handbook of Discourse Analysis: Disciplines of Discourse. London: Academic Press.

Vasquez, R.

1988 El curanderismo: Terapia y participación de clases sociales en la costa norte del Perú—Trujillo. Universidad Nacional de La Libertad, Trujillo, Peru. Tésis de bachillerato, antropología.

Walkup, J.

1987 Introduction. Social Research 54: 1.

Wallace, A. F. C.

1967 Identity Processes in Personality and Culture. *In* Cognition, Personality and Clinical Psychology. R. Jessor and S. Beshbach, eds. Pp. 62–89. San Francisco: Dorsey Press.

Weigert, A., J. S. Teitge, and D. W. Teitge

1986 Society and Identity. Cambridge: Cambridge University Press.

Westen, D.

1985 Self and Society: Narcissism, Collectivism and the Development of Morals. Cambridge: Cambridge University Press.

White, G. M., and J. Kirkpatrick

1985 Person, Self, and Experience: Exploring Pacific Ethnopsychologies. Berkeley: University of California Press.

Wiener, P., ed.

1958 C. S. Pierce: Selected Writings (Values in a Universe of Chance). New York: Dover Publications.

Wikan, U.

1984 Shame and Honour: A Contestable Pair. Man 19: 635–652.

Wolf, E.

1955 Types of Latin American Peasantry. American Anthropologist 57: 452–471.

Guardian Angels and Dirty Spirits: The Moral Basis of Healing Power in Rural Haiti

By Paul E. Brodwin

INTRODUCTION

Medical pluralism—the co-existence of diverse and often competing healing traditions within a single community, region, or national culture—is a central concern of most ethnomedical investigations. After all, there are very few settings which offer only one way to conceive of the body and its suffering, or where people rely on only one brand of therapy. In most parts of the world, both afflicted individuals and those responsible for their care must negotiate between several healing practitioners who typically represent different religious, ideological, ethnic, political, gender-based, or economic class interests in a society.

Countless ethnographies have documented the interplay between biomedicine, other literate or "cosmopolitan" medical traditions, and the more localized practices of herbalists or religious specialists, while a related line of research traces the history of medical pluralism in specific settings.[1] Although it is foolhardy to summarize such a vast literature, two areas continue to receive the most attention: (1) the health care seeking process, i.e., how people negotiate among healers in the context of local illness categories, political economic constraints, and on-going social roles; and (2) the cultural organization of medical knowledge, i.e., the symbolic constructions of the body, self, and affliction proposed by co-existing forms of healing, how they articulate with wider social and ritual orders, and how they inform the diagnostic and healing activities of specific practitioners (see Rubel and Hass 1990).

Behind these two popular topics lies an equally important but less-studied question which I take up here: How shall we classify the range of non-biomedical practitioners within a plural medical system? Although I investigate this question in the context of rural Haiti, it also illuminates some conceptual confusions surrounding the general study of medical pluralism. Just as health care seekers routinely deal in many different "medical idioms" over the course of a single illness episode, practi-

PAUL BRODWIN *is an Assistant Professor of Anthropology at the University of Wisconsin-Milwaukee, P. O. Box 413, Milwaukee, WI 53201. His current fieldwork examines the links between Pentacostalist healing and wider social transformations in rural Haiti.*

tioners may also mediate between several conceptions of the source of healing power. The struggles of these healers to authorize their own therapeutic knowledge and challenge the legitimacy of competing options is the topic of this chapter.

I profile below two individuals—both "secular herbalists/midwives," in the conventional classification--widely known as effective healers among the residents of a small village in southern Haiti. By narrating their life-histories and accounting for their particular expertise, each healer takes up a specific position in a plural moral universe. That is, they each appropriate a certain notion of upright ethical action in order to authorize their own therapeutic practice as both effective and morally correct. These healers stake their moral claims in religious terms; in particular, by drawing on the plural discourses of popular Haitian religion about the moral value of angels and spirits.

Before presenting the ethnographic argument, however, let me justify its relevance to the broader study of medical pluralism. Patients, their families, and their therapy managing groups (Janzen 1987) routinely negotiate between distinct medical traditions. They may even self-consciously reflect on the competing claims to truth and efficacy advanced by particular healers, and they usually perceive little conflict between treatments which strike us as logically incompatible (see Janzen 1978 and Amarasingham 1980). This much is a fundamental axiom of medical anthropology, and it continues to inspire current research (e.g., Nichter and Nordstom 1989).

This approach highlights the multiplicity of therapies which co-exist in a single social field. Indeed, some regard such diversity as the mark of an adaptive and culturally powerful therapeutic system (Leslie 1976: 10, Kunstadter 1975). A plural set of cosmologies, discourses on the body, and healing practices help the medical system as a whole to remain vital and responsive to cultural, political, and even epidemiological change. However, the entire argument proceeds from the point of view of health care seekers, not practitioners. It implicitly assumes that a given healing specialist will cleave to a single reading of the disorder and recommend a single form of treatment. The specialist's clientele, on the other hand, will have sifted through the ambiguous and contradictory readings of suffering proposed by several different healers. In most depictions of medical pluralism, therefore, healing specialists provide a stable background of discrete ideologies and techniques. What seems problematic (and most interesting) are the strategies people employ to choose between them and the consequences of their choice.

The discourse of Catholic herbalists and midwives in rural Haiti challenges these assumptions. As these healers describe their own treatments and draw the relevant differences between each others' practice, they rely on their own set of multiple and over-lapping criteria. In Haiti, the healers' perspective on medical pluralism can be as ambiguous and contradictory as the health care seekers'. Of course, their concerns differ; while patients and their kin search for appropriate, powerful therapies, herbalists and midwives attempt to secure their status as good Catholics and thus ensure their personal moral worth. In this chapter, therefore, I examine not the movement of people among healers (cf. Amarasingham 1980), but rather the movement of healing specialists between different accounts of therapeutic power. The shifting moral discourses deployed by these midwives and herbalists resist any simple, static classification of their healing practice: secular or sacred, "Catholic" or "Vodoun."

THE DIVERSITY OF HEALING SPECIALISTS
IN RURAL HAITI

The two healers introduced below live in Jeanty: a densely-settled village of approximately 2500 individuals near the southern provincial capital of Les Cayes, Haiti.2 On the one hand, Jeanty resembles many rural Haitian villages of this size: linked to regional and national economies by private bus-lines, most people survive on a meager income from the sale of crops in the twice-weekly market, petty commerce, or remittances from relatives working in Port-au-Prince and abroad. On the other hand, residents of Jeanty enjoy several advantages over other rural dwellers: the region has escaped the worst forms of deforestation and erosion common elsewhere in Haiti, and an energetic, committed citizens' council has brought limited electrification, a potable water project, and a small state-operated biomedical dispensary to the village during the past 15 years.

The residents of Jeanty consult a remarkably large array of non-biomedical healers. In fact, the local plural healing system includes the entire range of the practitioners mentioned by other Haitian and American anthropologists working in southern Haiti. For example, Coreil (1979), following Weise's field study (1971), lists six types of non-biomedical practitioners near Jeremie: midwives, bonesetters, herbalists, injectionists, *bokor* (which she translates as "sorcerers") and *houngan* and *mambo* (male and female Vodoun specialists). Clerisme (1979) describes five categories of healers active in the Petit Goave region: herbalists, injectionists, midwives, *houngan*, and herbalists/*houngan*. Working in the Grande Anse, Conway (1978) examines the practice of herbalists, midwives, two types of *houngan*, as well as Pentecostalist pastors.

Each researcher relies on different criteria to classify these healers. Conway privileges theories of etiology; according to him, religious specialists such as *houngan* and pastors are "personalistic" curers, who treat diseases caused by human or non-human agents, whereas herbalists and midwives are "naturalistic" curers (cf. Foster 1976). Coreil groups them into primary, secondary, and tertiary levels, based on the disorders treated, the cost of treatment, and practitioners' technology and level of training (Coreil 1983). Subsuming Haiti in the entire Afro-Caribbean region, Laguerre proposes three categories of "folk" practitioners: non-religious curers (including midwives and bonesetters); faith healers, inspired by God or spirits; and other morally ambiguous servitors of the spirits who both heal and cause illness (Laguerre 1987: 55). Finally, Hess classifies non-professional healers into three sectors—domestic medicine, Creole medicine, and mercantile medicine—based on the social context of their practice and the disemic codes of Haitian culture (Hess 1981, 1983).

According to all of these schemes, herbalists and midwives are secular healers, in contrast to the religious specialists who rely on the power of either the Christian god or the *lwa* (African-derived spirits who populate the Vodoun cosmology). However, when I began my fieldwork in Jeanty in 1987, herbalists and midwives invariably mentioned an invisible spiritual entity called an *anj gadyen* (literally, "guardian angel") from our very first interviews. They referred to the *anj gadyen* in order to trace their career as healing specialists and to account for their unique healing power.

Although they construct the *anj gadyen* in different ways and with different degrees of sophistication, their talk about it accomplishes much the same purpose. Catholic herbalists and midwives invoke the *anj gadyen* as part of a strategy to differentiate themselves from the immoral *houngan*, who serve not beneficent angels but rather the satanic *lwa* (also excoriated as "dirty spirits.") This is how herbalists and midwives justify their moral worth and legitimate their therapeutic power. Through this discourse of guardian angels and dirty spirits, we see that the practice of presumably secular healers is shot through with moral and religious concerns.

JEAN MILOT AND THE CATHOLIC CONDEMNATION OF SPIRITS

Take the example of Jean Milot, a 65-year old Catholic herbalist (*dokte fey*, or "leaf doctor") who lives with his wife just across the shallow river bordering Jeanty. His home is sparse but sturdily built, and large enough to house several of his four children when they return home between attempts at finding work in Les Cayes or Port-au-Prince. Of all the herbalists and midwives I interviewed, Jean has the most personalized reading of the *anj gadyen*, and his position on the *lwa* exemplifies a widespread Catholic reading of the moral components of the self.

Jean begins his explanation of the *anj gadyen* (or *anj*, meaning simply "angels") by depicting them as the seat of individual autonomy and judgment:

Each child of God has an *anj*, which was created with you, which directs you. The *anj* will tell you what to do, it will protect you. For example, the *anj* brought you here to my house. If you didn't have the *anj* which God placed in your head, you wouldn't know which route to take.

However, the *anj* (which Jean also refers to by the synonymous term "good soul," or *bon nanm*) does not alone make up the person. It is joined by a bad soul (literally, *gwo nanm*, or "large soul"), and in this Manichean reading of the self, the two souls co-exist in the same individual's body. The *bon nanm* represents the source of virtuous and effective action, whereas the *gwo nanm* is the cause of immoral behavior:

Each person has a *bon nanm* and a *gwo nanm* . . . The two are together in your body. The *bon nanm* was given to you by God, and it doesn't do things which are not good . . . The *gwo nanm* represents the other side of you . . . If you do something which is bad, it is the *gwo nanm* which makes you do it.

But then you think about it, you mull it over, and you say that you shouldn't have done that. That's when the *gwo nanm* leaves your body, and the *bon nanm* appears. It understands the sin, it understands that you shouldn't have done that. When the *bon nanm* re-enters you, you see clearly.

This style of psychological and moral theorizing may well have characterized rural Haitian life throughout much of the 20th century. The *anj gadyen* which Jean describes is roughly equivalent to the *ti bon anj* (the "small good angel"), a standard category of Haitian ethnopsychology mentioned by most researchers along with its complement, the *gwo bon anj* (the "big good angel"). Drawing on fieldwork in the late 1940's, for example, Metraux writes that the *ti bon anj* watches over the sleeper and, after death, accounts for the sins of the person who was in his charge (1972: 303, 258). The *gwo bon anj* has an almost physical substance; it can be removed from someone's head and stored in a bottle to protect it from enemies, and after death it can linger, ghost-like, in the places the person lived (Ibid.: 306, 258).

Maya Deren (1953) provides a more speculative, metaphysical reading, but it better captures the moral concerns expressed by Jean and the other healers. The *ti bon anj* represents an impersonal conscience or the universal commitment towards the good. It is detached from the pressures of daily life, and impervious to development and corruption. The *ti bon anj* is thus a constant of the human condition (1953: 26). The *gwo bon anj* is a person's soul understood as the repository of her history, abilities, and intelligence. The activities of daily life—including the possibility of mental confusion or evil—depend on constant communication with the *gwo bon anj* (Ibid.: 27, 35).

To return to Jean Milot's own words, recall that he describes the *gwo nanm* as the complement, and moral inverse, of the Catholic *bon nanm* (the *anj gadyen*). He traces a person's decision to act unethically and then re-evaluate one's sin to the waxing and waning influence of the two souls. These ethnopsychological categories thus carry a moral force, and in a double sense. They constitute the self as both a purposeful agent who exercises full self-control, and an ethically upright, morally correct person.

Jean thus deploys the moral rhetoric of good souls and bad souls (*bon nanm* and *gwo nanm*) in two ways. He first describes the chaotic and meaningless behavior typical of someone under the exclusive domination of the *gwo nanm*:

The *gwo nanm* is crazy. When people start to run around, to break things, to roll on the ground, they call him a crazy person. It is the *gwo nanm* that is directing him. The person doesn't have his *bon nanm* any more.

If you didn't have the *anj*, you could have ended up in the river [separating Jean's house from Jeanty]. The *gwo nanm* would leave you in the water; it's an old soul, an old rebellious soul[3] . . . I know that the Christian *bon nanm* is in you, because you are writing down everything I say. If the *gwo nanm* were in you, you'd be writing nonsense.

According to Jean, the *gwo nanm* is responsible for people's unruly, disordered behavior. But it also incites immoral or unethical conduct: it leads you to do "something bad," "something which you shouldn't have done." In this second respect, the bad soul is both a morally-inflected component of the self and a personified spiritual being. In the above passage, for example, Jean identifies the *gwo nanm* as an "old rebellious soul," and opposes it to the Christian *bon nanm*. On another occasion, Jean classified the *gwo nanm* as a "rebellious angel," and then proceeded to say that a rebellious angel is a Satan. The bad soul (and, likewise, the guardian angel) represent more than conventional names for ethical principles; they are spiritual entities with their own quasi-separate existence, and Jean embeds them in the conventional moral structure of village Catholicism: the opposition between Catholic worship and the service of the spirits, or *lwa*.

Haitian religious pluralism is enormously complex, comprising the formal, state-sponsored Catholic church, numerous Protestant sects, and that syncretic amalgam of West African practices and French Catholicism which most non-Haitians know as Vodoun (but is usually referred to in Creole by such terms as "to serve the spirits [*lwa*]" or "to serve the mysteries"). These different components cross-reference each other and even share key icons and forms or worship, and a full treatment of the entire system obviously lies beyond the scope of this paper. However, Jean (like most other residents of Jeanty) repeatedly insisted to me that he is a Catholic who emphatically does *not* serve the spirits. The particular position he takes up in this plural religious landscape must be briefly sketched out here, since it directly implicates his healing practice.

Jean clearly defines himself as an Catholic herbalist or *dokte fey* (literally, "leaf doctor"), as opposed to an *houngan*, the expert in serving the *lwa*. He extends his discourse on angels, spirits, *bon nanm*, and *gwo nanm* to describe the source of his expertise and the origins of his healing career. To begin with, Jean relies on the *anj* in the preparation of specific herbal remedies:

When you come to me, I consult you, I see what you have. We agree to meet tomorrow, for you to bring me money for the medication. Tonight, I'll see what I should do with you . . . When I sleep, the *anj* bring me all the ways to treat somebody. I can even answer them, saying "I'll do it." As soon as I fall asleep, I see how to act, which medications to buy.

The *anj* do more than simply bless the remedies or categorically ensure that his therapeutic actions will be effective. According to Jean, the *anj* tell him which *fey* to use for each specific case. Thus he once stated that because of the knowledge of the *fey* possessed by his *anj*, "it really isn't me who treats people, it's the *anj conducte*" (the "conducting angel," a term synonymous with guardian angel).

This reading of the *anj* as distinct spiritual beings also appears in the Jean's story of the beginnings of his career as a *dokte fey*. Jean underwent two types of apprenticeship before taking up his own healing practice. He learned about herbal treatments from his mother, a midwife and sometime herbalist. When Jean was in his early twenties, he began to substitute for her in deliveries and cases of illness. When she died, he continued to treat some of her old clients. He also learned "magic" and the treatment of a specific class of disorders called "Satanic sicknesses" from an *houngan* named Luc Sinwa.

Although Jean gained his empirical knowledge from these apprenticeships, the immediate cause of his beginning work as *dokte fey* was a call from his *anj*:

I began treating people when I was 30 years old. An *anj conducte* told me how to do it while I was sleeping. I didn't want to do it at all, but then one day I injured myself with a knife while I was working. I saw in my sleep that it was the *anj* who had made me cut myself, because of my refusal to do the work they wanted.

[Why didn't you want to do what the *anj* showed you?] All of my children are in Catholic school, and my wife takes communion and she confesses, so I don't want to have anything to do with that stuff. But when I saw that it was something serious, that they wanted me to be a doctor, I stuck to it.

Why did Jean originally refuse to follow the calling of his *anj conducte*? Jean mistook the *anj* for invisible beings of another sort— that is, for *lwa* who presumably wanted him to serve as a devotee or *houngan*, engaged in the elaborate ceremonies of temple-based Vodoun, providing food to nourish the *lwa* or even his own body for them to enter. His original refusal echoes the public repudiation of the *lwa* common among Catholic villagers (see below). For Jean, the spirits stand for everything opposed to the kind of upright life which is sustained by participation in the Catholic sacraments. His refusal to work for the *lwa* thus testifies to his own moral virtue.

However, Jean eventually decided that the call he heard in his sleep came from his guardian angel, not the *lwa*, so he began practice as an herbalist, not as a *houngan* who serves the spirits. He continues his moral devaluation of the realm of the *lwa* in the following contrast between his own healing practice and that of an *houngan*:

People who are *houngan* make good money. They push away God, and take up with Lucifer, with Ogoun,[4] in order to become wealthy. An *houngan* will make 200 gourdes, you'll only make 50. But you're better than he is. It is only in this world that the *houngan* has his mandate; after death, he's nothing. He's going under the feet of Lucifer . . . But if you are an herbalist, it's the work of God that you're doing.

By demonizing both the *lwa* and those who serve them, Jean positions himself squarely on the side of the Christian God. Recall that he drew a moral opposition between the two constituents of the self—the good soul and the bad soul—and then identified the bad soul as a "Satan." By analogy, he also opposes guardian angels to the *lwa*, and the herbalist to the *houngan*. The *houngan* literally sell themselves to the Devil. They may earn more money in this world than an herbalist, but they will be robbed of the after-life in heaven that a good Catholic can expect.

Jean Milot here takes up a position I encountered often among the Catholic residents of Jeanty. If villagers approvingly regard the *anj gadyen* as the source of morally upright action, they take just the opposite position towards the *lwa*. For many people, the *lwa* represent the antithesis of Christian virtues. They often responded to my inquiries about the *lwa* with an incredulous question of their own: why was I interested in such dirty, Satanic matters? Even asking about it placed me under suspicion. They (half-jokingly) accused me of using the information to send a sickness upon someone or even to try calling the *lwa* myself.

In countless conversations, people expressed their genuine, visceral disgust with the *lwa*. Their reactions constitute one possible public reading of the relationship between the realm of the *lwa* and formal Catholicism. Most people easily identify the *lwa* with bad souls. They use the term "Satan" to denote not only the *lwa* but also the *houngan* who serves them, the maleficent spirit they send upon their victim, and the resulting afflictions ("Satanic sicknesses").[5] In general, most people describe *houngan* as dirty, untrustworthy characters who invoke their spirits primarily to send sickness, but also for other immoral and unsavory purposes which no upstanding Catholic would even care to speculate about.

What accounts for this public demonization and denunciation of the spirits? For a full answer, we must first examine my fieldwork situation in light of the religious history of Haiti and the social divisions it embodies. In Jeanty, most people perceive me as a high status outsider, who presumably practices only formal Catholicism. Loudly denouncing the *lwa* is the same strategy they adopt in dealing with the only other foreigner living in the village, the French Catholic priest. Many people figured that I subscribed to the same hostility towards non-Catholic practices that has typified the colonialist European clergy (and Europeanized elite) in Haiti for most of the past 200 years (see Metraux 1972: 323–359, Breathett 1983). In their dealings with me, they understandably choose the Catholic-inflected condemnation of the *lwa* as the appropriate idiom to portray themselves as reputable and morally trustworthy people.

Publicly denouncing the spirits is a strategic move in this plural religious system. In doing so, people associate themselves with the Catholic church: one of the most powerful sources of formal social value and prestige in rural Haitian society (and far more legitimate than its closest rivals, the government and army). In these public declarations of religious affiliation, people pose the choice in dichotomous terms: you can serve either Christ or the *lwa*, and in serving one, you thereby repudiate the other. Obviously, this argument does not merely describe the situation; in its stark oppositional logic, it reproduces the historically dominant Catholic position. People like Jean Milot thus explained the powers of the *lwa* to me and condemned them at the same time. However, people's actual religious practices better fit a continuum model, in which exclusive attendance either at services for the *lwa* or formal Catholic mass represent the rare extremes (cf. Drummond 1980). In private interviews with individuals who do not need to defend their reputations as morally upright healers (unlike Jean Milot), many people easily describe themselves as Catholics who also serve the spirits.

The widespread, if publicly unstated, awareness of this admixture of Catholicism and service to the spirits explains a second reason for people's strident denunciation of the *lwa*. Most residents of Jeanty (approximately 85%) are Catholics who regularly attend Sunday Mass and, if they can afford it, are baptized, confirmed, and married in the church. They are concerned for their reputations as good Catholics not only to me, but also to their neighbors, and perhaps to themselves. The strategy of condemning the *lwa* thus emerges not only where Haitians confront (presumably) Catholic foreigners, but also in many other contexts of village life where people position themselves as more enlightened (*eklere*), more educated, or more powerfully connected than their peers (cf. Wilson 1973).

However, when people explained their own reasons for condemning the *lwa* as "satanic," they did not explicitly refer to either the social prestige of Catholicism or the intricacies of religious affiliation. Their discourse was much more pragmatic and immediate; it focuses mainly on the *houngan*'s immoral and maleficent use of their *lwa*. I first encountered this attitude indirectly, in the form of people's seeming ignorance of the *lwa* and the activities of *houngan* and their sensitivity to my overly insistent questioning. On one occasion, an elderly woman, the senior member of a prominent Jeanty family, denied any knowledge of the *lwa*. When I next asked whether she ever visited an *houngan*, she quickly and defensively replied "Why should I? I don't have problems with anybody!" She took my question as a challenge, almost an accusation, and her response reflects the general understanding of why one consults an *houngan* or be familiar with their activities.

According to many villagers in Jeanty, people seek out an *houngan* for one of only two reasons: to send an affliction upon an enemy, or to learn the cause of one's own affliction. Either motive can endanger one's reputation as a good Catholic who leads a morally upright life. Obviously, trying to send a sickness paints one as willing to murder others for personal gain, since jealousy over material resources (money, jobs, possessions) is one of the prime reasons to send a sickness. But even consulting an *houngan* for one's own affliction can carry a moral stain. Since the *houngan* is the only specialist who can identify a sent sickness, seeking him out suggests that one has potential enemies, who might have good cause to launch a malicious spiritual attack; for example, to revenge for a prior wrong. This explains perhaps the most common response to my question, have you ever visited an *houngan* for a sickness? "No, I'm innocent. I don't need to."

This concern with innocence and guilt pervades people's attitudes towards *houngan* and their healing powers. Any engagement with an *houngan* entails a suspicion of guilt. To hold the *houngan* in utter disrepute and loudly to proclaim one's ignorance of them powerfully attests to one's innocence. This is why *houngan* are despised and conventionally associated with the figure of Satan, the inverse image of Christian morality (cf. Hawkins 1984: 349ff). Because the *houngan* owes his special maleficent power to these spiritual beings, people identify the *lwa* as satans, as well, and denigrate them in equally strong terms.

Jean Milot follows this very same strategy. By practicing as an herbalist, he explicitly advances his claim as an ethically upright individual. To begin with, he positions himself as a Catholic who turns away from the temptation to profit from the immoral activities undertaken by an *houngan*. Moreover, he attributes his healing power to the *anj gadyen*, not the spirits, and he says that he would not have endangered his family's Catholic virtue by following the *lwa*. The conventional moral divide between Catholicism and the realm of the spirits thus underlies Jean's self-presentation as an innocent herbalist, who draws on only the angels' power to heal, not the satans' power to send sickness.

CALLING THE SPIRIT: MME. BEAUMONT AND *ERZILI*

Marie Beaumont, a well respected midwife, is a vigorous 55 year-old woman who lives with three daughters, her husband, and her husband's father in a large home near the center of Jeanty. She adopts yet another morally-inflected position towards the *anj gadyen*, the *lwa*, and their influence on human behavior. In many respects, her position overlaps with the one taken by Jean Milot. However, Mme. Beaumont surveys these issues from a privileged perspective: unlike Jean, she can become possessed by various *lwa* virtually at will. On several occasions, Mme. Beaumont was entered by Ogoun and Erzili (two of the most important *lwa* in Haiti), and I was able to speak extensively with these embodied spirits.[6]

Mme. Beaumont considers herself a good Catholic. Although she acknowledges that the *lwa* enter her, she refuses to draw upon their power in her healing practice. This is a contradictory and problematic position to occupy. Simply by having *lwa*, she risks being associated with other types of dirty, Satanic activities, such as the immoral and disorderly behavior caused by the bad soul (*move nanm*) and the houngan's malign skill at sending sickness. In her discursive attempts to resolve this contradiction, she invokes two different accounts of the *lwa*: one rooted in the Catholic oppositional scheme invoked by Jean Milot, and the other in the domestic cult of ancestors—a core component of popular Haitian religion. She selectively draws from both these religious idioms in order to narrate the origin of her healing practice and legitimize it as morally correct.

Mme. Beaumont's contradictory position first appears in her talk about the *anj gadyen*. She describes the *anj* in the same personalized terms that Jean employed, and her experience of them is even more vivid. Mme. Beaumont relates how she learned the skills of a midwife from the *anj* who came in her sleep:

I saw people telling me, 'do it this way, do it that way' . . . In my dreams, the anj gave me a scissors to cut the umbilical cord, they gave me thread to tie it off. I saw it as if in broad daylight with my eyes wide open. Each night I was doing a delivery, so finally I said to myself, 'Okay, I'll make that my profession.'

Like Jean Milot, Mme. Beaumont was initially confused about the identity of these beings who spoke to her in her sleep. Were they *anj* or *lwa*? Jean decided that it was the *anj*, after all, who wanted him to do the godly, beneficent work of a herbalist, not the *lwa* calling him to the Satanic activity of serving the spirits. But when I asked Mme. Beaumont the same question, she did not make as sharp a distinction. Over her husband's objections, she told me, "Yes, the *anj* is like a *lwa*," and then hastened to add

But I don't accept it. If I wanted it, that would be that. But I don't want it. The situation would be the same with my child: if she wanted to serve the *lwa*, she would serve the *lwa*, but she doesn't want to. . . .

If some guy comes to chat with me and I want to talk too, I'll answer him. But if I don't want to talk, I don't respond. It's the same thing.

Mme. Beaumont easily allows that the *anj* who instructed her in the midwife's trade resembled *lwa*. But on this issue, as on several others examined below, she adopts a position towards the *lwa* which successfully deflects the moral taint usually created by traffic with the spirits. In a partial break with the conventional Catholic scheme, Mme. Beaumont does not demonize the *lwa*. Merely having spirits does not mark her as evil, in league with Satan, and opposed to the godly Catholic realm. She chooses another strategy to establish her moral worth: she privileges not the absolute opposition between *anj gadyen* and *lwa*, but rather her own response to the importunings of the *lwa*.

On this point, Mme. Beaumont is absolutely clear: she has decided not to serve them. As she says in the above passage, this is simply a matter of choice, and no more difficult than refusing to interact with other human villagers. The *lwa* are not so powerful that they can force Mme. Beaumont's devotion against her will. Although she definitely has *lwa*, she retains the ability to refuse to serve them as a *mambo*, that is, to draw on their power for religious or therapeutic ends.[7] Through her vehement refusal to serve them, Mme. Beaumont distances herself from the evil and disorder which, according to the standard Catholic viewpoint, inevitably result from contact with the spirits.

Mme. Beaumont thus exploits one of the subtleties of the Catholic condemnation of the realm of the *lwa*. Like many other villagers, she does not claim that the *lwa* are evil, but rather that the *houngan* are tricky and unsavory characters, and that any engagement with them carries particular risks. Unlike Jean Milot, she does not condemn the *houngan* categorically for relying upon the spirits. Indeed, she acknowledges that by calling up their *lwa*, *houngan* enjoy certain powers that she lacks. This is chiefly the power to treat cases of Satanic sickness, and Mme. Beaumont reports her standard piece of advice for victims of this class of disorders: Go back to the *houngan* who sent the sickness upon you, so he can take it off again. Nonetheless, she generally thinks it is wiser for most of us to avoid dealing with *houngan*.

Mme. Beaumont employs an even more persuasive strategy to ensure her moral worth. She does not classify the *lwa* which enter her as members of the same set which includes Satan, the *gwo nanm*, and the crafty and untrustworthy *houngan*. To the contrary, she locates them in her very own family. These *lwa* come from my family line, they come from my ancestors, she repeatedly told me. Mme. Beaumont here embeds the *lwa* in a radically different framework from the conventional Catholic scheme. She defines the *lwa* in terms of the family cult of ancestral spirits, a vital component of religious life for many Haitian villagers which lies outside of both formal Catholic worship and attendance at the *houngan*'s healing ceremonies.

By invoking the ideology of the domestic cult of ancestors, Mme. Beaumont can escape the Catholic rhetoric of moral condemnation. In this cult, the *lwa* are conceived of as quintessentially local spirits, associated with one's ancestors and tied to one's family lands. Ancestors further than two generations back (one's grandparents' generation) typically become assimilated to the "generalized archetypes" of *lwa* which most students of Haitian religion mention: Ogoun, Erzili, Damballah, etc. (Smucker 1984).[8]

"Serving the spirits," in this context, means satisfying the sensual desires of the spirits and fulfilling one's familial obligations to the ancestors. The *lwa* are not demonized as the moral inverse of *anj gadyen;* on the contrary, people grant them a series of ordinary human traits. Metraux, for example, writes that they are "wily, lascivious, sensitive, jealous, and subject to violent attacks of rage which are quickly over . . . (1972: 94). In Jeanty, people assume that these *lwa* have much the same tastes as human beings: they enjoy drumming and dancing at the ceremonies held in their honor as well as the sweet foods and alcoholic beverages which people place on small household shrines to their family *lwa.*[9] If neglected for too long, a *lwa* can bother various family members by causing sickness or a run of misfortune which continues until the schedule of offerings is resumed (cf. Lowenthal 1978).

Mme. Beaumont cannot help that her family's spirits chose her (or that they continue to "dance in her head"), but she refuses to satisfy them with ceremonies, feed them with offerings, or do the *mambo's* work of divination and healing. Within the Catholic framework, it is easy to understand her rejection of the *lwa;* they represent the undesirable inverse of Catholic virtues. However, within the idiom of the cult of domestic spirits, she rejects the *lwa* for a less momentous reason: she simply doesn't like them. They are attracted to her, but she does not return their attention. Since this is a legitimate idiom for one's relationship to the *lwa* within Haitian popular religion, she does not elaborate this dislike. This second idiom assumes that the *lwa* are attracted to her for obscure and capricious reasons, so her refusal of them is equally uncomplicated. Even when she casts their claim on her in kinship terms, her rejection is unproblematic:

The *lwa* exists, but I don't acknowledge it as my own.[10] It's like a child who was born without a father . . . I don't recognize him as my child . . . I make the *lwa* into an orphan.

Mme. Beaumont says that she has abandoned the *lwa* and does not acknowledge its claims upon her. She refuses to nurture it or even to acknowledge that she is related to it, and for her, that settles the case. But because she does not demonize *lwa,* Mme. Beaumont made no attempt to hide her ability to call the spirits, either from me or from the many other villagers who have personally witnessed the *lwa* "dancing in her head." Not surprisingly, when her *lwa* speaks it offers quite another opinion on Mme. Beaumont's rejection of it. It also reveals that, contrary to all of her protests, Mme. Beaumont does rely on the power of the *lwa* when faced with difficult deliveries.

Mme. Beaumont can call up Erzili with minimal preparation and ritual apparatus. On one occasion, she poured a few drops of water on the ground as an offering, while saying in a normal tone of voice, "Erzili, there is someone who is calling for you." Returning inside, she sat down again, took off her glasses, and lay her head in her hands. After only a few minutes, Mme. Beaumont (or, rather, Erzili) looked up and shook both left and right hands with everyone present (a distinctive greeting only used by the *lwa* when the first enter their human servitor).

I was thus able to interview Erzili on the same range of topics as the other healing specialist in Jeanty: I asked her what herbal remedies she knows and what sicknesses she is able to treat. However, the *lwa* soon brought the conversation around to her own central themes: her annoyance that Mme. Beaumont refuses to work for her, and her fond memories about the better days when she was served by her the midwife's grandparents:

I'm not in the habit of treating people. My horse [i.e., Mme. Beaumont] doesn't want to do it. I could take off an old Satanic sickness . . . If you're sick, I could tell if it's a Satanic sickness upon you. I could take it off today, and tomorrow you'd go home.

If my horse wanted to do it, I could make her a big-time *mambo* . . . If my horse wanted to receive me, they way her grandmother did, she would be really wealthy . . . But she would rather talk with the white to make her money.

Erzili here boasts about her healing powers and complains that they remain unused because Mme. Beaumont has not become a *mambo*. She seems absolutely mystified by her horse's decision, and elsewhere she calls her horse stupid and lazy. But the *lwa* is not genuinely vindictive. Although Mme. Beaumont has abandoned her, Erzili will not revenge herself upon her horse or her horse's children. The *lwa* says that she would only punish someone who had once served her but then stopped, and that exempts Mme. Beaumont.

Despite her poor treatment from Mme. Beaumont, the *lwa* has apparently not abandoned her horse. In a story about a delivery in Jeanty, Erzili describes how she entered Mme. Beaumont, and thereby actually saved her life. This story sheds new light on Mme. Beaumont's vehement claims that she refuses to call upon the *lwa*'s power in her healing practice.

Erzili relates that her horse went to the home of a pregnant woman a few months ago to attend a delivery along with Octavia, the other prominent midwife in Jeanty. The woman delivered her child without complications, but then could not deliver the placenta, and soon afterwards went into convulsions, lost consciousness, and died. Erzili claims that the death resulted from a sickness sent upon her by some enemy in the village:

[How did you know it was a sent sickness which troubled her?] She delivered easily, without any problem. And she had delivered her two other children with no problems. But that night, when she delivered, a sheep and a goat died right in the middle of things . . . I don't know why [she got the sent sickness] She could have sworn at somebody, caused trouble for some people. That could have made them get her. She was pregnant, so she was easy to do in.

According to Erzili, as the woman lay dying, the same maleficent force overflowed its original target and attacked Mme. Beaumont as well as Octavia, and the two midwives were overcome by nausea and vomited. At that moment, Erzili entered her horse and Octavia's *lwa* appeared as well. Erzili says that they would have been killed without the protection which she and Octavia's spirit provided.

This story reveals the complexities of Mme. Beaumont's relationship with her *lwa*. To begin with, the account replicates some aspects of the oppositional Catholic moral scheme. Erzili characterizes the episode as a Satanic sickness, probably sent by human enemies who sought revenge for the victim's own hostile and immoral actions. However, since Erzili herself told the story, she casts herself in the opposite role from the one the *lwa* conventionally plays in the Catholic idiom. Most villagers would classify the *lwa* as an intrinsically evil analogue to the *move nanm*, a member of the same ungodly set as the dirty *houngan* and Satan. In the story which Erzili tells, however, she is the protector from evil rather than its source.

During the delivery, the *lwa* actually plays a role closer to the *anj gadyen*, ensuring that no harm comes to Mme. Beaumont. Erzili even remarks, "If my horse had truly not accepted me in her head, she would have died along with the mother of the child." However, the protective presence of the *lwa* does not ultimately challenge Mme. Beaumont's vehement position that she does not serve the spirits. As

Erzili recounted the events of the delivery, she never once described her horse calling upon her. She instead characterized her relationship with Mme. Beaumont in the following ways: "I helped my horse do a delivery; when she's involved in her work, I come; If I see it's something my horse can't do, I enter her." Erzili comes of her own volition, not in response to Mme. Beaumont's request. In this way, Mme. Beaumont preserves her identity as a midwife, not a *mambo*; as someone who may receive the spirits' protection, but does not actually serve them.

CONCLUSION

How should we characterize the healing specialties of Jean Milot and Mme. Marie Beaumont? Most anthropologists would classify them both as "secular" practitioners. Because of their reliance on herbal medicine and the empirical techniques of midwifery, they seem to differ categorically from the range of religious healers in rural Haiti: *houngan* and *mambo* who draw their power from the spirits, Protestant pastors who heal only when possessed by the Holy Ghost, and lay Catholic groups who rely on prayer and exorcism in their ceremonies for the afflicted (see Brodwin 1991).

However, the actual stories told by this herbalist and midwife suggest another answer. To begin with, they continually impressed upon me that they are good Catholics: neither servitors of the spirit nor members of Protestant sects. They take up a determinate, and emphatically non-secular, position in the plural Haitian religious system. More importantly, in the very descriptions of their healing practice, Jean and Mme. Beaumont invoke a range of invisible spiritual beings: guardian angels, good and bad souls, the *lwa* as malevolent "dirty spirits," and the *lwa* as ancestral shades. They draw on this religious rhetoric both to explain the origins of their healing careers and to account for the power of the their treatments. They compare themselves to other healers not as secular *vs.* sacred, but rather as inspired by angels *vs.* servitors of the spirits.

The argument here complements Harrell's recent conclusions about medical pluralism and cultural meaning (1991). Harrell demonstrates the near-impossibility of separating sacred from secular non-biomedical healers as he traces the multiple treatments offered to a 16-year old girl in Taiwan suffering from convulsions and dissociation. First of all, a single healer typically advanced several discrete and seemingly contradictory explanations, running the gamut from natural illness (secular) to attack illness (sacred). Secondly, certain healers included ritual medicines, charms, offerings to various deities, simple companionship, and moralistic exhortations in their range of treatments. Disputes about possible causes and appropriate cures remained long after the illness was over.

Harrell draws our attention to the ambiguous and contradictory meanings informing the practice of non-biomedical healers in a plural medical system. He concludes with a caveat: consensus regarding cultural meanings is actually not necessary to the process of healing. I have demonstrated much the same for rural Haiti, but by examining a different aspect of ethnomedicine. This chapter addresses not the multiple explanations advanced for a particular cases of sickness, but rather the moral claims which healers make within the multiple discourses of popular Haitian religion.

Jean Milot and Mme. Beaumont draw upon several idioms to ensure their moral worth. They both deploy a morally-inflected ethnopsychology to portray their practice as inspired by the principle of mature, orderly, and controlled behavior. Jean then constructs the guardian angel in specifically Catholic terms, as the moral inverse of the *lwa*, in order to characterize himself as a morally correct healing specialist, as opposed to the immoral *houngan*. Mme. Beaumont, however, chooses another strategy, based on another possible position within popular Haitian religion. The crucial point for her is not whether she has *lwa* (which she assuredly does), but whether she chooses to serve them. Although she refuses to call upon her spirit, Erzili still extends protection and perhaps even healing power to her. In their separate ways, these healers authorize themselves as ethically upright actors who have made the right choice among competing moral worlds.

ACKNOWLEDGMENTS

Fieldwork in southern Haiti (1987-1988) was made possible by a Travelling Fellowship from the Fulbright Foundation and a Doctoral Student Award from the Health Services Improvement Fund, Inc. (New York City). I gratefully acknowledge their support. I would also like to thank Professors Mark Nichter, Arthur Kleinman, Byron Good, and Robert Levine, and Mr. Guy Christian Jussome, for their comments on earlier versions. Of course, I alone am responsible for any errors. Portions of this paper were presented at the panel on "Cultural Pluralism and Healing in the Caribbean," at the 1990 Annual Meetings of the American Anthropological Association, in New Orleans, Louisiana.

NOTES

1. Several important studies of therapeutic pluralism have been carried out in the Latin American and Caribbean region: see Cosminsky and Scrimshaw 1980, Fabrega and Silver 1973, Foster 1978, Laguerre 1987, Crandon-Malamud 1991, and Staiano 1986. For research in Asian societies, see Amarasingham 1980, Kakar 1982, Kleinman 1980, Kleinman et al. 1978, Leslie 1976, Lock 1980, Nichter 1980, Unschuld 1985, Zimmermann 1978. For reports from African settings, see Comaroff 1980, Janzen 1978 and 1987, Janzen and Feierman 1979, Mullings 1984, and A. Young 1976; and from the Middle East, see Crapanzano 1973, Good 1976, Early 1988. This is far from an exhaustive list. The topic appears in virtually every issue of the major journals in medical anthropology: *Culture, Medicine, and Psychiatry; Social Science and Medicine; Medical Anthropology Quarterly;* and *Medical Anthropology.*
2. "Jeanty" is a pseudonym for the village and parish where I continue to conduct research. In order to protect people's anonymity, I have changed the names of all the healers described here.
3. In the Creole phrase he uses—*se youn vye nanm, youn vye nanm rebel*—the word "old" (*vye*) has a strong pejorative connotation. People often use this word when discussing the *lwa* or the activities of houngan, and they invariably say it with the same air of disgust: e.g., "I'm Catholic, and I don't believe in it. I don't want anything to do with those dirty old things" (*Se katolik mwen ye, m pa kwe ladan. M pa okipe m ak vye bagay sal sa yo*); "When he sings those spirit songs, it's a bunch of old words he's saying" (*le l chante chante lwa sa yo, se youn paket vye pawol l ap di*);
4. Ogoun is the name of one of the most common and most powerful *lwa*, cf. Barnes 1989.
5. In this context, "Satan" symbolizes much more than the evil spiritual actor from French Catholicism. In a process typical of Latin American societies, residents of Jeanty have appropriated Catholic icons and concepts, and then inserted them in a recombined and synthetic religious framework, without ceasing to consider themselves as Catholic (cf. Taussig 1980; Warren 1978: 38, 47; Watanabe 1990).
6. To describe the spirit as "entering" Mme. Beaumont is the most common English rendering of several Creole expressions: the spirit mounts her horse (*lwa-a monte chwal li*), the spirit dances in her

head (*lwa-a konn danse nan tet li*), the spirit takes her (*lwa a pran ni*), or, most simply, she has spirits (*li gen lwa*).

7. *Mambo* refers to the female equivalent of an *houngan*. The terms I heard most often in Jeanty for these religious specialists were *houngan* (or a close variant, *ganga*), *mambo,* and the French–derived labels *divino* (male) and *divineuz* (female). I encountered the designation *bokor* must less frequently, although it is commonly cited in the literature on Vodoun (cf. Courlander 1960, Hurbon 1987, Laguerre 1979, Maximilien 1945, Simpson 1970).

8. Students of Haitian religion often distinguish between the domestic forms of worship *vs.* public temple–based cults. Most classic works (e.g., Metraux 1972, Deren 1953, Simpson 1970, Bastide 1971, and Rigaud 1953) focus primarily on the public cults. These are more common in Port–au–Prince and the surrounding area (the Cul de Sac Plain) than in other regions of the country. They involve more elaborate and expensive rituals as well as a social hierarchy comprising *houngan* and several lower grades of devotees who enter through initiation rites. The detailed classifications of various *lwa* and their traits presented by the above authors reflect the knowledge of the *houngan* leaders of these public cults (cf. Metraux 1978; Courlander, personal communi–cation). However, the meanings Mme. Beaumont assigns to the spirits arise from the domestic form of popular Haitian religion, which closely resembles an ancestral cult (cf. Herskovits 1937, Murray 1977, Lowenthal 1978, Smucker 1984, Brown 1991).

9. While God (*Bondye*), understood largely in Christian terms, rules the entire universe and endows humans with the *bon nanm* which makes possible moral action, the *lwa* are concerned only with humankind and their ordinary afflictions and desires. Villagers have a relatively distant relationship with the exalted Christian god. Communication with this god is mediated by the Catholic priest and the rituals of the mass. Communication with the *lwa* is much more direct, since the *lwa* more closely resemble their human worshippers. Human beings can appeal directly to the spirits / ancestors and even influence their actions.

10. *Lwa–yo existe, men m pa rekonnet yo.* The verb *rekonnet* comes from the French "reconnaitre," and retains the meaning of recognizing the relatedness of a child and one's obligations towards him.

11. People such as Mme. Beaumont, who admit to some engagement with the realm of the *lwa*, commonly represent the spirits in a Catholic framework which lacks the damnatory quality of the conventional moral divide described above. The most well–known example is the analogy between spirits and saints established through visual icons and peoples' talk (see Begot 1983, Leiris 1953, and Metraux 1972: 325). People may also refer to the spirits as "mysteries" or even "angels," as in one of the expressions denoting possession: the angels mount him (*zanj–yo konn monte l*).

BIBLIOGRAPHY

Amarasingham, Lorna Rhodes
    1980   Movement Among Healers in Sri Lanka: A Case Study of a Sinhalese Patient. Culture, Medicine, and Psychiatry 4: 71–92.

Barnes, Sandra (editor)
    1989   Africa's Ogun: Old World and New. Bloomington, Indiana: Indiana University Press.

Bastide, Roger
    1971   African Civilisations in the New World. New York: Harper and Row (Torchbook Library).

Begot, Danielle
    1983   La Peinture Vaudou Comme Ecriture. Etudes Creoles (published by the Comite International des Etudes Creoles) VI (2): 9–28.

Breathett, George (editor)
    1983   The Catholic Church in Haiti, 1704–1785: Selected Letters, Memoirs, and Documents. Salisbury, North Carolina: Documentary Publications.

Brodwin, Paul E.
    1991   Political Contests and Moral Claims: Religious Pluralism and Healing in a Haitian Village. Ph.D. Dissertation, Harvard University, Cambridge, Massachusetts.

Brown, Karen McCarthy
    1991   Mama Lola: A Vodou Priestess in Brooklyn. Berkeley: University of California Press.

Clerisme, Calixte
    1979   Recherches sur la Medecine Traditionelle. Port–au–Prince, Haiti: Ateliers Fardin.
Comaroff, Jean
    1980   Healing and the Cultural Order: the Case of the Baralong boo Ratshidi of Southern Africa.
            American Ethnologist 7: 637–77.
Conway, Frederick
    1978   Pentecostalism in the Context of Haitian Religion and Health Practice. Ph.D. Dissertation,
            American University, Washington, D.C.
Coreil, Jeannine
    1979   Disease Prognosis and Resource Allocation in a Haitian Mountain Community. Ph.D. Disser-
            tation, University of Kentucky, Lexington, Kentucky.
    1983   Parallel Structures in Professional and Folk
Health Care: A Model Applied to Rural Haiti. Culture, Medicine, and Psychiatry 7: 131–151.
Courlander, Harold
    1960   The Drum and the Hoe: Life and Lore of the Haitian People. Berkeley, Cal.: University of Cali-
            fornia Press
Cosminsky, Sheila and Mary Scrimshaw
    1980   Medical Pluralism on a Guatemalan Plantation. Social Science and Medicine 14B: 267–278.
Crandon-Malamud, Libbet
    1991   From the Fat of Our Souls. Berkeley, Cal.: University of California Press.
Crapanzano, Vincent
    1973   The Hamadsha: A Study in Moroccan Ethnopsychiatry. Berkeley: University of California
            Press.
Deren, Maya
    1953   Divine Horsemen: The Living Gods of Haiti. New Paltz, New York: McPherson and Co.
            (Documentext).
Drummond, Lee
    1980   The Cultural Continuum: A Theory of Intersystems. Man (n.s.) 15 (2): 352–374.
Early, Evelyn A.
    1988   The Baladi Curative System of Cairo, Egypt. Culture, Medicine, and Psychiatry 12:65–84.
Fabrega, Horacio, Jr. and Daniel B. Silver
    1973   Illness and Shamanistic Curing in Zinacantan: An Ethnomedical Analysis. Stanford, Cal.:
            Stanford University Press.
Foster, George
    1976   Disease Etiologies in Non–Western Medical Systems. American Anthropologist 78: 773–782.
    1978   Hippocrates' Latin American Legacy. In Colloquia in Anthropology, E.K. Wetherington, ed.
            Volume 2: 3–19. Dallas, Texas: Southern Methodist University, Fort Burgwin Research Center.
Good, Byron
    1976   The Professionalization of Medicine in a Provincial Iranian Town. In Transcultural Health
            Care Issues and Conditions, Madeleine Leininger, ed. Pp. 51–65. Philadelphia: F.A. Davis Co.
Harrell, Stevan
    1991   Pluralism, Performance, and Meaning in Taiwanese Healing: A Case Study. Culture, Medi-
            cine and Psychiatry 15: 45–68.
Hawkins, John
    1984   Inverse Images: The Meaning of Culture, Ethnicity, and Family in Postcolonial Guatemala.
            Albuquerque, New Mexico: University of New Mexico Press.
Herskovits, Melville
    1937   Life in a Haitian Valley. New York: Alfred A. Knopf.
Hess, Salinda
    1981   The Semiotic in Medical Anthropology. Papers of the Canadian Ethnology Service, No. 78:
            40–53.
    1983   Domestic Medicine and Indigenous Medical Systems in Haiti: Culture and Political Economy
            of Health in a Disemic Society. Ph.D. dissertation, McGill University, Montreal, Quebec.
Hurbon, Laennec
    1987   Dieu Dans le Vaudou Haitien. Port–au–Prince, Haiti: Editions Henri Deschamps.
Janzen, John M.
    1978   The Quest for Therapy: Medical Pluralism in Lower Zaire. Berkeley: University of California
            Press.

1987   Therapy Management: Concept, Reality, Process. Medical Anthropology Quarterly 1(1) (new series): 68–84

Janzen, John M. and Steven Feierman, editors
1979   The Social History of Disease and Medicine in Africa. Social Science and Medicine (special issue) 13B: 239–356.

Kunstadter, Peter
1975   Do Cultural Differences Make any Difference? Choice Points in Medical Systems Available in Northwestern Thailand. *In* Medicine in Chinese Cultures, Arthur Kleinman, et al., eds. Washington D.C.: U.S. Government Printing Office for Fogarty International Center, N.I.H., DHEW Publication No (N.I.H.) 75–653.

Kakar, Sudhir
1982   Shamans, Mystics, and Doctors. New York: Alfred A. Knopf.

Kleinman, Arthur
1980   Patients and Healers in the Context of Culture. Berkeley, Cal.: University of California Press.

Kleinman, Arthur, Peter Kunstadter, E. Russell Alexander, and James L. Gale
1978   Culture and Healing in Asian Societies: Anthropological, Psychiatric, and Public Health Studies. Cambridge, Mass.: Schenkman Publishing Company.

Laguerre, Michel
1979   Etudes sur le Vodou Haitien: Bibliographie Analytique. Travaux du Centre de Recherches Caraibes. Montreal: Presses de l'Universite de Montreal.
1987   Afro–Caribbean Folk Medicine. South Hadley, Massachusetts: Bergin and Garvey Publishers, Inc.

Leiris, Michel
1953   Note sur l'Usage de Chromolithographies par les Vodouisants d'Haiti. *In* Les Afro–Americains, Memoires de l'Institut Francais d'Afrique Noire, Dakar, Senegal. No. 27: 201–207.

Leslie, Charles
1976   Asian Medical Systems. Berkeley: University of California Press.

Lock, Margaret
1980   East Asian Medicine in Urban Japan. Berkeley: University of California Press.

Lowenthal, Ira
1978   Ritual Performance and Religious Experience: A Service for the Gods in Southern Haiti. Journal of Anthropological Research 34 (no. 3): 392–414.

Maximilien, Louis
1945   Le Vodou Haitien: Rite Rada–Canzo. Port–au–Prince: Imprimerie de l'Etat

Metraux, Alfred
1972   Voodoo in Haiti. New York: Schocken Books

Mullings, Leith
1984   Therapy, Ideology, and Social Change: Mental Healing in Urban Ghana. Berkeley: University of California Press.

Murray, Gerald
1977   The Evolution of Haitian Peasant Land Tenure: A Case Study in Agrarian Adaptation to Population Growth. Ph.D. Dissertation, Columbia University.

Nichter, Mark
1980   The Layperson's Perception of Medicine as Perspective into the Utilization of Multiple Therapy Systems in the Indian Context. Social Science and Medicine 14B: 225–233.

Nichter, Mark and Carolyn Nordstrom
1989   A Question of Medicine Answering: Health Commodification and the Social Relations of Healing in Sri Lanka. Culture, Medicine, and Psychiatry 13: 367–390.

Rigaud, Milo
1953   La Tradition Voudoo et le Voudoo Haitien. Paris: Niclaus.

Rubel, Arthur J. and Michael R. Hass
1990   Ethnomedicine. *In* Medical Anthropology: Contemporary Theory and Method. Thomas M. Johnson and Carolyn F. Sargent, eds. Pp. 115–131. New York: Praeger Publishers.

Simpson, George
1970   Religious Cults of the Caribbean: Trinidad, Jamaica, and Haiti: Rio Pedras, Puerto Rico: Institute of Caribbean Studies.

Smucker, Glenn
1984   The Social Character of Religion in Rural Haiti. *In* Haiti — Today and Tomorrow: An Interdis-

ciplinary Study, ed. by Charles Foster and Albert Valdman. Pp. 35–56. Lanham, Md.: University Press of America

Staiano, Kathryn Vance
   1986   Interpreting Signs of Illness: A Case Study in Medical Semiotics. Hawthorne, New York: Aldine de Gruyter.

Taussing, Michael T.
   1980   The Devil and Commodity Fetishism in South America. Chapel Hill, North Carolina: University of North Carolina Press.

Unschuld, Paul
   1985   Medicine in China: A History of Ideas. Berkeley: University of California Press.

Warren, Kay B.
   1978   The Symbolism of Subordination: Indian Identity in a Guatemalan Town. Austin, Texas: University of Texas Press.

Watanabe, John M.
   1990   Fram Saints to Shibboleths: Immage, Structure, and Identity in Maya Religious Syncretism. American Ethnologist 17 (1): 131–150.

Weise, H. Jean
   1971   The Interaction of Western and Indigenous Medicine in Haiti in Regard to Tuberculosis. Ph.D. Dissertation, University of North Carolina, Chapel Hill, North Carolina.

Wilson, Peter J.
   1973   Crab Antics: The Social Anthropology of English–Speaking Negro Societies of the Caribbean. New Haven: Yale University Press.

Young, Allan
   1976   Internalizing and Externalizing Medical Belief Systems: an Ethiopian Example. Social Science and Medicine 10: 147–156.

Zimmermann, Francis
   1978   From Classic Texts to Learned Practice: Methodological Remarks on the Study of Indian Medicine. Social Science and Medicine 12: 97–103.

Deciding How to Decide: Possession-Mediumship in Jalari Divination

Charles W. Nuckolls

INTRODUCTION

The research discussed here is the result of several years' fieldwork among the Jalaris, a Telugu fishing caste people who live on India's southeast coast. Its purpose was to examine Jalari "spirit possession" in the context of Jalari divinatory practices. The findings indicate that the Jalaris, like other North and South Indian groups, experience possession as a response to stress which is both psychic (the effect of traumatic loss) and social (the effect of role-dependent expectations). I discuss the individual experience and social ontology of possession elsewhere, using a psycho-analytically informed approach (Nuckolls 1991b). Here I focus on possession-mediumship, which Claus, in his study of another South Indian society, the Tulus, defined as "the legitimate, expected possession of a specialist by a spirit or a deity, usually for the purpose of soliciting the aid of the supernatural for human problems" (1979: 29). My principal question is, quite simply, how do mediums and their clients achieve satisfying explanations of these problems?

This discussion, though generalizable in its results to other South Indian communities, is specific in its details to a Jalari caste fishing village on the northeastern coast of Andhra Pradesh State. There are at least two million Telugu-speaking Jalaris who live in villages which dot the eastern coast of India, from north of Puri (in Orissa) to south of Madras (in Tamil Nadu). The village where I worked is Jalaripet, a coastal hamlet near the port city of Visakhapatnam. The men are fisherman and fish in the Bay of Bengal for sharks, sardines, and salt-water mackerel. The women collect the fish on the beach and sell it in the city. Since the port was opened to sea-going container vessels in 1970, many Jalari men have turned to smuggling. Few, however, have moved away from the village.

In the first part of this paper I shall describe Jalari divination as an explanatory process which helps people make decisions about the causes of and remedies for illnesses and occupational failures. Possession-mediumship is described as an aspect of this process. In the remainder of the paper I shall draw upon native ethnographic information to try to explicate certain elements of the explanatory process in possession-mediumship. A case study is presented to relate and exemplify these elements. The paper concludes by advocating the further study of possession-mediumship as an explanatory process.

CHARLES W. NUCKOLLS *is Assistant Professor of Anthropology at Emory University, Atlanta, GA 30322. His research interests include ethnopsychiatry, the cognitive and psychoanalytic study of inference, and medical decision-making. He has done fieldwork in South India and Central Kentucky.*

APPROACHES TO THE STUDY OF SPIRIT-POSSESSION

There is an abundance of literature on South Asian possession (e.g., Freed and Freed 1964; Harper 1963; Claus 1979; Gough 1959; Kakar 1982; Kapferer 1983; Obeyesekere 1981; Opler 1958). Yet answers to the question "How does it work?" are limited, for the most part, to "psychological" and "sociological" perspectives that have been around for years. The Freeds, for example, interpret the experience of possession in a fifteen-year-old girl as a result of the girl's ambivalent attitude toward sex. Possession releases the tension at the same time that it signals to family members that there is something wrong (Freed and Freed 1964). Harper (1963) likewise, views possession as a problem-solving mechanism through which individuals in low-status positions voice otherwise inexpressible feelings. From psychological perspectives such as these, possession "works" because it releases and expresses pent-up desires and feelings. Claus (1979), by contrast, admits that psychological processes are important but stresses that possession states occur among people who are defined as vulnerable. He recommends interpreting the cultural meaning of possession states and their significance within religious systems. Kapferer, also an apologist for sociological interpretation, criticizes approaches to possession which "seem to pass immediately from cultural ideas to the inner working of individual psychology and back again (1983: 198). He recommends a social interactional approach which focuses on the ways private attitudes are processed into the world of social action. From sociological perspectives, such as these, possession is successful because the experiences it provides fulfill role-dependent social expectations.

The purpose of this paper is not to make or support claims for perspectives that are psychological or sociological, but to address what seems to be an important oversight in both: Possession is, after all, a phenomenon which usually expresses itself *in* language and which people interpret *through* explanation. This is most clearly evident in possession-mediumship, in which clients approach practitioners for help or advice in addressing immediate personal and social concerns. The question "How does it work?" then, must at some point come down to a question of how client and practitioner construct an explanatory account that is satisfying to both.

It might seem that we already have a set of workable analytic constructs in the theories of ritual healing advanced by Claude Lèvi-Strauss, Arthur Kleinman, and most recently, Loring Danforth (Lèvi-Strauss 1963; Kleinman 1980; Danforth 1989). Certain subtleties aside, that hypothesis reduces to the following proposition: ritual healing deploys powerful cultural tropes with which patients identify, symbolically transforming and healing themselves at the same time. Danforth, for example, shows that Americans who feel alienated and ineffectual may be attracted to New Age movements which reconfigure loneliness as a spiritual exercise in personal fulfillment. In one such movement, American firewalking, such fulfillment is achieved through the use of fire as a highly condensed symbol of courage, attainment, and spiritual release. Successful firewalkers transform themselves in one deeply meaning-laden ritual act in which fear and victory over fire become metaphors for fear and victory over the self and its shortcomings. Similar findings, from healing contexts as diverse as shamanism and psychoanalysis, are to be found. But little attention has been given to explaining the psychological and cognitive mechanisms that make ritual healing possible.

Absent from the discussion on ritual healing and symbolic transformation, probably because it seems too "rational," is the subject of inference and decision-making. Because *we* make distinctions between emotion and thought, choosing to locate the phenomenon of ritual healing in the former and not in the later, rational processes like these seem out of place. Everyday experience indicates otherwise. The American courtroom, for example, is a powerful ritual site resplendent with potent cultural symbols. Yet, the outcome of what happens there—a strong belief, let us say, in the guilt or innocence of the defendant—is achieved through rational argumentation under strictly enforced rules of inference and evidence. One would not want to argue that courtroom procedure is non-ritualistic, because of its rationality, or non-rational, because of its ritual. It is *both* highly ritualized *and* highly rationalized. So it makes sense to examine both as crucial aspects of the process. Yet this requires two things not commonly found in studies of curing and healing: an analytic approach sensitive to inference-making and discourse in which instances of inference-making take place.

The study of possession-mediumship as an inferential process helps us understand how possession-mediumship works. First, it focuses attention on the mechanisms of explanation by means of which practitioners and clients constitute meaning. Second, it provides a framework for describing these processes as context-specific phenomena by proposing that explanatory knowledge exists in a kind of "repertoire" and that people choose among the constituents of this repertoire to achieve explanatory ends. Third, it shows how cultural systems are operationalized by linking beliefs and ideas with the context-dependent characteristics of causal interpretation. The approach employed here thus offers insights into the medical divinatory process that are otherwise hard to detect (let alone interpret) through conventional psychological and sociological approaches which typically focus just on outcomes.

One indication that this kind of analysis has not been done so far is the almost complete absence of extended discourse analysis in discussion of South Asian spirit-mediumship. Such an analysis is, by its very nature, difficult to perform and difficult to process, because of the level of detail that it involves. The reader is thus forewarned: to understand the process of making inferences, it is essential to actually see them being made in the details of verbal exchange. My interpretation of Jalari possession-mediumship examines it as a constructive process in which participants make and evaluate explanations—a process recoverable only through the painstaking study of naturally occurring divinatory discourse.

JALARI DIVINATION AND DECISION-MAKING

Moral Hostages and the Logic of Indirect Attack

Jalari divination determines the causes of disruptions in physical health and occupational success, making no etiological distinction between the two (see Nuckolls

1991a, b, c). This means that discussion of Jalari divination cannot be limited to matters we term health-related. Remedies are sought in social relationships, in adjustments to interpersonal relations that are necessary to correct the precipitating causes of disorder. This makes the study of divination as a form of ethnomedicine problematic, since it could just as easily be thought of as a form of ethnolegal or ethnopolitical explanation. This analysis takes the position that such discriminations—between what is or is not health-related or ethnomedical—are unimportant, as long as the discussion focuses on the causes of distress, their explanation, and their means of redress.

Not all or even the majority of disruptions result in divination. The more a disorder contrasts with a person's expected or desired state, the more likely it seems to him and to others that he is the victim of spiritual attack. Anyone not past his prime and not chronically disabled is a candidate. But among these people some are more likely to be attacked by spirits than others. The Jalari concept of *baravu* ("weight") helps to explain why. *Baravu* in this context means "responsibility." Spirits attack neither arbitrarily, choosing their victims at random, not directly, inflicting suffering on the transgressors alone. Spirits select an "innocent" victim— a person who, by virtue of his visibility, value, and clearly undeserved pain, morally compels the responsible individuals to act.

The ill or suffering person is thus always a moral hostage to someone else. Young children and pregnant women are the most innocent and valuable persons and therefore the persons most vulnerable to spiritual attack. But the intended focus of the spirit's wrath may be more than one degree removed from the actual victim. In the case study presented later, a child was attacked to compel his father to break off relations with the father's younger brother, *in order* to compel the younger brother to break off relations with an affinally related household.

Initial Divination: The Search for "Efficient" Causes

Consider the case of a pregnant woman with a sudden high fever. Household members call the *dāsuḍu* ("shaman") to come to their house and examine her. The *dāsuḍu* picks up the patient's left hand by the wrist, pressing his left thumb against it to detect the arterial pulse (*nāḍi*). His goal is to identify the immediate or "efficient" cause of the woman's distress. Efficient causes are always spirits. The *dāsuḍu* therefore invokes the family goddesses and asks each one to confirm or deny its role as the attacking agent. A distinctive quickening of the pulse confirms a spirit's responsibility. Disconfirmation of the household spirits' role forces the *dāsuḍu* to consider the role of "outside" spirits (*pai ammavāḷḷu*) and to seek confirmation from them. If these spirits, too, deny responsibility, the *dāsuḍu* may conclude that the illness is a *dāktar jabbu* ("doctor illness") and advise the patient's family to seek medical treatment or to do nothing at all.

Confirmation that a particular spirit has attacked concludes the diagnostic portion of the inquiry and initiates the segment devoted to the prediction of future results. The *dāsuḍu* asks for some money, which he ties into a small cloth bundle and holds aloft as he re-invokes the goddesses. He tells them that the money is a *muddura*—the tangible representation of the family's intention to make good its promise to offer. But the family will make the offering only *after* all signs of illness abate, usually within a specified period of time, and *after* they have identified and redressed the event's precipitating causes. The *muddura* is removed and buried outside. All that remains is to wait and watch.

Initial Divination: The Aftermath

The outcome of an initial divination is the identification of attacking spirits as the event's "efficient" cause. Depending on "where" the spirits came from, inferences are made concerning the "precipitating" cause, which is always assumed to be social. For example, if the spirits are the victim's own household spirits, people infer that the spirits attacked because family members were arguing among themselves and therefore could not make offerings to the household spirits. Thus, the efficient cause was "offertory neglect," which resulted in the spirit's attack, and the precipitating cause was "family disharmony," which resulted in the failure to offer in the first place. Testing these inferences is crucial, in order to persuade people (either within or between families) that something needs to be done. Subsequent divination fulfills this need, by providing a forum in which people consider and redress the social precipitants of spirit attacks.

If symptoms subside during the period stipulated in the pulse divination, family members concluded that the diagnosis was correct. But they do not fulfill their side of the bargain (to make promised offerings to the attacking spirits) until they evaluate the event's *precipitating* causes. Why not consider "efficient" and "precipitating" causes at the same time and by means of the same diagnosis? In initial divination, clients and practitioners focus on restoring the sick person to health or (in the event of poor fishing) on restoring the fish catch to its previous level of abundance. Because they do not have to probe further at the preliminary stage to achieve these results, they do not. Only *after* success validates the primary diagnosis—indicating to the *dāsuḍu* and his clients that they are "on the right track"—do they inquire further into precipitating social causes.

Subsequent Divination: The Search for "Precipitating Causes"

In "subsequent" divination, the social situation of the client's family is examined for disruptions that could have precipitated the spirits' attack. The goal is not only to identify but also to address these disruptions. This can be done only through the painstaking development of a complex "argument structure" made up of inferences whose logical links to each other have been investigated and confirmed. Such a structure is meant to be convincing. Without it, people cannot be persuaded to rethink their social relations and adjust them to avoid future spirit attacks. Rigorous argumentation therefore assumes high prominence.

There are two forms of subsequent diagnosis. In one, called *cūpa rāyi* ("seeing stone"), the *dāsuḍu* comes to the affected family's house and is given a stone (the *cūpa rāyi*) which the family keeps for such occasions. The *dāsuḍu* sits on the floor with his right elbow balanced on his knee and the stone suspended from his right hand. He asks the spirits questions and they "answer" by making the stone swing back and forth. Swing means "yes" and not swinging means "no." In the second form, called *kāniki*, the *dāsuḍu* and his client visit a practitioner (also called *kāniki*). The *dāsuḍu* asks the spirits a question and the practitioner drops a handful of rice into a vessel filled with water. If the rice floats, it means "no." If it sinks, it means "yes." The *kāniki* diagnosis is performed outside, in full public view, and almost always in the presence of observers whose honesty everyone respects.

Precipitating social causes which clients believe are less severe, less threatening, or less difficult to solve are evaluated by means of the "seeing stone." Validation through the public performance of an outside practitioner is not required. Social causes which people believe may be more serious or more difficult to remedy are addressed by means of the *kāniki*. Here, the participation of an outside practitioner and the presence of independent observers validate the diagnostic results—a validation necessary in situations where the client needs to marshall public opinion behind him in the resolution of the precipitating social dispute.

POSSESSION-MEDIUMSHIP IN THE DIVINATORY PROCESS

Jalari possession-mediumship (*pati*) occupies an intermediary position in the divinatory hierarchy. Clients consult possession-mediums after an initial divination reveals the identity of the attacking spirits, but before they inquire into precipitating social causes, in subsequent diagnosis. The *pati* is an advisory forum which villagers use to work out tentatively formed hypotheses before they are submitted for more rigorous scrutiny by methods that are productive of visible and verifiable proof (the seeing-stone and *kāniki*). An analogy can be found in the American legal system. A prospective client approaches a lawyer with a problem he thinks may require legal handling. The lawyer examines the relevant case law and presents the client with the scenarios he thinks both meet the client's goals and accommodate the details of the case. Together, the client and his lawyer evaluate and choose among the available scenarios. Depending on what they find, the client might decide: 1) to approach the offending party and reveal his argument, hoping that the other person will simply give in; 2) to take the matter to trial, hoping that his argument is sound enough to persuade the judge and jury; or 3) to drop the case entirely and/or consult another attorney.

By presenting alternative legal scenarios, the lawyer helps the client "decide how to decide" among different redressive strategies. Jalari possession-mediumship is similar. The practitioner presents her client with alternative explanatory scenarios, to which she fits details relevant to the case at hand. If the "fit" is good and the argument sound, the client might feel confident enough to pursue the matter by making his argument publicly known, hoping that that will be enough. If, for example, the argument shows that the client's brothers are to blame for causing their family goddesses to attack, then the client may simply have to make this known in order to make his brothers take corrective action. If that does not get the job done— and if his confidence in the argument is still high—he might decide to validate it in the *kāniki*, in the presence of witnesses. An argument so validated is much harder to ignore, and the client's brothers would be forced either to capitulate or (in an equally probable scenario) to come up with an alternative argument that shifts the blame from them to someone else. Of course, following his consultation with the possession-medium, the client might decide that he has no argument and drop the matter immediately; or, he might decide to consult another practitioner.

Only the *pati* practitioner is possessed by the spirits he/she invokes: they "sit on his/her head," as the Jalaris say. In that state, the spirits, not the *pati* practitioner, answer questions and suggest interpretations to the client. *Pati*-s take place in the houses of the possession mediums, in an area set aside for the worship of household spirits. There is usually a shrine (*sadaru*) which contains spirit idols and other ritual paraphernalia. The medium faces the *sadaru*, not her clients. The session begins when she occupies a sitting or fully prone position on the floor, her head towards the *sadaru*. In a slow, rhythmical chant, the medium invokes her tutelary deity. Jalari mediums, who are women, undergo possession by the spirits of their own male children (called *iruḍu*-s, *irababu*-s, or *iranna*-s, from the Sanskrit, *vira*, "hero") who died in infancy or early adolescence. One or more of these spirits "possess" (*digu*, "descend on") the practitioner and speak through her to the clients who sit nearby.

Household spirits, including goddesses and deceased relatives, constantly monitor the client's affairs, sometimes intervening and other times protecting the client from intervention by outside spirits. To determine the causes of his distress, the client must communicate with his household spirits and seek their counsel. But this cannot be done directly because, Jalaris say, ordinary people lack the ability to speak and understand the spirits' "language." They must rely on specialists, such as possession-mediums, who are divinely "chosen" to mediate between spirits and humans. But the possession-medium's role is still secondary to that of her deceased son who, as her tutelary spirit, in turn mediates between her and the household spirits of the client. The tutelary spirit "invites" the household spirits to participate and the spirits consent, Jalaris say, because the tutelary spirit is "one of them."

Communication between the practitioner and the client takes place through verbal and non-verbal exchanges. The possessing spirits frame their utterances as generalized possibilities, which become more and more specific as the client responds by supplying additional information. To the client, of course, the spirits seem to possess unlimited knowledge and access to his private affairs. But the client conveys vital information through his responses, though these sometimes amount only to grunts and yawns and incomplete phrases. The spirits use this information to select and elaborate a scenario which eventually looks (to the client) like an explanatory account that is the unique creation of the spirits and not the joint creation of the practitioner and the client.

The tutelary spirit's first task is to identify the client's household spirits by name. Although omniscient, the spirit accomplishes this by trial and error, listing likely names for household goddesses and deceased family members and waiting for the client to agree or disagree. After identifying the client's household spirits, the medium's tutelary spirit invokes them, so that they, too, can assist in addressing the client's concerns. In the divinatory session that follows, the household spirits of the client and the tutelary spirit of the medium speak and respond to questions. Knowing which spirit is speaking at any one moment is sometimes difficult, since spirits do not always identify themselves.

The client's household spirits make statements which provoke the client's verbal and non-verbal responses. They suggest that the client neglected to make offerings to his household spirits. If the client makes no response, they propose that another family's goddesses are attacking. Depending on the outcome of these subtle inquiries, the household spirits ask more detailed questions: Did the client neglect the offerings because others in the family would not cooperate? Each time the client answers, verbally or non-verbally, he supplies the practitioner with information she needs. The "spirits" who speak through the practitioner, use this information to further narrow the range of possibilities and to finally construct an explanatory account the client will find satisfying.

Unlike other kinds of accounts (e.g., in the *kāniki*), explanatory accounts constructed in the *pati* always end up being highly contingent: *If*, they state, the client will act in a certain way, *then* certain events will follow. The *pati* is an advisory forum and its technique is exploratory, not evidentiary. Clients do not seek "proof" (as in a *kāniki* divination) but specific recommendations on how to act, how to overcome specific social difficulties, and how to avoid, if possible, taking the matter all the way to the *kāniki*. The most successful recommendations are those that fit the facts as presented and that accord with the client's own interests which, until articulated in the *pati*, may not have been well formed or well understood.

The Organization of the *Pati*

The *pati* is a process of identification and synthesis: identification of relevant scenarios and synthesis of presented information. In this process the practitioner and the client check and confirm each other's understandings, to achieve results that satisfactorily explain the relevant events. A typical session follows this progression:

1. Identification of client's household spirits
2. Diagnosis: Identification of efficient causes
    Synthesis
Initial Scenario
3. Diagnosis: Identification of precipitating causes
    Synthesis
Secondary Scenario
4. Prediction: Solution and Final Synthesis

In the first stage, "identification of household spirits," the practitioner recites a list of names from the Jalari pantheon. The client indicates which are relevant by making small verbal gestures of approval. In the second stage, "identification of efficient causes," the practitioner instantiates two "initial" scenarios, which represent the most probable "efficient" causes of diagnosed events. One, the "inside spirit attack" scenario, traces the efficient cause to the client's own failure to propitiate his household spirits. According to this scenario, the inside spirits then attack and cause illnesses among members of the client's family (usually, members of the same sublineage group). The other, the "outside spirit attack" scenario, traces the efficient cause to a problem between the client and another family. According to this scenario, outside spirits attack and inflict illness on the client's family members. The terms "inside" and "outside" may be inelegant labels, but they do reflect Jalari understandings of where spirits come from: one's own spirits, it is said, come from "inside" (*lōpala*) and other people's spirits come from "outside" (*pai*).

In the third stage, "identification of precipitating causes," the practitioner investigates the social antecedents of the (inside or outside) spirit's attack on the client. If the preceding inquiry demonstrates that "inside" spirits are responsible, then the practitioner assumes that social disputes within the household are to blame. She constructs a "secondary scenario" which attributes the failure to offer to the household spirits as a result of disputes within the household. Invariably, such a scenario focuses on relations between the male heads of the household whose arguments (usually over household resources) prevent them from joining together and making the required offerings to "inside spirits." On the other hand, if the preceding inquiry demonstrated that "outside" spirits are to blame, then the practitioner assumes that some kind of controversy between households is responsible. She constructs a "secondary scenario" according to which a dispute occurred and caused the spirits of one household to attack the members of the client's household. This scenario usually focuses on relations between affinally linked households, among whom arguments frequently erupt over the provision of material support or the planning of (cross-cousin) marriage arrangements.

Once a "secondary scenario" has been constructed, the practitioner begins the fourth and final stage, predicting the consequences of the client's future acts to redress the causes of his distress. Addressing the "efficient" cause is a straightforward matter: the client promises to make offerings to the attacking spirit as soon as the attack ends. Addressing the "precipitating" cause is more difficult: the social dispute which caused the spirit to attack in the first place must be corrected. Until that is done, and the promised offerings made, the attacking spirit may attack again. Attention is focused, therefore, on selecting strategies for social action. The selection process can take some time, however, as the practitioner proposes and as the client accepts, amends, or rejects various alternatives for corrective action. At the end, the practitioner assimilates the accepted solution to the argument structure and re-presents it to the client as a complete diagnostic and predictive scenario which, if it is any good, successfully incorporates all the details that the client considers relevant to the case.

THE CASE OF CINTIPILLI TATARAO

Teddi and Cintipilli are two Jalari patrilineages or clans. They are allied through cross-cousin marriage relations. Three sub-lineages, designated by the names of their founding male members, are involved in the present case: the sublineage of Teddi Ramudu (now deceased), now presided over by his son, Teddi Muntata; the sublineage of Teddi Naidu; and the sublineage of Cintipilli Tatarao. Sublineages are not necessarily residential units. Here, all three are considered "joint" not because their members live with each other, but because they worship goddesses and ancestors at a common "big house" (*peddillu*). The two Teddi sublineages are related to each other as agnates (father, sons, etc.) and the Cintipilli sublineage as affines (father-in-law, son-in-law, etc.).

The most important person in the senior generation is Teddi Naidu, formerly the village *pujari* or "priest" and presently the most feared man in the village because of his suspected occult powers. In the next generation, important individuals include Teddi Naidu's classificatory "sons" (*kōdukulu*), who are the sons of his elder brother, and his classificatory "sons-in-law" (*allallu*), who are the sons of his married sister. Among Naidu's "sons" are Teddi Muntata, now the village *pūjari*, and his younger brothers, including Ellanna, who figures prominently in the present case. Among Naidu's "sons-in-law" are two brothers, Cintipilli Tatarao and Cintipilli Paidanna. They are the sons of Teddi Naidu's elder sister. The older brother, Tatarao, is married to Teddi Naidu's daughter and is classified as a "real" (*sōnta*) "son-in-law." The younger brother, Paidanna, is married to a woman from another village. The youngest generation (not all indicated in Figure 1 below) consists of young children who play no role in the case except as innocent victims of spirit attack.

Until ten years ago, Teddi Naidu was the village *pujari* ("priest"). The priesthood is an inherited position among the lineal male descendants of the Teddi Ramudu sublineage. Teddi Ramudu himself, the previous *pujari*, died in 1965. His eldest son, Muntata, was too young to succeed him and so the position went to Ramudu's surviving younger brother, Naidu. When Muntata reached adult age, Naidu was supposed to relinquish the priesthood to him, but he refused. A long and divisive battle began, which finally ended in Naidu's forced removal from office. Naidu then entered the subsidized rice trade, setting up the first government rice store in the village, and later won election to the Visakhapatnam Municipal Council. He went on to amass considerable wealth and political power. He even built one of the village's first concrete houses.

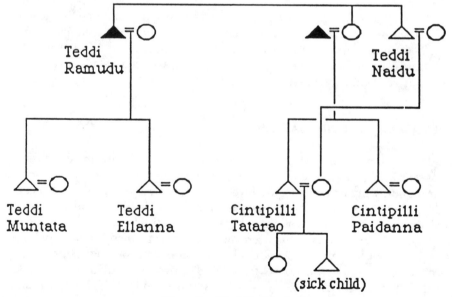

Figure 1.   Kindship Chart

What Naidu lost in giving up religious office, he sought to regain in other spheres. But by the early 1980s, he had lost both the government rice store and his municipal office. He no longer possessed great wealth. And his house, once the showplace of the village with its three rooms and tile floor, was in disrepair and long surpassed in opulence by others. The less Naidu possessed, the more he struggled to hold on to what he had—most especially, to the power and prestige he once enjoyed as village priest and head of his extended family. Moreover, Naidu claimed that he *still* controlled the village goddesses, especially the fiercer ones, Gatilamma and Ramana Mutyalamma. He said he could dispatch the goddesses to attack anyone who made him angry. Most villagers believed him and feared them; he was, they said, a "witchcraft man" (*cillingi vāḍu*).

Naidu avoids situations that might give rise to witchcraft accusations. To assert control over people—and most particularly over his own and affinally related sublineages—he uses indirect means. The present case is an illustration (see also Nuckolls 1991c).

The Teddi clan, made up of many sublineages (including the two mentioned above) has two competing centers of authority: the once dominant Naidu and his successor, Muntata. Members of the two constituent sublineages (Naidu's and Muntata's) maintain or achieve authority partly in relation to how many collateral relatives and affines they can bring within their spheres of influence. The affinal families nearest to both Naidu and Muntata are those of the two Cintipilli brothers. For Naidu or Muntata, to control these brothers would represent an extension of personal authority. Naidu has already achieved some success, in marrying his daughter to Tatarao, the elder brother. Tatarao is known throughout the village to be in Naidu's camp. But authority over the younger brother, Paidanna, is in the process of being lost to the "other side." This is evident, so the villagers say, in the fact that Paidanna and Muntata's younger brother, Ellanna, are close friends. The two are often seen in each other's company and in the company of Ellanna's sublineage group members, including Muntata. Naidu resents this and means to change it. The *pati* is the first step.

The *Pati* Divination

On January 28, 1985, a group of men including Cintipilli Tatarao (the client), Teddi Parasayya (Tatarao's friend), Teddi Naidu, and Ramulu Nukali (Naidu's friend) visited a possession-medium, a Jalari woman and Cintipilli lineage member from another village. They had come to find out what to do about Tatarao's son. The child had a serious fever which, under the circumstances, made it seem likely that a goddess had attacked him. By "circumstances" I mean two things. First, illnesses among people whom the Jalaris define as particularly valuable and vulnerable (especially male children and pregnant women) automatically become suspect as spiritual attacks. Second, as I explain below, people were aware of a situation that now existed that could explain the goddess's decision to attack. They hypothesized that Teddi Ellanna (see figure 1) did not perform his annual offering to his household goddess, Sati Polamma. Then Sati Polamma became angry and attacked Tatarao's child. Tatarao discovered this in a previous (pulse) divination, and promised his own offerings to Sati Polamma when she would stop attacking his child. To date, the promise remains unfulfilled and as a result, Sati Polamma has attacked Tatarao's child again.

To grasp the logic of this hypothesis, we must return to the Jalari principle of indirect attack, according to which relatives and friends of the transgressor—and not the transgressor himself—suffer the spirit's wrath. This makes sense, Jalaris say, because the responsible person can always ignore and conceal his own suffering if a spirit attacks him. But he cannot so easily ignore the suffering of others, especially if the victims are women and children. Not coincidentally, therefore, no matter how indirect the path, spirit attacks almost always fall (ultimately) on women and children.

Ellanna had neglected to make offerings to Sati Polamma. We do not know the reason why and, for the purposes of this divination, it does not matter. The goddess, disappointed that her offerings were not made, responded angrily, focussing her attack *not* on Ellanna, but on Ellanna's friend, Paidanna. Her intention, as the Jalaris interpret it, is to inspire in Paidanna the realization that to mitigate this attack and avoid others he must give up his friendship with Ellanna. Isolating Ellanna in this way will shame him into making the required offerings. But, by a further elaboration of the logic of "indirect attack," the goddess acted at yet another step removed. Instead of attacking Paidanna directly, she attacked Paidanna's brother, Tatarao, *to force him to make* Paidanna isolate Ellanna. And, finally, by third extension of indirectness, the goddess attacked Tatarao's children, in order to "shame" Tatarao into acting quickly. Remember, the intended victim is Ellanna.

But a problem developed. Tatarao could not persuade his brother, Paidanna, to quit seeing Ellanna. Tatarao, therefore, could not claim to have solved the social situation which precipitated the goddess's attack on him in the first place. And because of that, Tatarao failed to fulfill his promise to make offerings to Sati Polamma—offerings required any time a spirit attacks. That is why the goddess attacked him again, by afflicting his child with illness. Thus, we return to where we began. To protect his child, Tatarao *must* figure out a way to make the required offerings, and to do that, he must persuade his brother, Paidanna, to stop seeing Ellanna. That is why he has come to the *pati*.

It is a very complicated hypothesis, though certainly not unduly so, at least by Jalari standards. But to Tatarao, it easily explained the "efficient" and "precipitating" causes of his child's sickness. There were, however, many possible solutions, all with different implications for Tatarao. Tatarao and his allies have come to the *pati* to evaluate these implications and determine what to do next. They could, for example, decide to pursue the matter through the *kaniki* or other forms of divination. Or, they could decide simply to drop it. Possession-mediumship will help them decide how to decide by focussing their attention on the most crucial questions and limiting their options to the few most likely to achieve success.

Organization of the *Pati*

The *pati* divination for Cintipilli Tatarao is examined below in detail. It consists of several sections, in which the practitioner and the client investigate causes and proposed solutions. Within sections, phases exist in which the participants consider specific issues. The analysis below follows these sections and their constituent phases. Numbers refer to statements of the practitioner, the client, and the client's friends. A complete transcript containing all the numbered passages in sequence follows in Appendix A.

Section One: Identification of Household Spirits (# 1–20). The clients consulted this practitioner once before, when they identified Ellanna's goddess as the attacking spirit. They promised offerings to her that were contingent: 1) on the resolution of the attack's precipitating causes, and 2) on the goddess's ceasing to attack. The *pati* practitioner's knowledge of the case means that she can proceed quickly to identify the client's household spirits with a minimum of trial and error. The only household spirit to actually speak through or to the practitioner is the family's principal household spirit, Mutyalamma.

Section Two: Identification and Elaboration of Primary Causes (# 21–36) The practitioner speaks "as" her tutelary spirit, a deceased male child, whom she calls *"iranna"* ("hero"). She refers to her "sweet grandson," the client, who has collected "a quarter seer of unhusked rice" for making an offering but then has "gone back" (# 21). This means that the client's most immediate problem results from his failure to make an offering he promised to make.

Teddi Parasayya, Cintipilli Tatarao's friend and spokesman, speaks for Tatarao in addressing and responding to the possessing spirit. Parasayya is known for his powers of deduction and analysis. In his first response to the spirit, he clarifies their reason for coming to the *pati:* "From that day the child . . . has had injuries. His eyes do not reach the sky and his hands do not reach the earth" (# 22). The "child" is Tatarao's son—the patient in all of this—who has been sick with fever for some time. The practitioner responds in the broadest terms: "North and South are present. Near ones and enemies are present. Grandmother and grandfather are present" (#25). "North" and "near ones" refer to relationships within the patriline and "South" and "enemies" refer to relationships to other, probably affinally related families. These are very general possibilities. The practitioner simply proposes that relationships of one kind or the other are to blame for the client's failure to offer the "unhusked rice."

The practitioner's reasoning is not hard to follow. Earlier, when Tatarao consulted her, he promised to make an offering of "unhusked rice" to the spirit which had attacked his son. The promise remains unfulfilled. The practitioner has to determine why, by assessing the sequence of events that followed the making of the promise. She assumes that somewhere in this sequence a problem of some kind developed which prevented the client from making the offering of "unhusked rice." Her remark about "North" and "South" is an invitation to the client and his spokesman to participate in the reassessment, in order to find out where things went wrong.

The practitioner does not rush through the available alternatives. She begins with simple possibilities, which the client can consider and either accept or reject on his way to more difficult issues. This is a standard practice in all Jalari divination, not just in the *pati*. The elimination of simple alternatives precedes inquiry into more complex causes as precipitants of the client's distress. The simplest of these alternatives has to do with the divination itself. After the last *pati*, the client should have made an offering to *iranna*, the performer's tutelary spirit. If he did not, *iranna* could be the spirit attacking Tatarao's son. Parasayya claims, on Tatarao's behalf, that he did make the offering. (#30) This possibility is thereby eliminated.

The second possibility involves the influence of women who have married into Tatarao's sublineage. (#31) The practitioner asks if they are happy. Affinal women are notorious sources of discord, recalling a theme common throughout Hindu South Asia. If they are not happy, they can cause the goddesses of their natal households to attack their husbands' family. This inquiry also represents a standard divinatory practice of considering outsiders, especially wives and affines, first as possible precipitants. Parasayya, however, dismisses it and claims that the wives are happy. (#32)

Finally, the practitioner refers to the anticipated offerings the client, Tatarao, promised to make to the attacking outside goddess at the time of the last divination: Is it possible that the family decided not to offer the sacrifice of "male animals"? (# 33) The nature of the offering is not at issue; "male animals," like "unhusked rice," are divinatory euphemisms which stand for offerings of all kinds. The issue is the offering itself, and whether or not Tatarao plans to make it. Parasayya denies that they have decided not to make it, and adds the crucial information that the issue is not the animal sacrifice but "the child." They will make the offerings, he says, "if the child is seen." (# 34) The "child" in this case is the client's brother, Paidanna. Because he is "not seen," i.e., not present in his own house but, by implication, in Ellanna's, they cannot fulfill their side of the bargain and make offerings to the attacking spirit. In other words, the original problem remains— Paidanna is still disobeying the goddess's wish that he stop visiting Ellanna—and that is why the spirit has attacked again. The practitioner recognizes this as a central issue and begins a new and much more detailed exploration of precipitating causes in the next section.

Section Three: Identification and Elaboration of Secondary Causes (# 37–57) Parasayya's remark signals to the practitioner that she should concentrate on the "offerings." She therefore returns to an issue that must have come up in the previous consultation: "I told you to keep the *muddura* (token of the promise of making offerings) in the house. Did you keep it or not? I stood on the *muddura*. I caused happiness. Again difficulties will not occur." (# 37) The *muddura* (a cloth bundle containing money to be used in an offertory ceremony) is a tangible token of the intention to make an offering to the attacking spirit. We know that Tatarao offered the token to signify his intention to offer to the Sati Polamma (Teddi Ellanna's household goddess) after she attacked his son. The performer's remark suggests that Tatarao did not live up to his obligation to make the promised offering.

Parasayya's statement that the offerings would not be made "until the child is seen" indicated to the practitioner that a social dispute within the Cintipilli sublineage group was to blame for Tatarao's failure to live up to his promise. She knows the Cintipilli group—she is, of course, a member of the Cintipilli patriline—and knows that this particular sublineage consists of two brothers (Tatarao and Paidanna). She thus quickly establishes that the issue of the *muddura* is the issue of "the brothers." (# 41)

She then narrows the scope to the principal issue: "Did he go to their house?" (# 43) "He" is Paidanna and the "house" is Teddi Ellanna's house. Parasayya agrees with the practitioner's description of Paidanna's behavior and confirms that "he is going." (# 44) The practitioner's next reference links Paidanna's visits to Ellanna's house ("because he is roaming . . .") to attacks by "their" (Ellanna's) goddess. (# 45) But the practitioner does not immediately accept this argument, even though she herself constructs it. She asks the client, "Did you stay in the house?," to suggest that he, not Paidanna, might have visited Teddi Ellanna's house and thus caused Ellanna's goddess to attack. Parasayya (who speaks for the client, Tatarao) answers that he did not. This is not an unusual inquiry. Sudden reversals occasionally provoke unexpected revelations from clients who want to believe, but who do not emotionally accept, the developing argument structure's imputations of blame. If Tatarao *had* visited the forbidden house, but blamed his brother anyway, he might have admitted it here, in response to the practitioner's sudden question. But Parasayya denied it. This is important, too, since the client can now feel certain that he is on the right track.

The possession-medium returns to the matter of the *muddura*, linking it to the issue of Paidanna's visits to "their porch" and implicitly to the continuance of the goddess's attacks on Tatarao's children. (# 47) Then she focuses on the crux of the matter: "Can't you make those two brothers climb the porch?" (# 49) Defining the problem thus, as a matter involving "the brothers" and "the porch," transforms it into a problem of fraternal unity. Paidanna and Tatarao are co-members of the same sublineage and co-residents of the same *peddillu* ("big house") whose "porch" they "climb" together, signifying their unity. The *peddillu* is the ritual center of the family, where meals are prepared and where household spirits are worshiped. It symbolically represents the whole sublineage group. Thus, any discussion about the "big house" (and by extension, its "porch") is actually a discussion about sublineage solidarity. Defining Paidanna's visits to Ellanna as acts which distance him from the "big house" converts his visits into assaults on the integrity of his sublineage group. Eventually, as we shall see, this will make it necessary for Paidanna to choose between his friendship for Teddi Ellanna and his allegiance to the sublineage group he and his brother constitute.

Let us consider what the *pati* has achieved so far. In just four steps the practitioner has constructed an explanatory account of the precipitating and efficient causes of Tatarao's child's illness:

1. She begins with the assumption that Tatarao's present difficulty (his young son's illness) results from his failure to make the offerings he promised to the attacking goddess of another household.

2. She determines that Tatarao did not make the offerings because his brother, Paidanna, is still visiting Teddi Ellanna's house. That is the reason the goddess attacked in the first place and that is the reason she is attacking now. Tatarao cannot address the "efficient" cause (by making offerings to the attacking goddess) until he resolves the "precipitating" cause (by stopping Paidanna's visits to Ellanna).

3. She summarizes the present situation: Tatarao will not fulfill his promise to offer to the attacking goddess until Paidanna stops visiting Ellanna's family.

4. She states the current problem: Tatarao must find a way to stop Paidanna's visits because the visits constitute an affront to the integrity of the sublineage he and

Paidanna constitute. Conversion of the problem into an issue involving fraternal solidarity is crucial, and lays the groundwork for the proposals to follow.

The practitioner's analysis is framed according to a cultural logic which links causes and effects through the principle of "indirect attack." Paidanna, according to this analysis, should not visit Teddi Ellanna's house. The reason is that Ellanna has not made offerings to his goddess, Sati Polamma. If Paidanna visits Ellanna, the goddess will attack Paidanna for interfering with her plan to isolate (and thus shame) Ellanna. The logic of indirect causation explains why. The goddess will attack Paidanna because his visits to Ellanna represent (to the goddess) support for the individual who has offended her. The goddess hopes that her attack will prevent future visits, isolating Ellanna, and thus shaming him into making the required offering. But Paidanna continues to make his visits. Therefore, the goddess attacks him, but only indirectly, by attacking his older brother, Tatarao. Here too, the goddess intends to cause shame—but this time her target is Paidanna. Again, the principle of indirect attack is at work. The goddess does not attack Tatarao directly, but attacks his child in order to shame Tatarao into taking action against his brother.

What all of this is supposed to achieve is this: *If* Tatarao persuades Paidanna to stop visiting Ellanna, then Tatarao's child will recover. *If* Paidanna stops visiting Ellanna, Ellanna will be shamed into performing the necessary offerings. Then the goddess will be satisfied.

Section Four: Prediction and Proposed Solutions (# 58–end) Phase A (# 58–67) Exchanges between the practitioner and Parasayya consist of restatements and summaries until # 62, when the practitioner makes her first concrete proposal. Paidanna, she says, should "pay homage" that he will never "climb the porch," i.e., Paidanna should promise never to visit Teddi Ellanna's house again. Tatarao accepts the general idea but dismisses the proposal as unworkable. Paidanna would never accept it. In # 64, therefore, the practitioner—speaking as Tatarao's household goddess, Mutyalamma—suggests that they should threaten Paidanna by making him choose between his own family and Ellanna's: "Will you stay with me or will you stay with them?" This strategy was anticipated in the conversion of the problem to an issue involving fraternal unity. Parasayya, Tatarao, and Nukali assent to this proposal (# 65–67). The remaining segments of the *pati* evaluate the implications of this proposal.

Phase B (# 68–75) What if Paidanna refuses to be threatened with the breakdown of his sublineage group? The practitioner anticipates their concern and replies in # 68: "If he says 'no', then by leaving the one who said 'no', you stay separately, without having any friendship with him." The client, in other words, should fulfill his threat and isolate Paidanna. The client agrees and Teddi Parasayya, his spokesman, restates this conclusion in his own words: "Call the son [Paidanna], convince him, and then ask him three times. If he says 'no' all three times, I will throw him away and abandon him."

Phase C (# 76–103) The investigation of alternative outcomes continues. What, for example, will happen if Paidanna visits Ellanna's house secretly or simply speaks with Ellanna outside his house? The practitioner and the client consider these possibilities, in order to define and delimit the solutions proposed earlier. Tatarao begins in # 76: "Today the brother (Paidanna) will agree. But then he will go like a thief and again there will be problems." The practitioner repeats her earlier decree: "Let him go or let him stop. Now I am saying that he should not make friendship with that man (Ellanna)." (# 77) The client and his friends agree. Repetition and refinement is not unusual in a divination. Usually the client just wants the proposed solution to be stated more inclusively, in order to give it more force.

The same is true of Tatarao's next concern: "Not to the house! Just because he talks on the road she attacks." (# 83) The goddess already confirmed that Paidanna's visits to Ellanna's house must be stopped. But Tatarao believes that Paidanna might continue to have social relations with Ellanna's group (by talking to Ellanna "on the road") even if he stops visiting Ellanna's house. He wants to preclude that as a possible "way out" by asking a question which invites the goddess to extend her stricture to virtually every social contact between his brother and Ellanna.

Before the goddess can answer, Parasayya interrupts and reframes the argument in terms of their ultimate goal: To bring Paidanna within the orbit of Naidu, his mother's younger brother and Tatarao's father-in-law: "Now leave aside the matter of the *peddillu* (the issue of Paidanna's visits to Ellanna). The father-in-law is there. The two brothers should live happily with him. That way, you'll be happy, right?" (# 84) The "father-in-law," of course, is Naidu, who is related to the Cintipilli brothers as their mother's brother. The goddess agrees ("that's what I am saying") and states that, if they will obey the commands of their household spirits, then all will be well. (# 85)

This is one of the few references to Teddi Naidu in a *pati* which, at the highest level of generality, is all about Naidu and the Cintipilli brothers' relationship with him. The fact that such a reference is made is a little surprising, since it is not really congruent with the argument's developing logic. Up to this point, Tatarao and his spokesman, Parasayya, have argued that the reason Paidanna should stop visiting Ellanna is to protect his brother, Tatarao, from further attacks by Ellanna's goddess. The remainder of the *pati* is the same: arguments against Paidanna are framed exclusively in terms which make him responsible for his brother's well-being as well as for the continued survival of the family that he and his brother constitute. But Parasayya's remark reminds us that there is a subtext beneath all of this and reveals that, at least occasionally, that subtext can be transparent in divinatory discourse. It is clear that Tatarao, the client, wants very much for his brother to join him in alliance with Teddi Naidu.

At this point, the participants return to their earlier argument, elaborating the consequences of his action, should Paidanna refuse to sever his connection with Ellanna and his faction. The goddess synthesizes these comments and re-presents them to the clients: To Paidanna they should say, "If you like, stay with me, or if not, then as soon as you fly away, don't stay with me, if you make friendships with them." (# 96) This is an ultimatum. Paidanna should align himself with his own family, thus affirming his devotion to the sublineage and its "big house," or with Ellanna, thus (by implication) countenancing the dissolution of this sublineage.

Tatarao refers (in # 97) to the *muddura* he never offered. He wonders when he should fulfill his promise to offer, now that they have decided to give Paidanna another chance to rejoin the family. The practitioner answers rather curtly: "So you shouldn't offer it, mindless fellow." She means that there is no need to make the offerings to Sati Polamma until the situation provoking her attack is finally resolved.

(# 98) She states that they must not "untie the *muddura*-s" (# 100) until they have spoken with Paidanna.

The effect of this apparently unnecessary reference ("these are all known things," as Tatarao remarks) is to initiate the final stage of the *pati* in which the performer summarizes the divination: "You make the two of them (Tatarao and Paidanna) sit down and then ask them three times. Then along with the grand-children you will be able to be happy. Then you can untie the *muddura*." (# 103) The brothers, Tatarao and Paidanna, should be brought together and convinced to live as a joint family under Tatarao's authority. If they do, then offerings to the attacking spirit can take place, and the child who now suffers the consequences of the spirit's attack will recover. The practitioner has returned to where she began—that is, to the problem of the unfulfilled promise to offer—having traced the line of causality from efficient to precipitating causes and then back again, showing precisely what must be done to correct the situation.

Phase D (# 104–127) The client prefers to linger in the preceding stage, exploring the implications of the proposed strategy: As Parasayya says, "there may be some further difficulties." (# 104) At first he simply wants to be reassured that the attacking goddess, Sati Polamma, will not attack Tatarao again if Paidanna's recal-citrance continues. He wants to be sure that his household goddess will protect Tatarao against the further "indirect" attacks of the outside goddess. The household goddess assures him that she will, but only if he promises never to speak with Paidanna again (# 112). This, of course, is exactly what the client wants: He can excuse distancing himself from his brother Paidanna, by saying that he has no choice if he is to avoid spirit attacks.

In # 117, however, Tatarao returns to the question of the property now owned jointly by him and his brother, Paidanna. This, too, can be used to threaten Paidanna. If Paidanna prefers the company of Ellanna and his sublineage group, then Tatarao will threaten to divide the joint family's property between them and thus dissolve the joint family. This is no small matter. But is has the advantage of showing Paidanna that they mean business.

Division of a family is a difficult subject for Jalari men to contemplate. By elevating Paidanna's behavior to an issue affecting fraternal solidarity, Tatarao and his friends raise the stakes on both sides. Regardless of the merits of the case on other levels (the "rightness" or "wrongness" of Paidanna's visits per se), escalation of the case to this level ultimately forces both sides to decide how much they value solidarity. Tatarao and the others wager that Paidanna will reject Ellanna, and thereby choose solidarity over division and, by implication, allegiance to Teddi Naidu instead of Teddi Muntata. If they are wrong, then they will have to live up to their threat—in which case they, and not Paidanna, will be responsible for the division.

Phase E (# 128–end) "Now there are no problems," (# 128) says Parasayya, indicating that the *pati*'s main business is over. Either Paidanna will obey and "live happily with the father-in-law [Naidu]" or he will not, in which case "they [Paid-anna and Tatarao] will go away, like birds, each spreading to a tree." (# 132) The *pati* practitioner takes this as her cue to sum up, resuming the process she began earlier, before Parasayya introduced new issues. Recall that she had begun to restate the diagnosis, proceeding from the problem of Paidanna's visit to the fulfillment of the

the obligation, represented in the *muddura*, to make offerings to the attacking goddess. She returns here, finally, to the issue of the offerings: "If you pay homage to the attacking goddess, I will stand. I will keep the attacking goddess in the palm of my hand." (# 135) This is where the session ends.

The *Pati* and its Aftermath

It is time to consider the subtext in more detail, to understand how the explanations and strategies achieved in the *pati* fit in.

Cintipilli Tatarao and Paidanna are brothers. Tatarao is married to Teddi Naidu's daughter. Naidu is Tatarao's mother's younger brother, making Tatarao's a cross-cousin (MBD) marriage. When Paidanna, Tatarao's younger brother, married, Tatarao and Naidu both assumed that he would marry into Naidu's family, either to Naidu's remaining daughter or to some girl in "daughter" relation to Naidu. Instead, Paidanna married a completely unrelated woman. To Naidu, this signified transgression against his authority.

Paidanna began spending more time with his mother's older brother's family (Teddi Muntata and Ellanna) than with his mother's younger brother's family (Teddi Naidu and his own brother, Cintipilli Tatarao). That offended Naidu and bespoke a further erosion of his authority. Not only had Paidanna rejected one affinally linked household (Naidu's own) as a source of a bride, he had chosen the other affinally linked household (Muntata's) as the source of friendship and support. This added to Naidu's long-standing grievance against Muntata, who had taken his place as the village priest several years before. Naidu decided to use "events" to his advantage, either to win Paidanna into his camp, thereby diminishing Muntata's sublineage group, or, to destroy Paidanna's sublineage by precipitating a division between Paidanna and his brother, Tatarao.

Then, Tatarao's child became ill. Illness of a child very often becomes the locus of divinatory concern, and of disputed social relationships, as people attempt to identify and correct the illness's precipitating causes. Naidu seized on this event to suggest to Tatarao an ingenious hypothesis, according to which his brother (the errant Paidanna) was to blame because of his relationship with Ellanna, a member of Teddi Muntata's group. It is a complicated strategy, to be sure, but one entirely consistent within the Jalari principle of indirect attack. Tatarao's *pati* divination confirmed it. Naidu could then say to Tatarao, "Either force your brother to stop seeing Teddi Ellanna and his family, or you will suffer more spirit attacks." And Tatarao could then say to Paidanna, "Either stop seeing Teddi Ellanna and his group, or our group will break down."

What actually swayed Paidanna, however, was not just the weight of his brother's argument. His own children became ill shortly after the *pati* took place, suggesting that Sati Polamma had bypassed his brother and attacked him at closer range. This was the turning point. Paidanna immediately abandoned all resistance and accepted Tatarao's argument completely. He also stopped visiting Ellanna and aligned himself with Naidu. Naidu even bragged that he would "send Paidanna's foreign wife away" and remarry him to a girl of his own choice. From anyone else, that would be an incredible boast. But from Naidu, it seemed more like a prediction.

CONCLUSION

Jalaris visit *pati*-s to formulate social strategies whose immediate precipitant is usually illness. Less pressure exists to construct air-tight argument structures in the presence of ever-watchful and rigorous observers, as in the *kāniki*. There is freedom to ask open-ended questions, to argue, and to debate. The *pati* here is a case in point. Its purpose was to formulate an argument structure as the basis of a consensus among Tatarao, Naidu, and the rest of their faction. They achieved this purpose and returned to the village with a coherent perspective and a plan. This was no small accomplishment. In any debate, the party whose argument demonstrates the most logical cohesion and internal consistency has a better chance to win. The strength of the argument constructed in the *pati* probably made Paidanna's incorporation into the Naidu faction more likely than it would have been otherwise.

By looking at the *pati* as an explanatory process, we see how it works to achieve such ends. A Jalari client, like Cintipilli Tatarao, approaches a practitioner with a partially formulated explanatory hypothesis. The practitioner chooses among the constituents of her explanatory repertoire and calls up the ones she considers most applicable. She and the client then test the proposed scenario, to see if it fits the case at hand, and to assimilate case-specific details to its structure. Of course, the finally completed scenario should explain events in a manner that is favorable to the client's goals. If it does, then the client uses it as the basis of his decision either to pursue the matter through more rigorous divination (as in the *kāniki*) or drop it altogether. The *pati* helps him to make these decisions.

In the past, anthropological approaches to South Asian possession-mediumship have looked at it as a tension-relieving or role-fulfilling experience. My research does not challenge these views. It simply advocates a shift in analytic attention from the *outcome* to the *process*, i.e., from what possession-mediumship achieves to how it achieves it. The approach I adopt, therefore, focuses on divinatory discourse and on how practitioners and clients construct causal accounts. There are three objectives: first, to describe the structures which represent knowledge about cause and effect; second, to show how such structures are used in constructing and evaluating causal arguments; and third, to demonstrate that explanations based on such arguments are socially significant as crucial determinants of change. Perhaps some readers will assert that such objectives belong more properly to the domain of conflict resolution than to medical anthropology. What studies like this demonstrate, however, is that there can be no hard and fast distinction between the two.

ACKNOWLEDGMENTS

This work was supported by grants from the American Institute of Indian Studies, the National Science Foundation, the National Endowment for the Humanities, and the Charlotte W. Newcombe Foundation. I thank Professor Janis Nuckolls (Departments of Anthropology & Latin American Studies, Indiana University), Professor Richard Shweder (Committee on Human Development, University of Chicago), Professor Byron Good (Department of Social Medicine, Harvard University), and four anonymous reviewers for their comments. I especially thank one reviewer for providing the felicitous expression "moral hostage." The usual disclaimers apply.

REFERENCES CITED

Claus, P.
  1979   Spirit Possession and Spirit Mediumship from the Perspective of Tulu Oral Traditions. Culture, Medicine, and Psychiatry 3(1): 29–52.
Danforth, L.
  1989   Firewalking and Religious Healing. Princeton, NJ: Princeton University Press.
Freed, S., and R. Freed
  1964   Spirit Possession as Illness in a North Indian Village. Ethnology 3(2): 152–171.
Gough, K.
  1959   Cults of the Dead among the Nayars. *In* Traditional India: Structure and Change. M. Singer, ed. Philadelphia: The American Folklore Society.
Harper, E.
  1963   Spirit Possession and Social Structure. *In* Anthropology on the March. B. Ratnam, ed. Madras: Social Science Association.
Kakar, S.
  1982   Shamans, Mystics and Doctors: A Psychological Inquiry into India and its Healing Traditions. New York: Alfred Knopf.
Kapferer, B.
  1983   A Celebration of Demons. Bloomington, IN: University of Indiana Press.
Kleinman, A.
  1980   Patients and Healers in the Context of Culture. Berkeley: University of California Press.
Lèvi-Strauss, C.
  1963   The Effectiveness of Symbols. *In* Structural Anthropology. New York: Anchor Books.
Nuckolls, C.
  1991a Culture and Causal Thinking: Prediction and Diagnosis in a South Indian Fishing Village. Ethos 19(1): 3–51.
  1991b Becoming a Possession-Medium in South India: A Psychocultural Account. Medical Anthropology Quarterly 5(1): 63–67.
  1991c Notes on a Defrocked Priest. *In* Ethnopsychiatry. A. Gaines, ed. Buffalo, NY: State University of New York Press (forthcoming).
Obeyesekere, G.
  1981   Medusa's Hair. Chicago: University of Chicago Press.
Opler, M.
  1958   Spirit Possession in a Rural Area of North India. *In* A Reader in Comparative Religion. W. Lessa, and E. Vogt, eds. Evanston, IL: Row Peterson and Co.

Appendix A.

TRANSCRIPT OF THE *PATI*

Format
1. Numbered passages are statements by the practitioner, the client, and the client's friends.
2. Expressions in parentheses represent comments by participants and observers.
3. Invocations, which precede questions and which describe the invoked deities, are deleted because of their length and because they have nothing to do with the development of the argument structure.

Section One: Identification of Household Spirits

1. Salutations! Oh, Dhanakonda [goddess name], are you in their house?

2. (No! If she were there, we'd say so: Cintipilli Tatarao—client)

3. (If she isn't there, why would he [the medium's tutelary deity] speak? If she is, he would say that she is: Ramulu Nukali—friend)

4. Are you there, Mutyalamma [a household goddess]?

5. (She is there: Cintipilli Tatarao—client)

7. It seems Cintipilli Appayya grandfather [a family ancestor] is there . . .

8. (He is: Cintipilli Tatarao—client)

9. He is there. Is Sati Polamma [the attacking goddess] there?

10. (It is, it is: Cintipilli Tatarao-client)

11. I, Paidamma [a household goddess], came. I, Appayya, came. Along with the sweet grandson [ancestor], along with the sweet *peranta*-s [deceased household women], *viranna*-s [deceased household men] came.

12. (We have *viranna*-s?: Cintipilli Tatarao-client)

13. (We have *peranta*-s: Cintipilli Tatarao-client)

14. Didn't your parents burn [i.e., aren't your parents included among the dead ancestors]?

15. (Yes: Cintipilli Tatarao)

16. Mutyalamma! This human has come for some reason. Hey, in your house . . . It seems there wasn't happiness.

17. (Why wouldn't there be? Aren't we worshiping the ancestors?: Cintipilli Tatarao)

18. (If there is happiness, then why would we be here?: Ramulu Nukali)

19. (Aren't the ancestors present?: unidentified speaker)

20. I am saying that they are.

Section Two: Identification and Elaboration of Primary Causes

21. The name of the father is Mutyalu. Tata [another ancestor] is there. Appanna [another ancestor] is there. Having kept a quarter seer of unhusked rice, did you not go back?

22. (From that day the child . . . has had injuries. His eyes do not reach the sky and his hands do not reach the earth. If you are Mutyalamma, or if you are Paidi Talli [another household goddess], or Cintipilli Tatarao [an ancestor], then lift up the son, lift him up!: Teddi Parasayya—friend of client)

23. I'm speaking, so just wait! This is Mutyalamma. Cintipilli Appayya grandfather is in the east. They are in the west.

24. (So what!: Ramulu Nukali)

25. North and South are present. Near ones and enemies are present. Grandmother and grandfather are present.

26. (They'll tell us what's going on: Teddi Parasayya—friend of client)

27. Please ask them.

28. (You tell us! We came for you to tell us: Teddi Parasayya—friend of client)

29. Having come to *iranna* (the practitioner's tutelary spirit) . . . you didn't offer half a quarter of rice, for the homage you paid.

30. (We did: Teddi Parasayya)

31. The women weren't happy, it seems, sweet grandson.

32. (Yes, they were: Teddi Parasayya—friend of client)

33. Again the human did not roam. Food was not given. Male animals were not burned.

34. (Well, if not today, then tomorrow we will make the offerings. If the child is seen
. . .: Cintipilli Tatarao—client)
35. Then I will stop it in the house [i.e., then I will protect you from the attacking
goddess].
36. (Let's hear more about that: Ramulu Nukali)

Section Three: Identification and Elaboration of Secondary Causes

37. I told you to keep the *muddura* in the house. Did you keep it or not? I stood on the
muddura. I caused happiness. Again difficulties will not occur.
38. (Then tell us why those things are happening!: Teddi Parasayya)
39. Are there still problems?
40. (How many problems are coming!: Cintipilli Tatarao)
41. Mutyalamma! Are not the brothers present?
42. (He is present: Teddi Parasayya)
43. Did he go to their house?
44. (He is going: Teddi Parasayya)
45. Because he is roaming . . . Did their goddess attack them? Did you stay in the
house, human?
46. (No. I did not: Teddi Parasayya—friend of client)
47. Did you offer the *muddura*? Did it [the goddess] get mad because they are
climbing their porch? Grandson, even if you go the *kāniki*-s and *pati*-s, you will not
find the way.
48. (Then you tell us!!: Teddi Parasayya—friend of client)
49. Can't you make those two brothers climb the porch?
50. (But they are climbing: Teddi Parasayya—client)
51. Now, as soon as they climb . . .
52. (But what will we do?: Cintipilli Tatarao—client)
53. (Then, Mutyalamma, we will stop them: Teddi Parasayya—friend of client)
54. (The brothers are dividing. What about that!: Cintipilli Tatarao—client)
55. (Say something!: Ramulu Nukali—friend)
56. (If you tell them to, they will live together somehow: unidentified speaker)
57. He [Paidanna] won't stay, even if you tie him up.

Section Four: Predictions and Proposed Solutions

Phase A
58. If that man [Paidanna] steps on the porch, then their goddess comes and attacks
my house.
59. (If the man does not step on the porch, then this [goddess] won't come: Teddi
Parasayya—friend of client)
60. That goddess is attacking.
61. (What should we do?: Cintipilli Tatarao—client)
62. Saying, "I will not climb the porch," can you make him pay homage?
63. (No, how can we do that. He will not agree: Cintipilli Tatarao)
64. Make him sit down and tell him this: "In our house this is what's happening. If
you step on their porch, a goddess is attacking us. So, will you stay with me or will
you stay with them?" Can't you ask him to answer this, grandson?

65. (They will ask: Teddi Parasayya—friend of client)
66. (We will ask: Cintipilli Tatarao—client)
67. (Ask!: Ramulu Nukali: friend)

Phase B

68. If he says "no," then by leaving the one who said "no," you stay separately, sweet grandson, without having any friendship with him.
69. (Ask the goddess if she will raise or not: Ramulu Nukali—friend)
70. (She will raise: Cintipilli Tatarao—client)
71. (Ask anyway!: Ramulu Nukali—friend)
72. (According to what you told us to say, we told the male child. I explained to him that because of what he is doing, Sati Polamma is attacking us: Teddi Parasayya)
73. (Sooner or later he'll see it that way: Cintipilli Tatarao)
74. (Call the son, convince him, and then ask him three times. If he says "no" all three times, I will throw him away and abandon him: Teddi Parasayya)
75. If he climbs that man's porch and makes friends with him—if the goddess attacks?

Phase C

76. (OK, it attacks. Today the brothers will agree. But then he will go like a thief and again there will be problems. Ask Cintipilli Appayya and Mutyalamma that: Cintipilli Tatarao—client)
77. Let him go or let him stop. Now I am saying that he should not make friendship with that man.
78. (Just so. He will talk with them: Teddi Parasayya—friend of client)
79. (First ask them: Ramulu Nukali—friend)
80. (If he says "no," then get rid of him: Teddi Parasayya—friend of client)
81. (Leave him!: Ramulu Nukali—friend)
82. (Ask if the son is going to the *peddillu* and if Sati Polamma is attacking: Teddi Parasayya—friend of client)
83. (Not to the house! Just because he talks on the road she attacks: Cintipilli Tatarao—client)
84. (Now leave aside the matter of the *peddillu*. The father-in-law is there. The two brothers should live happily with him. That way, you'll be happy, right?: Teddi Parasayya—friend of client)
85. That's what I am saying. If you obey the order given of the household spirits, then obey.
86. (They will obey: Teddi Parasayya—friend of client)
87. (True, eventually he'll see it our way: Teddi Parasayya—friend of client)
88. (Yes, he must: Ramulu Nukali—friend)
89. (Pay homage to the attacking goddess. If you talk it out with him and pay homage, then these two brothers will again be able to live together: Teddi Parasayya—friend of client)
90. (Now the two brothers [Tatarao and Paidanna] should be together. We will tell this to that human [Paidanna]. When he says "no," then . . . .: Ramulu Nukali—friend)
91. (He already said "no,": Cintipilli Tatarao—client)

92. (Even if he says "no," he feels nervous. He knows he might next: Cintipilli Tatarao—client)

93. (He feels that. We will abandon him: Ramulu Nukali—friend)

94. (Shall we stay or shall we go? If we stay with the younger father-in-law [Naidu], then will we live happily . . . he will immerse in water and immerse in milk [i.e., perform the kāniki]: Cintipilli Tatarao—client)

95. (He will say "no." This man will say "no." "You stay at this end and I will stay at that end," he will say: Ramulu Nukali—friend)

96. Say this: "If you like, stay with me, or if not, then, as soon as you fly away, don't stay with me, if you make friendships with them [i.e., Teddi Ellanna's group], I will say."

97. (I will tell him, goddess. From Monday we will offer the *muddura*-s: Cintipilli Tatarao—client)

98. So you shouldn't offer to them, mindless fellow.

99. (Having untied it, will you raise this man and this man?: Teddi Parasayya—friend of client)

100. Now, until you ask these two people, don't untie! Don't untie the *muddura*-s, sweet grandson, listen to me.

101. (We know all that: Cintipilli Tatarao—client)

102. (Well, if you know so much, why did you come here, to the *pati*?: Ramulu Nukali—friend)

103. You make the two of them sit down and then ask them three times. Make the two brothers sit down and ask them three times. Then, along with the grand-children, you will be able to be happy. Then you can offer the *muddura*.

Phase D

104. (There may be some further difficulties: Teddi Parasayya—friend of client)

105. Neither that of the east nor that of the west, the *cillingi* [witchcraft] human . . .

106. (OK, the human [Paidanna] will say no and "I will live by myself." Ask her if she will raise us: Ramulu Nukali—friend)

107. For the word spoken at *viranna* [i.e., for the diagnosis given in the *pati*] when happiness was about to be given, you went to kāniki-s. They may have fouled you up, is it not?

108. (No, see here: in that way we will call the him and ask him three times. The [Paidanna] will say no. "Whenever you say no, then you can live on your own and I will live on my own." Holding his uncle [Naidu], he [Tatarao] will live. Then will you lift your son [Tatarao] and daughter [Tatarao's wife] and raise them?: Teddi Parasayya—friend of client)

109. I am saying that I will raise them. I will get rid of the goddess attacking the household. I will hold my child in my hand and I will raise him. I am Cintipilli Appayya.

110. (What if she doesn't raise?: Teddi Parasayya—friend of client)

111. (We should pay homage: Cintipilli Tatarao—client)

112. You should not talk at all with the human [Paidanna] who roams.

113. (I won't even look at this house!: Cintipilli Tatarao—client)

114. (Ask this: "I will divide [the property] of those two. I will not live [with Paidanna and his family] at all." Ask that: Teddi Parasayya—friend of client)

115. (When he says "no," right?: Ramulu Nukali)
116. (On the day he tells me to hand over his money, on that day I'll just throw it at him. But until then I won't hand over the share: Teddi Parasayya—friend of client)
117. (I won't keep it in my house. Now it is in my house. I will hand it over: Cintipilli Tatarao—client)
118. (Now who will hand over the share?: Ramulu Nukali—friend)
119. (He [Paidanna] will say "no": Cintipilli Tatarao—client)
120. Now you are asking about the share, sweet grandson. Now, when the human says "no," you should take it [the money] and throw it at him.
121. (When he says "no," we should take it and throw it at him: Ramulu Nukali—friend)
122. (Then?: Cintipilli Tatarao—client)
123. (Give the money to him—his share: Teddi Parasayya—friend of client)
124. (If he [Paidanna] doesn't give in, then his money will go to him and our money will go to us: Teddi Naidu—uncle to client)
125. (When he says "no"?: Cintipilli Tatarao—client)
126. (If he says "no," then they will divide up the money: Ramulu Nukali—friend)
127. (I will give the money and distribute the pots: Cintipilli Tatarao—client)

Phase E
128. (Now there are no problems: Teddi Parasayya—friend of client)
129. If not, then please go.
130. (According to what you said we will fold our hands and pay homage: Teddi Parasayya—friend of client)
131. (Again it will come to the brothers. Again it will come to the brothers: Ramulu Nukali—friend)
132. (They will go away, like birds, each spreading to a tree: Teddi Parasayya—friend of client)
133. You are not afraid.
134. (It will happen like that: Ramulu Nukali—friend)
135. Listen to me, sweet grandson. If you pay homage to the attacking goddess, I will stand. I will keep the attacking goddess in the palm of my hand. The *māyadāri* ("dreammaker") comes by night, comes into the dreams, and mixes them up. I will send that away. Do you understand or not, sweet grandson?

"Unclean Deeds": Menstrual Taboos and Binding "Ties" in Rural Jamaica

E.J. Sobo; Case Western Reserve U., Dept. of Anthropology

INTRODUCTION

Traditionally, Jamaican people are cautious about eating: they would rather go hungry than accept food when unsure about the "cleanliness" of the cook. Hygiene is a particularly sensitive issue when cooks are menstruating. Menstruating women should not cook and if they do no one should eat the food that they prepare because to do so would be highly dangerous. But "uncleanliness" and the traditional ban on menstruants' cooking involve more than mere hygienic fears: menstrual blood provides women with a potential source of coercive power. The menstruant's power and mentrual taboos may be understood through an examination of the culturally constructed role that fluxing menstrual blood plays in reproduction, kinship, and general health.

ANTHROPOLOGICAL APPROACHES TO MENSTRUATION

Menstruation is commonly mentioned in the ethnographic literature. Most scholarship on the topic has been devoted to the meanings that surround it (e.g., Laws, Hey, and Eagan 1985; Lindenbaum 1972; Olsen and Woods 1986) but little reference is made to the ethnophysiological construction of the process of menstruation itself (for exceptions, see Newman, ed., 1985 and Snowden and Christian 1983). Many works focus on menstruation's negative symbolism (e.g., Delaney, Lupton, and Toth 1987; Golub 1985) and, following Douglas (1975), the concept of menstrual pollution.

In their review of the literature, Buckley and Gottlieb point out that many anthropologists too quickly attribute menstrual taboos to the somewhat tautological notion of the "inherent pollution of the female principle" (1988: 39). Because of this and since the "pollution theory" used to illuminate menstrual taboos has itself been fashioned on data concerning these same taboos, past work has "tended toward redundancy" (p.4).

With this paper, I argue that deeper exploration of the "uncleanliness" allegedly "inherent" in women is necessary: many authors stop short of making real contri-

ELISA SOBO *is a post-doctoral research fellow at Case Western Reserve University in Cleveland, Ohio. She is currently researching the benefits of unsafe sex perceived by inner-city women and runaway teenagers in Cleveland.*

butions to the literature on culture and menstruation because they do not attend to emic understandings of the menstrual process and its symbolism. Also, this symbolism's positive meanings (Skultans 1988) and the fact that women may benefit from certain menstrual taboos (Lawrence 1988) have, until recently, too rarely been explored.

Another shortcoming of past work identified in Buckley and Gottlieb is the reliance on universal, monocausal explanations for what is more likely to be "overdetermined by a plethora of psychological, ecological, and social facts" (p.24). Examples of this are seen in the cross-cultural studies of Bock (1967), Young and Bacdayan (1965), Montgomery (1974), Paige and Paige (1981), and Stephens (1961). As Buckley and Gottlieb go on to say, "Menstrual taboos are cultural constructions and must first be approached as such" (p.24). This essay takes such an approach. Further, it argues that cultural constructions of menstruation are linked to ethnophysiological notions and cannot be understood fully until this is taken into account.

The idea that the meanings of menstrual blood are related to ethnophysiological explanations of its reproductive function has been ignored in much of the literature (some exceptions are Martin 1987 and Wright 1982). And the influences of kinship ideologies on menstrual taboos remain completely unexplored.[1] Kinship beliefs frequently inform the constructions of procreation from which menstrual blood gains meaning and so they need to be considered. Blood's other ethnophysiological functions can also greatly influence the meaning it takes on when passed as menses and this, too, needs attention. This essay demonstrates the importance of these dimensions for analyses of menstrual symbolism.

Buckley and Gottlieb point out that "to transcend the limitations in received theory demands a more balanced and comprehensive ethnographic base than that which has been available"(1988:5). While theoretically informed, this paper provides the kind of ethnographic specificity that they call for. That is, beside contributing to the literature concerning the relations between the meaning of menstruation and ethnophysiological notions, demonstrating the shortcomings of superficial glossings of menstrual or female pollution, and adding to the literature on the social uses of menstrual taboos, this paper adds to the ethnographic record. It provides new data on Afro-Caribbean gender relations and ethnophysiology; information on the latter is particularly sparse. As I show, traditional Jamaican notions about the power of menstrual blood are associated primarily with its role in procreation and kinship and, secondarily, its role in general health and bodily purification.

SETTING AND METHODS

The data discussed in this essay were collected during the course of a larger study of discourse related to procreation, health, kinship, and magic (Sobo 1990; In press). The interviews that the essay is based on were done with males and females, individually and in both mixed and sex-segregated groups. They were both formally structured and informal, as conversations. They took place in community settings and private yards; some were done in clinics. Actions taken in regard to the body and informants' drawings of its inner workings were also analyzed. Participants were mainly impoverished rural Jamaicans, most of whom are of West African descent. Many are Christian; most believe in an enchanted world full of ghosts, spirits, and magic. Hereafter, I refer to these folk as "Jamaicans."[2]

Unemployment and underemployment run high throughout the island. In 1987, the per capita income was barely $1000 (U.S.). Where I resided, a village of eight hundred people just east of Port Antonio, one-third could find no work (STATIN 1982). Many villagers engaged in small-scale agricultural pursuits yet few could "manage" with this income alone. To supplement these earnings, they also took in wash, hired themselves out for small construction jobs when such work was available, engaged in part-time petty trade like selling oranges, and relied on relatives for resources. Almost all villagers belonged to extended kin networks (but factors such as migration to cities and overseas have weakened many family ties despite norms for reciprocity between kin).

A typical rural Jamaican village consists of people brought together by ancestry, or by proximity to a shop or postal agency. In some cases, a village is organized around an estate where villagers sell their labor. Houses generally lack plumbing and electricity, and are made of wood planks and zinc sheeting. They are built as far apart as possible but are usually still within yelling distance of a neighbor. Even though kin solidarity is valued, assumptions about the wickedness and "coveteousness" of human nature lead people to guard their privacy and exert caution in most social dealings.

Households are often matrifocal (see R.T. Smith 1988: 7–8) and non-legal marital unions are common. In a study of contraceptive practice in Jamaica, Brody found that 84% of his subjects (mainly impoverished, reproductive-aged, sexually active women) were in such unions. Not all couples live together: 43.3% of his subjects were in "visiting" unions. Brody regards unstable conjugal relations as a "salient feature" in the lives of fecund young women (1981: 187–8).[3]

Jamaican gender relations are typically "consumed by strategies or 'games playing'" (Henry and Wilson 1975: 165). Impoverished men and women see each other instrumentally (*cf.*, Brody 1981: 188; R.T. Smith 1988: 142). While men are seen as irresponsible and unreliable (*cf.*, Brody; R.T. Smith pp.192–3), women are perceived as "smart, clever, and devious" manipulators in "constant search for a male on whom they can rely" (Henry and Wilson: 193, 172).[4]

Men are allowed to express power overtly but women must remain secretive about the control they try to assert over the resources of others (Freilich 1968). Concealed like their genetalia, women's covert power can be "dangerous" for men. Women seek to benefit by manipulating men, but men feel violated when their free wills are interfered with. Gender-linked role expectations and ideas about the dangers of relationships are expressed and perpetuated through the use of menstrual taboos, as will be shown.

DISCUSSING MENSTRUATION

Menstrual taboos have deep meaning for those who enforce and abide by them. Like most of Jamaican culture, these meanings are not formally taught. People glean knowledge of menstrual power from conversations had and overheard, by listening to people "run joke," and by paying attention to discussions concerning dangers and fears. Cultural facts are implied as often as stated and, despite the tenor of formal education (which emphasizes rote learning), Jamaicans learn to "study a thing" by observation—to "pick sense out of nonsense."

Because of the selfish, "unnatural," and antisocial (as well as revolting) ideas connoted, many feel uneasy talking explicitly about the ways that red pea soup and other dishes get tainted with blood in women's bids for power over their men. "Me no business with that," people say, wary of what an inquirer might think. Until trust has been established, people often hide their knowledge by simply calling menstruants and their blood "unclean." But this word carries a clear message about social and moral affairs.

"CLEAN" LIVING

"Clean" living is "good" living—altruistic living which perpetuates the social and moral order. While sociable people do ask things of others, they do not "take advantage" or do they seek to control people through magic or sorcery. Decisions are left up to individuals; social pressure is the only coercion applied. Good people appeal to the understood rights and obligations that inhere in relationships. The "unclean," however, use deceitful means to gain their desires. Using various techniques and poisons, "unclean" men and women harm competitors or manipulate others' "minds."[5]

Healthy, sociable relationships are mutually beneficial. Wicked individuals initiate self-serving relationships or alter healthy ones to suit themselves. They pay no heed to the fairness of exchanges or others' rights to autonomy. Often, the wicked rely on "unclean deeds" to keep their skewed relationships going.

Those "right with God" have been washed of the self-centered sinfulness that the "unclean" wicked retain. Because "sin" would undermine the social and moral order, it is denigrated and targeted for purges. "Sin" also undermines physical well-being, as do blockages and other disagreeable substances; purging such matter from the body is essential to health in Jamaica, as is later seen. Incorrigibly wicked individuals are sometimes "run" from a community. Like "dirt," they get swept away by the broom of social opposition. Social pathologies and individual physical pathologies are homologous (*cf.* Taylor 1988).

Antisocial feelings often gain covert expression. A full discussion of the psychology behind this is beyond the scope of this paper but it is important to note that childhood training promotes the rechanneling of antisocial aggression from superiors toward other targets. It also engenders ideas about manipulating would-be bosses so that one's own wishes can be realized. Children learn early that the very food that "builds" a person can be used to covertly convey "unclean" substances, like poison. Uncomfortable about their own antisocial feelings, people project them onto others. They know that despite an overt belief in the value of altruism, "bad mind" wishes of others who "take advantage" are rampant. As a result, children grow up wary of everyone (See Cohen 1955).

CLEANLINESS AND EATING

Jamaicans, feeling very vulnerable to the evil intents of others, worry about eating food that has been purposefully handled improperly. Eating can be perilous. Some food caution certainly has to do with ordinary concerns about sanitation. But Jamaicans primarily fear the wicked use of black magic and poisoning: they fear "unclean deeds." Added to food, certain chemical preparations, minerals, and herbal concoctions can poison. Anything associated with decay also can poison, rotten things being the negation of life and health.

Menstruation's association with "uncleanliness" has to do with belief in the ability and inclination of women to use their menstrual blood wickedly as magical "compellance" poison, to "tie" others to them (the mechanism behind this is explained below). "Uncleanliness" indexes antisocial possibilities in the menstruants themselves, not just the connections between "raw" menstrual blood and sepsis, rot, or death. So references to "uncleanliness" may be employed to check women's claims to ascendency. If a woman gets "bright" or uppity, one need only "remind her of the last thing she wore": her "raas clat" or "pussy clat"—her menstrual cloth or pad.

Menstrual symbolism, then, involves much more than simple pollution. The "uncleanliness" associated with menstruants has important moral and social implications. A full appreciation of these dimensions demands the discussion of traditional Jamaican beliefs concerning physiology. The "uncleanliness" of menstruation and the power of menstrual blood to "tie," as well as its mundanely septic nature, are based in Jamaican beliefs about blood.

TRADITIONAL HEALTH BELIEFS

Traditionally, Jamaicans see the body as an open system that must stay "equalized." Ideally, the body maintains itself at a certain, warm temperature. But, because it has pores and is permeable, the body's temperature may be thrown off by thermal changes in the external world. Although dangerous, especially for the "tender" or those not "fit" (the physically vulnerable; the infirm), permeability is necessary for proper heat exchange and for the dispersal of waste matter. Keeping the system clean and thermally regulated is required for health maintenance.

Permeability is also necessary because the body must take in food to build the components of its structure and replenish those lost through work and other aspects of living. Food[6] goes from the mouth through a tube to the "belly," the large inner cavity, which resembles a big bag and holds (among other things) a "maw" or "grinder." Different foods turn into different bodily components as needed, and the purity of these components depends upon the nature of what gets ingested.

BLOOD TYPES

Blood is the most vital and meaning-invested component of all and it comes in several forms. When unqualified by adjective or context, the word "blood" means the red kind, built from thick, dark liquid items such as soup, English-style stout, and porridge, and from reddish edibles such as tomatoes. Some feel the blood of "meat kind" such as pork or "mutton" (goat meat) is directly incorporated into human blood; others say that its juices "build" blood. Wild hog meat, redder than regular meat, is seen as super-nutritious and vitality-boosting because wild hogs feed on characteristically pure, red-colored roots, said to be beneficial blood builders.

"Sinews," another form of blood, comes from okra, fish eyes, and other slimy foods with light-colored, gelatinous ooze, such as egg whites and cow "foot." "Sinews" includes but is not limited to synovial fluid, which does resemble egg whites and lubricates, making joints "sipple." The eyes are filled with "sinews" and glide in their sockets with its aid. "Sinews" is also associated with the "nerves" and with procreation. Many call it "white" blood in comparison to the red. Both kinds of blood are needed for "fitness," which shows itself through good health, fecundity, and a body's moist and juicy plumpness.

CLEANLINESS

Good health depends on and is exhibited with plumpness but, as with healthy relationships, a balance between intake and outflow must be maintained. All that gets taken into the body must be used or expelled as "filth" or "dirt" because unincorporated excess begins to swell and decay. This knowledge leads people to associate superfluous or unutilized food, fat, sexual energy, and such with filth and the inevitable process of decomposition. Some Jamaicans speak of "good fat" and "bad fat"; the good is firm like a "fit" mango and the bad is "soft," hangs "slack," and denotes declining "fitness" as if a person was an overripe fruit, beginning to break down or rot.

A body that does not efficiently rid itself of excess and rotting waste can turn septic inside. Because of the inevitable cycle of life, sweet and useful things turn bad and sour; those that decay in the body and stay too long will bring sickness.

Not all foods are transformed into specific components like "sinews" or blood, and some are not utilized in the "structure" at all. Some things simply go to waste: extra liquids become urine, and solid "food" turns to "didi" or feces, which move out from the "belly" cavity through the "tripe" or intestinal tube until expelled. Urine and feces "must stink" because they are waste, a young girl explained. People who do not use the toilet often enough literally fill up with waste: a mother asked her five year old daughter why the white missionaries always had such soft and overfat bellies, and the little girl offered that "the tripe them fulla didi." The mother translated: "They fulla shit."

Some substances are not recognized as waste until incorporated into the body. Usually, they work their way out in sweat, called "bad water" when super-saturated with toxins. Some say that sweat forms from water drunk and it carries toxins from the flesh, picking up waste as it makes its way to the skin for expulsion through the "pulps" or pores. Curry, for example, comes out in the sweat, people say, turning it slightly yellow. Working hard is good because it makes the body sweat, and so cleanse itself, but "pulps" clogged with dirt cannot serve as passages. Keeping skin clean aids the expulsion of toxins in sweat. Because it carries waste, sweat can be redolent; bathing serves to "freshen."

Most blood-borne toxins are purged with bowel movements and urination, but people can take special preventative steps to ensure blood cleanliness. Health-related concern over the state of one's blood is typical among descendents of the African diaspora. So is the practice of cleansing it: "bush" or herbal teas commonly serve as blood purifiers (Laguerre 1987; Snow 1974). For Jamaicans, the bitterness of a brew indicates how effective it will be. Cerasee (*Mimordica charontia*) tea is an island favorite. Tea of ground bissy (*Cola acuminata*) also removes strong toxins. Most tea brewed for breakfast has preventative blood-purifying action.

Many things can make the blood impure. "Dirty" blood can result from eating something disagreeable, such as soured food or "fertilizer [laced] food." The sickness "bad blood," a generic sexually transmitted disease, involves taking in poisons from another person's genitals.[7] "Dirty" blood can also come from breathing in poison, such as insecticide which is associated with cancer in the chest. "Dirty" blood signals "slackness" in "caring the body," as in failing to follow preventative measures such as drinking "bush tea."

INNER ANATOMY

Blood is the primary and most thought about bodily component, but the most important part of the inner body or "structure" is the "belly." This big cavity or bag extends from just below the breast to the pelvis, with tubes leading out at its bottom. The "belly" is full of bags and tubes, such as the "baby bag" and "urine tube." A main conduit leads from the top of the body through the "belly" to the bottom (not from bottom to top), with tributary bags and tubes along its length. Sometimes, tube and bag connections are not thought of as tightly coupled. A substance improperly propelled can meander off course and slide into an unsuitable tube or bag, lodge, and cause problems.

WASHING OUT THE "BELLY"

Portions of food not converted into bodily components are expelled. Substances that remain inside too long become foul, upset the body's balance, and cause sickness. Waste must be kept flowing downward and out through the pores and other orifices.

Most sickness gets started in the "belly" because of the central roles this space plays in the incorporation (that is, the conversion into bodily components) of substances taken in and the concomitant expurgation of foreign matter, whether the wasted part of food or drink, medicine, air, poison, or even another's bodily substance (such as sexual effluvia). This is one reason for the strong reliance on "washouts" or laxative purges for maintaining health. Such reliance is also found among other Afro-Caribbean people (Laguerre 1987); it is "legion" among African-Americans (Snow 1974: 87). Taylor (this volume) argues that an emphasis on maintaining a continuous, unimpeded flow through the body is common among those who value reciprocity and emphasize the obligation kin have to share with each other, as Jamaicans do.

"Washout" should be taken frequently. Once a month, just like menstruation, is advised. The model for health is gynocentric: periodic cleansing is recommended for all.[8] Every household medicinal supply includes, if nothing more, a purgative of some sort such as epsom salts, cathartic herbs, or castor oil. The Jamaican emphasis on the "belly" and on blood purity explain why so many mistake medical life-support devices seen in hospitals, such as the "nose tube," as mechanically effecting "washout"-like cures.

When Jamaicans say "belly working," they mean it is laboring to wash an excess of disagreeable things down and out. Maintaining good health depends on proper "belly" function. This is enhanced through preventative measures such as the ingestion of purifying teas and cleansing purges, and the purity of the person and his or her blood and system as a whole depends on it. Offending substances must be "operated" out—"cut" from the system with purgatives. The link between the usage of these words and the idea that surgeons operate, cut, and remove things to restore proper health is clear.

SICKNESS

Sickness results when the body's internal equilibrium is upset by the entrance of disagreeable foreign substances that trigger stress reactions, so the body's permeability must be guarded. Sickness also results when something mistakenly slips into the wrong bag or tube and lodges and rots or clogs the system. A lack of attention to proper, timely nutrition and blood that gets unbalanced (too dirty, too full of sugar, too thick, etc.) can also "bring problem."

The idea is not so much that battles for power and territory are being fought between alien germ forces and armed white blood cells (*cf.* Martin 1991 regarding metaphors used in the U.S.A.) but that sickness is caused by reactions that lead to the festering rot and rising gas typical of decomposition. These reactions are reminiscent of the life-cycle of fruit which, like the body, is at its peak or "well fit" when "full" and firmly juicy. They bespeak a lifestyle in which people know the decay of corpses, carcasses, garbage, and papaya first-hand. Sickness—these reactions—will occur when something that can disturb the balance of the body happens or finds its way in and is not "cut," "operated," "worked," or removed efficiently enough or in a timely fashion.

MALE AND FEMALE BODIES

The general principles behind reproduction and sex follow from the ethnophysiological model described. Male and female bodies differ only in that each has some unique sets of tubes and bags which the other does not, and also because females must take in matter—semen—that contains others' wastes. The female body can handle the trauma of receiving semen, while the male body cannot. This belief does not mean that women are more "fit" than men. However, because "normal" men do not receive, women can be branded as less clean.

ANAL INTERCOURSE AND AIDS

"Unclean deeds" that dirty the blood and bring sickness include sexual acts that Jamaicans deem "unnatural." Support for such judgements can be expressed in ethnophysiological terms. Jamaicans explain that anal intercourse is "unnatural" because the vagina is built to take in semen but the anus is not.

Ned, my Jamaican "sister's" boyfriend, claimed that AIDS troubles homosexual men because semen, which normally moves from the vagina to the womb, has no natural destination when ejaculated into the anus. Moreover, the rectum does not have an easy opening (like the vagina) for draining out matter that lingers. Nor do men have a natural monthly "washout" like menstruation. Semen that enters the rectum always gets lost inside and rots, Ned explained, causing AIDS. Ned's inventive use of traditional health beliefs to illuminate a new health threat is one example of the creative way that traditional models get extended as people attempt to come up with plausible explanations for new problems.[9]

Anal intercourse, with a man or a woman, harms the body. In addition to the "natural" physical toll it takes, its immorality makes it dangerous. It constitutes a behavioral infraction against the moral order in which procreation is the aim of sex,[10] and it violates the understanding that humans should be responsible custodians for the bodies God lends them. Those who traumatize the body unduly are "careless" and so less deserving of divine protection. Spiritual consequences can follow.

Anal sex shows itself on as well as in the body. One grandmother, observing a thin and not "well-shaped" woman walking on the road before her house, declared, "As I look upon the gal's batty [bottom], I know say the man trouble the gal's batty. What sin, eh? The lord God did give him [sic] the batty hole to pass out the dung—didn't give it for nothing to go into." The "gal's" flat "batty" and her knock-kneed walk indicated a habit of anal sex.[11]

Anal intercourse is all the more harmful and "careless" when between men. Still, the Jamaicans I talked to and island media coverage indicated that most Jamaicans do not share Ned's American-influenced idea that AIDS attacks only male homosexuals (Ned was in America during the early years of the AIDS epidemic). In actuality, half (49%) of all cases (ninety-six had been reported in Jamaica by March of 1989) have been traced to heterosexual contact and women account for one of every three sufferers (*Gleaner* 1989). Those who have heard that, internationally, most people with AIDS are black either believe this is a racist fabrication (some say to conceal a white plan to exterminate black nations) or, giving into the color prejudice engendered by colonialism and slavery, construe it as "proof" that blacks are "slack" and immoral.

Because traditional ethnophysiological beliefs are applied creatively to new problems in efforts to understand and manage them, AIDS patients are believed to be covered with burst sores and pustules full of impurities being "worked out" of the blood through the skin. One woman told of a patient who, due to the extent of her suppurating sores, had to be ensconced in plastic wrap before she was transported to a Kingston hospital. AIDS spreads through contact with the decaying matter excreted in these sores as well as through contact with sexual waste or effluvia.

Most villagers believe AIDS was introduced to human circles by people who have sex with animals. Animal effluvium which penetrates the body causes an adverse reaction, not only because it is animal (and so extremely foreign and toxic to humans) but also because it contains waste. Like ejaculated semen that does not meet an egg, it is out of place in the human body.

"DISCHARGE" AND "DISCHARGING"

Bodily excretions that are improperly deposited or disposed of constitute a significant health risk. Women "dirtied" by the non-reproductive presence of semen must expel it. A man's own semen causes problems only when stored in his body for too long. "Germs" (sperm) "germinate" in the "seed bag" (scrotum). When a man ejaculates, sperm (along with impurities that have collected in the groin) moves up and out from this storage place. "Sinews," stored above and behind the "seed bag" in a tube called the "line" in the lower back, ease its passage. Alternatively, some suggest that semen is stored with the "sinews" itself in the spine (or in a bag behind the spine) and is propelled directly from that location, bypassing the "seed bag." Some say the "seeds" are simply there, as they are in fruit such as the avocado pear.

Sperm, "sinews," and waste matter combine to make "discharge," which leaves the body at orgasm. Sperm fattens women, making them sexually appealing and attractive. Girls grow plump in their teen years as a perceived result of becoming sexually active. To support their claim for the health-enhancing value of sperm, many people say that prostitutes and other women who dip so low as to perform oral sex[12] get fat; names are often named.

But sperm cannot always be easily incorporated into a receptor's body to fatten. Blood types differ and those of each lover cannot always blend. Also, semen can lodge in spaces not accessible to the red blood with which it might otherwise mix. Once outcast, "discharge" quickly decomposes and, like decaying matter of any sort lodged in the body, it causes sickness if not disposed of. In support of this, many say the toxicity of "discharge" makes prostitutes "pull down"; they refer to specific thin women in making their point.

"Discharge" defiles the receptor. The waste it contains is toxic, fouling, and all the more noxious because it was already rejected by another body. But Jamaicans assume that sex itself necessitates the deposit of one's substance into another: tradition has it that even lesbians couple as "man" and woman, the "man" having supposedly "stretched" her external genitalia into an insertable pseudo-penis with the aid of an oil made for this purpose. As long as the person receiving the fouling matter is female all is fine; women can menstruate and so cleanse their inner spaces of rotting "discharge."

Male justifications for frequent intercourse include the belief that without it "discharge" piles up. Overfullness with aging "sinews" and unexpelled waste has deleterious effects. The male body corrects small imbalances through wet dreams, but excesses can harden up in the spine, causing back pain and sexual problems. Men emphasize the importance of "clearing the line" during sex. It is assumed that men will find partners and so need never masturbate to "clear the line." Women who stay celibate too long may get "nerves" problems as "sinews" balances come undone. "Discharging" "equalizes" and cleanses the body, promoting as well as signaling good health. People—mostly men—use this knowledge to justify frequent sex and to coerce others into partnership.

Sex is healthy but also dangerous because it "heats" and so "opens" the body, leaving it vulnerable to foreign intrusions. "Hot" from "the work," "bloodstrings" dilate and joints loosen. The opening to the womb expands, facilitating conception. The thrusting action of the penis "opens" women further. This makes the use of condoms risky: they can shoot off of the penis (a "gun in a baggie") during sex, lodge somewhere, rot, and cause sickness. If a condom clogs a woman's "tube" (unqualified, "tube" refers to the vagina), infertility and those problems associated with a backlog of blocked, decomposing menses would ensue.

MENSTRUATION

Heterosexually active women cannot avoid "discharge" which, from the time it leaves a man until its incorporation into a baby's body, is potentially dangerous and defiling. When sperm and egg "catch," all is well. The man and woman involved become "babyfather" and "babymother" to each other. The fetus is a conglomeration of blood and semen. If conception does not occur, gravity "runs" semen from the "tube." But leftovers in the womb can rot. So women menstruate, flushing out decomposing, unused semen.

Having a baby sweeps out impurities that build up within the reproductive bags and tube(s) even better than the menses do. Because of this, childbearing promotes good health. Mothers can claim "Me clean," insulting childless others by insinuating that they are physically impure. Post-menopausal women, have "closed" wombs; "discharge" cannot lodge within them to pollute them. It runs out the vagina, unused.

Some Jamaicans believe that intercourse brings on menarche (the onset of cyclic menstruation) by "opening" a girl's womb and exposing her to the danger of trapping male "discharge." However, as others observe, menarche can occur before first intercourse. All agree that menstruation carries out more than just semen. It releases excess blood which would otherwise accumulate and bring on "pressure." But, more importantly, it cleanses the body of toxins and excess "sinews." While females, like males, do "discharge" during intercourse and their "discharge" also contains impurities and "sinews" (and, some believe, "germs"), menstruation is necessary for a full cleansing.

Having many lovers can cause menstrual irregularity. Semen from several men tax the body much more than one man's "germs" because each sort has its own toxicity and one may "disagree" with another (as vinegar curdles milk), speeding decay and compounding the likelihood of sickness. This, as well as the other physically traumatic effects of having multiple partners, each of whom "pushes" the vagina into a different shape, keeps many women from seeking "outside" partners. A woman's regular mate appreciates this.

Men do not menstruate and so have no routine body purge but this is not problematic. People simply say that men's bodies are different; they are not designed to purge others' "discharge." Normally, men have no need for monthly flows: the nature of men's work leads their bodies to sweat more than women's, leaving fewer impurities inside. Also, many of the male's impurities are eliminated with "discharge." Additionally, male bodies do not tend to accumulate blood, which leads to "pressure," like women's do. Still, for the sake of prevention, men follow women's lead and try to take "washout" once a month to purify the blood and cleanse the system. And, in addition to cleansing teas, they drink "plenty beer" to flush out poison.

PRECAUTIONS

Because they do not menstruate, men are safe from the dangers of the "hot state" it entails. During menstruation, the womb, vagina, and blood vessels "open" to increase the flow of cleansing blood. A menstruating woman is "loose" and "hot" and should not take a "washout" because it would increase the flow from her already "open" womb and "bloodstrings," causing hemorrhaging, and possibly death.

Menstruants must avoid cold baths and must stay out of drafts: the chances to "catch up cold" or take in pernicious matter increase in "hot," "open" periods. During the rest of the month, wearing panties and keeping one's skirt down and tucked between one's legs when sitting is sufficient, but now extra precautions must be taken. Menstrual pads, whether "clat" (cloth) rags or store-bought sanitary napkins, do more than absorb blood. They also offer protection from drafts and other intrusions that might penetrate the vagina and get "caught" in the womb during this vulnerable period. Because their vaginas are so "open," menstruants are easily impregnated.

THE "HEALTH" AND SICKNESS

Menstrual blood itself is pure and clean; it is the waste matter and semen carried down by the blood that is "unclean." The belief that semen is polluting exists in other cultural contexts (Eilberg-Schwartz 1990: chapter 7; Gregor 1990; McClain 1989: 75), as does the belief in blood-borne waste (Farmer 1988; Laguerre 1987). Accordingly, the belief that menstrual blood's actual polluting quality inheres in its contents may exist in other cultures but this can go unnoted when no effort is made to probe beneath the surface of informants' statements about menstruation's uncleanliness.

For Jamaicans, the dark chunks and strings of "clotty-clotty" in menstrual blood contain the actual impurities and waste material: things being worked out of the circulating blood, bunches of semen, and clots of "cold" (mucous) which would otherwise accumulate and block the tube(s). One old woman used an analogy: the river is clean but the mud at the bottom is dirty. The vagina is a river-like conduit in which water equals clean blood, and mud equals semen. The blood of menstruation, like the water of sweat, is itself pure and clean; "dirt" is what it carries.

Cyclic menstruation is desirable (*cf.* MacCormack 1985) and menstruating is often called seeing one's "health." With the exception of menstrual blood (for reasons soon explained), effluvium free of toxins and expelled from a "clean" person is, in its purity, health-promoting. A "clean" individual is pure both physically and morally, such as a churchyard healer who practices when "fresh" or just-bathed and when spiritually clean from a period of fasting, praying, and celibacy. "Clean" healers can rub patients' bodies with their own sweat as part of a cure. The cleansing, curative action of the blood of Jesus is expounded in churches throughout the island (indeed, a North American who visited me during my fieldwork noted, "They seem a little preoccupied with blood"). One's own urine can cure one's own pink eye and one's saliva can "well" one's cuts but only the truly pure can, as Jesus did, share effluvia to cure without endangering recipients, whose bodies would otherwise reject these fluids as foreign matter.

Healthy bodies recoil against decay, and things not purged on time, as by menstruation, fester inside. The body reacts to the insult of decomposition by, in attempting adjustment, becoming sick. A body in the process of cleaning itself, as with fever (which, put simply, "melts out" toxins), is sick. Menstruants can therefore claim to be "sick" and often do so when avoiding daily duties. Calling menstruation "sickness" also serves to keep women from pursuing certain activities and it highlights the pollution they carry.

THE DEEPER MEANING OF MENSTRUAL "UNCLEANLINESS"

When contaminated, as they normally are, effluvia that transport waste out can cause sickness. They can also compel, by altering the "minds" of others into whose bodies they get incorporated. But if too much of what is essentially decomposing matter and thus noxious poison is given, the targeted person could become sick enough to notice and even sick enough to die. As one might expect, this sort of sickness begins in the "belly." It is but one form of "bad belly," the generic Jamaican gastro-intestinal complaint.

Women, as a way to "tie" men to them and thus secure their love and money, can collect their own menstrual blood for use in cooking.[13] This is easily done by squatting over a steaming pot. The hot steam helps gravity to ease out some of the menses. Sometimes, used menstrual rags are soaked in water to loosen the blood which is then "queezed" or wrung out. It can be collected and stored for later use.

The most commonly adulterated food is rice-and-peas, a reddish-brown dish. A woman can steam herself directly over the pot as she finishes cooking this. Red pea soup, "stew-peas," and potato pudding are also known as potential menses carriers. All are the correct color and commonly eaten. Some men are so frightened of ingesting menses that they refuse even red herring, a dried fish which they say takes its color from having been killed when menstruating. As careful as men are, menstrual blood diluted in food cannot be tasted. As one woman said, laughing about the teaspoonful needed to compel, "Cho—you think that little bit can flavor pot?"

UNCLE'S CASE

One man, Uncle, sensed strife in his relationship with his common-law wife and soon became alarmed by chronic "belly" pain. In the kitchen, he stumbled upon a vial of dark, viscous liquid. A visit to a magic specialist confirmed his suspicion that because she loved him so much and with such jealousy, his wife had been trying to "tie" him to her by cooking with her menstrual blood. This explained the strife (not being fully "tied," he felt "contrary") and the "belly" pain, and justified Uncle's concern. Had he not put a stop to things, the buildup of menstrual toxins in his "belly" would have killed him.

Menstrual rhetoric is often made to serve what Foster calls a "validating role" (1988); it is used to confirm or legitimize claims concerning preexistent, problematic relationships. In Uncle's case, it seems that the "wife" had become too demanding; Uncle felt that their relationship had ceased being mutually beneficial and fair. The "bad belly" physically represented his sense that too many demands were being made of him. Indeed, his partner's desire to control his decisions regarding what he would do for her brought the sickness on to begin with.

Behavioral changes can indicate "tying," but not everyone becomes aware of these changes. The ingestion of menstrual blood signals itself in a "bad belly" that seems to have no cause and looks "funny" (due to its shape, accompanying symptoms, persistence, etc.). Massive overdoses can bring death. Women must exert care when trying to "tie." They take comfort knowing that, because of its "natural" quality, ingested blood evades the medical doctor's or coronor's detection.

MEN FEAR "TYING" MORE THAN WOMEN DO

Because of their reproductive role, women have access to the most potent means to "tie" and so to compel action.[14] Menstrual taboos stem from this "natural" fact. While women cook for themselves, men normally do not. They must trust the women who prepare their meals to do so with high regard for "cleanliness." But it is not just the sexual division of labor that causes men to fear "unclean" food more than women do. Traditionally, men hold the resources that people might "grudge," covet, or take advantage of. Moreover, "tying" is built on notions about interdependence, kinship, procreation and parent/child relationships that raise questions concerning dependence and selfishness, which are more of an issue for men.

Conditions that make it hard for men to fulfil the expectation that they provide financially for partners and children leave men wary of contracting obligations, which any social tie involves.[15] So do developmental factors. During childhood all children are well-bound to their mothers, who encourage their dependence. Girls do not grow as ambivalent about this interdependence as boys do (Chodorow 1978). They lack the male's role expectation of independence (although they can and do attain it) and have less fear of the relational bonds that "tying" represents. Furthermore, ascribing more than procreative power to semen is rare.[16] Menstrual blood is far more notorious as a device for "tying." Women can control men with the effluvia of their own bodies but men must work magic with outside sources.

Women do fear being "tied" through "Obeah" or sorcery by men who have nothing to give them but beatings. Many take precautions, such as not drinking from opened bottles because drinks may be adulterated, and guarding their underclothes which, if ritually buried in a man's yard, can compel a woman to stay with him. But because women are seen as plentiful "like rice grain" and since men tend to overtly express power, the likelihood of this scenario is low and people know it.

Men, who must eat from women and whose bodies cannot handle foreign "discharge," are not as safe.

KINSHIP AND BLOOD

As babes are bound to mothers through the intake of mothers' blood both in the womb and at the breast, so too are those men who unknowingly eat blood-infused food bound to the women who provide it. The sociable mother/child kin-bonding model underlies the powerful connotations of blood, adds to the significance of commensality, and accounts for "tying's" mechanism.

Real kinship is material, concrete, and consubstantial: it is based on shared blood. Conception occurs when male and female bloods "mingle"; the "lump" that becomes a fetus is made up of sperm and mother's blood. The kinship bond between a mother and a child is "tied" with her blood which, incorporated into the body of the child, physically compels the child to behave altruistically in relation to her. People of "one blood" share "one mind" and are of "one accord."[17]

The creation of kinship is not fixed or finished at conception. The growing fetus "eats," with its mouth, food ingested by its mother as well as its mother's blood. If she is having intercourse, it eats semen too. Once born, a baby continues the consubstantiation process that creates kin by drinking his or her mother's milk. Since breast milk is made of bodily substance, its ingestion can tie a baby to an otherwise unrelated wet-nurse. While experiencing the "hot" of labor and delivery is central in establishing maternity rights when they are in question, traditional Jamaicans subscribe to an attenuated form of what Watson (cited in Meigs 1987: 120) refers to as "nurture kinship": kinship that can be altered after birth by what Meigs calls "postnatal acts."

Adopted children can become as good as related; to feed is also to "grow" a child. The significance of food-sharing in confirming relatedness, as between spouses, stems from ethnophysiological understandings of consubstantial connections. These understandings give meaning to using food as a vehicle for substances that "tie." And they underlie the "compellance" power of menstrual blood.

Fed to desired husbands by aspiring or insecure surrogate mothers/wives, menstrual blood works as it does for the biological mother who uses it to "grow" her fetus. The incorporation of a woman's menstrual blood "ties" a man to her just as it "ties" an unborn child to its mother-to-be. Moreover, men ingesting menstrual blood selfishly (even if not through their own volition) eat what should have nourished their own offspring, an idea that causes more distress.[18]

VOLUNTARY RELATIONS

While the irrevocable ties of kinship and the rights and obligations that ensue are expected to accompany a parent/child relationship, spousal bonds should be elected. As with other voluntary relationships, spouses should not be so tightly bound together that partners suffocate. A good relationship turns bad when partners lose their sense of connectedness with others outside of that relation or feel that they have forfeited their freedom. A menstrually "tied" man has had his auton-omy usurped: his sense of obligation is not really his own and his "willingness" is taken advantage of. Arrived at by "unclean" means and being for the benefit of the other instead of the two, this kind of "tie" is "unnatural" and undesirable.

The fear of lost liberty and the resentment of forced action that surface in reac-tions to "tying" reflect ideals for relationships that are, in part, a reaction to the leg-acy of slavery. This fear and resentment is seen also in relation to contracts. Men dislike the sense of being bound or indebted by contracts of any kind (including the marriage contract) and hesitate to sign them. "Big men" are supposed to call in debts, not pay them off. "Big men" rule their women, not the reverse—as happens in cases of "tying."

SOME OTHER TABOOS

The mechanism of "tying" underlies the traditional taboo on a "babyfather" eating food prepared by his "babymother's" postpartum helper. Traditionally, a new mother's mother takes over for her during her baby's first nine weeks or so, giving her time to "knit up" her loosened joints and safely "close" her stretched "tube." Childbirth and the need for support it entails can motivate a woman to "tie" a man, and afterbirth blood could work as a "high power" "tying" agent. Its connection with procreation and fetal nourishment is patent. The helper would have this blood on her hands from washing the "babymother's" clothing and maternity "clat" (blood rags) and might contaminate food as she cooks.

The belief in "tying" also underlies traditional advice against letting a menstru-ating woman hold a baby. The decaying waste menstruants release causes a sick-ness reaction in a baby's body. The implicit association between menstruation and the state of non-pregnancy and the fact that menstrual blood can be used to control others may be related to the importance placed on minding this taboo. In a society where children are highly valued and baby-stealing is feared, a menstruant who wants to hold another's baby might be perceived as attempting to control the child's affections.

MENSTRUAL TABOOS: A NEW VIEW

Men refuse to eat from the pots of "unclean" women because of a fear of "unclean" deeds. It is a mistake, however, to equate this kind of "uncleanliness" with simple pollution. Menstrual taboos are much more complex than that (cf. Buckley and Got-tlieb 1988). In rural Jamaica, an "unclean deed" involves sorcery or magic and self-ish intent. Temporal uncleanliness does figure in menstrual beliefs, but the scrupulousness with which cooks wash hands indicates that "slackness" would have to be intentional. The possibility of having and acting on this intent in order to "tie" is central to menstruating women's "unclean" state. Many informants say that taboos gain most support today from men, who are understandably adamant about keeping menstruants from preparing food.

Several other factors underlie the male distaste for menstruation. Its benefits to the female body notwithstanding, menstruation confirms that semen is being washed out instead of "ingrafted" and this upsets men. In addition to being psychologically disturbing (Bettleheim 1954; Weigle 1989), it is unbecoming to have to acknowledge any lack of procreative power; siring children is a sign of masculine potential. Jamaican men like the thought of reproducing more than Jamaican women do. On the average, men beginning their reproductive careers desire 2.8 children; by contrast, women want only 2.2 (Powell and Jackson 1988: xv).

Menstrual taboos can also ease men's procreative and sexual burdens. They encourage female shame about their genitals and help instill in them a lack of willingness to even think about their reproductive organs. This (along with health concerns) leads many women to do little to guard themselves from pregnancy, which benefits men who want to impregnate them. It also means that many women do not think to ask for sexual gratification, which benefits men unable or unwilling to comply. Also, those men uninterested in having (or unable to take on) many lovers can point to the threat of menstrual "tying" to justify their choices as they try to safeguard their reputations.

HEALTH, PRAGMATISM, AND MENSTRUAL TABOOS ON SEX

Typical men seek sex but even a "stallion," "ram goat," or "most high nature" man would never have intercourse with a menstruating woman—or at least he would never admit to having done so knowingly. Upon menstruation, muddying semen washes down and out of the vagina, making sex at this time "careless" and "unclean." Any contact with menstrual blood is dangerous due to the weight of compelling and sickening poisons it contains. Taboos on sex during menstruation keep men from direct physical contact with harmful, polluting substances and the powerful, obligating blood of reproduction.[19]

Knowing a mate's cycle helps a man stay undefiled and un-"tied." But many women do not bleed punctually. Noticeably irregular schedules are attributed to infidelity. The body, confused by so much different foreign matter, purges itself irregularly. Knowledge of this keeps many women faithful; none want to risk having their "outside" love affairs physically announced with each capricious period. Moreover, men can justifiably and openly leave mates who keep "outside lovers" (even if these "lovers" have been invented to explain what are genuinely irregular periods).

WOMEN AND MENSTRUAL SEX

In addition to fears of sickness and "tying," other reasons lead people to avoid sex during menstruation. Taboos give women a justification for refusing to allow men to "climb pon belly," whether disinterest in sex stems from the cyclical changes that can make penetration painful or from other factors, such as fatigue, messiness (wash is women's work), or boredom with a man's technique. Taboos also protect women, "open" from the "heat" and "looseness" menstruating entails, from "catching up draft" and "taking up cold."[20]

But even menstruating women may need "the work." Prostitutes can supposedly stop their periods by drinking laundry bluing diluted in water or by inserting it vaginally when they "see the blood." It seems that bluing whitens the blood of the menses as it bleaches stains from clothing. The belief that women put bluing in their vaginas to "sick" men probably exists as an extension of this: even "clear" (light colored) menses must carry contaminating things and may still be able to compel action. Unmarked—not reddish—it might gain entrance to the "belly" of a man with his guard down. This belief reveals, as do most beliefs pertaining to menstruation, the prominent male fear that women will abuse their trust.

The violation of another's autonomy through deceit and the reliance on magic or "unnatural" (and therefore sinful) means makes a deed "unclean." Because of the dual nature of the word, calling menstruating women "unclean" mystifies women's power and at the same time shames them. It moves attention away from their "natural" procreative abilities to the fact that menstrual blood emanates from their lower regions, where waste leaves. It associates menstrual blood with dirt (a very temporal kind of "pollution") and so lowers women's self-esteem, highlighting women's "nasty" state and "trickify," antisocial character. Rather than celebrating the positive aspects of their powers, it associates them with those "unclean" people who deal with "black magic."

WHY WOMEN SUPPORT MENSTRUAL TABOOS

Fearing women's power (and intention) to "tie," men promote taboos that keep menstruants away from their food. This requires the collusion of women, and collude they do—where they see the benefit. A shopkeeper would not close shop, nor would a woman with no one to help cook put away her pot. Taboos can easily be broken because people cannot always know who is menstruating. People do not advertise their cycles. Also, malnutrition, conception, lactation, depression, and other conditions can suppress ovulation. Regular, four-week periods are far from inevitable.

Miss Reeny laughed when asked if menstruating bothered women: "If anything, they glad to see it. Means they can left from fireside." The ban on cooking during menstruation allows women a period of rest from this chore while also attesting to women's inherent power. Rural Jamaicans do not say that menstruation brings relief by confirming non-pregnancy. Nor do they dwell on cyclic bodily irritations. Women do have aches, as folk knowledge shows: marigold (*Bidens reptans*) tea eases cramps and sinkle bible (*Aloe vera*) tea or a drink made by soaking its scrapings in water eases nausea and other small "belly" troubles. But Jamaican women do not think about dysmenorrhea until reminded and even then not much unless they experience unusually severe discomfort. Instead, they think about the pleasures and drawbacks which accompany being "unclean."

As noted in regard to sex, menstrual taboos have social uses beyond those that stem directly from the ethnophysiological ideas and the suspicion of "bad mind" in others. Old women can exercise power over younger ones by demanding they submit to the taboos. The high status that post-menopausal women enjoy rests, in part, on their "cleanliness," which they highlight by emphasizing the "uncleanliness" of young women who might otherwise usurp their positions. Moreover, by keeping girls ignorant of all but the barest details of menstruation, older women invest it with the sacredness that accompanies secrecy, making knowledge of it a valuable tool for female bonding.[21]

Women make use of the terror their vaginas and vaginal secretions inspire in other ways, too. A woman stepped over a pan of food and exposed it (and its owner, her brother) to the "unclean" power emanating from her vagina, rendering it unhealthy (not to mention potentially obligating), and sending a definitely aggressive message to him (he did not eat it).[22]

By making men aware of the threat inherent in menstrual blood, women try to reduce the chances of their men taking food (and sex) from unknown women who might steal them away by "tying" them. Even without the blood and for reasons stated, food-sharing symbolizes relatedness. A woman sharing food with an unrelated man indicates the likelihood of intimacy. Men expect to give women something useful in exchange for cooking and sexual services; still, women can add blood to ensure that this happens. It is women's hope that the fear of this will keep their men coming home for dinner and keep them from readily creating new relationships (and so incurring "outside" financial obligations) by sharing a "next woman's" food. Ideally, the fear of menstrual "uncleanliness" helps keep a man's money flowing to his regular conjugal partner.

Women have a vested interest in male beliefs in their power for it promises to help them control and "hold onto" their men. Talk of the danger of menstruation mobilizes the male anxieties mentioned earlier and so promotes the female ideal of male sexual and financial fidelity; the threat of "tying" should work like the threat of menstrual irregularity that helps keep women faithful. But the structural function that menstrual symbolism should serve in advancing conjugal stability and so ensuring the continuity of resource allocation is undermined by other cultural factors such as the expectation (upon which male reputations depend) that men have many lovers.

While they may not be able to stop adultery, women at least can lower the social standings of their competitors through gossip about "nastiness" and "bad habits." They can try to ensure that their rivals be excluded from female reciprocity networks and social circles by convincing members that these rivals are dangerous and will try to usurp their men. Attempting to protect their interests and manipulate social relations, women use menstrual rhetoric against each other. In ruining others' reputations, women represent themselves as morally upstanding and respectable; they make the claim that, unlike the maligned rivals, they pose no threat to other women and so are worthy of social support.

In using talk of "unclean" female power to control members of their own gender group and gain status women unwittingly participate in a system of oppression and male dominance that limits their authority and leads them to consider "tying" men to begin with.[23] But this dimension of menstrual discourse generally remains unseen, overshadowed by the more immediate and practical benefits that menstrual taboos bring women and also by the psychological value of the belief in female power.

Women's talk of their power can fuel a sense of independence from men similar to that which, according to Brody (1985), talk of reproductive autonomy promotes. Women's support of menstrual taboos perpetuate similar "ideas of self-management and autonomy" that substantiate women's "collective self-representation

(Brody 1985: 176)" as powerful social actors who are, in certain circumstances and to a certain degree, able to control their lives.

CONCLUDING REMARKS

The menstruant's power flows from traditional Jamaican ethnophysiological understandings about the role of blood, especially in relation to reproduction and kinship. It also involves blood's internal cleansing function as well as traditional notions about others' "bad minds" and their tendency to use black magic for selfish reasons. The fruition of an integrated approach to menstruation—one that investigates both traditional understandings of the physiological processes behind menstruation and the taboos that surround it, instead of focusing only on one of these —has been demonstrated, as the deeper meaning of menstrual "uncleanliness" and the mechanisms by which menstrual blood endangers have been exposed.

As I have shown, Jamaican menstrual taboos involve more than simple hygienic fears. Traditional Jamaican explanatory models for sickness involve things that modern medical models (and many U.S. folk-models) fail to consider. More importantly, for traditional Jamaicans "cleanliness" is not just a temporal or "natural" physical matter; its moral dimensions are paramount in certain contexts.

The traditional Jamaican cultural construction of menstrual symbolism entails much more than temporal or "matter out of place" pollution. The polluting, "unclean" state of a menstruant involves her "evilous" potential to "tie" and so to take advantage of her spouse. The blood flowing periodically from her "tube" is supposed to flow; menstruation signals and brings good health to women.

Matter such as menstrual blood, vaginal secretions, and breast milk continually moves in and out of women's bodies. While one may exert some (admittedly context dependent) control over certain expulsions and penetrations (such as urination, "discharge" or orgasm, eating, or genital intercourse), women have no power over vaginal and breast secretions. The female body is inherently and perpetually leaky and the perception of what leaks as "matter out of place" seems to take the male body as its point of "normal" reference. It also seems to assume that all other cultures do so too.

Menstrual blood is welcome in traditional Jamaica and menstruation is considered healthy. The same is true in other cultural contexts (cf. Browner 1985; Newman 1985: 15; Skultans 1988). In the Jamaican case and, as I have suggested, in possibly many others, menstrual blood cleanses the body and is clean itself but the semen it carries is rotten and "dirty." However, the blood becomes "unclean" and polluting, in two senses, when used to "tie." Firstly, menstrual blood is indeed "matter out of place" when in a man's "belly." Secondly, and more importantly, it becomes "unclean" when used for coercive purposes.

"Tying" is an "unclean" deed; "uncleanliness" here refers directly to black magic and immorality. While "natural" ties and obligations are fine and generally desirable (indeed, social adulthood cannot be attained without them), "ties" created through deceit are evil and "unclean." The essence of traditional Jamaican menstrual symbolism revolves around moral—not simple temporal—pollution.

It is "Jamaica style" to not "talk straight." Words with double meanings are favored because they offer protection: ambiguity enables a speaker to extract his or herself from uncomfortable situations by denying a listener's interpretation. This is why menstrual taboos are discussed through the idiom of "uncleanliness"—of simple, mundane hygiene concerns.

Especially when speech play is culturally encouraged, care must be taken so that the meanings that hide beneath the literal surface of discourse do not go unheeded. In Jamaica, if a listener has a "deep" understanding of "unclean's" meaning (as all Jamaicans do) s/he can infer concerns over "evilousness." Those insufficiently familiar with traditional Jamaican culture will assume that the blood itself is dirty. But, as all Jamaicans know, menstrual blood is a purifying agent and only its use in black magic and its contaminants—semen—are unclean.

ACKNOWLEDGEMENTS

Research for this essay was carried out under the guidance of F.G. Baily, to whom I owe great thanks. I am also indebted to William Wedenoja, Mark Nichter, and Yossela Moyle.

NOTES

1. While some studies of menstrual taboos take cultural beliefs about the value of having children into account, none explore the effects of ideas about how kin are constituted.
2. Classic works on Jamaica include those by Clarke (1957), Beckwith (1929), Henriques (1963), and Kerr (1952). A collection of life histories is found in H. Smith, (1986), and health and healing are discussed by Wedenoja (1989) and Laguerre (1987). Other pertinent works include those by Foner (1973), Hudson and Seylor (1989), Seaga (1969), and Wilson (1973).
3. Census data from 1982 indicates that while 43% of Jamaica's adult population is married, 33% of adults are cohabiting or in "visiting" unions and 24% are not involved with a partner (STATIN 1989: 85). However, my project does not concern widows or "independent" women uninterested in forming unions, for they would not "tie." Also, it deals only with the poor, who are much less likely than the rich to marry (married people are tied by law and are less likely to resort to magic). For these reasons, Brody's figures are preferred over census data.
4. In addition to Henry and Wilson (1975), see Justus (1981), Massiah (1986), Mohammed and Shepherd (1988), Roberts and Sinclair (1978), and Senior (1991) regarding women's status in the West Indies.
5. The "mind," located near the heart, provides motivations and generates emotions. It is the seat of volition. Factual matters like "maths" are dealt with by the brain.
6. Although I use "food" to mean all comestibles, to Jamaicans the word refers only to tubers and belly-filling starches; other edibles have more specific names, such as "meat-kind" and "salting."
7. The poisons that cause sexually transmitted diseases are sometimes called "germs" (see Mitchell 1983: 843), but in this paper "germs" refers to gametes or germ cells: eggs and sperm. (Mitchell's informants probably linked venereal disease transmission to the transfer of germ cells themselves.)
8. Women take care of primary health needs in many if not most societies (see McClain 1989). The tendency for women's ethnophysiological understandings to be modeled on their own bodies needs further exploration, as do the effects this has on the household production of health.
9. In a similar fashion, a group of men attributed a (verified) rise in throat cancer to an increasing "slackness" with regard to oral sex (see notes twelve, fourteen, and sixteen). The associations seen between insecticide and fertilizer and "dirty" blood and cancer (see "CLEANLINESS") also demonstrate the creative ways that traditional understandings get used to explain how certain illnesses occur and also to express opinions regarding modernization.
10. Although sex can be recreational, the possibility of procreating should be inherent in the act. Because of this (and for a few other reasons not relevant here) non-genital sex (and contraception) can bring shame. See notes twelve, fourteen, and sixteen.

11. The woman telling me this had reason to look for negative qualities in the passer-by. Some years ago, the two women had quarrelled regarding the ownership of some coconut trees. They have never resolved their differences.

12. Oral sex is overtly non-procreative and so it is shameful. I pointed out in note ten that sex can be recreational as long as the process of procreation is not hindered. But with oral sex, the "white" blood lost has almost no chance of finding the right "tube" and becoming a baby. All who give oral sex are called "cannibals"; they are antisocial beings who invert the preferred order by "eating" potential children.

13. No woman I knew admitted to doing this herself and all the information I have is hearsay. Whether or not "tying" occurs often or at all, its island-wide cultural salience and the fear that it inspires make it "real" enough to warrant discussion.

14. Ingested female "discharge" can obligate just like menstrual blood. A man performing oral sex (to "eat under the two-legged table") can eat his lover's discharged egg and incorporate it into his own body. Having no womb, he cannot "grow" it into a baby. He could, however, mesh with what would have been his lover's child, thus becoming like her son (as he would if he ingested her menstrual blood). So cunnilingus can "tie man like donkey" just as menstrual magic can. Men use this knowledge (and also point to the danger of ingesting another's waste) to promote genital sex.

15. These conditions include poor job prospects and also the pressures mothers place on grown sons for their loyalty and resources. But, moreover, men are brought up by women who expect them to be—and so treat them as—"irresponsible." Social learning leaves men less than fully capable of responsible action.

16. Semen is a relatively weak obligating substance because father/child ties are never as highly charged as mother/child relations. Women can perform fellatio with minimal fear of being "tied" by semen. Even so, many men say that they do not desire it. They belittle the women who give oral sex, calling them "vampires" because they suck blood, and "dirty" because their bodies are full of un-used, rotting semen (taken in vaginally excess semen runs out). "Vampires" must take "wash-out" extra-frequently to avoid sickness.

17. Although kin are separate and stand as individuals, their substance remains conjoined conceptually. Rozin and Nemeroff note that this continuing "continuity of substance" stems from a history of past contact, through a common ancestor. They argue that "kinship loyalty and affection is construable as an instance of contagion"—an instantiation of the cognitive style that contagious magic is based on (1990: 221, 219).

18. The data presented in this paper is well-suited for psychological analyses. For instance, the Oedipal Complex may be implicated in "tying" and the anxiety associated with it, as menstrual "tying" actually creates a kind of mother/son link between lovers. Repressed resentment over obligations to kin may also surface in the fear of "tying." But, given the scope of this paper, a full exploration of the psychological themes that suggest themselves must wait.

19. In avoiding intercourse with menstruants men also avoid the sight of blood on their penises, which can suggest castration. This terrifies men who, lacking other avenues to manhood because of cultural and economic barriers, locate their very masculinity and social adulthood in their genitals.

20. People abstaining from sex during menstruation avoid subjecting themselves to culturally salient "raw" odors, associated with decay and death. Sexual sweat and effluvia can be quite redolent—especially in the heat of the day or during or just prior to a woman's menstrual period (female villagers report that their body odors become "higher" then). People believe that the pungency of sex lingers to reveal their "business." During menstruation, the stench of sweat and sex would be "higher," "renker," and even more likely to bring shame. The maintenance of "respect" necessitates sexual abstinence during this period.

21. Mothers generally tell daughters little or nothing about menstruation before it happens, nor do they inform them about sex. MacCormack and Draper note that "a fecund young woman moves into a position to challenge the very status of her mother," who trys to hold onto power by witholding information (1987: 153).

22. The following tale makes clear the dangers associated with things the vagina harbors. A robbery occurred in which several "idlers" stole a large amount of cash from a woman who worked "in foreign" and had returned home to the village for a visit. One of the young thieves gave a big wad of bills to a lover, who decided to take a bus to Kingston. She hid the money inside her vagina, or so the story goes. On a tip, the police stopped the bus, took her in for questioning, stripped and searched

her. Luckily, they found and confiscated the money. Had they not, each dollar spent would endanger the life and the "mind" of the one who accepted it, due to where it was stashed.

For similar reasons, people were aghast at a tabloid account of a corporation where bosses searched women's vaginas for contraband in the canteen—a place where people must eat (*Weekend Enquirer* [Jamaica] 1989: 7). They worried over this and not the unfair and exploitative aspects of the practice.

23. Elsewhere (in preparation), I explicitly deal with the issue of female kin networks and the links between female solidarity and intergender tension and segregation.

REFRENCES CITED

Bettelheim, B.
   1962 [1954] Symbolic Wounds: Puberty Rites and the Envious Male. New York: Collier Books.
Beckwith, M.
   1929   Black Roadways. Chapel Hill: University of North Carolina Press.
Bock, P.K.
   1967   Love Magic, Menstrual Taboos, and the Facts of Geography. American Anthropologist 69(2):213-216.
Brody, E.
   1985   Everyday Knowledge of Jamaican Women. *In* Women's Medicine: A Cross-Cultural Study of Indigenous Fertility Regulation. L.F. Newman, ed. Pp.161-178. New Jersey: Rutgers University Press.
   1981   Sex, Contraception, and Motherhood in Jamaica. Cambridge: Harvard University Press.
Browner, C.H.
   1985   Traditional Techniques for Diagnosis, Treatment, and Control of Pregnancy in Cali, Colombia. *In* Women's Medicine: A Cross-Cultural Study of Indigenous Fertility Regulation. L.F. Newman, ed. Pp.99-123. New Jersey: Rutgers University Press.
Buckley, T. and Gottlieb, A., eds.
   1988   Blood Magic: The Anthropology of Menstruation. Los Angeles: University of California Press.
Chodorow, N.
   1978   The Reproduction of Mothering: Psychoanalysis and the Sociology of Gender. Los Angeles: University of California Press.
Clarke, E.
   1957   My Mother Who Fathered Me: A Study of the Family in Three Selected Communities in Jamaica. Boston: George Allen and Unwin.
Cohen, Y.
   1955   Character Formation and Social Structure in a Jamaican Community. Psychiatry 18:275-296.
Delaney, J.; Lupton, M.J.; Toth, E.
   1976   The Curse: A Cultural History of Menstruation. New York: E. P. Dutton and Company.
Douglas, M.
   1975   Couvade and Menstruation. *In* Implicit Meanings. Pp.60-72. Boston: Routledge and Degan Paul.
Eilberg-Schwartz, H.
   1990   The Savage in Judaism—An Anthropology of Israelite Religion and Ancient Judaism. Bloomington: Indiana University Press.
Farmer, P.
   1988   Bad Blood, Spoiled Milk: Bodily Fluids as Moral Barometers in Rural Haiti. American Ethnologist 15(1):62-83.
Freilich, M.
   1968   Sex, Secrets, and Systems. *In* The Family in the Caribbean. Gerber, S., ed. Pp.47-62. Puerto Rico: Institute of Caribbean Studies.
Foner, N.
   1973   Status and Power in Rural Jamaica: A Study of Educational and Political Change. New York: Teacher's College Press.

Foster, G.
  1988   The Validating Role of Humoral Theory in Traditional Spanish-American Therapeutics. American Ethnologist 15(1):120-135.
Gleaner (Kingston).
  1988 May 4, How AIDS Spreads in Jamaica. p.1.
Gregor, T.
  1990   Male Dominance and Sexual Coercion. *In* Cultural Psychology—Essays on Comparative Human Development. Stigler, J.W., Shweder, R.A., and Herdt, G., eds. Pp.477-495. New York: Cambridge University Press.
Golub, S., ed.
  1985   Lifting the Curse of Menstruation: A Feminist Appraisal of the Influence of Menstruation on Women's Lives. New York: Harrington Park Press.
Henriques, F.
  1963   Family and Colour in Jamaica. London: Macgibbon and Kee.
Henry, F., and Wilson, P.
  1979   The Status of Women in Caribbean Societies: an Overview. Social and Economic Studies 24(2):165-198.
Hudson, R.A., and Seyler, D.J.
  1989   Jamaica. *In* Islands of the Commonwealth Caribbean: a Regional Study. Medita, S.W., and Hanratty, D.M., eds. Pp.43-160. Washington D.C.: Department of the Army.
Justus, J.B.
  1981   Women's Role in West Indian Society. *In* The Black Woman Cross-Culturally. Steady, F.C., ed. Pp.431-450. Cambridge: Schenkman Publishing Co.
Kerr, M.
  1963   Personality and Conflict in Jamaica. London: Willmer Brothers & Haram Limited.
Laguerre, M.
  1987   Afro-Caribbean Folk Medicine. South Hadley: Bergin and Garvey Publishers, Inc.
Lawrence, D.L.
  1988   Menstrual Politics: Women and Pigs in Rural Portugal. *In* Blood Magic. Buckley, T. and Gottlieb, A, eds. Pp.117-136. Los Angeles: University of California Press.
Laws, S.; Hay, V.; Eagan, A.
  1985   Seeing Red: The Politics of Premenstrual Tension. London: Hutchinson and Company.
Lindenbaum, S.
  1972   Sorcerers, Ghosts, and Polluting Women. Ethnology 11:241-253.
MacCormack, C.P.
  1985   Lay Concepts Affecting Utilization of Family Planning Services in Jamaica. Journal of Tropical Medicine and Hygiene 88:281-285.
MacCormack, C.P. and Draper, A.
  1987   Social and Cognitive Aspects of Female Sexuality in Jamaica. *In* The Cultural Construction of Sexuality. Caplan, P., ed. Pp.143-161. New York: Tavistock Publications.
Martin, E.
  1991   Toward an Anthropology of Immunology: The Body as Nation State. Medical Anthropology Quarterly 4(4):410-426.
  1987   The Woman in the Body: A Cultural Analysis of Reproduction. Boston: Beacon Press.
Massiah, J., ed.
  1986   Women in the Caribbean. Social and Economic Studies (special issues) 35(2,3).
McClain, C.S., ed.
  1989   Women as Healers—Cross-cultural Perspectives. New Brunswick: Rutgers University Press.
Meigs, A.S.
  1987   Blood Kin and Food Kin. *In* Conformity and Conflict: Readings in Cultural Anthropology. Spradley, J.P. and McCurdy, D.W., eds. Pp.117-124. Boston: Little, Brown and Company.
Mitchell, F.
  1983   Popular Medical Concepts in Jamaica and Their Impact on Drug Use. The Western Journal of Medicine 139:841-847.
Mohammed, P. and Shepherd, C., eds.
  1988   Gender in Caribbean Development. Mona: University of the West Indies Women and Development Studies Project.

Montgomery, R.E.
  1974 A Cross Cultural Study of Menstruation, Menstrual Taboos, and Related Social Variables. Ethos 2:137-170.
Newman, L.F., ed.
  1985 Women's Medicine: A Cross-Cultural Study of Indigenous Fertility Regulation. New Jersey: Rutgers University Press.
Olesen, V. and Woods, N.F., eds.
  1986 Culture, Society, and Menstruation. San Francisco: Hemisphere Publishing Corporation.
Paige, K.E. and Paige, J.M.
  1981 The Politics of Reproductive Ritual. Berkeley: University of California Press.
Powell, D. and Jackson, J., eds.
  1988 Young Adult Reproductive Survey. Kingston: National Family Planning Board.
Roberts, G. and Sinclair, S.
  1978 Women in Jamaica. New York: KTO Press.
Rozin, P. and Nemeroff, C.
  1990 The Laws of Sympathetic Magic. *In* Cultural Psychology: Essays on Comparative Human Development. Stigler, J.W., Shweder, R.A., and Herdt, G., eds. Pp.205-232. New York: Cambridge University Press.
Seaga, E.
  1969 Revival Cults in Jamaica. Jamaica Journal 3(2):3-15.
Senior, O.
  1991 Working Miracles: Women's Lives in the English-Speaking Caribbean. Cave Hill, Barbados: Institute of Social and Economic Research (published in association with Indiana University Press).
Skultans, V.
  1988 Menstrual Symbolism in South Wales. *In* Blood Magic. Buckley, T. and Gottlieb, A, eds. Pp.137-160. Los Angeles: University of California Press.
Smith, H.F., ed.
  1986 Lionheart Gal: Life Stories of Jamaican Women. London: The Women's Press.
Smith, R.T.
  1988 Kinship and Class in the West Indies. Cambridge: Cambridge University Press.
Snow, L.F.
  1974 Folk Medical Beliefs and Their Implications for Care of Patients—A Review Based on Studies Among Black Americans. Annals of Internal Medicine 81(1):82-96.
Snowden, R. and Christian, B.
  1983 Patterns and Perceptions of Menstruation. New York: St. Martin's Press.
Sobo, E.J.
      One Blood: The Jamaican Body. Albany: State University of New York Press. N.d. In press. Abortion Traditions in Rural Jamaica. N.d. In preparation.
  1990 The Jamaican Body: A Study of the Use of Traditional Health Beliefs. Ph.D. diss., University of California at San Diego.
STATIN (Statistical Institute of Jamaica).
  1989 Statistical Yearbook of Jamaica 1989. Kingston: Statistical Institute of Jamaica.
STATIN.
  1982 Census. (Unpublished Portland information.)
Stephens, W.N.
  1967 [1961] A Cross-Cultural Study of Menstrual Taboos. *In* Cross Cultural Approaches. Ford, C.S., ed. New Haven: HRAF Press.
Taylor, C.
  1992 The Harp That Plays By Itself. This volume.
  1988 The Concept of Flow in Rwandan Popular Medicine. Social Science and Medicine 27(12):1343-1348.
Wedenoja, W.
  1989 Mothering and the Practice of 'Balm' in Jamaica. *In* Women as Healers: Cross-Cultural Perspectives. McClain, C.S., ed. Pp.76-97. New Brunswick: Rutgers University Press.
Weekend Enquirer (Jamaica).
  1989 May 5-7, Spread yu legs, mek a si if yu hide anyt'ing up de!! P.7.

Weigle, M.
  1989   Creation and Procreation. Philadelphia: University of Pennsylvania Press.
Wilson, P.J.
  1973   Crab Antics. New Haven: Yale University Press.
Wright, A.
  1982   Attitudes Toward Childbearing and Menstruation Among the Navajo. *In* Anthropology of
          Human Birth. Kay, M.S., ed. Pp.377-394. Philadelphia: F.A. Davis Company,
Young, F. and Bacdayan, A.
  1965   Menstrual Taboos and Social Rigidity. Ethnology 4:225-241.

The Harp that Plays by Itself

Christopher C. Taylor

INTRODUCTION

In the past several decades the discipline of anthropology has proliferated in a wide variety of directions and given birth to numerous subfields, including political, economic, symbolic, and medical anthropology. As a further corollary to this trend, each of these subfields has developed a characteristic vocabulary, a specific body of theory, and an empirical base which each considers its special province of intellectual concern. The labor of anthropology has become progressively more subdivided into smaller and smaller tasks whose accomplishment has become the responsibility of increasingly more specialized researchers. In this respect the production of anthropological discourse has come to resemble activity in every other productive sphere in capitalist society. Although the increasing division of anthropological labor and its "rationalization" (Weber 1958) have usually been justified in the name of greater efficiency, it is debatable whether this is a sign of intellectual ferment or merely the reflection of a fragmentary process that has characterized the quasi-entirety of Western culture and history (cf. Lukacs 1960 [1922]; Jameson 1981).

In sharp contrast to this atomistic tendency in the discipline, some studies have sought to transcend the boundaries separating anthropological subfields. These studies often explicitly, and justifiably, claim Marcel Mauss as an intellectual forebear, finding in his notion of the "total social phenomenon" (1967 [1925]: 1) inspiration for concepts such as "holism" (Dumont 1980) and "holographic symbolism" (Wagner 1986). Many neo-Marxist researchers have followed in this "holistic" vein (cf. Godelier 1986), realizing that Marx's analysis of the commodity (1977 [1867]) as the key to understanding capitalist society, presaged Mauss's insight into the nature of the gift. Although Marx concentrated his attention on the question of social relations while Mauss was more concerned with the question of cultural meanings, Marx did not neglect the question of meaning. This is clear in his notion of "commodity fetishism" (ibid. 178–79). Capitalist social relations, by turning human labor into a thing (commodity), transformed things (commodities) into entities endowed with animate powers. "Commodity fetishism" bears magico-religious significance as well as economic significance. In a sense, it is the analogical obverse of the concept of *hau* (Mauss 1967: 8–10). Since *hau* implies the persisting recognition of the producer in the object produced, it represents human labor in its non-alienated state.

CHRISTOPHER C. TAYLOR is an Assistant Professor in the Anthropology Department at the University of Alabama at Birmingham. His research interests include ethnomedicine, political economy, and AIDS. He has done fieldwork in Rwanda and in rural France.

Meaning-oriented anthropologists inspired by Marx have made frequent use of his concept of "commodity fetishism." For example, M. Taussig (1977), shows that for certain South American peasants, their perceptions of the workings of the cash economy were colored by their religious beliefs concerning the nature of evil. Enrichment for them became tantamount to renouncing morality and making a pact with the devil by treating money as if it were a human being—baptizing it in a religious service. In a longer work (1980), this same author emphasizes the radical division between perceiving the world through the lens of "use value" versus perceiving it through the lens of "exchange value" (Taussig 1980: 18). While he links pre-capitalist societies to "use value" perceptions—the social idea of "organic unity between persons and their products" (Taussig 1980: 38)—he links capitalist societies to "exchange value" perceptions—the social principle whereby human relations become a function of relations between things.

Despite the importance of Taussig's work as a source of inspiration to the present study, the division between "use value" and "exchange value" is rarely as neat and unproblematic in actual social practice as Taussig's studies intimate. There are probably no societies in the world based purely upon "use value" perceptions. Building a sociological typology on this distinction is thus somewhat crude. Nevertheless, in the context of a world where pre-colonial exchange paradigms continue to co-exist with those of the global market, there is merit in attempting to synthesize the insights of Marx and Mauss as Taussig has done. But a more successful attempt at this synthesis is that of Chris Gregory (1982), who demonstrates that both gifts and commodities with different cultural meanings circulate within the confines of a single but not atypical Melanesian society. Furthermore, gifts can sometimes be converted into commodities and commodities into gifts (Gregory 1982). The two concepts thus lie at opposite poles of a continuum, which, in contrast to Taussig's model does not imply strict separation between use value and exchange value.

Gregory's findings can be fruitfully applied to my own research on healing in Rwanda, for it is clear that people there are having to confront the demands and opportunities of the commodity world. People buy used American clothing, they ride in Japanese vehicles, and they raise coffee and tea for sale on the world market. Despite this, it is also clear that the concept of the gift remains a core concept in Rwandan culture. The term for man in Kinyarwanda, *umugabo*, as well as the term for manliness, *ubugabo*, are both derived from the root verb, *kugaba*, whose primary meaning is "to give" (Jacob 1984, vol. 1: 308). The quality of being a man, therefore, is first and foremost a social quality, the capacity to engage an "other" in a reciprocal relation. This is possibly the most compelling evidence that Rwandan indigenous categories reflect the concept of the gift as first propounded by Mauss, and later elaborated by Lévi-Strauss (1947) and Gregory.

In employing the gift/commodity distinction, I compare two different *logics* of production and exchange. If gifts and commodities can co-exist in the same society, gift strategies and commodity strategies can surely co-exist within the same individual psyche. When one conceptualizes a relation according to "gift logic," one is motivated by the ideal of establishing enduring reciprocal relations with others through the intermediary of things; when one is operating according to "commodity logic," one acts to acquire money and things through the intermediary of people. In actual practice, however, one set of values predominates over, but seldom excludes the opposing set of values. Moreover, in a society such as Rwanda where capitalist cultural values are beginning to be internalized, ambiguity between gift notions and commodity notions has become accentuated.

Gift logic incorporates notions of reciprocity and redistribution. Ideally, persons and things are exchanged in relatively continuous patterns. In Rwanda, this ideal of continuity receives expression through the exchange of liquid aliments (and bodily fluids). Such liquids both embody and represent the value of continuity; in that sense they are "symbols that stand for themselves" (Wagner 1986), in sharp contrast to money—the quintessential commodity—which represents but does not embody value (Wagner 1988).

Gift and commodity logic also differ with regard to social and biological reproduction. Reproducing the social relations of a commodity economy is contingent upon control over the means of production. Reproducing social relations in a gift economy, on the other hand, is contingent upon control over the means of consumption, for people produce each other through the gift of things which they consume. Gregory refers to this process as "consumptive production" (Gregory 1982: 71, 101). Food is both substance and symbol in a gift economy; it is nourishment as well as a meaningful gift. It is thus not surprising to find food employed as a central symbol in issues related to social and biological reproduction. Furthermore, while in a gift economy there is a tendency to convert wealth into social relationships, in a commodity economy there is a tendency to accumulate wealth in the abstract or objectified form of money.

Problems arise, however, when the choice between gift or commodity logic is ambiguous. In such instances if a person chooses to act in accordance with gift logic, he may lose materially; if he chooses to act in consistency with commodity logic, he runs the risk of undermining a social relation. Usually this dilemma is avoided because most social interactions contain "metamessages" (Bateson 1972) which enable social actors to correctly situate themselves at the same discursive level as their interlocutors. "Schizophrenogenic" (Bateson 1972) conditions result when a person is unable to perceive or properly respond to these "metamessages." This inability may be of a psychological nature and rooted in childhood experience, but "metamessages," I maintain, can also be misconstrued when the socio-historical context is contradictory, when the implicit rules and assumptions of interaction are in a state of flux (Sapir 1932: 521). If left unresolved, such situations may contribute to social conflict and illness.

In this paper, I explore concepts of pathology in local Rwandan therapies and discuss the central role of fluids in these concepts and in other aspects of social life. Following in the "holistic" tradition, I show that therapeutic concepts reflect religious, moral, and economic concerns. First, I consider these notions in early Rwandan society, and then in relation to the institution of divine kingship (which persisted in its pre-Christian form until 1931). Next, I briefly examine how fluids are conceptualized today. Finally, I consider the expression of this symbolism in two different modes of present day Rwandan popular healing: one which is a therapy of accusation, and another, of more recent origin, which is a therapy of confession practiced by a healer who calls himself "Nanga y'ivuza" ("the harp that plays by itself").

EARLY RWANDAN SOCIETY

Gift logic principles were more accentuated in pre-colonial and early colonial Rwandan society than they are today. These principles surface in Rwandan representations of personhood and hierarchy.

In the earlier ethnographic literature, Rwandan society was described (cf. Maquet 1954) as a rigid, castelike hierarchy, in which the pastoralist Tutsi minority (14% of the population) dominated Hutu cultivators (85%) and a small number of autochthonous Twa (1%). This situation led to violence in 1959–62, when the Hutu majority overthrew Tutsi dominance and the Tutsi monarchy. Although it is probable that the colonial strategy of indirect rule rigidified ethnic boundaries between Tutsi and Hutu and exacerbated inequalities between the two groups (cf. Newbury 1988), in central Rwanda the ethnic categories had validity as "social constructs" even before the arrival of colonialists.

In consistency with Gregory's observations concerning consumption, it should be emphasized that one core aspect of the social construction of ethnic identity concerned diet. In early Rwanda, the most prestigious diet consisted of liquid aliments. Part of the Tutsi claim to superiority rested upon the ability to drink liquid aliments rather than eat solid foods requiring cooking (de Heusch 1985: 115), for the Tutsi diet consisted largely of milk, mead, and honeyed sorghum beer. Some even claimed that they never ate solid foods (Maquet 1954: 31) while those who did, ate them with a sense of shame and behind closed doors. The agricultural Hutu ate mostly the solid foodstuffs they cultivated. They had less access to milk and honeyed beer, though many were able to consume lesser grades of beer and some milk, because as clients (*abagaragu*), they had received cows from Tutsi patrons (*abashebuja*). The Twa were the least favored of all in terms of access to liquid aliments. Although their diet was probably the most varied of the three groups, they neither possessed cattle, nor raised the crops necessary to make beer, for most of them earned their livelihood from pottery making, the least respected profession.

This hierarchy of consumption was also a hierarchy of production. The most esteemed labor was that which least involved the earth, pastoral labor, for the earth was associated with impurity. The least respected labor was that which directly involved the earth, pottery-making. The labor of the Hutu was midway between these extremes, for although they worked the earth, they worked it with tools, rather than directly with their hands.

According to a Rwandan legend (Smith 1975: 39), this state of affairs was justified by the different behaviors with respect to milk of the three brothers, Gatutsi, Gahutu, and Gatwa, sons of the mythical Rwandan king, Gihanga. Gihanga gave each of the brothers a pot of milk and told him to guard it during the night. But Gatwa became thirsty and drank his pot of milk. Gahutu became drowsy and in dozing off, spilled some of the contents of his pot. Only Gatutsi succeeded in keeping a full pot of milk until the next morning. For this reason, Gihanga decreed that Gatutsi should possess cattle and enjoy the right to rule. Gahutu would only be able to procure cattle as a gift from his brother, Gatutsi, in exchange for his labor. As for Gatwa, he would never possess cattle; alternate periods of gluttony and starvation were to be his lot.

Cattle and milk were important gifts in virtually every Rwandan rite of passage:

clientship, blood brotherhood, and marriage. One custom associated with marriage, which has completely disappeared, was called *kwambika umwishywa* (which means "to dress the bride with the flower, *umwishywa*"). Until the 1940s or '50s, the groom would adorn the bride with *umwishywa* (*Momoridica foetida*), a plant that was also used in the royal rituals. *Umwishywa* was clearly associated with fertility fluids, for its flowers are white and its small gourd-like fruit, at maturity, are red. In the marriage ceremony, the husband placed a garland of *umwishywa* around the bride's head, *kwambika umwishywa*. Then he expectorated a mixture of milk mixed with herbs either in her face or between her breasts, *gucira imbazi* (Ndekezi n.d.: 62–63).

This action of adorning the bride, then spitting milk upon her, evoked the fertility powers associated with milk and *umwishywa* as two powerful images of surrogate semen—one bovine, the other botanical. With regard to the garland of *umwishywa*, this represented the bride's becoming contained within a ring of "semen," her husband's patrilineal group, the group to whom her reproductive potential was being transferred. With regard to the expectorated milk, this suggested the husband's potential semen, the seed that the bride would contain in order to produce new life. As a wife, a woman was both container and contained; she was the container of potential new life, but her capacity to reproduce was contained within a patrilineal group. Milk and *umwishywa* were appropriate symbols of the transformation from maiden to wife, for once the bride received her husband's semen, her body swelled like the gourdlike fruit of *umwishywa* and became as "flowing" as a lactating cow.

Even at the end of life, milk was valued as the ideal liquid gift. In the past, Rwandans administered cow's milk to their agonizing elderly relatives as a measure of euthanasia. The dying person's family took milk and poured it into his throat until he choked. The most compassionate manner of dying in Rwandan cultures was thus, being drowned in its most cherished liquid aliment.

THE RWANDAN KING

Until 1961, a king (*umwami*) ruled Rwanda; until 1931, he was non-Christian. One of the most important religious functions of pre-Christian kings involved ceremonially regulating the fluids of production, consumption, and fertility. The king was Imaana's (the Rwandan supreme deity) representative on earth and Imaana was conceptualized as "diffuse fecundating fluid" of celestial origin (d'Hertefelt and Coupez 1964: 460). The Rwandan king catalyzed the descent of Imaana to the earth. He was the ultimate guarantor of the fertility of cattle, women, and land. In times of drought, famine, epidemic, or epizootic, the king could be deposed or called upon to offer himself (or a close familial substitute) as a sacrificial victim (*umutabazi*), so that the shedding of his blood would conjure away collective peril. The *umwami* mediated between sky and earth. He received the celestial gift of fertility and passed it downward to his subjects. It was said that the king drank the milk milked by Imaana, while ordinary humanity drank the milk milked by the king (Kagame 1951: 53–55).

The beneficence of Imaana was conceptualized as milk, rain, and fertility. The king as the earthly avatar of Imaana received this beneficence and channelled it downward to the rest of humanity. He was the kingdom's most giving being. The king's body, as a focal point of the "flow" process, could be compared to a hollow conduit. In effect, celestial beneficence passed directly through the king and in some mythical representations, directly through his alimentary canal. A story which is sometimes told about Ruganzu Ndori, a legendary Rwandan king, illustrates this principle very clearly. Here, fertility is restored to the earth by first passing through the *umwami*'s digestive tract. The following is the legend as it was recounted to me in Rwanda in 1987:

Ruganzu Ndori was living in exile in the kingdom of Ndorwa, a kingdom neighboring Rwanda to the north. There he had taken refuge with his FZ (*nyirasenge*) who was married to a man from the region. In the meantime, because the Rwandan throne was occupied by an illegitimate usurper, Rwanda was experiencing numerous calamities. The crops were dying, the cows were not giving milk, and the women were becoming sterile. Ruganzu's paternal aunt encouraged him to return to Rwanda, retake the throne and save his people from catastrophe. Ruganzu agreed. But before setting forth on his voyage to Rwanda, his FZ gave him the seeds (*imbuto*) of several cultivated plants (sorghum, gourds, and others) to restart Rwandan cultures. While en route to Rwanda, Ruganzu Ndori came under attack. Fearing that the *imbuto* would be captured, he swallowed the seeds with a long draught of milk. Once he regained the Rwandan throne, he defecated the milk and seed mixture upon the ground and the land became productive once again. Since that time all Rwandan kings were said to be born clutching the seeds of the original *imbuto* in their hand.

Other inferences to be drawn from this legend concern the implicit and explicit associations linking the king to the productivity of the soil, to milk, prosperity, fertility, and continuity. Several of these symbolic associations inhere in the meanings of the Kinyarwanda verb, *kwama*, and in the Kirundi verb *kwāma* from which the noun, *umwami*, is derived (Vansina personal communication; de Lacger 1959: 83). (Kinyarwanda and Kirundi are dialects of a single language.) In Kinyarwanda, *kwama* means: "to be famous, to be known by everyone; to have done something for a long time and to continue to do it, to have a certain habitual comportment; to be prosperous or to live a long time" (Jacob 1984, vol. 1: 17). In Kirundi, *kwāma* means: "to bear fruit, to fructify, to be fertile; to always be; to make or do something without stopping" (Rodegem 1970: 5–6). According to J. Vansina (personal communication), *kwāma* also had a popular meaning, namely, "to lactate."

Another verb in Kinyarwanda and Kirundi, *gukama*, means "to milk." In several interlacustrine regions the terms *mukama*, from *gukama*, and *umwami*, from *kwama* or *kwāma*, were used as synonyms (Rodegem 1970: 209). In the nearby interlacustrine kingdom of Bunyoro, the king was called "Mukama." Kinyoro and Kinyarwanda have the same term, *gukama*, meaning "to milk." When the Bunyoro "Mukama" died, a man would ascend a ladder, pour milk onto the ground and say, "The milk is spilt; the king has been taken away!" (Beattie 1960: 28).

The terms *umwami* and *mukama* thus encompass several crucial concepts which are central to Rwandan symbolic thought: continuity, productivity, fertility, prosperity, and their metaphorization in the popular imagination as a flowing process, lactation. Nevertheless, the verb *gukama* in Kirundi and in Kinyarwanda has yet another meaning which gives a hint that embedded within these representations is their contrary. Sometimes *gukama* means "to dry up" (Rodegem 1970: 209). In other words, in early Rwandan society one could not "milk" the environment without running the risk of depleting it; one could not have "flow" without "blockage," for the two were inextricably conjoined. The person of the *umwami* and his college of ritual specialists had to assure that the sky's fecundating fluid fell in sufficient quantity, but without washing the kingdom away. They had to control "flow," but they could only do this by "blocking" it. Similarly, in his clientship relations the king possessed the power to enrich or to impoverish; he could bestow gifts or withhold them.

Nevertheless, the institution of kingship and its accompanying rituals partially dissimulated the king's "blockage" function. These depicted the king as a boundless giver, a defender of the principle of "flow" and an enemy of "blockage." Again the king's body was a focal point of this principle. Ritualists saw to it that his physiological processes were kept in motion, for every morning the king imbibed a milky liquid called *isubyo*, which was a powerful laxative (Bourgeois 1956: 173). While the ostensible purpose of this matinal libation was to purge the king's body of any impurity (*ishyano*) he might have contacted, the reasoning behind the custom goes deeper than that. The *umwami's* enemies were the antithesis of "flowing beings;" they were beings who blocked production, exchange, and fertility.

One of the king's responsibilities in pre-colonial Rwanda was to eliminate beings who lacked the capacity "to flow." Two such beings included girls who had reached child-bearing age and who lacked breasts, called *impenebere* (d'Hertefelt and Coupez 1964: 286), and girls who had reached child-bearing age and who had not yet menstruated, called *impa* (d'Hertefelt and Coupez 1964: 286). In both cases, these girls were put to death, for one lacked the capacity to produce the fertility fluid, milk, while the other lacked the capacity to produce the fertility fluid, blood, which according to Rwandan ideas of conception joins with semen to congeal into new life. Such girls, "blocked" in their capacity to reproduce, were thought to be potential sources of misfortune to the entire kingdom, for their aridity could cause the sky to refuse to give its fertilizing rain.

Finally, however, the ultimate "blocking being" in early Rwandan society was the king himself. He could withhold his generosity from any of his subjects. He thus embodied both "flow" and "blockage."

FLUIDS IN HEALTH, ILLNESS, LOVE, AND DEATH

Today fluid imagery continues to permeate Rwandan popular notions of physiology and sociality. While this imagery is enacted in practices associated with healing—just as it was once enacted in the rituals of kingship—it is never verbalized in any explicit way. "Flow/blockage" symbolism is situated beyond language in metaphor and beneath language in the body. It can be discerned in the discourse of patients and healers from any of Rwanda's three ethnic groups, though it is somewhat less prominent in the explanatory models of urban Rwandans influenced by Western biomedicine. In another paper (Taylor 1990) I show the persistence of "flow/blockage" imagery in the reasoning of urban women who are aware of AIDS but yet eschew condoms on the basis that the condom might become lodged in the vagina and cause illness or infertility.

In rural Rwanda, where most of my field research took place, fluids are important as bodily humors, as gifts, and as symbols. The most important bodily fluid in cases of sorcery or "poisoning" is blood (*amaraso*). Poisons attack the blood first.

Frequently, people say that they interrupt the flow of blood between the heart and the brain (cf. Habimana 1988). The heart (*umutima*) and the brain (*ubwonko*) are thought to work together in producing and maintaining consciousness. When Rwandans speak of "losing heart," they mean loss of consciousness. The heart is the seat of reason, volition, and desire; the brain aids the heart in this function. Blood is the organ of tactile sensibility. Blood coursing through the veins allows the heart and the brain to sense whether something that one touches is hot or cold, soft or hard.

Healers state that poisons (*amarozi*) diminish the total volume of blood in the body; poisons dehydrate the body, or they cause blood to exit abnormally from a bodily orifice. A poisoning can decrease the volume of blood in the body by as much as one half without yet killing the victim. When someone dies from a poisoning (*uburozi*), it is because he has lost all his blood.

Male semen (*amasohoro*) is also thought to be blood, but in a purified form. Contained within semen (*amasohoro*) is its active principle, *intanga*, which means "gift of self," from the verb *gutanga*, "to possess, to give" (Jacob 1984, vol. 3: 271). Women also possess *intanga*, but theirs is in the blood. Healers say that the ideal condition under which male *intanga* and female *intanga* fuse together to produce new life is after both the man and the woman have had orgasm during coitus. The most likely time for conception to occur is within the first week after the woman has had her period. Rwandans conceive of sexual intercourse not only as an activity to procure pleasure, but also as a productive act. This is implicit in their use of the verb, *gutanga*, one of whose meanings is "to give," which links procreation to gift logic and to reciprocity. In sexuality, the two partners' "gifts of self" fuse together to produce a common product, a child.

For this reason, healers add that a couple must have frequent intercourse during pregnancy in order to permit the two "gifts of self" to continue to fuse. This is especially true during the later stages of pregnancy. Frequent intercourse during pregnancy is called *gukurakuza*. In other instances the term *gukurakuza* means "to agitate milk in order to extract the butter" (Jacob 1984, vol. 2: 304). Making a baby is like churning milk; one shake is not enough. Through the concept of *gukurakuza*, Rwandans metaphorically link procreation to a productive activity involving milk.

Milk and cattle are also important in mediating social transformations; cattle are the required bridewealth gift when a man wishes to marry. One cow, or sometimes two, is given to the bride's father as a brideprice (*inkwano*). Later when the bride-wealth cow calves, one female calf will be returned to the husband's father for each cow that he gave as *inkwano*. This return gift of a cow from the bride's father to the husband's father is called *indongoranyo*. Today the custom of offering this return gift is falling into desuetude, an indication that the system of prestations and counter-prestations (cf. Maquet 1954: 88–89), which once characterized relations between the families of the husband and the wife, is also disappearing.

One value which persists to the present day is concern for the new mother's milk. This regards not only the immediate family, but also the family's social entourage. The proper onset of lactation is dependent upon an exchange of gifts. After the eight-day period of seclusion which follows the birth of a new child, people come to see the new mother and bring her gifts. This custom is called *guhemba* (to recompense). The wife's parents perform a special kind of *guhemba*. They bring the couple a goat, cow's milk, beer, and especially, a quantity of sorghum porridge (*igikoma*). Both this custom and the sorghum beverage brought as a gift have the name, *igikoma cy umubyeyi* (the porridge of the relative). The idea behind this custom is that if the woman drinks sorghum porridge (*igikoma*) in sufficient quantity, she will have abundant maternal milk (*amashereka*), because sorghum porridge is thought to stimulate the production of milk. The wife's parents, therefore, will have aided their daughter's lactation through their gift of *igikoma*. Furthermore, they will have indirectly participated in the production of the child's body through this gift.

Maternal milk is the principal sustenance of Rwandan babies and children may continue to nurse until they are three or four, though most babies are weaned earlier, from 1½ to 2½ years old. A woman who lacks maternal milk is called *igihama*, a term which also applies to women who lack vaginal secretions (*amanyare*) during intercourse. Although someone outside the context of Rwandan culture might not see any connection between a woman who lacks maternal milk after child-birth and one who lacks vaginal secretions during intercourse, Rwandans not only see a connection, they equate the two women by using the same term to denote them. Both women lack an important bodily fluid, one which is important in the exchange between a woman and her child, and another which is important in the exchange between a woman and her husband. In both cases this lack of the requisite fluid compromises the woman's fertility and the household's ability to reproduce.

Vaginal secretion is extremely important, for the Rwandan fashion of making love, called *kunyaza*, requires that the woman produce copious secretions (*inyare, amanyare*) during intercourse. *Kunyaza* comes from the verb *kunyara* (to urinate) and means "to make urinate," i.e., the man is supposed to make the woman "urinate," cause her profuse secretion. In *kunyaza*, the man does not penetrate the vagina until after his partner has "urinated," i.e., begun to secrete *amanyare* in profusion. Ideally, intercourse causes both participants to produce a fluid contribution, for conception is said to be most probable after both partners have had orgasm.

While *kunyaza* is still practiced in Rwanda, other customs involving the married couple have completely disappeared including *kwambika umwishywa* and *gucira imbazi* (discussed above). Today, instead of these two rites, the husband and wife sit on opposite sides of a calabash of sorghum beer and drink from it at the same time. Then all the other participants at the wedding ceremony come forward and drink from the calabash in turn.

Drinking and the values which surround it are central to Rwandan notions of sociability. These notions continue to be important in present day rural Rwandan society. Drinking *urwagwa* (banana beer), *ikigage* (sorghum beer), or bottled pilsner beer remains the foremost social activity in Rwanda. Drinking is also the context where one may clearly witness the division between Tutsi and Hutu, on one hand, from Twa, on the other. Although Tutsi and Hutu will drink together and openly share the same container (*igicuma*) or the same drinking straw (*umuheha*) with one another, neither ethnic group will do so with Twa who happen to be present. Twa may drink and receive a beverage in the company of Hutu or Tutsi, but the containers and straws that they use must be separate.

When someone comes to visit, the host will usually offer the visitor beer to drink. If the host possesses beer, but refuses (*kwima inzoga*) to offer some to a guest, though others are present drinking, this is a very serious affront, tantamount to saying that good social relations no longer exist with that person. This is an example of how fluid exchange is important in the most ordinary context of social interaction.

FLUIDS IN POISONING

Today values related to fluid exchange continue to underlie Rwandan concepts of "poisoning" (*uburozi*).[1] Poisoners are those who do not abide by reciprocity. They are those who take, but do not give. Breaching the morality of "gift logic" compromises social relations and can lead to illness. Witches act in two basic ways: either they interrupt exchange or they siphon away things destined for others. Rwandan poisoners are "blocking beings" who make women sterile and men impotent by stopping their flow of generative fluids. Or, they are vampirish, anthropophagic beings who parasitically suck away the vital fluids of others. There are thus two basic expressions to pathology: "blocked flow" and "hemorrhagic flow."

Both these forms figure prominently in popular therapies that rely on techniques of accusation. In these accusatory therapies, the healer or diviner first establishes whether an illness is ordinary or extraordinary. If it is extraordinary, he attempts to determine if the illness is of spiritual or human origin. These two categories are not mutually exclusive, for humans can enlist the aid of various spirits to afflict others. If the sickness has been sent by another person, the healer attempts to discover who that person is, and how the charms or poisons used can best be neutralized. This type of therapy orients the sufferer's suspicions towards those with whom he has problematic social relations. It is a therapy which emphasizes a "persecutorial" view of misfortune (cf. Zempleni 1975).

Such a therapy is practiced in the northern Rwandan commune of Butaro, which has been transformed less quickly than most parts of central and southern Rwanda. Here, despite the inroads of the commodity world, many pre-colonial social arrangements have persisted. This particular form of therapy is called *kuraguza amahembe* ("to divine by horns"). The procedure involves "sending" a small animal horn to bring back the voice of one's poisoner, so that the patient and healer can interrogate it. First, the patient spits on the horn and then states his name and problem. The healer invokes the spirits of the horn and instructs them to find the voice of his patient's sorcerer. Questions to the voice concern the poisoner's motivation and his mode of operation: What does he begrudge his victim? What poisons has he used? How can these be neutralized?

One example of a poisoning which is quite commonly treated by Butaro healers who employ *kuraguza amahembe*, is that called *kumanikira amaraso* (which means "to suspend blood"). In this poisoning, a fluid is taken from the intended female victim: either her menstrual blood (*irungu*), her urine (*inkari*), or some of the fluid which exudes from the vagina after parturition (*igisanza*). The poisoner takes one of these fluids, adds medicines to it, puts it in a packet and suspends the packet from the rafters of a house, or among rocks on the summit of a high hill where rain cannot touch it. If menstrual blood or urine has been taken from the woman, she will be unable to conceive. If blood from childbirth, *igisanza*, has been taken from the woman, she will be able to conceive, but unable to deliver the baby. The foetus will become turned transversally in the womb or it will move upwards toward the heart. In both variations of this poisoning, whether the woman is pregnant or not, the female victim's reproductive capacity becomes arrested or "blocked." Another variation of this spell, sometimes called *umuvu*, entails throwing the packet with the woman's menstrual blood or urine into a fast-moving stream. In this case the woman's menstrual flow becomes excessively abundant or prolonged.

In effect, by suspending a woman's blood or other fluids involved in sexuality or reproduction, the woman's reproductive functions are also "suspended." Either she becomes unable to deliver the baby already in her womb, or menstruation stops and she becomes sterile. By suspending the woman's bodily fluids in a position between sky and earth, or in a place where rain cannot touch them, the woman's body becomes "blocked." When her fluids are put into a body of fast-moving water, her menses become dangerously abundant, an example of "hemorrhagic flow."

Treatment

Healers vary in their treatment of this poisoning, nevertheless these variations possess features in common.

One healer has the woman lie on her back while naked. He takes medicines and sprinkles them in a line from the woman's forehead, over the middle of her face, over her chest and abdomen, down to her genitals. The logic behind this treatment appears to be that movement must be encouraged from the top of the body to the bottom.

A healer named Antoinette uses another method of cure, but her treatment of *kumanikira amaraso* (to suspend blood) follows a similar line of symbolic reasoning to the previous one. Antoinette's procedure, however, engages more elements from the macrocosmic sphere in which the female body, as microcosm, is embedded: house, earth, sky, and rain.

Antoinette has the woman lie naked on the floor of her house. Her abdomen faces upward. Someone climbs onto the roof of the house, parts the thatch, and then pours an aqueous mixture of medicines through the opening onto the woman's abdomen. Another person, inside the house, rubs the woman's stomach with the medicinal mixture before this drains to the earthen floor. In this treatment the blockage within the woman's body is considered as if it were a blockage between sky and earth, for it is counteracted by someone's actually moving to the sky position—ascending to the roof of the house—and pouring fluids earthward. This time, however, the downward movement of fluids includes the woman's body in the circuit of flow from sky to earth. The cure is virtually a one-to-one homeopathic reversal of the symbolic operations accomplished in the poisoning, which removed the woman's body from the circuit of moving fluids by "suspending" her blood between earth and sky. In this cure, an analogic relation is established between the reproductive processes of the female body and the elemental forces of nature.

Baudouin, another Butaro healer, treated *kumanikira* in a symbolically comparable way. In one case he gave his patient, who was unable to deliver despite being pregnant, water with a piece of hippopotamus (*imyubu*) skin in it. In addition, he gave the woman a remedy concocted from the *umuhaanga* plant (*Kotschya ae-schynomenoides; Kotschya strigosa* var. *grandiflora; Maesa lanceolata*) (Jacob 1984, vol. 1: 449). The name of this plant comes from the verb *guhaanga* which means: 1) to create, to restore, to invent; 2) to occupy a place first; 3) to germinate, to blossom; 4) to have one's first menstrual period. He also gave her a plant called *umuman-urankuba*, a name which comes from the words: *kumanura*—to make something descend, or to depend on; and *inkuba*—thunder. The full meaning of the name of this plant would be: "to make thunder descend, to depend on thunder," i.e., to make rain fall.

Once again this is an image of restoring the sky to earth movement of rainfall, and by analogy, restoring flow to the woman's body. In restoring this flow, the healer renders the woman capable of creating, capable of blossoming. The use of the hippopotamus follows the fact that it is an aquatic animal, whose bellowing resembles thunder.

NANGA Y'IVUZA

While *kuraguza amahembe* (to divine by horns) is widely practiced in the Rwandan commune of Butaro and other areas of the north, in the central and southern areas of Rwanda, one frequently encounters therapies that integrate aspects of confessional techniques. The most outstanding example of confessional therapy that I witnessed was that practiced by a healer who called himself "Nanga y'ivuza." To my knowledge, only this healer and five wives of his who lived in various parts of southern Rwanda placed such emphasis on confession.

The name "Nanga y'ivuza" comes from *inanga* (harp) and *kwivuza* ("to sing or to play by itself"), hence "the harp that plays by itself."[2] This name was used by a syncretistic religious sect which originated during the 1950s in Burundi and then was brutally suppressed in 1967 when 30 of its members were hanged (Rodegem 1970: 547–550). Criminal charges against the sect included: the ritual murder of children, the drinking of blood, incest, and cannibalism. Note that these charges represent antitheses to gift logic, while they are also images of "closed circuit flow," i.e., things that stay in, instead of being shared out. They evoke the stereotype of the witch: one who wants to consume without sharing, one who wants to produce himself but not others. Incest, for example, is the sexual consumption of a consanguine, a category of kin which is normally destined to be sexually consumed by an alliance partner. Cannibalism is a form of endogamous consumption: it is eating within the species rather than outside of it. Drinking blood could also be thought of as endogamous consumption, for it means consuming the product of one's own body. To kill one's children is to refuse to give them to the next generation, to refuse to reproduce society.

The "Nanga" that I met had once been part of the sect, but had fled from Burundi to Rwanda to avoid persecution. Here he practiced as a healer, but he did not attempt to revive the cult's organization and win new converts. He continued, however, to use the term "Nanga y'ivuza," but as a title for himself; people addressed him as "Nanga." Each of his five wives lived in a different part of south-central Rwanda and each operated her own healing establishment. All had been his former patients. Nanga spent a great deal of his time traveling from one wife's residence to another, where he would participate in healing sessions with the patients and attending to business affairs.

Nanga's therapy differed significantly from the northern healers discussed above, for he believed that the immediate cause of illness was fear (*ubwoba*) and that the ultimate cause was sin. Sin abrogates the normal relation of protection that personal "saints" (*abatagatifu*) exercise over someone. Nanga explained that the *abatagatifu* were essentially equivalent to the Rwandan idea of ancestral spirits or *abazimu*. Unlike *abazimu*, though, they did not require sacrifices to be offered in their honor. One maintained their benevolence simply by avoiding sin.

Usually one's own sins breach the relation of protection, but sometimes it is the sins of the older generation whose consequences are visited upon the children. Sins include: violation of any of the Ten Commandments, the practice of traditional rites, such as the veneration of one's ancestors, participation in the traditional religious cults of Ryangombe or Nyabingi, the wearing of protective talismans, or attempting to do witchcraft. Jealousy was also considered to be a sin, and naiveté, while it was not a sin, could also bring on suffering. Contrary to traditional belief, Nanga denied that *abarozi* (poisoners) could ever harm anyone through non-empirical means. To Nanga, belief in a spell such as *kumanikira amaraso* was the height of foolishness. Nanga thus rejected the validity of the "flow/blockage" model as a social principle.

Nanga's treatment centered on confession. He interviewed each patient one by one, asking him if he knew such and such a person, such and such another. Often he went through a long list of Rwandan names, as his patient usually responded, "Ndamuzi" (I know him/her). Occasionally he mentioned an incident or some other very specific fact about his interlocutor and discussed this briefly. Then, he lapsed into a kind of glossolalia which seemed like a mixture of bits of French, Kiswahili, Kinyarwanda, Kirundi, and other less intelligible sounds. This was the language of the "saints" (*abatagatifu*); Nanga claimed to be able to heal because he understood the language of the *abatagatifu*. These latter would reveal everything about the patient to Nanga including the patient's sins. In the face of such omniscience, the patient was induced to confess all his sins, for it was only by confession that one could reopen the channels to one's *abatagatifu*. Often a patient's parents attended the healing session so that by their confession their children would recover.

Nanga used only two medications: a purgative and a sudorific (sweat-producing medicine), but these could be seen as analogous to confession, for they evacuate the body, just as confession evacuates the soul. These two medications, moreover, continue to follow the "flow/blockage" model of physiology. Nanga occasionally used these two medications, but he preferred to believe that the key to cure resided within the patient himself. "Each patient comes with his own medicine and he leaves with it," he was fond of saying. In other words, the cure is already inside oneself.

Nanga's patients usually spent only a few hours or a day with him, but others lived with him or with one of his wives for weeks or months. One patient, named Felicity, consulted Nanga because she was 28 years old and not yet married. Being single at this age is a cause of serious consternation for a Rwandan woman. Felicity had given birth to two children from previous affairs, but had not married either child's father. She worked as a secretary at the Université Nationale du Rwanda and lived in Butare in a small two room apartment with her young son and a cousin who had come to live with her to attend school in Butare. Many of her relatives perceived her as rich because she had a salaried job, despite the fact that she just barely made ends meet. One day a distant "aunt" showed up with her baby, expecting to be sheltered and fed for an indefinite period of time. Felicity did not know how to deal with this woman, nor with any of her other demanding relatives.

Nanga treated Felicity, advising her that her problem was not one of sin as much as naiveté. She should be firmer about saying *no* to people, even if it meant that relatives would accuse her of being selfish. If she had a job and they did not, it was not her fault, but theirs if they became jealous of her. People need not feel they're doing wrong by trying to earn money, Nanga maintained, instead it was wrong to be jealous of someone who had a job or who was earning a good living. People should be responsible for themselves, he claimed.

Many of Nanga's patients had problems similar to that of Felicity, many were young and had salaried jobs, whereas their parents were peasants. Often they appeared trapped in the same kind of bind, a bind where relatives and friends perceived them as rich, even though they had very little disposable income above and beyond their living expenses. They were people living in the commoditized, cash economy world in terms of employment, but whose origins lay in the gift economy world of domestic production and patron-client relations. They were caught on the horns of a dilemma: whether to act according to gift logic and risk impoverishment, or to act consistently according to commodity logic and risk being accused of selfishness, or even witchcraft, by friends and relatives.

Nanga was able to treat patients whose problems stemmed in part from the gift/commodity "double bind," because he had found a personal solution to this dilemma for himself. Through personal experience with illness, he had internalized his culture's most salient conflict. Then he had found a means of resolving it by discovering in the "Nanga y'ivuza" cult, a restructured version of the "flow/blockage" dialectic—one which apparently favored "blockage" over "flow." As a consequence, Nanga could then morally choose commodity logic over gift logic and thus resolve his personal crisis. Furthermore, he could eventually apply this "revelation" to his method and theory of therapy. Just as "blockage" could come to eclipse "flow," so could the commodity eclipse the gift. This shift of emphasis forms the symbolic basis of Nanga therapy. In conceptual terms, Nanga could assume the role of "culture broker" for commodity logic by offering a moral system based on the concept of sin, but which integrated elements of "flow/blockage" symbolism. In this respect, he provided patients with an ideological structure which did not appear radically new to them, even though it implied significant rejection of gift logic. Nanga's therapy could bridge the gap between gift logic and commodity logic by offering a symbolic system which was cognitively intermediary between the old system of ritual and myth and the new symbols of the market place.

Nanga's own life provided his patients with an example of what could be gained by assuming a destiny intimately linked to the possibilities afforded by the cash economy. Besides healing, Nanga grew coffee, raised bananas which were brewed into commercially sold banana beer (*urwagwa*), and occasionally cut trees to sell as construction lumber. From these activities and from the fact that he had numerous patients (who paid relatively high fees by Rwandan standards), Nanga was quite well off by local standards. He was a model African small capitalist farmer, an entrepreneur, as well as a healer, and he was very successful.

Nanga, in my opinion, implicitly understood that the therapeutic problem under commodity logic was guilt, guilt from excessive retentiveness, and concomitant social isolation through failure to observe reciprocity. Nanga's healing function was partly one of disculpation. He helped patients make the transition to commodity logic by purging them of their guilt, for according to gift logic, to accumulate and not share is to be a "witch" (*umurozi*). According to commodity logic, on the other hand, to make a profit and yet share too much is to misuse one's capital. When one chooses commodity logic, one is forced to be retentive. Using a restructured version of "traditional" Rwandan symbolic imagery, Nanga could treat patients confronted with choosing "blockage" over "flow," profit motive over reciprocity. Nanga's answer to those faced with this dilemma is thus understandable: witches do not exist, and jealousy of those who are wealthier than oneself, is wrong. This reasoning may also explain why he perceived a conflict between the older and younger generation even to the point of attributing the latter's illnesses to the former's sins. The older generation was more likely to attribute credence to traditional practices and to gift logic. Hence, as in Freudian therapy, parents "cause" their children's illnesses.

The transition to commodity logic implies a different notion of the person, a more individualized and autonomous person, but one in danger of isolating himself from others by being retentive or acquisitive to excess. Hence, there were two major strategies to Nanga's therapeutic interventions. In response to guilt and retentiveness, Nanga offered purgation. This we see in the practice of confession, for confession reduces the burden of accumulated sins. It was also manifest in his use of laxatives and sudorifics. Nanga's therapy emphasized illness causes internal to the person. Instead of external causes, i.e., poisoners and spirits, the patient should look within himself for the source of his cure.

This idea is expressed in Nanga's name as well: "the harp that plays by itself," which is clearly an image of autonomy. This representation resembles that of the body in Nanga's therapy, for instead of a body metonymically and metaphorically connected to the things and persons that it touches—which is the idea underlying the therapy of the Butaro healers—the principle of Nanga's therapy is the self-afflicting, self-restoring body. The body is thus an instrument, which, like Milton Friedman's idealized free market economy, supposedly regulates itself. Furthermore, Nanga passionately disagreed with traditional healing practices intended to cause blood to flow through cupping (*kurumika*) or through small incisions (*indasaago*) made on the skin. Blood must not be shed in this way, Nanga would say, it must be kept within the body. While Nanga continued to treat sweat and feces according to "flow" imagery, he refused to shed blood as a therapeutic measure. Blood, I would aver, is in Nanga's therapy the body's most capital humor. It must not be diminished; it must be saved.

As to the second aspect of Nanga's therapeutic strategy, the reduction of social isolation, this was countered in several ways. First of all, patients often lived with one of Nanga's wives for several weeks or months. They interacted with each other and participated together in cooking meals, cleaning the compound and their living quarters, brewing *urwagwa* (banana beer), and sometimes working in the field.

Once or twice during the day, they gathered together and Nanga's wife treated them. They talked about themselves, their illnesses, all the incidents in the past when they had had similar feelings of malaise, etc. Sometimes they received massages from Nanga's wife or from each other. All these techniques served to reestablish feelings of connectedness to others. Furthermore, part of Nanga's therapy seemed to be aimed at educating people to the possibility that they could form meaningful social ties outside the constraints of traditional morality and gift logic. These group therapy sessions allowed Nanga's patients to experiment with this possibility.

Given the economic situation in southern Rwanda where more and more people are participating in cash cropping and wage labor employment, Nanga's therapy has attracted a wide following, because it is adept at curing the disorders of people who are living increasingly according to commodity logic, but who still feel subject to the moral constraints of gift logic. This dilemma, though more pronounced in southern Rwanda, is the entire society's overarching "double bind."

The therapeutic strategies of the Butaro healers and Nanga are virtually antithetical: where the Butaro healers seek out the "witch" in one's social nexus, Nanga healers seek out and purge the "witch" in one's self, i.e., sin and guilt. This may be the reason why "Nanga y'ivuza" cult members back in Burundi were perceived as people who advocated "blockage" instead of "flow," and were charged with crimes which were images of "closed-circuit flow." Nanga healers have attempted to resolve the psycho-social contradictions associated with accumulating wealth in a society which has traditionally emphasized the conversion of wealth into social relationships through the giving of gifts. The problem which they confront could be formulated as: How can one accumulate wealth and not be considered someone who blocks the flow of gifts, i.e., a "witch"? They have resolved this dilemma by reducing the pertinence of "flow" imagery from the social group to the individual body. Given this shift, the therapeutic problem becomes one of seeking out and expunging "blockage" within the self, rather than "blockage" within the group. Thus, their therapy is one of confession, rather than one of accusation.

CONFESSION

Nanga's focus upon confession is also interesting because of the fact that in Western history, confession was not codified as a sacrament in the Catholic Church until the Lateran Council of 1215 (Foucault 1980: 58). Moreover, as the importance of confession as a means of establishing guilt increased, the importance of accusatory techniques declined. Interrogation and inquest gradually supplanted "ordeals" and testing rituals such as duels and "judgments of God" (Foucault 1980: 58). This trend, Foucault argues, was associated with the rise of individualism in the West.

For a long time, the individual was vouched for by the reference of others and the demonstration of his ties to the commonwealth (family, allegiance, protection); then he was authenticated by the discourse of truth he was able or obliged to pronounce concerning himself. The truthful confession was inscribed at the heart of the procedures of individualization by power. [Foucault 1980: 58–59]

Confession as a psychological and social technique presupposes a relationship to authority. "The confession is a ritual of discourse in which the speaking subject is also the subject of the statement; it is also a ritual that unfolds within a power relationship, for one does not confess without the presence (or virtual presence) of a partner who is not simply the interlocutor but the authority who requires the confession, prescribes and appreciates it, and intervenes in order to judge, punish, forgive, console, and reconcile" (Foucault 1980: 61–62). Thus, it is not surprising to find confession sometimes wielded as a hegemonic tool, where the subject becomes the object of his own condemnation, a condemnation which merely apes the precepts and beliefs of the authority extracting the confession. Consider, for example, what was perhaps the first efflorescence of confession ritual in Western history, the confessions of witchcraft extracted by means of torture during the 16th to 18th centuries, a period which also witnessed the expansion of capitalism in Europe (Wallerstein 1976) and the decline of holistic theories of pathology (Thomas 1971).

Confession has become institutionalized as a "core symbol" in modern rituals of political repression. In these rituals (i.e., in torture), bodily pain and disfigurement become the primary means of inscribing the "verity" of a particular ideology upon the subject's own words (cf. Scarry 1985). Confession has also thrived as a therapeutic technique in the West, for it is central to the practice of psychiatry. While confession has never been absent from the African therapeutic context (cf. Jackson 1989), its use has usually been overshadowed by accusatory techniques. Some authors (cf. Augé 1975; Zempleni 1975) interpret the recent appearance of confession in African therapy as the manifestation in the therapeutic and religious domain of the society's transition to capitalism, a transition which involves a "monadization" (Augé 1975) of the person.

Certain categorical distinctions are peculiar to capitalist culture, for example, the distinction between the home and workplace, between who a person is as a member of a familial group, and what he does to gain his livelihood. In Maine's terms the transition from traditional to modern society involves the movement from "status" to "contract." In Marx's terms the transition from pre-capitalist to capitalist society involves the combination and tension between "use value" and "exchange value" in the core artifact of capitalism, the commodity. Under capitalism, this combination comes to imply the separability of "use value" from "exchange value," for the home becomes the locus for the realization of "use values," and the market place becomes the locus for the realization of "exchange values." Under capitalism "exchange value" predominates over, but does not completely extinguish "use value."

In like fashion, with regard to pre-colonial Rwandan symbolic thought, I have attempted to show that the ideology of "flow" was positively valued over "blockage," its paradigmatic opposite. Despite this, the imagery of "flow" was inseparable from the imagery of "blockage"—the institution of kingship seems to tacitly acknowledge their conjoined nature. What appears to be occurring today, however, as evinced in "Nanga" therapy, is that "flow" imagery has begun to separate from "blockage" imagery. While Nanga can still nominally uphold the validity of the "flow" model in cognizing some therapeutic measures—as in his use of purgatives and sudorifics—beyond the body, the modality of "blockage" prevails, for in social life one should attempt to make a profit and accumulate wealth. The circle of relations to which the individual applies the social analog of "flow" imagery has begun to diminish, become restricted to the household. This is why Nanga therapy continues to underline the causal relatedness of parental actions to children's sicknesses. The household is becoming the last social sphere in which market ideology does not govern interaction, and where "flow/blockage" ideology can persist. Beyond the household—as Nanga therapy leads its patients to acknowledge—the model of "flow" as a social principle is losing its significance. This is indicative of the historical process occurring in Rwanda, its incorporation into the world economy.

Confessional therapies are a corollary to this historical process, for they tend to reflect and to reinforce the dichotomization of the person into one who is, i.e., "substance," versus what one does, i.e., "code for conduct" or "contract" (Barnett and Silverman 1979; Schneider 1968). Nanga's therapy tends to replicate capitalist culture's distinction between matters of substance and matters of contract (or code for conduct), for it purports to act only on phenomena located within the person (i.e., substance). This idea is evidenced in Nanga's telling remark, "Each patient comes with his own medicine and he leaves with it." In like fashion, such therapies de-emphasize pathological causes external to the person, a notion exemplified in another of Nanga's assertions, "Witches and evil spirits do not exist."

When misfortune becomes a question of qualities internal to the person, i.e., judgments of "substance," it becomes difficult to sustain therapeutic notions and procedures which implicate the person in wider schemes of causality. These wider schemes of causality include at their most encompassing level, representations of the cosmos. At their least encompassing level, they concern moral representations of human bodily organs—e.g., the heart is the locus of volition, the liver is the seat of passion—where a model of social emotions becomes transposed to the realm of physiology. Between the level of the body and that of the cosmos, one encounters representations of social life in its relation to health and well-being, including beliefs concerning the motives of others, as in witchcraft and sorcery. Although holistic theories of the body and of the cosmos may persist in capitalist culture, such theories have historically been marginalized by the dominant discourse concerning the nature of pathology, a discourse which privileges microscopic, particulate reality, as in the "germ theory" of illness, over cosmogonic, relational reality. While the "germ theory" separates and excludes, holistic theories conjoin. When "substantialized" theories of the person and of pathology come to predominate over holistic ones, the separation between persons and things, family and work, mind and body, comes that much closer to appearing like a natural property of the universe.

Nanga therapy takes the "conjoined" symbolism of the "flow/blockage" dialectic and separates it into spheres of pertinence. While Nanga affirms the desirability of a "flowing" or at least, "unblocked" body and a harmonious household, he does not affirm reciprocity and redistribution in everyday social life. On the contrary he affirms the virtues of profit making and capital accumulation, i.e., "blockage," a principle which runs counter to "traditional" Rwandan values. This shift of emphasis could be compared with the Marxian observation that, under capitalism, "use value" and "exchange value" become separated between the home and the market place. While Marx describes this historical transition in terms which make sense in the context of Western culture, Nanga makes this separation comprehensible through symbols which derive from Rwandan culture. Moreover, by tacitly affirming the principle of "blockage" in social life, Nanga, in a sense, makes it all the more probable that there will be "blocked" souls and bodies in need of confession and purgation. Nanga's therapy reflects and reproduces both the ideology of "commodity logic," and the pathologies that it engenders. Nevertheless, by culling from "traditional" Rwandan "flow/blockage" imagery while limiting its pertinence, this therapy provides a mediate zone where people caught in the agony of the transition between gift logic and commodity logic, can articulate and sometimes alleviate their suffering.

ACKNOWLEDGMENTS

I would like to thank Fred Damon of the University of Virginia and Jean Comaroff of the University of Chicago for their comments on earlier drafts of this article.

NOTES

1. "To poison" is the closest approximation to the Kinyarwanda verb, *kuroga*, even though a Rwandan *uburozi* ("poisoning") does not always have to be introduced into the body by ordinary empirical means.
2. Readers familiar with the ethnographic literature on popular healing in central and southern Africa may note the similarity of the name, Nanga, to the term, *nganga*, which is used in some areas to designate a healer. In this case the resemblance between the words is accidental for their etymology is different. The closest cognate of *nganga* in Kinyarwanda is the term *umuganga*, which is used to designate biomedical practitioners. Popular healers are called *umuvuzi*, *umucunyi*, or *umupfumu*.

REFERENCES CITED

Augé, M.
    1975   Logique lignagère et logique de Bregbo. *In* Prophétisme et thérapeutique. Pp. 219–238. Paris: Hermann.
Barnett, S., and M. Silverman
    1979   Ideology and Everyday Life. Ann Arbor, MI: University of Michigan Press.
Bateson, G.
    1972   Steps to an Ecology of Mind. New York: Ballantine.
Beattie, J.
    1960   Bunyoro. New York: Holt, Rinehart and Winston.
Bourgeois, R.
    1956   Banyarwanda et Barundi, tome IV religion et magie. Brussels: Académie Royale des Sciences Coloniales, Classe des Sciences Morales et Politiques, Mém. in-8°, nouvelle série, tome IV, fascicule 2.
de Heusch, L.
    1985   Sacrifice in Africa. Manchester: Manchester University Press.
de Lacger, L.
    1959   Ruanda. Kabgayi (Rwanda): Vicariat Apostolique.
d'Hertefelt, M., and A. Coupez
    1964   La royauté sacrée de l'ancien Rwanda. Tervuren: Musée Royal de l'Afrique Centrale.
Dumont, L.
    1980   Homo hierarchicus. Chicago: University of Chicago Press.
Evans-Pritchard, E.
    1937   Witchcraft, Oracles and Magic Among the Azande. Oxford: Clarendon Press.

Foucault, M.
  1980   The History of Sexuality, vol. 1, An Introduction. New York: Vintage.
Godelier, M.
  1986   The Making of Great Men. New York: Cambridge University Press.
Gregory, C.
  1982   Gifts and Commodities. London: Academic Press.
Habimana, E.
  1988   Envie comme cause d'attribution dans les maladies mentales *ibitega*. Unpublished Ph.D. dissertation, l'Université du Québec à Montréal.
Jackson, M.
  1989   Paths Toward a Clearing. Bloomington, IN: University of Indiana Press.
Jacob, I., ed.
  1984   Dictionnaire Rwandais-Français. Edition abrégée. Kigali (Rwanda): l'Institut National de Recherche Scientifique, Imprimerie Scolaire.
Jameson, F.
  1981   The Political Unconscious: Narrative as a Socially Symbolic Act. Ithaca, NY: Cornell University Press.
Kagame, A.
  1951   La poésie dynastique du Rwanda. Brussels: Mémoire de l'Institut Royal Colonial Belge, Section des Sciences Morales et Politiques Vol. XXII, no. 1.
Lévi-Strauss, C.
  1947   Les structures élémentaires de la parenté. Paris: Mouton.
Lukacs, G.
  1960 [1922]   Histoire et conscience de classe. K. Axelos and J. Bois (translators). Paris: Editions de Minuit.
Marquet, J.
  1954   Le système des relations sociales dans le Ruanda ancien. Tervuren: Musée Royal de l'Afrique Centrale.
Marx, K.
  1977 [1867]   Capital. vol. 1. New York: Random House.
Mauss, M.
  1967 [1925]   The Gift. New York: Norton.
Ndekezi, S.
  n.d.   Ubukwe bw 'abanyarwanda. Kigali. (Rwanda).
Newbury, C.
  1988   The Cohesion of Oppression. New York: Columbia University Press.
Rodegem, F.
  1970   Dictionnaire Rundi-Français. Tervuren: Musée Royal de l'Afrique Centrale.
Sapir, E.
  1932   Cultural Anthropology and Psychiatry. Selected Writings of Edward Sapir. *In* Language, Culture, and Personality. D. Mandelbaum, ed. Pp. 509–521. Berkeley: University of California Press.
Scarry, E.
  1985   The Body in Pain. New York: Oxford University Press.
Schneider, D.
  1968   American Kinship. Englewood Cliffs, NJ: Prentice-Hall.
Smith, P.
  1975   Le récit populaire au Rwanda. Paris: Armand Colin.
Taussig, M.
  1977   The Genesis of Capitalism Amongst a South American Peasantry: Devil's Labor and the Baptism of Money. Comparative Studies in Society and History 19(2): 130–150.
  1980   The Devil and Commodity Fetishism in South America. Chapel Hill, NC: University of North Carolina Press.
Taylor, C.
  1990   Condoms and Cosmology: The Fractal Person and Sexual Risk in Rwanda. Social Science and Medicine. 31(9): 1023–1028.

Thomas, K.
  1971   Religion and the Decline of Magic. New York: Charles Scribner's Sons.
Wagner, R.
  1986   Symbols That Stand for Themselves. Chicago: University of Chicago Press.
  1988   The Fractal Person. Paper presented at a symposium on "Great Man and Big Man Societies," Paris.
Wallerstein, I.
  1976   The Modern World System. New York: Academic Press.
Weber, M.
  1958   The Protestant Ethic and the Spirit of Capitalism. New York: Charles Scribner's Sons.
Zempleni, A.
  1975   De la persécution à la culpabilité. *In* Prophétisme et thérapeutique. Pp. 153–218. Paris: Hermann.

The Production of Self and Body in Sherpa-Tibetan Society[1]

Vincanne Adams, Princeton University

One of the hallmarks of modernity is the joint project of representation and intervention (Rabinow 1991). Representations generate truth claims about certain subjects which in turn become targets of various instruments and technologies of social control. Subjects, in other words, are both constructed and ultimately disciplined through representations that claim to assert truth about them. The best examples of the way representation and control work together in medicine come from the writings of Michel Foucault. He suggested that during the 17th century in European society a discourse emerged about the body which was essential to both a new type of power and new ways of controlling individual bodies and populations.

Modernity, Foucault argued, is marked by its use of knowledge-power instruments to exercize social control, and its decreased reliance on coercive mechanisms of control that used force, such as physical coersion, the police, or militia. Knowledge, and consequently truth, about the body, its sexuality, and its physical movements, for example, were increasingly produced through apparatuses like psychoanalytic confessionals and through panoptic surveillance techniques found in social welfare agencies and other institutions (prisons, hospitals, schools) (Foucault 1973, 1977). Foucault called the modern technique of power "bio-power," because it implemented its disciplinary strategies through health dimensions of both individuals and populations.[2] A discourse of norms and normalcy was produced by the feedback between "confessing" individuals (patients, prisoners, students) and the institutions devoted to writing and producing knowledge about these individuals. This discourse in turn became a subjective text used by individuals to regulate their lives, increasingly potent as truths about subjectivity were increasingly produced (Foucault 1980). Populations disciplined by agencies of social welfare increasingly implemented social programs that managed mortality, morbidity, and fertility through self-regulatory techniques. In a subtle form of inverted benevolence, the agencies supported by populations because of overt altruistic purposes ended up being the very institutions which regulated their lives (Armstrong 1983). Power in modernity operated on a principle of less force for greater control, which was in part dependent upon the eventuation of knowledge in "techniques of the self," or disciplinary strategies effected by the self on the self. Altogether, these arrangements formed the modern nation-state, according to Foucault, since it was no longer a monarch or his monarchial arrangements of coer-

VINCANNE ADAMS *is an assistant professor in the anthropology department at Princeton University. She is currently researching medicine, modernization, and late capitalism in the Buddhist Himalayas.*

cive power which were the effective locus of power, but rather the "order of things" that was the state and hence the modern locus of power. As O'Neill aptly noted, "[t]hese discourses evolved in the shift from medievalism to mercantile and industrial capitalism when the mechanisms of social control had to be redesigned to administer individuals more closely than church, parish and family authority could accomplish" (1986:24).[3]

Bio-power was deployed through "concrete arrangements" such as institutions of medicine, prisons, schools, and the military, all of which codified information about the body and populations and thereby produced their "truths." Such truths were used as instruments of knowledge-power around which interventions were contrived. This type of control depended upon an increasingly problematized *subjectivity* of self, counterposed to the self's ability to see itself as an *object* that could be regulated through self-discipline. Bodies, discursively objectified, were made to offer up their hidden truths for self (and ultimately public) scrutiny. An example of this in medicine is the way medical representations of the anatomical body could only emerge once the *body as an object* was conceived, which in turn was made possible in part through techniques of penology; (public displays of hanging and quartering of the criminal in eras of monarchy gave way to theatres of anatomical dissection and surgery in modernity). Here, the construction of the body as an object was joined with the act of punishment and, consequently, social control (see also Bryan Turner 1987, Comaroff 1982). The plural act of self-revelation and self-discipline was accomplished. In the clinic, and through other health and welfare agencies, the body's hygiene, health, and sexuality became the targets of various indirect disciplinary strategies that were made possible through a well-established subjectivity.

Finally, for Foucault, bio-power replaced already existing techniques for producing truth found in Christianity such as the confessional. Submission to Christian "games of truth" were motivated by desires for salvation and effected through renunciation. Above all, "truth" was constructed around moral mandates in Christianity. In arrangements of bio-power, on the other hand, motivations derived from desire for health, sanity, and safety, without promise of other-worldly gains and without moral imperatives. These motivations were on the whole products of a type of rationality rather than morality, suitable to an emerging capitalist bourgeoisie whose citizenship had to be unceasingly reconstructed. Willing consent to techniques of bio-power was effected through motivations for self improvement. Truth in this process was always destabilized by the fact that it was always reconstructed. As more of the hidden details of the self were exposed, so were its truths forever rediscovered (or reinvented).

In this paper, I explore how Buddhist medico-religious practices in the contemporary and historical Tibetan setting emerged from pre-existing medico-religious forms as fundamentally new practices of self which resembled in some ways those that existed in the European "modern" project. First, Buddhist healing systems produced individualized and subjective patients whose objectified bodies were self-regulated through medical knowledge, rituals, and everyday actions aimed at achieving a healthful existence, but through a rhetoric of enlightenment. Forms of modern power in Europe were contingent upon subjectivity — a subjectivity that evolved prior to modernity (Foucault 1984, 1986). My research looked at the emergence of subjectivity as a Buddhist project, and then at the way Buddhist healing systems implemented a type of productive power that resembled forms of power in European modernity. Gaining an understanding of the existence of this type of power in the Tibetan cultural setting enhances our ability to understand how modern health development projects arriving as part of the expansion of the capitalist nation-state through biomedicine at the periphery can be approached in anthropology. We might ask, in other words, what forms of power preceeded the modernity of the colonial era in Tibetan societies? In a related vein, we might ask, are there elements of modernity in the civilizations outside of capitalist, European-American society?[4]

One way to observe the way power worked in the historical project of Buddhism was by looking at the changes over time in representations of the self and of the body, since in medicine it was upon the body and through the image of self that healing techniques and, consequently, power found their most potent effects. By focusing on healing, I gained insight on the way different representations of the self and the body were produced and sustained over time as "interlocutors" between state and self-control, or as a means through which the state could come into existence. One might argue that the archaic state emerged in historic Tibet as a pre-capitalist "order of things" contingent upon medical apparatuses for producing knowledge about the body and the self.

Among the culturally Tibetan Sherpas of northeast Nepal studied over two years first in 1982 and again in 1986-87, I found that the "self" was tripartite: social, physical, and mental. This tripartite conception of self reflected the historical growth of certain socio-political principles of organization which directly and indirectly emphasized the body and reconfigured the image of self in Tibet through techniques resembling productive power. The very gradual emergence of the modern centralized state in Tibet by the 13th century corresponded with the rise of Buddhism and a heightened individualism which accentuated social, fiscal, and intellectual independence and eventually produced a de-socialized, reified body.[5] Ideas about a healthy life emerged in the Buddhist era out of pre-existing concepts of life which linked ruler to ruled, allegiance to submission, self to other. In Buddhism, these concepts were supplemented by images of a healthy life based on transcendence of social bonds, independence and detachment, and self-discipline/ awareness. The proliferation of concern for identifying the "self," and beyond that the composition of self as consciousness (or cognition) *and* body, created the opportunity for an apparatus for the Tibetan state. Unlike the supposed break from monarchial, Christian eras to modernity in the European context, however, Tibet's monarchial and pre-Buddhist institutions continued to exist alongside and sometimes within emergent forms of productive power in the new arrangements of governmentality.[6] Rather than subverting the "social self," its foundations in acts of reciprocity and the social formations which depended upon it, individualism and independence were to some extent subsumed within the "social self."[7]

SHERPAS AND TIBETANS[8]

Khumbu Sherpas were a culturally Tibetan ethnic minority living at the Tibetan border southeast of Mount Everest in Nepal.[9] They had for the last 450 years depended largely upon overland trade between Tibet and regions south, animal husbandry, and to a limited extent agriculture on high altitude fields carved into hillsides and small plateaus. They were most renowned for their successful participation since the turn of the century in high altitude Himalayan mountaineering expeditions as guides and porters.

Ascending via plane and eventually on foot into the high altitude Sherpa villages from the country's capital in Kathmandu, one moved progressively from Hindu to Tibetan culture. The villages of Khumbu were clustered into small snow-peaked Himalayan valleys and plateaus just beyond the edge of Tibet proper. Since the turn of the 19th century, the villages of Khumbu were juxtaposed between two cultural, social, and state systems. On the one hand, they were a frontier Tibetan society whose main sources of income, sources of literature, models of government, clothing, medicine, economy, language, and knowledge nearly all originated in Tibet (see Aziz 1978). Even after the region built its own monasteries (dgon pas) at the turn of the century, the healing and religious orientation of these institutions was to Tibet. On the other hand, the Khumbu region has been part of the Nepalese kingdom for the over two-hundred years of the country's existence as a kingdom. Until Westerners who came through the Khumbu en route to Everest in the early 1950s paved avenues for later full penetration of Nepalese infrastructure in the region, the presence of the kingdom was minimal. Foreigners built airstrips, wider trails, hospitals and health posts, and schools. Later, the controlling arms of the Nepalese monarchy made themselves more omnipotent through these institutions and through police stations, border checkposts, national park headquarters and outposts, river hydro-electric projects, banks, and postal services scattered throughout the region. Gradually, the schools and medical facilities were (and are still being) turned over the Nepalese government. These agencies exerted their control largely through laws and restrictions imposed directly from ministries in Kathmandu working, until 1990, under his Majesty the King of Nepal.[10] Despite the Khumbu Sherpas' obedience to laws of trade and taxation imposed by the Nepalese government, however, they had only token involvement with the monarchy over the years. They were a frontier peasant community in the kingdom of Nepal, but more significantly they were a frontier peasant community in the culturally-defined Tibetan state.

Trade relations guaranteed steady movement of Sherpas between the Khumbu and Tibetan cities, as well as further south and east in northern India and Sikkim. The local Tibetan governmental systems served as models for Sherpas, with *pembus* (*Tibetan:dpon pos*), headmen, serving as tax collectors for the Nepalese kings. Their closest equivalents were Tibetan feudal estate overlords (Carrasco 1959) since *pembus* were always wealthy men of the oldest households in the Khumbu. But the feudal arrangement of Tibet never entirely took hold in the Khumbu, where despite large differences in wealth and property ownership most householders were of relatively equivalent economic status in comparison to frontier villages of Tibet proper. By 1963, the *pembu* system of taxation had given way to the elected *panchayat* (*Nepali:*council of five) system implemented by the Nepalese government, but even though the arrangements and titles changed, the clans of the former *pembus* still dominated membership in the *panchayat*. Although Sherpas were not part of the feudal society of Tibet, the arrangements of power by which their lives were ordered came from Tibet, and were expressed particularly through practices of medicine and concepts of personhood.

SHERPA CONCEPTS OF SELF

Contemporary Sherpa sickness was thought to arise from: social offenses against the dead or living of the natural or celestial world; from negligence, accidents, and *karma* which disrupt the body; and from states of consciousness. Sherpa beliefs about the nature of affliction and its remedies suggested a tripartite conception of self as social, physical and mental. Sickness was believed to arise from tensions between 1) individual and social self and 2) within the individual between mental and physical being.

The concept of *chi nang sang sum* (*phyi, nang, gsang gsum*) helped elucidate Sherpas' "self" constructs. *Chi* meant outside, *nang* meant inside, *sang* meant secret, *sum* meant three. The concept was applied to many facets of Tibetan and Sherpa life. An example of its use was that those outside the monastery and uninitiated were considered *chiwa*; *nangwa* were monks initiated and living inside the monastery. *Sangwa* were those monks who had undergone initiation into the more advanced, secret levels of practice and *sum* was the constitution of the three as a unit. The notion was also applied in esoteric contexts to pathogenesis: sickness arose from outer demons appearing as "real" (which meant anything from weather, astrology, bacteria, viruses, food poisoning, or for the laity, real spirits which they had offended); inner demons released through incorrect actions (which translated to bad diet, bad *karma*, and other faulty behaviors promulgated by the individual and affecting the body in a negative way); and secret demons that arose from faulty control of the life wind (*rlung*) (conceived as one of the body's three humours and conceived by the laity as the condition whereby one could think oneself into sickness; madness was considered a disorder of *rlung*) (see also Tucci 1970:175).

The Sherpa laity put the concept of *chi nang sang sum* to their own use. Sherpas suggested that the concept served to delimit boundaries between the spheres of their social and personal lives. These boundaries were maintained in daily *and* ritual acts. I was told that "*Chi nang sang sum* meant to outside and inside one we talk different. There are outside and inside secrets that we must keep." Sherpas explained that someone who told many people about his or her problems was someone who knew no *chi nang*. Some things could be told to one's family, and some things one would have to keep secret even from them. If one had *chi nang*, one knew when to share knowledge with others *and* when to withhold it. Having *chi nang* was considered empowering to the individual, but also protecting; not sharing secrets protected you since "what others didn't know couldn't hurt you." At the same time, having *chi nang* also meant knowing when to share with others as a structural complement to avoiding social bonding. It was as important to know when, with whom, and what to say as it was to know when and how to avoid talking to certain others. The boundaries between self and world were commentary that Sherpas believe that one had to regularly balance being part of the group and at the same time be independent of it. This idea emerged again in the comments of one Sherpa, recorded by Ortner: "If my neighbor is in a bad mood, I must have done something wrong, and if I am in a bad mood I must have done something wrong" (Ortner 1978a). The self was at once connected causally to others but self-contained at the same time—an individual in a socially effective aggregate. Failing to sustain a balance between the extremes of a continuum between self and other caused health disorders.

For example, sickness was caused by witches, *pem*. *Pem* were usually living females with whom one had contact. All women were thought to be capable of causing sickness in others in two ways: "over-liking" and "under-liking." The woman who "over-liked" another was either "loving someone too much" or envious of his or her possessions, qualities, etc., and was forced to be this way by her *gyaptak* (a personal god which *forced* certain sentiments in those in whom it resided). The woman who "underliked" another, conversely, was usually angry with that person. Both situations caused sicknesses of equal discomfort. The idea that sickness stemmed from "over-liking" (expressing desires and attachment or inter-dependence) was another way of stating the importance of social independence. On the other hand, the idea that sickness stemmed from "not liking enough" (expressing hostility and detachment or independence) was another way of stating the importance of social bonding and socio-centricity. Spirits and deities had the same problems with humans. These included *lha* (gods), of 1) mountains associated with clan ancestors, 2) one's personal gods, and 3) earthly gods of trees, rocks, rivers, and mountain passes. It also included *shrindi* (spirits), *norpa* (ghosts, or persons held in the intermediate state after death before rebirth), and occasionally the earthly spirits called *lu, tsen, du* (spirits of places of nature) These deities and spirits caused sickness if they were "under-liked" out of neglect or hostility, and if they "over-liked" due to great attachment to certain humans with whom they came into contact.

Sherpa medical practitioners played a critical role in configuring the "Sherpa self." Their practices included: shamanism, called *lhawaism*;[11] and lamaism, which included scholarly *amchi* medicine.[12] For the last thirty years, Sherpas also had biomedicine in both Khumbu and Kathmandu.[13] Sherpa shamanism pursued a dialogic, relational remedy for its patients through reciprocal relationships that encouraged communality, such as in gift-giving to spirits and etiologies based on real social conflicts. The healing performances of Sherpa shamans, like those of other shamans in Nepal discussed at length in the edited volume by Hitchcock and Jones (1976), attempted to resolve, or at a minimum bring into the open, ailments stemming from disorders of the "social self."[14] Lamas and *amchis*, on the other hand, claimed the ability to cure disorders of the body and consciousness stemming from individual action and attachment to the physical world. Bodily afflictions were the consequence of mental obstructions due to excessive anger, greed, and ignorance. Lack of discipline resulting in attachment to the physical and social world because of greed, anger, and ignorance also caused afflictions. Lamaism pursued a course of instruction in individualism and non-attachment, and it built effigies to help patients visualize their mental obstructions and give them a symbolic material shape. Lama *amchis* also catered to the individual self, but principally through the site of the physical body by means of an elaborate physical diagnostic system and pharmacopeia.

The Sherpa healers emphasized different aspects of the Sherpa self: social (shamans), mental, and physical (lamas, including *amchis*). As it happened, however, Khumbu Sherpa sentiments of social identity enfolded the other two, since lamas' symbolic messages about the individual mental and bodily selves were most often subsumed within a context of communality concerned with the social self; their effigies were re-interpreted as gift-offerings to spirits causing disorder, and *amchis'* treatments were manipulated by patients so as to maximize the treatments' social reciprocity value. The individualized mental and physical selves of Khumbu Sherpas were thus constantly thrust back into a context of sociocentricity. Over the last years of field and archival work, I too came to the conclusions suggested by others[15] that the Sherpa imagery of self as social derived from a historical epoch of shamanism, whereas the imagery which divided the individual into bodily/mental being originated with the arrival and rise of Buddhist lamaism in Tibet. Of interest was how the discourse about the self shifted as new forms of society took shape and as the need for new forms of power were generated.

Several aspects of Sherpa medical pluralism were thus of interest to me. First was the historical gradual emergence of a concept of self as a subject, separate from others and self-regulating. Second was the way the individualized self emerged as both a subject *and* object—that is, as a self with a detachable, physical and objectified body. Third was the significance of the transition to Buddhism as a turning point from on the one hand a social system held together through idioms of family and collectivities in feudal arrangements but reliant for cohesion upon monarchial military force, to a society that was held together through individual self-will using productive power and feudal coercive arrangements but with an absence of military force. Foucault found that for modern Europe, the emergence of a discourse of self was essential to a modern state which needed to exert control through non-coercive, self-willed means. I suggest that the discourse of self in Tibet was also linked to the growth of a loosely structured state system that could not exert control through coercive means alone but rather had to rely also on knowledge-power instruments to exist. In Europe, bio-power and "governmentality" largely substituted monastic power and feudalism. In Tibet, strategies of power which resembled productive power and arrangements of governmentality were part and parcel of monastic theocratic power. In the remainder of the essay, I explore the emergence of subjectivity through increasing textual attention to the self as a problematic notion in specific ways in historical Tibet. I then briefly look at the mechanisms whereby the Tibetan public, like Sherpas, were brought into arenas of observation where under scrutiny they could produce truths by and about themselves. In the summary, I explore the similarities and differences between bio-power and the kind of power seen in historical Tibet.

PRE-BUDDHIST TIBET[16]

Oral histories recorded in written form after the 9th century in Tibet claimed that Tibetan kings descended to earth from the heavens by means of a sky-cord. This cord was then used again to pull them back to heaven at the end of their reign (Snellgrove and Richardson 1968:49-53, Choephel 1978, Macdonald 1984). When the sky-cord of the king Dri Gum was accidentally cut, so began the reign of earthly beings over other earthly beings. Some twenty six or so generations later, King Srong-brtsan sgam-po (c.640 A.D.) introduced Buddhism to Tibet.

It was probably the time period between Dri Gum and Srong-bstam sgam-po which witnessed the emergence of a pantheon of sky and celestial beings to whom the mundane of the earth paid homage (Tucci 1955). These deities emerged on top of a host of earth deities and demons fixed to specific mountains, trees, rivers, lakes, and boulders. It is this earthly and heavenly pantheon of demons and deities which is still represented to this day in shamanic practices of Sherpas and Tibetans.

The few historical records from pre-Buddhist Tibet, that is Tibet before 7th to 9th centuries, suggest that Tibetan society variously consisted of warring chiefdoms and at times larger kingdoms organized on the basis of simple ranked kinship units, held together through ritual social reciprocity in patron-client linkages, and backed by military force. The lack of a written language limited the size of kingdoms, since the kingdom would only grow as large as that area which the king could visit in a year's time to collect taxes and corvee and to garner allegiance from populations which in some cases were the vanquished and unallied populations. Rulers of this time were vested with responsibility for ensuring the rainfall, protecting their people from epidemics, ensuring fertility, and generally "maintaining the cosmic and social order intact and in due working order" (Tucci 1955:200). Rulers establishing their rule and expanding their territories relied on the services of pre-Buddhist priests. These priests were able to contend with deities and demons who inhabited the earth (the *saptak*) and heavens (the *lha*), and who were potentially pathogenic to the general social order (Ekvall 1964, Stein 1972, Snellgrove and Richardson 1968).[17] The most prevalent of the spirits capable of disrupting the social and cosmic order, the *saptak*, (*sa bdag*) were opposed to the "civilizing" tendencies of the kingdoms since these tendencies disturbed the spirits' homes. These disturbances included building castles, timbering for permanent homes, cultivation, irrigation and mining for ores used in the production of armor—tendencies which were crucial for state-building (Stein 1972). Rulers, in this sense, made claims to authority through military power (or coersion) but also through the legitimizing power of priests who enabled negotiation with demons and deities and who thereby safeguarded the public (Blondeau 1977).

Ritual practices, not surprisingly, effected cures through acts of reciprocity and social bonding, often relying on representations of the ideal family as an inter-dependent unit. In ancient Tibet, one can surmise that retribution for failing to maintain harmonious social relations was sickness; and priests who could cure the sick used effigies, diagnostic explanations, and rituals that required family participation in order to restore social harmony. The centerpiece of the priests' rituals was the *lu* (*glud*) or ransom, offered in exchange for cure or prevention. The ransom was often a sacrificed animal or other goods offered as a means of contracting an oath with deities and demons, analogous to the oath-binding transactions between kings and subjects (Karmay 1975, Snellgrove 1967:37, Snellgrove and Richardson 1968:55).

Pre-Buddhist notions of the soul gleaned from these ceremonies show it as a site at which social linkages were made obvious. The soul was a collection of protecting gods through which the status of the person was constructed. These gods derived from clans associated with place of birth and sacred places of nature at these natal sites such as mountains, rivers, trees (Stein 1972:227). Sacred mountains were the *bla-ri* (soul mountain) of those communities who worshipped them as ancestral deities, probably because in ancient times lineage heads were buried near to or in these mountains, following the custom of entombment of early kings inside of large plateaus constructed to resemble mountains. The funerals for these kings also reiterated family linkages through the distribution of family wealth to guests on the basis of kinship and social distance from the deceased (Richardson 1949, 1953, 1963,

Lalou 1952, Karmay 1987, Rona-Tas 1955). Tibetologists also note that the etymology of the terms *lha* (deity and the term used for clan deities), and *bla* (soul) show them to have been originally the same (Samuel 1985).

Pre-Buddhist cosmology configured the self around notions of the family, the family house and the village (Ekvall 1964, Stein 1972, 1957a and b). The family house was modelled after the image of a socio-centric self, housing a lineage unit within a social space which had, collectively, a central courtyard opening to the heavens, like that at the top of the head of the person through which the soul was believed to be connected to the heavens. Nomadic tents had similar holes at the top, and villages, too, were linked through their central axis (the site which would later become the *gompa*) to the world of celestial deities (Ekvall 1968).[18] It was the location of the soul of the sociocentric self, family, and village which existed along this central axis. If the former was stolen (by deities or demons) or absent for any long period of time, the household (like the self) ceased to exist (Karmay 1987). The self was its *social* identities, and these were fixed in physical and social time and place. As with the imagery projected by Sherpa shamans, pre-Buddhist conceptions of self were relational and dialogic, defined through others.

Contemporary Sherpa shamanism provided interesting glimpses of what the ancient shamanic rites (among others) may have looked like. In the case which follows documented in my field notes, called a *labeo* or lashu (*bla-bslus*, soul ransom or seduction), two Sherpa brothers who lived alone with their mother called a shaman to negotiate the moving of a demon called a *saptak* (*sa bdag*, earth spirit) who lived in a tree near their home.

The elder brother was planning to build a home for himself and his new bride, and their fear was that a *saptak* demon might live in the tree that they planned to chop down. If disrupted, he would cause sickness and misfortune for his new family.

What the brothers did not discuss openly was the fact that one of the most common sources of conflict in the Sherpa community was that between brothers who had "split" their home when the elder took a wife and the younger stayed behind with the parents in the family home in a pattern of ultimogeniture. The problems were largely economic in origin, since the elder brother took his income away from his natal family from that point onward, investing it in his family of procreation. Mother-in-law fought with daughter-in-law (*iwi/nama*) over the resources of the son/husband and invariably this ended up pitting brother against brother. The conflicts manifest themselves as diseases, accidents from violence, and financial misfortune.

The shaman, of course, did find a *saptak* demon living in the tree and agreed to attempt to persuade him to move. On the evening of the possession, the shaman came with his wife, who served as a translator, and with a "village" lama (a monk who had broken his monastic vows). We ate a large meal together and soon after, the shaman constructed an effigy of the *saptak*. It was a small dough figurine with a large head, opened mouth, and outstretched hands and feet. It was crowned with a "god's eye" that represented the "net" in which the demon's spirit would be caught. The shaman's altar was set with bowls of rice, butter, a polished brass plate mirror, his large drum, and a headdress. He first became possessed by his tutelary god, who ushered him into the realm of other gods that he could see in his mirror plate.

Finally, the shaman was possessed by the *saptak* and the audience welcomed the demon with invitations to come, drink his favorite distilled beer, and eat his favorite foods. The demon demanded to know why he was being called, and he then asked why his favorite drinks that we offered were not warmed to his liking. We addressed him as *saptak rimpoche* in an attempt to appeal to him. (*Rimpoche* is the title used for revered reincarnate lamas, although it can also be used as an honorific for persons outside the religious context). And, we warmed his beverages. We learned that he had a wife, a *lu* (*klu*, water goddess) who would also have to be moved with him, and so we promised to move her as well. For this, we had to construct an effigy of her. The spirits both finally agreed to move but only just before dawn, and since that was several hours away, the shaman came out of his trance.

We tried to sleep, but failing that, the shaman suggested we eat another meal. The boys cooked another meal which we ate together, and then we laughed and talked until it was time to prepare for the move. Finally, at nearly four in the morning, the shaman went back into his possession trance and we met the *saptak* again. This time he demanded branches of the tree he was moving from. His wife, the *lu*, asked for flags of her favorite colors and a small butter lamp. After an hour more of coaxing and offering the spirits with gifts, they finally agreed to move. Quickly, quietly, the spirits left the shaman and went into the effigies, and we ran with them across the fields to their new home outside the village where, blessed with burning juniper and with promises that we would respect them, we left them together.

The ceremony ended back at the home, when the shaman became possessed in the last few moments by his tutelary lama and prognosticated on the health of the family and their livestock at the younger brother's request.

The ceremony was a success, and the elder brother was able to go forward with his plans to build a new home. The parallelism between the patients' needs and those of the spirit entities is not uncommon. That the ceremony required the construction of a new home for the demon and his wife made sense, since the ceremony ultimately aimed to create the possibility for the elder brother to construct a new home for himself and his wife without disagreement from his brother or mother. The format of the ritual was uninterrupted reciprocity; the meals we ate together were acts of hospitality from the brothers to each other and their friends, just as the feeding of the demons was intended to create hospitality for them. The cermony was filled by a symbolic repertoire of reciprocity. The promises were made in order to entreat a reciprocal promise by the spirits, and vice versa (pace Ortner 1978a).

Also in ancient Tibet cooperation of spirits was gained through reciprocity and the creation of social bonds patterned after the implicit (though not always reliable) bonds of trust between kin. Retribution for failing to sustain good social relations with others was sickness. This instantiated a repressive mechanism of social control. It was not desire for normative health but rather fear of the wrath of spirits that made the shaman powerful. Concepts of self revolved around the family and society as an inclusive extension of self. It is upon this foundation that Buddhism rose to prominence in Tibet beginning in the 7th century.

THE RISE OF BUDDHISM: 8-13th CENTURIES

With the rise of Buddhism in Tibet we see for the first time a codification of behavioral codes in a written language about the self. The self was a problematic concept for Buddhists, and they devoted considerable time to writing texts that explored/produced its truths.[19]

Once represented, the self became an object of intervention. More importantly however, once represented the problematized self became the locus for subjective intervention or self-disciplinary efforts which indirectly allowed the loose Tibetan "state" to exist.

Buddhism was introduced in the early 7th century and grew in popularity among elites until the mid-9th century. At the same time Tibet grew from a small kingdom in the Yarlung valley into a huge empire vaster than the Tibet of before 1950. Buddhists were persecuted after the mid-9th century and the empire collapsed into scattered principalities for another four centuries. By the 12th century Buddhism had become a popular religion and monasteries were "virtually everywhere" (Stein 1972:66, 75). The second, popular diffusion of Buddhism was seen as giving rise to the theocracy of Tibet, which continued to retain its autonomy by cleverly engaging foreign powers as patrons of its religious orders for the next seven centuries (Stein 1972, Snellgrove 1987, Snellgrove and Richardson 1968, Tucci 1970, Carrasco 1959, Macdonald 1984).

In the period between the first and second diffusions, the tensions between types of religious practice and the institutional forms Buddhism took (which partly explain the fall of empire in the 9th century) were exacerbated (Snellgrove 1987). On the one side were the wandering *tantrists* whose methods were highly magical, whose practices were highly symbolic, and who claimed the ability to conquer and/or recruit the support of demons and deities more deftly than existing pre-Buddhist priests. This sort of Buddhism was more closely aligned with the cosmology of the oldest branch of Buddhism, *ningmapa* (*rnying ma-pa*), and one could still find hereditary lamas living as *yogic* adepts in small *gompas* outside villages in Eastern Tibet and the Himalayas, even among Sherpas. On the other hand, there were the monastics, whose form of practice was less magical, more scholarly and ascetic, and who emphasized teaching others, unlike *tantrists* who stressed secrecy and retreat. This form of Buddhism had its contemporary counterparts in the monasticism of *gelukpa* (*dge-lugs-pa*) branch, the youngest of the current five branches and recently the most powerful in Tibet.

The monastic practices were the more stable elements contributing to the diffusion of Buddhism (Snellgrove 1987:504-5, 510), and practices of *tantra* were seen as corrupting influences to this stability. However, *tantrists* were probably the more convincing of the practitioners to the laity whose social order was still based on notions of reciprocity and social negotiation with demons. The *tantrists* were magicians whose teachings were more like shamanism than monastic Buddhism. This ironically probably explains both the rapidity with which *tantric* Buddhism took hold in Tibet *and* the resistance to it by monastics. Monastics held popular appeal to nobility and aristocracy because of their promulgation of good social behaviors through a wealth of exoteric practices, a codification of behaviors which integrated well with productive activities such as agriculture and trade, and an emphasis on writing and record-keeping. But *tantrisms'* specialized religious cults whose orientations were inward and esoteric and whose ideas about demons resembled pre-Buddhist shamanism made *tantrists* appealing to the public. Some pre-Buddhist priests became *tantric* adepts because of the similarities in practice and belief (Snellgrove 1987:399). The conversions must have been in opposition to the practices of monasticism, which in their own turn opposed whatever institutional control priests still had over local and national governments and nobility (Samuel personal communication, Tucci 1970:163-4).

Eventually, the teaching in *tantric* consecrations provided much of the material for Tibetan monastic ceremonies devoted largely to medico-religious interventions (Snellgrove 1987:510), but in the process of incorporation, the tensions between the two enfolded into the monastery itself. For example, *Boddhisattvas* and reincarnate teachers of monasteries deal with the internal struggle between withdrawal, retreat, secrecy, and mentalist practices versus altruism through teaching and performance on behalf of others, and exoteric exercizes intended to both document and teach methods of self-perfection (Snellgrove 1987:512-14). The theocratic "state" itself benefitted most from the enfolding of the two knowledges into the monastery; the monasteries were crucial to the implementation of new types of power which relied on self-regulatory mechanisms, but the content of the practices allowed for a smooth transition from widespread pre-Buddhist beliefs about magic and the supernatural.

The theocracy of Tibet eventually "threaded together" the feudal society predating the rise of Buddhism. In the long run, based on what was known of the Tibet from roughly the 14th to 20th centuries, Tibet was really no more than a loose weave of regions under the control of a variety of monasteries of different sizes and sectarian orientations. They shared this control with local nobility whose power was legitimized by monasteries which the nobility themselves founded and supported (Samuel 1982, Stein 1972, see also Ortner 1989). Nobility held onto property through protective laws of inheritance. Many of their lands were farmed by farm servants (khol-po), who received their own inalienable plots of land in exchange for farming services on the noble's estate. A large percentage of the population was tax paying peasants (khral-pa) who obtained land of their own through purchase or through grants given to their families for government service. Some land owners avoided government taxes by turning their properties over to the government as monastery holdings. Monasteries were usually tax exempt, yet they survived by collecting their own taxes from villagers and by obtaining sponsorship funds from villagers whose children were being reared by them in monastic-run hostels and schools (Carrasco 1959). By at least the 19th century, there were communities of married nuns and monks (ser-ky'im) who were granted lands which they farmed for themselves in exchange for tribute to an estate overlord, whether this be a monastery or a member of the nobility (Aziz 1978), and this was unlike other religious communities. The ser-ky'im were forbidden opportunities to trade and herd, but they were able to earn income by serving nearby patron communities through ritual services which required literate practitioners. The dual occupation of cultivator/religious scholar of the ser-ky'im signalled the close relationship in general between monastic institutions and land cultivation, for monasteries held the most extensive land holdings in all of Tibet. Finally, by its later period, Tibetan Buddhism had many sects which vied for central control. This meant that some regions had several monasteries, one of which had popular support in a region and provided the region with religious services. The other monastery in such cases was often the monastery linked to the governmental sect in power in Lhasa; this monastery was able to requisition monks from each household and provide educational services that would propell these monks into higher ranks of the government bureaucracy.

Monasteries were also one of the main loci of cultural life for Tibetans. They were the only educational facilities and they were always near to the centers for commercial exchange (including long-distance trade and local sale of crafts, animals and produce). The monasteries were also administrative centers in the sense that since they housed the principal literate persons and resources, they kept records about local populations and produced texts for dissemination to other regions of the country and abroad. They were scholarly institutions, likened to institutions of Oxford or Cambridge, and they also provided medical services to the public by either allowing the infirm to stay in monastic homes of relatives or guest houses during their treatment, or by visiting to the homes of the infirm for ceremonies intended to eradicate the disorders. The surveillance abilities of the monasteries were not only a result of their ability to house Tibetans (particularly monks) and collect information about them and their families, or of their ability to disseminate normative codes through monks returning to their family homes for vacations and private religious ceremonies, but also a result of their strategic location in and near population centers which they served with medical practices.

The monasteries were not the only resources for medical care, since private physicians who passed on their skills to their family members also practiced out of their homes and were tax exempt because of their service to the state (Rrinpoche 1973). Finally, medical teaching hospital/colleges were built by the 17th century and the government provided scholarships to students from all of the regions' provinces, who, in turn, were obliged to practice their medicine in a region of the country designated as needy by the central government (Rinpoche 1973). In the college, patients were treated free of charge on a daily basis. There, the patients were also observed and used as pedagogical resources. Once out of the college, students on government scholarships were replaced by other students from their "home" monastic region.

The state was constructed around Buddhist knowledge and practice, the spiritual and symbolic apex of which resided eventually at the Potala Palace in Lhasa. The knowledge system linking together regions was more important in defining the state than were fiscal or military systems. To some degree, the variability of religious institutions and their differential abilities to both appeal to and gain support of local populations resulted in great social rifts, often formed along sectarian lines. This is why, for example, efforts to implement directives from the central government through the regional administrations outside of Lhasa usually failed, and why external agencies encroaching on Tibet could find inlets through sectarian differences. On the other hand, the sectarian differences and regional variability gave the institutions of Buddhism added strength. They were flexible enough to be locally adaptable while sustaining a universal discourse about the self and social life that was conducive to national unity and self-disciplinary uniformity among its particularized units. The flexible character of Tibetan Buddhism accounted for the plethora of interpretive schools and texts on Buddhism that emerged from Tibet's scholars; it also accounted for the process whereby new versions of "truth" were regularly generated by these scholars as a bi-product of their observation of a changing society.

The imagery that came to us about the arrival of Buddhism showed Tibet as a giant ogress whose limbs had to be pinned down by the *stupas* built in support of Buddhism (Macdonald 1984). The ogress signalled the image Buddhist translators held of the untamed and barbaric peoples of Tibet. Tucked into the civilizing agenda of Buddhism was an unwritten effort to undermine those qualities of pre-Buddhist Tibet that did not acquiesce to Buddhist ideals of independence, of self-discipline, and of conscious control over corporeal desires and attachments. The discourse of Buddhism aimed to produce subjectivity: individuality where there had been collective identities; *self*-control where there had been control by *peers*; a bifurcated self where there had been a unified, social whole; and a supercedence of conscious (mental) over physical being, which ultimately meant constituting a body as a non-social object upon which self-strategies could be put into effect in the effort to obtain self-perfection. This was despite Buddhism's ultimate goal of over-coming subject/object dualism.

The Buddhist project, like that preceeding and during modernity in Europe, cre-ated a discourse about the self which could disclose its "true" nature in the uni-verse. To do this, it had to re-create the self in a form which coalesced Buddhist and pre-Buddhist thinking. Buddhist translators and practitioners had to convert their religious teachings into teachings which made sense to their public. They did this in a number of ways. To begin with, they actively competed with pre-Buddhist priests for the role of legitimizing local rulers by adopting into their cosmology the notion of demons and deities *local to the region*, and after finding a place for these super-natural beings, they claimed to possess superior ability to control them (Ortner 1978b). Below, I explore five aspects of the Buddhist discourse during this transi-tion time.

Demons, Self, and Non-Self

Buddhism reasoned that sickness and other misfortunes were the consequence of individual action, and more significantly *thought*, rather than *social conflict*, by con-structing a model in which various levels of interpretation could be accomodated. For example, some demons were taken as symbolic extensions of the notion of failed self discipline in this life (ignorance) or in one's past life (*karmic* inheritance, *las*).[20] Buddhism at once acknowledged the presence of spirits and then designed a form of practice which depotentized them in a discourse about the omnipotent sen-tient consciousness. We can see, for example, the ritual practices of *cho* (*gcod*) which were intended to allow oneself to visualize the demons and battle with them (Gyatso 1985). David-Neel explained this through a description of a monk she se-cretly watched while he practiced *cho* rituals on a hillside:

> Meetings with these demons is deliberately sought in order to challenge [them], to turn the experience into one of liberation from fear, boundless compassion, complete detachment and spiritual illumina-tion. . . the monk is attacked by demons. They eat him, the lama says. This is his training. . . he must learn the demons are himself. . . He who does not believe in demons would never be killed by them (1937:148-152).

The evil demons were, at the esoteric levels of practice which everyone was sup-posed to hope to achieve, turned into manifestations of the evil which one ulti-mately would strive to eliminate (Snellgrove 1987:467-68). Disorder was seen as caused not only by failed social interaction with demons and deities but also by failed discipline of the consciousness. Bodily ailments were representative of the sentient mind's inability to see and understand the "true" nature of reality. Lamaism never eliminated from its texts the imagery of demons and deities as in some sense "real" because *chiwa* (uneducated) minds' awareness of demons and deities as inner qualities required a *sangwa* (secret understanding) sentient mind or consciousness for dealing with them. For the *sangwa* practitioner, demons and dei-ties were sometimes mental conceptualizations because all things were, in some sense, mental conceptualizations, at that level. Buddhism applied to disease, a flexible knowledge which could, for strategic purposes, represent itself as a cosmology of demons and deities while at the same time rendering some of these spirit entities illusory.

Practitioners visualized themselves as deities with supernatural powers and destroyed the lesser deities and demons through combat. Examples of the ritual therapies of contemporary Sherpa lamas and monks elucidated these practices, again taken from my fieldnotes:

Onchu was a wealthy Khumbu villager who suffered general pains over his whole body—a condition Western physicians diagnosed as arthritis. He hired ten monks for an entire-day ceremony. The centerpiece of his healing ritual was a set of effigies *lu* (body, *lus*): one of Onchu and one of his wife, dressed to resemble them as closely as possible, even using their hair clippings and snatches of cloth from their clothes. These effigies sat at the center of an altar constructed of conical *torma* (figurines) representing the Buddha, offerings to the Buddha, butter lamps, and around the outside of the altar on each of four sides three rows of pyramidal *torma* representing lesser demons and deities (each side painted a different color affiliated with each of the four directions).

The altar was very important because it represented a *mandala*. Buddhists arriving to Tibet in the 7th century generated a model for the universe which served both as a meditative aid for achieving perfection in enlightenment and as a model of that state of perfection. The *mandala* was not a rendition of the universe as it existed but rather the universe as it should exist. *Mandalas* were usually symmetrical and four-sided, representing the geographic directions of the universe radiating from a central locale—usually an image of a single *buddha*, *boddhisattva*, or divine being. The mandala was used by practicing Buddhists as a meditative aid, fixing their sentient mind on the central figure enabled skilled practitioners to essentially become the pictured entity in their minds. This practice was carried out by the monks rather than the patients, but patients who were capable were expected to read along and practice the ceremony with the healers. By becoming the being from which the universe radiated, practitioners were believed capable of great spiritual and mundane accomplishments, including eradicating the ailment through teachings. *Mandalas* also served as architectural blueprints for monasteries, bringing the conceptual into life and framing the life of the monastics with a conceptual ideal. In *kurim* (bskyed-rim) curing ceremonies like this one, the *mandala* altar was intended to reconstruct the origins of the universe, abolishing temporal fixity in the minds of ritual participants, making the participants timeless, and collapsing history into a present construction of the practitioners.

The ceremony itself entailed recitation in unison from texts, punctuated by the sounds of cymbals, horns, drums and bells. Each of the movements was indicated in the texts that read like scripts of a drama performance. Throughout the day the patient sat and watched the event, and occasionally his wife filled the monks' tea cups. The recitations were first made as invocations, consecrating the effigies as representatives of spirits, persons, and deities, and inviting the demons and deities to symbolically enter their figures on the altar. The ceremony was meant to be a sort of "party" for them, I was told. The rest of the recitations were devoted to a symbolic battle between the monks taking the form of the Buddha and the symbolic demons who were meant to be enticed to the bodies of the human effigies. The lesser demons and deities surrounding the humans were recruited by the monks to help in combat; they were the "soldiers" ready to do battle.

The ceremony ended after each effigy was removed from the alter and admonished individually. The house was then emptied and a sole monk walked with the final effigies of the deconstructed altar backward along a trail of *tsampa* out of the house. The trail was quickly swept up after his footsteps, leaving no trace of a return path to the home. The entourage of monks and effigies was paraded outside the village where, amidst final purifications with smoldering juniper, the altarpiece/effigy was burned.

From the perspective of the lama and some of the more educated monks who performed *kurims*, the meaning of the *kurim* was multiple. There were different levels of practice, they explained, which were tailored for different levels of knowledge and awareness. Performances which were for the laity had to rely on a

widespread symbolic paraphernalia which put the meaning of the ritual into
layperson terms, according to the professionals. In the long run, the ceremony was
intended to educate the patient about the nature of inner disorder or "inner demons" (*gdon*).

One monk explained to me that laypersons who had little or no monastic education had to be educated through the use of symbols and analogy:

We do this [the *kurim*] to obliterate obstructions and send them out. The *torma* is a thing, but really it is an
idea in our mind. If we get sick, bad things happen, or if people say bad things about us—gossip—this is
to send these obstructions away. The *torma* is for visualization of what is in the mind—the obstacles.

The cure thus entailed a visual drama of how specifically the patient could cure
his disorder: by imagining himself as a Buddha, combatting his inner demons by
imagining them as real demons attacking him, and then fooling them to come to
take his effigy rather than him. Sherpas also believed the ceremony was more effective if the effigy was dressed with real items owned by the patient. The final lesson
the patient was meant to grasp was one of detachment. The demons attracted to the
effigy were set ablaze at the moment the patient was meant to realize his own detachment from his physical being—the physical being which was dependent on
others for food, shelter, sexuality, and companionship.

In ancient Tibet this knowledge about demons and deities as sometimes conceptualizations of the uneducated consciousness was implemented on the Tibetan laity. For the laity which still believed in demons however, lamas claimed to conquer,
control, and eventually destroy rather than negotiate with the demons through a
philosophy about the imagination. Samuel elaborated on this,

Tantric Buddhist practice involved meditation on the so-called Tantric "deities". . .These were not deities in a conventional external sense. The Tibetans referred to them by the same word, *lha*, as they used
for "real" deities thought to exist within the material world and in the various heavens of the Indian and
Tibetan cosmology (the term is used to translate Sanskrit *deva*). However, the tantric deities were not so
much forces external to the individual as potentialities within the individual, as within everything that
exists (1990:128-9).

The *lha* were often the same that linked the individual to the collective through
household, lineage, clan, community, estate, and country. But they were reconcep-
tualized as inferior to Buddhist adepts who, in shedding their attatchments to such
identities, proved capable of obtaining ultimate health through enlightenment.
Moreover, Buddhist adepts showed themselves to be more successful than shamans in the mundane sphere; since these *gurus* were paid great sums of money,
they were able to establish vast displays of their wealth by commissioning artwork,
constructing temples, reproducing books, and sporting expensive robes. All of
these acts were included in the repertoire of merit-acquisition, transcendent exercises leading to perfection in enlightenment (Tucci 1970). This was attractive to a
laity which placed great value on material wealth.

One of the interesting things about the Buddhists' multi-modal[21] approach to
reality is that it had to problematize notions of the self. Whereas pre-Buddhist concepts of the self as at once body *and* soul were predicated on the notion that the soul
actually existed but was inseparable from the body, Buddhism had to submit that
the two were separable, given the illusory nature of self. Because characteristics derived from awareness of the "ego" of self were the source of suffering, the self must

also be dissolvable. This, in effect, was contrary to the notion of a soul. Theories of "no-self," which argued that all personality was transient or imagined character came up against the belief in the transmigration of some essence of self in reincarnation (around which principles of *karma* and *dharma* revolved). They thus had to re-invent the soul in a type of consciousness principle, which they did in the notion of *nam-shi* (*nam-shes*).22 Buddhists first emphasized the notion of the individual over the social self by deconstructing the socially significant symbolism of demons as pathogenic sources of disorder. Second, Buddhism problematized the nature of self by deconstructing and then reconstructing notions of the soul in principles of consciousness. Since pre-Buddhist concepts of the self entwined soul and body, problematizing the "soul as a component of self" would be important to another project of Buddhism that will be discussed later, namely the rendering of the body as a controllable and ultimately a disposable entity once the *nam-shi* could be liberated from it.

As successful as Buddhism was at introducing a heightened sense of individualism through its theory of demons and a "non-self," however, it failed to eliminate belief in real demons and a "social self." In fact, Buddhism was really only successful at posing alternatives to pre-Buddhist notions of the self and the supernatural. Of significance was that by posing an alternative to collective identity, Buddhism opened up a means of designing systems of self-regulation. To be sick meant to be ignorant of one's inner self, and so the quest for truth about the inner self was set into motion through Buddhist healing techniques. Exposed, the inner nature of the self could thus be observed and ultimately disciplined. The more patients presented themselves for preventive and curative treatments, the more closely the state could exist through the self-controlling actions of its public. The more often the Tibetan presented him or herself for services or medical treatments, the more closely entwined with monastic systems of power they became. Before turning to an examination of the production of truth, we need to return to the process on which this was contingent, namely the creation of subjectivity.

Reciprocity Versus Individualism

As part of its effort to deflect attention from socio-centric groups, Buddhism also introduced alternatives to the high value placed on reciprocity. Rites of animal sacrifice which underlay reciprocity were reinterpreted as paganish by Buddhist teachers (Ekvall 1964). Killing was demeritorious (saving lives was virtuous) and "feeding" the demons, since they were actually expressions of one's ignorance, would be tantamount to enriching one's sickness. Lamaism stressed the impermanence of all things, epitomized by the fact that death was imminent and enlightenment meant recognizing this fact. By achieving detachment from the material world on which the physical body depended, one could thus ultimately conquer death with enlightenment. Impermanence militated against social interdependence since impermanence implied a transitory nature of social commitments and obligation rather than long term, morally binding obligations to others. To be indebted was to be attached to physical needs, a position which was not only repugnant but also sickness provoking.23

Indoctrination was carried out in and through monasteries. Whereas patterns of reciprocal exchange had always guaranteed social and personal success, as exemplified by the success of kings' exchanges, monasteries presented opportunities for "disinterested giving" as vehicles for ultimate success. Almsgiving and the founding of monasteries were constructed as exercises in detachment. They were meant to be "true gifts" in the sense that Parry (1986) noted, ". . .ideally given in secrecy and without any expectation of worldly return" (1986:467), a concept which undermined entirely the goals of reciprocal gift-giving and establishing social bonds (pace Mauss 1937). Moreover, because monasteries were receptacles for both almsgiving *and* local taxation, they blurred the lines between fiscal responsibility to the state and individual responsibility for health and well-being. In a subtle form of power focused on populations and productivity, the *gompas* in some areas deftly conflated good health with taxation.[24]

However, according to Sherpa society, as with most of the Buddhist discourse, almsgiving became subsumed within a set of ideals about social reciprocity so that while laypersons used contributions to specific monks and abbots to demonstrate their ability to transcend money in a non-reciprocal sense, they also interpreted their gift giving as attempts to "purchase merit" for their next lives and as a means of engaging in reciprocal exchanges with the community. Favors of food, money, and shelter were tabulated at communal ceremonies held at the monasteries. Villagers demanded that the monks make public announcements of contributions so as to record information about the relative prestige "debt" owed to each contributor. Moreover village *gompa* festivals presided over by lamas and monks were sponsored by villagers on a rotating basis. In past years the networks of reciprocity multiplied since rising costs of food made it impossible for any family to meet the entire expense of sponsoring events.[25] Productive forms of power emerging through the knowledge practices of Buddhist clergy were accompanied by a form of repressive power in which fears of becoming social outcastes through failure to participate in reciprocal exchanges persisted. While Buddhism did represent the self as ideally individualized rather than subsumed within kinship or reciprocal alliances, it was only successful as a counter-representation to pre-existing, stubborn conceptions of the ideal self.[26] Of importance was that this self-determining identity was part of equation by which the monasteries helped Tibetan populations regulate themselves. Other factors also played important roles in the creation of subjectivity.

Alternatives to Family

Buddhism not only posed alternatives to reciprocity, it also challenged the family as an organizing principle for society. If the deities and demons of nature were rendered purely symbolic and subdued, as discussed above, then the lineages and clan groups they represented were also made less important. The hierarchical relationship between heavenly deities and earthly deities and demons was yet made to conform to the notion of a still more powerful resource—the consciousness. Buddhism supplemented these locally defined deities with more universal role models in actual persons who were representatives of the Buddha's achievement—the *bodhisattvas*: lamas, and their students, the monks, who represented the accomplishments of the individual, disciplined sentient mind. The lamas emerged as central figures in Buddhist iconography, surrounded in paintings by the less significant local deities of the regions where villagers lived. The individual rather than the so-cial unit was represented as *normal* in performed acts and textual and aesthetic ma-terials that symbolically defined and reproduced the culture.

Since reciprocity was itself, in some part, used to bring non-kin into kin-like rela-tionships which were based on implicit bonds of trust, it makes sense that family was also scrutinized and challenged. For example, *bonpo* priests in the pre-Bud-dhist period reinforced kinship units by officiating at funeral services that were in-tended to secure heavenly afterlife for lineage heads, and they thereby secured the well-being of the lineage (Lalou 1952).[27] Buddhist lamas, however, argued for indi-vidual responsibility at death and later in one's next life, tabulated on the basis of accumulated merits. In death, they posited, one "walked alone," relying only on the preparations made in this life for the next.

A monk of Khumbu explained the emphasis on the individual at the time of death as the story told in the Mani Rimdu annual ceremonial dance by the character Tolden:

When you are born, you must die. Everyone gets sick, but this [process] shows one the physical body. It will get sick, disease and die. The main idea is that you must meditate. Otherwise, you are wasting your time. Tolden says the lama, shaman, doctor—none can save your life. They will care for sick people, but we are all mortal—*jiktenba* (*'jig rten pa*)—destructible bodies. At that time of death, nobody can save you. Not even your relatives can help you then. You must leave your body behind. Then you must walk by yourself.[28]

Belief in reincarnation, which became the "pivot" of both religious and political life, emerged in the late 11th century (Blondeau 1977:15)[29] as a most serious subtle challenge to the system of kinship and practices of inheritance which legitimized it, since reincarnation cut across blood relations. Although it was slow in coming, and although some sects never fully implemented a system of reincarnate abbots, the system eventually took hold on a large scale. It would be difficult to find any Ti-betan who did not believe it possible that his or her child could be born as a reincar-nation of a highly respected religious scholar (*trulku*) or a lama (*bla ma*).

We know, however, that reincarnation theories did not destroy the patterns of inheritance or kin reckoning, since hereditary lamas whose sons inherited their role in their *gompa* (*dgon pa*, religious house) existed throughout Tibet. More important, ideas about family continued to challenge the authority of reincarnation through patronage bonds established between brothers inside and outside the monaster-ies.[30] Even reincarnate abbots were influenced by their families, whose status be-came elevated upon the abbot's "enthronement." Patron-priest relationships persisted not only among those monastic sects who were largely founded, sup-ported and controlled by aristocratic families, but also in those sects where reincar-nation played a decisive role in governing (Snellgrove 1987:515).

The family was no longer the only locus of the self but merely one of the contexts in which the independent self might function. Monasteries which recruited vast numbers of Tibetan youth did not reconstitute the family; they posed an alternative to it. Their alternative stressed not affinal and consanguineal notions of personhood but rather methods of personhood that devolved to a method of self-discovery and deconstruction. The monasteries were in some sense conduits for individualized self-awareness. They were also two way conduits: monks learned the truth about themselves, then they carried these truths back to their family homes for ritual services and holidays, making possible the transmission of knowledge-power instruments into almost all Tibetan households. The link between the hierarchical, administrative centers of government and average households in Tibet was thus made possible in many areas through infringements upon the importance of the family unit and an increasing emphasis on the exoteric pedagogical role of the clergy.

Self-Discipline

Theories of self discipline formed an important part of the creation of both subjectivity and discourses about the body as an object. The most convincing of the early Buddhist practitioners were *tantrists*, who posited the most elaborate theories of the individualized self. For *tantrists*, the self had two distinct components: the body and the consciousness. They preached that the body encompassed the universe; the ability to control the body with the consciousness was thus equated with the ability to control the universe (Basham 1963). Hence, disciplines of the *body* were also devised and elaborated in Tibetan Buddhism. Buddhist healers had to take theories about the healthful perfection of the self and the sources of disease (borrowed wholesale from Sanskritic sources) and systematize the knowledge about correct behaviors that could help one to obtain this healthful perfection. These theories began with awareness of the twelve causal "enchainments" (of cause and effect) of suffering:

(1) Ignorance (of the vanity of the phenomenal world: *avidya*) is the production ("occasion of production") (*nidana*) of of the physical constructions which will be avoided or dissolved by consciousness. (2) The physical constructions (*samskara*) produces representation (*vijnana*). (3) This causes individuality, characterized by a name and a form (*namarupa*). (4) Individuality causes the play of the six sensory domains (the five physical senses and the subtle cognitive sense) which in their own turn (5) permit contact with the object of sense. Touch (6) causes the sensation which (7) evokes thirst (desire). Desire (8) causes appropriation and this, in the form of sexual union, produces (9) an embryonic existence (semen of the parents where arrives the incarnation of a psychical individuality). The embryonic existence turns into (10) birth and this (11) to old age and death. The psychical individuality does not disappear after death. Void of ignorance (*avidya*), it is "'pushed" (12) by the impulses and thirst conditioned by past acts, toward a new phenomenal existence, its suffering and its end (Fillozat, J. 1970 in Meyer). It is this series of twelve productions (*nidana*) which is represented in the rim of the Wheel of Life (*srid-pa'i 'khor-lo*) with which the Tibetans adorn the facade of their temples. At the center of the wheel are represented the three forms of ignorance (the three poisons): aggression, mental obscurity, and desire in the form of a serpent [anger], a pig [ignorance], and a cock [greed] (Meyer 1988:63-5 my translation).

Tantrists argued that breaking the cycle of rebirths and obtaining enlightenment could be accomplished. Practice for the *tantrists* and monastics entailed rigorous devotion, regular and proficient meditation, control over mental conceptualizing, correct recitation of *mantras*, and performance of ritual gestures (*mudras*) with the instruments of *vajra* (*rdo-rje*) and bell. Above all, it entailed following the *Eightfold Pathway* espoused as a key to enlightenment, practicing:

. . .correct views, correct intention, correct speach, correct action, correct effort, correct and ardent vigilance, and correct contemplation (Meyer quoting Silburn 1988:62 my translation).

Moreover, the powers gained by proficient practice were believed to be on the one hand universal and on the other hand emergent from within the individual. As Samuel (1990) noted, the goal of rigorous practice was the "awakening" of inner "potentialities":

These potentialities (=states) could be awakened or actualized by appropriate practices. The development of these potentialities was complemented by other practices, concerned with becoming aware of and controlling the various psychic centres and flows within the body . The two sets of practices together led to the ultimate goal of Tibetan Buddhism, the attainment of the enlightened state believed to have been achieved by the historical Buddha and his successors. . . . The potentialities acquired as part of the "path" were thought to convey powers of healing, defence against misfortune, prediction and divination, and these poweres were highly valued by Tibetans in their own right (Samuel 1990:129).

The Buddhist thus emphasized *self*-control, which meant first taking refuge in the Buddha and then *devoting oneself to the study of oneself* in meditation. The objective was in some measure to liberate one's consciousness hitherto hidden from view from its confinement within the physical body and within a thick cloud of mental attachments. The body was of the following character: the material body or *rag pa'i lus* (body of touch, sense) supported an inner, innate or peculiar body or *gnyug ma'i lus*, which consisted of two components *rlung* (vibratory power) and *sems* (sentient mind or consciousness, also called "mind-light" from which derives the term enlightenment). *Sems* was responsible for creating *samsara* (the endless cycle of rebirths) being an instrument for objectification, but it was also capable of transforming itself into transcendent consciousness, *ye shes lus*, which went beyond the duality of existence—non-existence, or I—Not I. Practices of meditation and self-discipline were capable of transforming one's sems into transcendent consciousness. The sems was of similar nature to the mental body or *yid lus*, containing the dichotomizing faculty (I-not I). It was attached to its physical being and therefore subject to the perils of *karmic* inheritance (*las*). The *ye shes lus* or body of transcendent consciousness was free from attachment and defilements and therefore without material form (Tucci 1970), thus it was capable of infinite compassion because it had no desire attached to it.

The *yid lus* or mental body was the house for "inner weaknesses" which could be overcome by the awareness possible of the *ye shes lus*, transcendent consciousness, obtained through self-disciplinary techniques, including the commissioning of *kurims*. Thus certain schools emphasized the inverting of a "discovered" inner weakness into a strength. Desire and especially desire manifest as libidinal passion, for example, were thought of as a negative "potentialities" until they were used for the purposes of self-discipline (Snellgrove 1987:121,129-30). In some schools this meant, for males, fully exerting libidinal desires toward an *image* of a beautiful female and then deconstructing the image created there, limb by limb, these were practices of the *maya* body (*sgyu lus*) which was itself a condition of the potentiality of moving from *sems* to *ye shes*. One of the hallmarks of *tantrism* was the emphasis on using ritual techniques to achieve enlightenment by adepts rather than for purely dramaturgical purposes. They assumed, for example, that performances carried out correctly would produce beneficial effects in propelling the self toward enlightenment. Those who lacked enough self-discipline to perform such rituals themselves, such as an audience, would still benefit from the ritual. However, these observers would reach the goal of enlightenment much more slowly than practitioners themselves, utilizing many more lifetimes. Celibacy was considered a practice which expedited movement toward enlightenment in monastic schools, and the gains from this practice would carry over to the rest of the population. However, other schools at various times continued to practice sexuality as an exercize in sharpening one's mental dexterity. Their logic was that it was not sexuality that was undisciplined so much as the passion of sex, since it was passion that signalled desire. Intercourse with others was carried out to extend one's passions to the limit without desire—that is preventing ejaculation; ironically, sex was a means of exploring the limits of one's ability for self-control. For monastics who found the life of celibacy did not suit them, breaking one's vows and becoming a married village nun or monk was always possible, thereby they could retain their religious role for the laity without living in the monastery itself. For the educated laity, the same intentions were aroused. For both the educated laity and the different schools of monastics and other practitioners, sexual intercourse was seen as a most potent source of self-scrutiny allowing one to gain both mastery over desire and knowledge about the self and the transient nature of reality.

While the monasteries were concerned with the reproduction of knowledge systems, the lay populations and ex- nuns and monks occupied themselves with the reproduction of human repositories into which this knowledge could be placed; these repositories were potential reincarnates, students, and sponsors. The fact that medical practitioners espoused a theory about the potential medical problems for women who did not have children by the time they were 25 years of age begins to point to the productive qualities of Tibetan Buddhist medical practices (explored below). The consequences of monastic arrangements in terms of social control were many. Populations offered to monasteries intimate demographic information concerning their reproduction and productivity. This information was tabulated as part of a taxation system by monasteries, where monasteries held regional control, and by local aristocratic families where they held feudal control.[31] However, even aristocratic families gained insight on such things as productivity among families by observing monastic support by the laity when they enrolled their children in monastery schools and when they made outright donations. Since local aristocratic families were closely tied to some of the monasteries, obtaining information through monasteries was not a problem for them. Detailed record keeping concerning monastic contributions in advance of ceremonies they were pledged for were a hallmark of Tibetan monasteries. But, monasteries also exercized control through less obvious techniques resembling productive power. Buddhism's incitements to action were focused upon gaining more complete understanding of the inner self, bringing its inner truths out into a conscious arena where they could then be controlled. Control of one's inner being enabled control over the universe. The product of the practice, then, was a self-willed regimentation according to a schedule of attitudes, behaviors, thoughts, and intentions. These disciplines were both in the realm of the moral and ethical as well as in the realm of the rational. *Karma*, or *sonam*, worked as a moral principle among the laity, compelling behaviors which prohibited such things as killing, stealing, cheating, dishonesty, treachery, etc. For a promising rebirth, one submitted to the repressive regimes of *karma* which worked through *sems*. On the other hand, a principle of *lung ta* (*rlung rta*, wind horse) worked along the lines of a productive power. Symoblized by the act of causing a prayer flag to be placed so that its prayers would flow into the air in one's absense, *lung ta* signalled a type of religious protection that awareness of the importance of prayers would bring. *Lung ta* was though among Tibet's laity to be a quality of the person—lamas possessed enormous amounts and the layperson possessed much less but could gain more through religious practices like prayer or meditation. *Lung ta* was not something one was born with or something inherited from past lives. It had to be acquired in this life and was of use in this life for obtaining health, and thus it also worked through the principle of "inner vibratory power," the *rlung*, or "wind" bodily humour (the light of the transcendent *sems* rides on the *rlung* vibratory power). The person with much *lung ta* was considered the most capable of staying healthy since *lung ta* signified the strengthening of one's vibratory power through actions of religious value, one of the characteristics of enlightenment is the presence of light, and it is upon the *rlung* (breath) that this light rides (Tucci 1970:64).. Finally, the disciplines of Buddhism compelled actions that propelled one toward transcendent consciousness or enlightenment (a unity of consciousness and light), and in this state, because it was free from attachment, unlimited compassion was possible. Below, we will see how this translated into notions of medicine for the Buddha.

The final component of self-regulatory control in Tibet was the objectification of the body in terms which would allow it to be worked on for the benefit of the state. In the case of European society, Foucault noted that anatamo-politics of the body increased its docility and its usefulness, its productivity and its "integration into efficient and economic controls." In Tibet, the body was objectified but it was not celebrated as the locus for identity. Its inner anatomies and functions were elaborated as temporary locations for emotional strength or weakness which emmanated from the mind, or mental body; ultimately however, the body was seen as an impediment as much as a means to ultimate health in enlightenment rather than as the location of the health itself. In the process of rendering the sentient mind or "consciousness" transcendent, however, Tibetan medical sciences represented the body's functions as linked to the natural universe. It became subjected to a type of social control mandated by the organic representations of the body, carried out in the name of health.

Medical Theories of the Body

Buddhism had dramatic effects in redefining concepts of self in its medical practices. It was in the medical theories that the identity of an objectified body seemed to have become most clearly enunciated. Tibetan medical theories placed into the context of Buddhist theories of transcendence a highly schematized anatomy of the body. In this theory, beliefs about the individual, non-social nature of disorder, the deconstruction of "spirits," a transcendent sentient mind and a physical, objectifiable body were espoused. Amchi medicine combined the practical medical theories of Ayurveda with the Tibetan variants of Mahayana Buddhism, the former of which focused on the physical qualities of life in the natural universe and the latter of which focused on the metaphysical aspects of life in a transcendental universe.

Buddhist doctors, or *amchis*,[32] thus began with the idea that ultimate healing was transcendence of *samsara*. Practitioners first had to transcend the cycle of unconscious death and rebirth by losing one's attachment to the physical body. *Amchi* medicine reasoned that since the body[33] contained the universe, it consisted of elements of the natural world and was subject to proximate causes of sickness which were seen as imbalances of the body's three humors lung, tiwa, pagin (*rlung, mkhris pa, bad kan*: wind, bile, phlegm). These humors were themselves internal manifestations of universal qualities of the natural world. *Amchi* medicine specialized in the treatment of proximate causes of humoral imbalances stemming from diet, climate, astrology, organic dysfunction, and *karma*. *Amchi* science reasoned that since the body was made of elements of the natural world, its functioning must then be manipulable at an intermediate level by intervention with elements of the natural world (Dash 1976, Dhonden and Kelsang 1983). Hence, *amchi* medicine developed an elaborate pharmacopeia using herbs, minerals, bones, flowers, barks, stones, animal organs, and foods. Its treatments however, were not restricted to pharmacology. They stressed "correct" behaviors (the Eightfold Path), dietary restrictions, meditation, commissioning of blessings, emotional control and self-discipline (especially in taming anger and greed as, for example, in the passions of sexuality), and physical movement (e.g., away from or toward a specific climate, or into or out of monastic regions of influence). Those with superior consciousness would not of course need pharmacological interventions because they would not get sick or if they did, they would cure themselves through mental prowess alone. In fact, Sherpas explained that this principle was, they surmized, one reason that the reincarnate lamas rarely got sick. At best, the pharmacological interventions provided temporary bodily relief for conditions which ultimately would have to be cured through total discarding of the body.

Buddhists represented the body as inherently flawed by birth, destined to suffer, and certain to find relief only with enlightenment. Because the healer was meant to provide not only medical care but also medical instruction, the healing *bodhisattva* in Tibetan Buddhism was meant to envision himself as a healing Buddha whose body was like a "tree" of medicine, capable of curing *upon decomposition* through consumption by others:

In another lifetime when he (the Buddha) was ill he uttered a vow to receive a body [like] a "tree of medicine"; all those who were ill—in seeing him, in smelling him or in touching him, or in consuming his skin, his blood, his flesh, is bone or his marrow—were healed of all illness. . .The "king of trees of medicine"is a tree whose wood permits one to see the vital organs inside the human body. The *Avatamsaka* describes it as a great tree whose root, trunk, branches and leaves heal patients who smell or touch them; it compares the tree to the body of *bodhisattvas* impregnated with great compassion (Tatz 1985:47).

The texts also conceptualized the body of the patient as a tree which was also intended for decomposition: the "root *tantras*" (*rtsa pa'i rgyud*) depicted etiology, diagnosis, and treatment schemata as trees. They were read by means of a narrowing of focus which began with large categories in the trunk and "read" through the branches until they came to rest on the particularities (symptoms, pharmacological properties) depicted as leaves. The root of diagnosis explained through the analogy of the tree, methods of observation (of urine, mucous), pulse diagnosis (of the three humours), and interrogation (of the patient regarding conditions which might have given rise to the disorder). The root of etiology offered again through the analogy of the tree, indications of the normal healthy body with its inherent three faults (being part of the world of *duksa*, suffering), and the unhealthy body with the movement of diseases through its various locations. Finally, the root of treatment explained through the analogy of the tree, treatment through diet, behavior, medication and external therapies (such as compresses, moxabustion, movement, etc.). The system of medical knowledge expressed by means of analogy first created the body as an inanimate, naturally occuring object, reified into the image of a tree composed of interrelated anatomical specificities and imminently destined to decompose. It thereby deconstructed the living body as an entity with tangible value in the long run. The *boddhisattva's* body was imbued with the spirit of compassion because of his transcendent acuity; the utility of the body itself then became most apparent upon its destruction, one of the fundamental laws of nature to which the body was captive.

In *amchi* medicine, the body as an object was exposed and elaborated en route to transcending it in order to obtain enlightenment. The regulation of the circulation of its humours, together with the balanced functioning of its organs and most importantly the moderation of its mental dispositions, were articulated by practitioners in texts written for instructing, intervening on behalf of others, or for exercise by patients themselves. A low level of intervention then recommended that people who suffered phlegm disorders, for instance, should change their diet or leave one region and move to another; people with great anger might be given a series of *mantras* to sit and recite in order to turn the intensity of their anger into equally intense compassion; people with chronic sicknesses might be told their condition resulted from actions in a past life which they could not escape in this life but which they might avoid in the next life by devoting themselves to the monastery as a monk or nun, or by performing numerous religious services over the upcoming years of their life. Finally, the practices of good health required the integration of the body with the natural universe around it, through careful ingestion and altering conditions of climate, but also through acts of cultivation and productivity which could translate into sponsorship of ceremonies by monks and lamas, who believed that ultimately benefits of their own discipline would help others through a principle of compassion.[34] For the monastic, meditation was an exercize which promoted good health, but for the secular majority who did not take the time to meditate, performing good acts through work regimens was considered a step in the right direction. The reproducibility of spiritual knowledge was made possible through theories of reincarnation and a corps of boddhisattvas which forever grew, but the real benefit, it seems was in the ways that these monks became sites not only for the investments of spiritual objectives but also real material currencies in crops and money from the laity. In this way, even though the body was ultimately an obstruction to enlightenment, it could, like passion, be put to use for the purposes of good health and the path toward enlightenment and for the purposes of sustaining levels of productivity among the laity.

In summary, pre-Buddhist notions of the body were inseparable from notions of the collective soul; the social universe defined the body as a part of its surrounding social environment. The Buddhist treatment of the body as an extension of the "natural" universe was thus probably easily made. However, the categorization and systematization of the natural body as an individualized object, subjected to the manipulations of mental effort, was new. Viewed from the perspective of shamans, and their attempts to construct patients' social anatomies to resolve sickness, *amchi* medicine could be seen as reconstructing patients' social anatomies into natural bodily anatomies. *Amchis'* emphasis upon transcendence of physical things reproduced a body *separable from and controlled by the sentient mind*, the "true" seat of the self. The type of body produced in Buddhism differed significantly from the type of body that seems to have predominated in pre-Buddhist times—a body constructed internally on the basis of the external social world of the person.[35] The new self, which was both mental and physical, contrasted wildly with the shaman's self which could only exist for and through others. The project of constructing the body as an object was made complete in *amchi* medicine. As an object, the body could thus be brought into the sphere of intervention by the "state" via the rhetorics and scholarly theories and practices of "self-discipline." In the long run, however, Tibetan concepts of self were sustained in all three forms, accomodating both shamanic and Buddhist knowledge. The self emerged as tripartite—bodily, mental, and social. But the body and consciousness were enfolded into the social self in the long run and this may have been why *amchi* medicine also eventually included a category of diseases which resulted from demonic attacks (Rinpoche 1973).

The importance of the emergence of scholarly materialist medical theories about the body was that despite the religion's ultimate attempt to transcend subject-object dichotomies, it constructed new objects of discursive interest, namely, the body and the consciousness, now treated as polar and highly problematized entities. *Amchi* medicine over time continually refined its medical strategies so that they focused not simply on the body in contrast to the norm, but also on specific types of bodies and specific emotional types: "the children," "the elderly," "the females," "the lethargic," "the insane," and "the accident prone," for example. Each of these categories of people constituted different types of practice in *amchi* medicine, since each was vulnerable to its own peculiar disorders (see, for example, Finckh 1976). Thus the shift in the medical gaze from families to the bodies of populations and the spaces between these populations was completed over time. First came the creation of normative grids by which social categories of persons could be seen as abnormal and medically deviant, therefore in need of medical intervention—grids which it should be noted combined both information collected from populations with norms already fixed in the image and practice of Gautama Buddha. Then came the refinements of practices devoted to the care of the children, the females, etc., all of which made further demands on these bodies to divulge their hidden secrets — to make them the object of inquiry and ultimately of self-control. It was not merely through one's social experience that one was able to identify one's self, as with shamanism, but now also through the normative grid of disease categories that one could identify one's self. A phlegmatic person was in a risk category of persons prone to disorders of the intestines, etc. It is important to note again, however, that the normative grid notion for Tibetan physicians was a notion that combined eternal truths fixed in representations of the Buddha and the state of enlightenment with new information that was ascertained about the norms of the body. Statistical collection of normative standards was, if collected, in this sense always placed back into the context of given religious/philosophical truths about the body.[36]

No doubt the monasteries had a significant role to play in defining populations in such categories since monasteries had responsibility for managing great numbers of male youths, females who were disallowed entry, usurping tenants who did not pay rents but whom they could not punish, and madpersons whose challenges to their authority must have been a constant source of discomfort given their own relativistic interpretations of reality and so who were disciplined through theories of excessive anger that required great mental discipline to control. In *amchi* and lamaist medicine, the first accomplishment was thus the creation of a body that could be managed by the sentient mind; the next step was refining its theories so that specific categories of people had techniques of self care peculiar to them. Techniques of power that were implemented on the national level through hospitals and the mandates to supply regions with physicians trained in amchi medicine (or by exempting lineages of physicians from taxation) (Rinpoche 1973). These techniques were crucial to the existence of the state.

THE PRODUCTION OF TRUTHS

The constitution of subjectivity was one of the major accomplishments of Buddhism in Tibet. A second was constructing arenas in which truth could be expanded through experimentation and observation. In post-Enlightenment European and American societies, theaters of experimentation were set up in medical clinics, asylums and prisons. Through observation of and experimentation on the human subjects at these locales, the limits of human truths offered themselves up for scrutiny. In Buddhist Tibet, no exact counterpart arenas were found in monasteries, or in the extension of monasteric services into private homes, except perhaps in hospital settings.

First, monastic settings were not designed as places of experimentation but as places of higher learning. Their scholarship depended upon a class of literati called *Gyeshes* (*dge bshes*) whose occupations included the production of interpretive texts which they themselves wrote. If examples from Khumbu sufficed to show the nature of their writings, then these publications included the recording of current events, history, political commentary, and treatises on the general state of the population, its health, concerns, religious apathy, or religious zeal. The information used by *gyeshes* in their texts came to them either through clients who visited the monastery or by visiting homes of clients where they performed diagnoses, preventive ceremonies and blessings. In both locales, clients exposed family and personal problems by commissioning services for themselves or for others who were in medical need. For example, services were sought for clients whose lives were endangered by working on risky Himalayan expeditions, alcoholism, financial ruin, or bodily disease. Monastics also collected information about populations through ceremonies which attracted the financial support of entire communities. Public sponsorship of ceremonies eventually turned into competition between villagers, in which financial promises escalated in public shows of personal success. These activities exposed to monastics the state of taxable income. The ability for the monastery to respond to newly produced truths about social reality was nowhere more clearly shown than in the Khumbu monastery's support of an altogether new ritual ceremony called *Bumtsho* ("a hundred thousand blessings"), which began for Khumbu Sherpas in Kathmandu in 1984 and was moved to the Khumbu several years later. In 1987, this ceremony amassed sponsorship from the laity amounting to three lakh (300,000 Nepalese rupees or $15,000. at the time), an enormous sum by Nepalese standards, given mostly by the wealthiest villagers. Gyeshes and lamas at the Khumbu monastery actually wrote new texts that could be used for Bumtsho, combining historical treatises with new treatises which allowed them to represent new population-level truths about the dangers of investing too much money in material goods and not enough in religious ceremonies (like the yearly recitation of the *bka gyur*, (original scriptures of the *Buddha's* teachings), or on how flying via helicopters is ultimately no different from walking in terms of the final goal, but only in terms of the pace at which one moves to get there, to explain through analogy the growth of Buddhism in popularity.

Monasteries took young boys from surrounding families into their scholarly ranks. Children in monasteries provided another crucial link between households and state apparatuses. Knowledge produced in monasteries found its way into the homes through monks and nuns on their visits home as well as through exoteric practices in the form of healing performed by these monks and lamas. Families usually called their children and relatives for the performance of ceremonies and in this way brought larger spheres of social life into the purview of the administrative monastic centers.37 The utility of monks as mediators for a type of confessional was, however, only possible through a deconstruction of family as a basis for identity. Without undermining family completely, the monasteries were able to make residual use of them through their links to sons (and daughters in the case of *ser ky"im*) in religious communities. Also of importance is recognizing that in Tibet it is not clear how much of the information monks were able to collect actually found their way into medical texts in the monasteries. More extensive studies of this feedback link would have to be made.

As aforementioned, the monasteries themselves were designed in the image of an ideal universe, the *mandala*, and as patrons entered the monastery, they also made possible the expansion of the monasteric project to the community. Architecturally, the *mandala* blended hierarchy with symmetry, fantasy with history. Overall, the representation intended to combine stability with movement, or consistency with adaptability. The effort to sustain given truths within Tibetan Buddhism (for example the invoking of the *kangyur*, *bka' 'gyur*, combined with the effort to innovate, improve and expand upon newly discovered truths (for example the voluminous texts on interpretations of the *kangyur*, called *Tengyur*, produced over the last millenium) is one of its striking features. The material medical practices of Tibet also showed this strong flexibility and innovation.

Whereas monastic arenas for the production of truth were not obviously engaged in experimentation but simple observation, the medical sciences did use experimentation. The development of the pharmacopeia of *Amchi* medicine with substances local to the Tibetan plateau and Himalayas was originally accomplished through experimentation on patients and the careful recording of findings in medical texts and manuals. To some extent, these data were fit into pre-existing models of the universe and nature determined in *Ayurvedic* and Buddhist schemas. But, they were also innovative and expansive given the ever-increasing stores of knowledge about the body and its relationship to the sentient mind uncovered through medical treatments. Contemporary Tibetan lamaist medicine and *amchi* medicine in Khumbu both showed such innovative capacity by incorporating into their diagnostic schemata new bodily elements derived from two sources: first, *amchis* innovated with knowledge gained from observation of clients who were using new medicines imported from both China and the West—this knowledge they represented in new texts and diagnoses; second, they incorporated biomedical knowledge that was being taught at local schools and introduced through international agencies, since clients themselves increasingly presented this knowledge on their own. *Amchis'* own theories of disease and health that served to produce truth through representations of the body were thus forever challenged to *both* sustain a subjectivity based on rather fixed, historical constructions of the self and at the same time expand notions about the self to incorporate new truths that the patients offered up. Even the most recent journals of Tibetan medicine distributed in the West show this expansionary tendency, since they make claims to *amchi* treatments for conditions for which biomedicine has had little luck—hepatitis, malaria, cancer.

In contrast to the sites of confession in European psychoanalytic clinics, hospitals, asylums, etc., the confessionals of historical Tibetan and contemporary society were rudimentary. Biomedical, lama, and *amchi* services engaged in roughly the same level of inquiry with patients, each noting details about pathogenic behavior, personal physiology, occupational stress, and disposition. These techniques presented a great contrast to shamans' techniques in which the shaman was expected to know details of the patient's life without the patient disclosing anything. (Ironically, the shamans *did not probe*, but they uncovered details of social life about patients; lamas and doctors *did probe*, but the details they uncovered were about personal, individual life and its internal anatomies rather than about their social lives). Also important is that the shaman did not use concepts of normative grids; cretins, for example, were not thought to be afflicted by their condition of deafness or muteness. It was only when cretins, like any other person in the community, disrupted social harmony or became victims of such disruption that they were designated as afflicted by the shaman. However, the techniques of *amchis* were apparently not as productive as those we have witnessed in the European modern context. The hospital or psychoanalytic record keeping processes which transformed themselves immediately into interventionary techniques in the European context were much more refined than the mode of transfering information between the *amchi* or lama and the scholars who created interventionary strategies in the Tibetan setting. The mechanisms by which truth was produced in Tibet historically were in many ways similar to those of the European modern context: they were contingent upon the creation of subjectivity which allowed for scholarly study of the self to be fully developed; it was also subjectivity which enabled *amchi* medicine and lamaist practice to deploy self-regulatory techniques on the population. However, although the end process was the same, the time involved and the mechanisms of transmission were different.

SUMMARY

Obeyesekere noted that one of the characteristics of worldly religions, as opposed to religious systems of tribal society, was their ability to ethicize everyday behavior by placing moral values on social actions (Obeyesekere 1968). The individual was accountable for his or her actions in this life and in the afterlife, or next life. In tribal society, immoral behaviors were sanctioned by immediate acts of retribution by supernatural entities. The task of the shaman was to appeal to supernatural entities in order to revoke their wrath. The task of the priest (or lama) was to remind individuals of the potential moral consequences of their behaviors. The development of theocratic Tibet from its scattered tribal principalities over several centuries was made possible through Buddhism, and this series of events in many ways followed this progression. The shift to a worldly religion and the emergence of a state, more-over, entailed revisions in the way that people thought about themselves and their society.

Where the family and its idiomatic social bonds once organized social life and defined the *self* in pre-Buddhist Tibet, the state had come to offer an alternative to the family in the institutions of Buddhism in Tibet. New models of personhood derived from individual self-work, study, and meditation were implemented through Buddhist discourse. Ultimately, the route to health and perfection for the Buddhists lay in further refinements of self, which distinguished the principles of consciousness from the physical entity. Shedding one's attachment to the body, made possible through death but also through the disciplines of the sentient mind, was the first and final step toward health. By arousing support for themselves, monasteries provided the opportunity to shed primary allegiance to the family by eliminating the significance of the body, since it was on the body that one's "social skin" was worn. In lay perspective, the body was, after all, made of bones, (*rus*), from one's father's lineage and flesh, (*sha*, for sherpas, *t'ag*, or blood, in Tibet), from one's mother's father lineage. The direct alliance between state and citizen (both created through the discourse) was, in this sense, effected through a discourse of individualism, consciousness, and body.

Tibetan Buddhism promoted a knowledge system which was aimed at ethicizing everyday behavior in order to regulate it. As the self moved from its social identities to individualized forms of identity, it also moved from peer-censorship to self-censorship and self-production in the effort to avoid being deterred from a self-projected path toward enlightenment. Like other worldly religions, Tibetan Buddhism relied on a system of self-disciplinary measures that were ethical in nature. Also like other wordly religions it promoted self-discipline through promise of an other-worldly reward in enlightenment (principles of *karma* or *sonam*). Unlike religions and more like the power Foucault identifies for late European society, however, power in Tibet was productive rather than repressive: its "truth game," if you will, was that of producing a forever expanding knowledge about the self, exposing it for scrutiny and allowing it to be acted upon in a self-disciplinary mode.38 Power was not simply effected as a biproduct of a moral endeavor; it was also a rational attempt to gain self-knowledge. *Lung-ta* or the ability to develop spiritual protection was a measure of one's religious knowledge for the more educated, and a measure of one's supernatural strength for the less educated. Either way, it improved one's health and chances for speedy enlightenment and was a rational complement to the disciplinary projects implied by notions of *karma* (*sonam*) which worked through ethical dimensions.

Also, Tibetan Buddhism implemented and produced its discourses about the self through a host of social apparatuses, including but not limited to monastic functions that appealed to morality. Indeed, the variety of monasteries and hermitages that produced the discourse were themselves part of the political, educational, aesthetic, architechtural, fiscal, and productive arena of the "state"; they organized "things" and "thoughts," because they functioned as schools, governmental offices, medical clinics, welfare agencies, and occasionally the sites for public discipline where both observation for collecting knowledge and disseminating truths about the population were possible.

Like the productive power of post-Enlightenment Europe, the discourses of self implemented through Buddhism and its institutions were not without a basis in productive and material relations. Samuel (1982) argued that Tibet was essentially a stateless society since there was no strong centralized political authority. With no effective or extensive military or police of its own, with the physical difficulty in exerting control over the arid geographic distances of Tibet, and with the local variation in lifestyles of these once warring and overland trade-dependent peoples more than half of whom were nomadic during part of the year, one must ask, then, of what the Tibetan state did consist? In contrast, I would argue that Buddhism provided the ideal arrangements for a "state." By allocating funds for the construction of monasteries, by recruiting members of the wealthy households as monks (and members of poor households as high reincarnate lamas), by exempting monasteries from taxation while allowing each to extract its own tithes and conscript its own monks, by constructing an individualized and asocial body through ritual and ideological apparatuses, by sustaining an extremely flexible apparatus for the production of truths, and finally by regulating behaviors and emotions through a self-disciplinary theology that aroused regulated "religious incitements to action," the loose governmental system of Tibet was able to create itself as a "state" through the self-disciplines of the populations that it served. However, Tibet had feudal elements, and individual inalienable rights were not as fully developed as in the modern European capitalist state. In this sense, the need for absolute control via the mechanisms of productive power, if they can be called that, were probably not as fully developed in Tibet, even though similar forms of power may have existed there. In other words, there was, in effect, no emergent bourgeoisie in Tibet whose disciplines had to be effected through a type of bio-power. The nomadic, small tenant, and elite populations of Tibet did, however, need forms of control which were not repressive, particularly in the absense of strong centralized government and extensive military control. There were enforced laws, punishable with tariffs, public stocks, and amputation of limbs (Rahul 1969), but these were less effective in sustaining the notion or experience of statehood than were the Buddhist discourses of self. It was in these discourses that the possibility for a Tibetan state existed,[39] but it was a state that did not achieve great material wealth and productivitity so much as spiritual wealth and productivity. The disciplines of Tibet's regimes of power were largely focused on producing spiritual knowledge and spiritual wealth,[40] and the disciplinary techniques of Buddhism aroused participation among the laity to achieve these spiritual ends.

Weber noted the crucial linkage between religious morality and Asiatic forms of archaic state authority, particularly for Confusianism and China, as well as for Hinduism and India. Tibet's ability to exist as a state was also contingent on a religious system—not one which relied on a pervasive repressive morality, though, but one whose mechanisms of power were partially productive, embedded in philosophical notions of selfhood and the pursuit of truth through self-discipline in monastery-based schools, clinics, and agricultural and government centers. As Tibet was feudal-like, however, other mechanisms of power were still in place there—mechanisms which were repressive. In final analysis, the concept of a productive power used by Foucault to understand European-American bourgeois rationality has some limited utility for the study of Tibetan society and culture, contingent as they were on a well-developed productive subjectivity; but it also suggests that power needs still to be seen as historically and culturally contingent. The Sherpa case showed that the conceptualizations of power in the modernity of locales and times studied by Foucault should be scrutinized then for their cross cultural relevance, specificity, and for determinations of how we might go beyond them.

As a final note, the Buddhist discourse was not unidirectional, and this may speak more broadly to the notion of historical discursive breaks versus genealogies of knowledge which are continuous over time. The attractiveness of Buddhism to the laity was that Buddhism provided a more effective means of controlling demons and deities than shamans did. Buddhism's conceptualizations of self were probably also attractive to the laity because the laity eventually needed a new notion of self *vis-a-vis* leadership. As leadership became dislodged from its kinship roots and as rulers were installed to regulate larger territories and populations over time, the idea of individual allegiance to a governmental body connected through neither kinship nor location to its citizens probably had to emerge, and Buddhism was there to galvanize it. Sherpa medical pluralism showed, however, that in the long run Buddhism neither subverted pre-existing notions about communality nor eliminated pre-existing beliefs in demons and deities, or the symbolic weight they carried for social bonds, so much as it presented options to these pre-Buddhist beliefs. This was probably in part because popular ideology and material survival still depended to a large degree on communality, reciprocity, and institutions of the family, even though at some level acknowledgement of and participation in the "state" did not.41 So, where the state needed individualized subjectivity of Buddhism in order to come into existence (fully by the 15th century), so too it could be argued that the state's survival depended on an ongoing perpetuation of the pre-Buddhist concepts of self and society, many of which are still visible today at the frontier of Tibetan culture in Sherpa Nepal.

NOTES

1. An earlier version of this paper was presented at the American Anthropological Association's 89th annual meeting in New Orleans in November 1990. The author wishes to thank audiences at the University of Keele, England, University of Arizona, Tucson, Queens College CUNY and the American Anthropological Association panel on Discursive Rituals and Ritual Therapies of the Himalayas, Sandy Macdonald for assistance at the Musee Guimet in Paris, Geoffrey Samuel at Berkeley, the University of California at Berkeley Department of Anthropology and the Fulbright-Hayes Foundation for field research awards and support, Mark Nichter, Francis Zimmerman, Aihwa Ong, Louisa Schein, John Norby, and an external reviewer for their constructive comments on earlier versions of this paper. I alone take responsibility for the information and interpretation presented here.

2. Medical and social sciences devoted to the study of the body by exposing its intimacies and anatomies participated in the discourse, not as repressive but as productive instruments. The more that was known about the body, the more avenues there were for intervention, each of which explored the possibilities for achieving human perfection as found in the imagery of European Enlightenment. Whereas monarchial power relied on agencies of force as in militia or police, bio-power worked through knowledge and its strategic uses. In Foucault's words, bio-power had:

    . . .two poles. . .[one] centered on the body as a machine: its disciplining, the optimization of its capabilities, the extortion of its forces, the parallel increase of its usefulness and its docility, its integration into systems of efficient and economic controls, all this was ensured by the procedures of power that characterized the disciplines: an anatomo-politics of the human body. The second, formed somewhat later, focused on the species body, the body imbued with the mechanics of life and serving as the basis of the biological processes: propagation, births and mortality, the level of health, life expectancy and longevity, with all the conditions that can cause these to vary. Their supervision was effected through an entire series of interventions and regulatory controls: a bio-politics of the population (Foucault 1980:139).

Bio-power's two simplified poles were: one which was focused on regulating populations through reproduction, mortality, and morbidity; and another which was focused on defining the qualities of a healthy life and then setting into motion a system of individualized self-regulatory behavioral measures which ensured this type of life. Rabinow also provides clarification here (1991:1,1989), along with Yang (1989:25-6).

3. Knowledge produced in the disciplines of medicine, psychology, penology and other social and natural sciences took the place of the state in regulating behavior so that formal governmental disciplinary bodies and laws fell into a secondary role in an arrangement of what Foucault calls "governmentality" (Foucault 1979, 1988, Rabinow 1989). Governmentality, or the "arts of government," were not concerned with territory and property (including the subjects who inhabited that territory) as were the monarchs. Rather, they were concerned with persons in relation to other persons, their relation to events (plagues, births, deaths, etc.), and the manner of their behaviors as individuals and as populations. Nor were the "arts of government" modelled after the family, whose ruler would managed a home as his kingdom, as were monarchs. Rather, they used the family as an instrument through which they could create and exercize power in acts of individual self-discipline. This included the family's production of statistics which could be used in the political sciences to construct social policies (Foucault 1979).

4. Ultimately, my work may lead to a problematization of the notion of modernity. As it stands, modernity is seen as invented by and implemented in the West. Like "capitalism" and "progress," in some analyses modernity is seen as exported to and imposed upon the rest of the world, and in that usage it runs the risk of substituting one sort of evolutionism for another. Perhaps other societies have thoroughly modern projects of their own. For the Tibetan case, the application of "modernity" is problematic and not, certainly, directly parallel. However, it brings up for discussion questions about the meaning of modernity and the degree to which comparative studies of power are possible. The essay here is exploratory rather than definitive.

5. Foucault introduced a method of historical analysis modelled after archeology. A discursive (rather than teleological) approach to history places ideological formations at the forefront rather than causal linkages and chronologies. Michael Taussig (1987), who followed Walter Benjamin, demonstrated a discursive method to history, which relied on notions of time as non-linear.

6. On governmentality, see footnote 3, above.

7. The method I explored in this research was linked to scholarship from Europe, Britain and the US on the way scientific (including medical) knowledge was socially produced, offering truth claims in the name of discovery. This approach began with the work of Kuhn (1970), and Latour and Woolgar (1986), Latour (1986). It was also linked to a history of scholarship on medicine as an agency of social control in the work of Parsons (1951), Ehrenreich (1978), and Zola (1978). The particular mechanisms through which medicine achieved its control drew from explications of ritual that appeared first in a nearly post-functionalist era by Turner (1964, 1968), who suggested the term liminality for that time of potential social change during sickness in which patients became vulnerable to suggestions about normative behaviors constituting or altering the social order. This was later elaborated by Frankenberg (1980, 1981), Comaroff (1985), and Mullings (1984) whose works demonstrated this approach to sickness in the context of contestation between emergent capitalist social orders and indigenous political economic formations. The emergent configurations of self demonstrate the way that the afflicted body became a site upon which competing versions of the social order are contested through medico-religious institutions and techniques. This notion was suggested in work by Lata Mani (1987), Lock and Scheper-Hughes (1987), O'Neill (1985) and writings by Michel Foucault, Ronnie Frankenberg, and Bryan Turner. It is at times when the body is most vulnerable in sickness that fundamental conceptions of the social order and the meanings of tradition are brought into question, as noted by Comaroff (1984) and V. Turner (1968). It is during sickness that the meaning of traditions are challenged by alternatives of the present. Sickness episodes thus emerge as illustrations not only of the changing social world in which patients live, but also of the history which helped to shape that world. Reading the narratives of sickness entails understanding the historical

constitution of the 'healthy body' and the way discourses of the self are generated and reconstituted over time. Foucault's model of bio-power and governmentality added a new dimension of subtlety to our understanding of sickness because these concepts focused on the construction of power in the medical event, the social construction of an expanding scientific knowledge about truth and finally, the links between the individual and state systems, where agencies of force do not constitute the state. Foucault's method focused at once on normalizing knowledges and specific techniques of physical control in physical spaces (see also Donzelot 1977, Hodges and Hussain, 1979). Because Foucault made important contributions to an understanding of power in the medical setting, exploring the applicability of his concepts outside of post-Enlightenment, European society seemed important. In the case presented here, his concepts were examined for their utility in exploring the complex society of Tibet and its representatives in northeast Nepal, the Sherpas.

8. The fieldwork and archival work upon which this work was based began in 1982, briefly and then continued in 1986. It included two years of research among Sherpas of Khumbu and Kathmandu Nepal and archival research thereafter.

9. Khumbu was the region where some 3000 Sherpas lived, in the Solu-Khumbu District, Khosi Zone, Nepal. It was directly southeast from Mount Everest, north of the "Pharak" area which was north of the "Solu" area in the district. Sherpas from this region played a predominant role in mountaineering and trekking through Himalayan trekking agencies, some of which the Sherpas themselves owned in Kathmandu. Khumbu Sherpas have been studied by Furer-Haimendorf, and a large group of geographers and ecology scholars and to some extent in Sherry Ortner's most recent book. There are also extensive writings on Solu Sherpas by Alexander Macdonald, Robert Paul and Sherry Ortner, much of which has great utility for studies of both Khumbu Sherpas and Tibetan society and culture in general.

10. In 1990, a popular democratic revolution overthrew the king of Nepal and established a constitutional parliamentary system in which the king plays a minimal role.

11. This is not to say that *lha pas* are or were the only shamanistic practices of Tibetan cultural groups. There are lengthy examinations of spirit possession in Nepal in the collected volume by Hitchcock and Jones (1976), A. W. Macdonald's collection of writings on healers in Nepal (1983, 1987), and in a recent book by Mumford (1989). As well, Ortner (1978a and b) and Paul (1976) examined the relationship between Sherpa shamanism and lamaism in particular.

12. Sherpas followed the orthodox *Mahayana* tradition of *rNyingMa Pa* Tibetan Buddhism, one of five sects (including modern *Bonpos*) of what some have called *Lamaism*. Sherpas emigrated from eastern Tibet some 460 years ago and although they were fully incorporated into the Nepalese state, they remained to a large extent culturally representative of frontier Tibetan society (compare with Aziz 1978, for example). Because of their relative isolation at the fringes of Tibetan society, it was likely that their shamans, some of whom emigrated to Khumbu from other Tibetan frontier regions, were representative of the type of Shamanism found in Tibet in its pre-Buddhist era (Samuel 1985) (see also footnote 15). Of course, Shamanism and Lamaism are syncretic today.

 Since there was an extensive historical and modern medical literature written by Tibetans to which I have not yet referred, I see my examination of this medical tradition as exploratory rather than definitive at this point. A more thorough examination of the systems of knowledge of *Amchi* medicine is warranted.

13. Biomedicine added another apparatus of social control for Sherpas, an apparatus closely linked to development capitalism in the region, but I discussed this issue elsewhere (Adams 1989), and I did not address it in this context.

14. The idea of a "social self" that can be contrasted with an "individualized self" is explored historically in this paper. It is a dialogic, referential notion of self which defines its identity through relationships to others, also discussed in works by Bahktin (1981) in a universal model, Dumont (1970) and Parry (1986) for India, McHugh (1988) for Nepal, and Yang (1989) for China.

15. Ortner (1984), and Samuel (1990) for Sherpas and Mumford (1989) for Gurungs and Tibetans in north central Nepal.

16. In history, claims to truth are hotly contested, since truths about the past are usually reconstructed to meet the agendas of the present (Hobsbawm 1983). Here too history was represented as an invention of and for the present. Histories of Tibet were no exception in this regard (Macdonald 1984). Those written after the 1959 flight of the Dalai Lama and some 100,000 Tibetans from Tibet, and the arrival of Chinese troops to Lhasa, usually reconstructed Tibetan history by *either* emphasizing Tibet's sovereignty as a nation *or* they emphasized its lack of independence vis-a-vis the empires of

China. The same was true of histories about ancient religions in Tibet. There were no written pre-Buddhist histories of Tibet, and the only written documentation of Tibet prior to the 7th century were manuscripts found in a cave at Dunhuang at the turn of this century, some Chinese sources, and several stone inscriptions written during the period of the first diffusion of Buddhism into Tibet. These documents and inscriptions pointed to the fact that pre-Buddhist religion was quite different than later versions claimed. Some argue today that *Bonpos* were a professional class of priests serving the monarchs of Tibet's imperial period. Later *Bonpo* historians who never converted to Buddhism, that is *Bonpos* of the last ten centuries, reconstructed and "Buddhized" their religion, inventing a history of it which mimicked that of Buddhism, and claimed that Buddhism was essentially an outgrowth of *Bon*. But even this is only one interpretation. Even the documents from Tun Huang were constructions. Who wrote them and what was their vested interest? We will never know. Just as we will never really know what life was like in pre-Buddhist Tibet. It was not surprising, however, that Tibetan histories and foreign histories of Tibet were so revisionist, given the relativistic and controversial nature of Buddhist epistemology which took as one of its starting points the transiency of notions of truth.

17. Tucci (1955) suggested that the ability to divine and to negotiate with deities and demons of the real world was also vested with the king himself, especially when he wore a helmet (headress) endowed for that purpose by the priests. Thus even here the priests probably played an important legitimating function according to Tucci.

18. Stein (1957a,b) explains the dualistic orientation of pre-Buddhist cosmology: the heavens were as opposed to earth, demons as to deities, existence as to non-existence. The family house was also believed to be the location of the family soul (*bla*).

19. This is not to suggest that the self was not problematic before Buddhism, but that literature on nature of its problems and methods of dealing with the problematized self emerge after Buddhism as a peculiar Buddhist project.

20. Buddhists also systematically assimilated the terminology and cosmology of pre-Buddhist religion to Buddhism (Stein 1972:127, Karmay 1975). It is important to note, too, that *tantrists* had already in their ideology the notion of symbolic demons (Stein 1972:143-44, 191,235).

21. Samuel (1990) usefully introduces this approach as one which may have more widespread utility in anthropological analyses.

22. Lessing explains, "Now it is a well-known fact that Buddhism denies the existence of a soul in any sense in which we understand it. The ensemble of phenomena which lead to the assumption of a soul substance or substratum is attributed in buddhism [sic] to some sort of actualism, a complicated dynamic interplay of conscious and subconscious forces, S.[Sanskrit] *Dharmas* , a term which has been translated by "elements," states "of consciousness," "essences," none of which is wholly satisfactory. I therefore use the rather colorless expression "data." These "data" are stimulated into function by *karma*. Early Buddhism enumerates six of these conscious states thus created, five of which are channeled through our sense organs, while a coordinated sixth "sense" is concerned with nonsensuous *dharmas* or "data." In later Buddhism an additional seventh "state of consciousness" was assumed, which relates these six states to an ego, also illusory. The last step in this development was the postulation of an eighth, not really conscious, but subconsious state, in which the germs of seeds of all our present or past actions are stored to await their resurgence as new states of consciousness when conditions are favorable. It is this "granary of consciousness" which survives death and shapes the personality of the next incarnation. This doctrine has been characterized as "psychological atomism" because it dissects each moment of the imaginary psychological continuum into a number of irreducible, momentary, unreal "data." It has no room for a soul as a permanent substratum of the personality. Nevertheless the Lamaists have contrived to equate the *bla* concept inherited from pre-Buddhist times with the granary of consciousness popularly called in Tibetan *nam-shi*. It is this *nam-shi* which requires the assistance of the lama in finding the most favorable exit from the body of the moribund" (Lessing 1951:265). Samuel notes that Lessing may be only partially correct. In particular, he suggests that *rnam shes* or *kun gzhi rnam shes* are in many cases not equated with *bla* but are rather clearly distinguished from each other. It seems that the notion of *bla* as a single principle gave way with Buddhism to a plethora of ways of talking about (and therefore knowing) the nature of the self and the soul principle. This is the point I am making—that there emerged a great deal of writing and discussion about the relationship between and conceptualization of the nature of the self and soul.

23. Ekvall commented on the individualistic orientations of Tibetans: "As a generalization, it may be stated that the doctrinal emphasis on impermanence seems to have weakened the will to create societal units of enduring strength. If we begin with the individual, it is immediately apparent that he is more important and occupies a position characterized by greater individual freedom in relation to the groups of which he is a part than many of the peoples of Asia" (1964:84).

24. Again, thanks to Samuel for reminding me that in some areas (Aziz 1978) villagers paid taxes to a *gelukpa* monastery but they went to other monasteries, *kagyupa* and *nyingmapa*, for religious services. One would assume that even in these circumstances, the laity was being doubly taxed—once for the main coffers of the Tibetan government under control of *gelukpas* and once for the support of the religious regimes which in some measure organized the lives of the rural Tibetans. Here, the blurring of monetary contributions with gaining spiritual rewards (whether as *spa yin*—benefits of *karma*, or as *rlung-rta*—religious knowledge protection) was still at work as disciplinary regimes which held together the "state."

25. *Dumje* is the Sherpas' largest celebration, marking the anniversary of the death of the patron lama of the region (see Paul 1976). *Dumje* sponsorship, for example, called on nine families of Khum Jung and Kunde per year for sponsorship. Each family provided money and uncooked rice, cooked food and labor for a three day event to which the entire population of both villages was invited. Because the cost of rice had risen so dramatically over the last ten years, a new "member" sponsorship system was instituted whereby families borrowed rice from one another during their sponsorship year. Later, they were expected to return an equivalent amount of rice when their supporters were in turn responsible for sponsoring Dumje. Each year nearly all households' reciprocity networks were mobilized.

26. In contrast to Ekvall's commentary on doctrinaire influences toward individualism, Stein (1972) noted that sociocentrism found first in the family continued to override doctrinaire and secular practices, which accentuated individualism: "Two principles exemplified in the family are found again when we turn to consider the structure of authority: cohesion and the strength of the group, on the one hand; the hereditary authority of one person and a keen sense of hierarchy on the other. Time and again one has the feeling that the second of these principles has won the day, but that the first continues to counterbalance it" (1972:125).

27. Historically, extending the power of the lineage was also vested in priests. They pronounced, for example, black magic curses against enemy groups to protect their clients in battles.

28. Like other practices, however, the individualizing funerary services of the lamas were in practice made collective. Tibetan funerals were followed by huge prestations of money and food from the deceased's family to the entire community in an effort, (according to Sherpas), to contribute to the merits of their beloved family member and to help secure a favorable outcome for the deceased in his or her next life.

29. Although Snellgrove wrote that documents from Tun Huang contained indications of reincarnation principles (1987:452), most documents suggested the idea of a heavenly terminus for the deceased in pre-Buddhist Tibet, and Samuel (personal communication) noted that it seems too early for the system of reincarnate lamas but too late for the notion of rebirth. Stein (1972:76) offered that it was the abbots of Drigung, the Karma-pa branch, who "started the system of successive reincarnations of the same person, which was later adopted for the Dalai and Panchen Lamas." This would place it at 1283. The Dalai Lama reincarnate lineages were designated in 1578 (by the Mongols) and traced retrospectively to two previous incarnations to the life of Gedu Gyatso (1475–1542).

30. This followed from a pattern of one brother marrying and the other going into the monastery. Powerful and wealthy families thus retained their positions through alliances with the monasteries.

31. Pointing to the persistence of repressive forms of power alongside those emergent productive forms of power.

32. Not all Tibetan doctors were Buddhist lamas or trained in the monastery, but their practices were all based on Buddhist knowledge.

33. Which was likely the composition described by Tucci (1970:56): "The individual in his psychophysical reality located in a particular time and place: including the material body (rag pa'i lus)—the *sems* plus the five components of the personality, sense organs, related perceptions, mental functioning and the faculty of cognition (yid); the subtle body (phra mo)—channels (rtsa), through which moves *rlung* and *sems*; the most subtle body (shin tu phra pa'i lus) and *sems*—called the innate body (ngyug ma'i lus) and the innate sems (gnyug ma'i sems); and finally the body of mental cognition (yid lus) in a

state of dreaming or of intermediate existence (*bar do*), a modification of body and *sems* in a more subtle (*phra pa*) state."

34. Again, the view of the body as a wholistic system interdependent with the natural universe distinguishes it from biomedicine which viewed parts of the body as discrete objects subject to their own interventions.

35. Zimmerman (personal communication) pointed out the difficulty in arguing that the body is reified in Tibetan medicine. He noted *amchi* medicine's Ayurvedic origins and the Ayurvedic conception of humoralism, he suggested, is a psychosomatic concept; passions of the mind produce bodily diseases. I suggest, in response, that there is in *amchi* medicine a notion of a body that is separable from self, (as espoused in theories of reincarnation and demonstrated symbolically in lama *kurims*). That the body and consciousness are linked such that emotions, for example, produce bodily responses is also true for Tibetan medicine. However, the goal of the practitioner, in Tibetan medicine, was to enable the sentient mind to supercede the body — to render the body illusory, as was believed for all things of the material world. The Tibetan knowledge system placed the sentient mind into a hierarchical relationship to the body, dominating it and rendering it rather insignificant in the progressive efforts toward enlightenment. Ultimately, the great feats of immaterial bodily transport claimed to be accomplished by lamas show how bodily existence is simply consequential to mental agility, rather than vice-versa.

    It is important to note the difference between the bodily conceptions in Buddhism and those of biomedicine. In the former the body is seen as part of the universe, interconnected to all elements of the universe and functionally interdependent upon them. In biomedicine, it was the ability to treat as separate and functionally independent various bodily parts which marked high modernism in medical practice. The difference is important since it shows how even though aspects of productive power were in place in Tibet, it was not able to achieve the high levels of marketability and penetration into so many areas of social life that we now see for biomedicine where such things as sexuality or heart disease are treated as organically separable and therefore profitable. One might argue that this later stage of biomedicalized bodies represents a form of postmodernism rather than modernism.

36. Here is a major difference with the techniques of bio-power, since in Tibetan Buddhism, the normative grids were never wholly divorced from the religious underpinnings and rendered relational only in terms of universal principles of science. However, I believe there is room here for a discussion about the difficulties of distinguishing between the religious, philosophical, and scientific in both Western science and Tibetan medicine.

37. Even where monasteries of different sects competed in a single region and where popular support was held by the monastery not directly under the administrative authority of the Lhasa government, information must have been shared between monasteries and religous practitioners as part of the scholarly endeavor.

38. Aihwa Ong usefully reminded me that the Asiatic religious traditions such as Confusianism, Islam and Brahminical Hinduism, also cultivated subjectivity and self-understanding, and this was explored by Weber and many others. These analyses examined how state systems, particularly tributary societies of imperial China managed populations through a system of morality that defined not only who individuals were but how they should behave on a daily, lived basis. I found that Foucault's conceptualizations of power were useful in expanding beyond the work of authors such as Weber our ability to understand how historical Tibetan society must have operated. Particularly useful were Foucault's observations of: the role of scholarly discourses that did not invoke the numinous to legitimize themselves, and the social agencies that grew from these scholarly works; the way that power was productive of a transient sort of truth rather than repressive, as was true for coercive forms of social control; and finally, the way that these sciences were contingent upon subjectivity.

39. Macdonald (1984:137-8) suggested that Buddhism was used as a "powermodel" to extend kingly control in Tibet's early expansion. Powermodels, he wrote, "are deliberately formulated and exploited by certain elites and are used as instruments of social control" (1984:133). In this case, the powermodel invoked, among other things, a history which gave the early dynasty a sort of unbroken continuity linked to even the empires of India. In the later years of Buddhism's development, monasteries were no longer instruments of kingly power so much as institutions of a decentralized state apparatus through which knowledge was produced about correct behaviors, right and wrong

sentiments, obedience, and discipline of the self that regulated the whole population. This power existed not in exclusion of tributary power, or power by threat of force or starvation, but alongside it. As a type of power that resembled bio-power, it was continually productive.

40. The advantage of using a postmodern method in this sense might be not in its ability to show us comparative uses of power but the possibility of multiple uses of power within multiple forms of economy. Tibet's economy revolved around productivity for spiritual gain—a form of symbolic capital that is what legitimized and allowed the monasteries to survive, alongside their material wealth. That is not to say that other forms of power were not also at work: it is not surprising that soon after the Mongols established the regency which was later to become the Dalai Lama, census taking apparatuses were implemented through the monasteries (Tucci 1970:27). Censuses constructed around the concept of myriarchies or twelve divisable units tabulated and surveyed populations and recorded levels of production, household sizes, occupations, movements from region to region and standards of living (Carrasco 1959). Coupled with the production of knowledge about appropriate behaviors which would lead to a healthful life, and a set of codes and regimens that would bring that life into existence, Buddhism seemed the perfect remedy for statehood. This included undermining notions of collectivity and family and configuring in their place individuals on the one hand and categories of people on the other: "the *sangwa*" (initiated secret monks),"*nangwa*"(initiated novitiate),"*chiwa*" (un-initiated non-monastic); "children," "females," "the elderly"; "the *phagin-wa*" (the phlegmatic), "the *tiwa-wa*" (bilious), and "the *lung-wa*" (those whose "air" is too active). Census-taking provided an ever-expanding apparatus for defining the location and nature of self "truths" but also allowed for the perpetuation of repressive techniques of control.

41. I have shown this was also true for Sherpas' involvement with tourism, where they absorbed forms of wage labor into a reciprocity-based economy rather than capitulating to "capitalism" as an external determining set of forces (Adams, 1992).

REFERENCES

Adams, Vincanne *Healing Buddhas and Mountian Guides: The Social Production of Self Within Society Through Medication in Nepal* Doctoral Dissertation Dept. of Anthropology UC Berkeley 1989.

Adams, Vincanne "Reconstituted Relations of Production in Sherpa Tourism" *Ann. Tourism Res.* 19(3); 1992.

Armstrong, David *The Political Anatomy of the Body* Cambridge: Cambridge University Press, 1983.

Aziz, Barbara Nimri *Tibetan Frontier Families* New Delhi: Vikas Publishing House 1978.

Bahktin, Mikhail *The Dialogic Imagination* C. Emerson and M. Holquist, trans. Austin: University of Texas Press 1981.

Basham, A.L. *The Wonder That Was India* New York: Hawthorn Books 1963.

Blondeau, Anne -Marie "Le Tibet, Apercu Historique et Geographique" In A. Macdonald and Y. Imaeda, eds. *Essays sur L'Art de Tibet* pp.1-22. 1977.

Carrasco, Pedro *Land and Polity in Tibet* Seattle: University of Washington Press 1959.

Choephel, Gedun *The White Annals* Dharamsala: Library of Tibetan Works and Archives 1978.

Comaroff, Jean "Medicine: Symbol and Ideology" In P. Wright and A. Treacher, eds. *The Problem of Medical Knowledge* Edinburgh: Edinburgh University Press 1982.

Comaroff, Jean "Healing and Cultural Trasformation: The Tswana of Southern Africa" *Soc. Sci. & Med.* 15B:376-78, 1984.

Comaroff, Jean *Body of Power/Spirit of Resistance* Chicago: Chicago University Press 1985.

Dash, Bhagwan *Tibetan Medicine* Dharamsala: Library of Tibetan Works and Archives 1976.

David-Neel, Alexandra *With Mystics and Magicians in Tibet* London: Penguin 1937.

Dhonden, Yeshe and Kelsang *The Ambrosia Heart Tantra* Tibetan Medicine No. 6 1983.

Donzelot, Jacques *La Police Des Familles* Paris: Editions de Minuit, 1977.

Dumont, Louis *Homo Hierarchicus/ The Caste System and Its Implications* Chicago: University of Chicago Press, 1970.

Ekvall, Robert *Religious Observances in Tibet: Patterns and Function* Chicago: University of Chicago Press 1964.

Ekvall, Robert *Fields on the Hoof: Nexus of Tibetan Nomadic Pastoralism* Chicago: Holt, Rinehart and Winston 1968.

Ehrenreich, John ed.*The Cultural Crisis of Modern Medicine* New York: Monthly Review Press 1978.

Finckh, Elisabeth *Foundations of Tibetan Medicine* Volume One London: Watkins 1978.

Foucault, Michel *The Birth of the Clinic: An Archeology of Medical Perception* London: Tavistock 1973.

Foucault, Michel *Discipline and Punish: The Birth of the Prison* London: Allen Lane 1977.

Foucault, Michel "On Governmentality" *Ideology and Consciousness* (6):5-21, Autumn 1979.

Foucault, Michel *The History of Sexuality Volume One* New York: Vintage 1980.

Foucault, Michel *The Use of Pleasure/ The History of Sexuality, Volume 2* Peregrine 1984.

Foucault, Michel *The Care of the Self/ The History of Sexuality, Volume 3* Vintage 1986.

Foucault, Michel "Technologies of the Self" in L.H. Martin, H. Butman and P.H. Hutton, eds., *Technologies of the Self: A Seminar with Michel Foucault* Amherst: University of Massachusettes Press 1988.

Frankenberg, Ronnie "Medical Anthropology and Development: a theoretical Perspective" *Soc. Sci. & Med.* 14B:197-207, 1980.

Frankenberg, Ronnie "Allopathic Medicine, Profession and Capitalist Ideology in India" *Soc. Sci. & Med.* 15A:115-125, 1981.

Gyatso, Janet "The Development of the Gcod Tradition" In Barbara Aziz and Matthew Kapstein, eds., *Soundings in Tibetan Civilization* p. 320-341, 1985.

Hitchcock, John and Rex Jones *Spirit Possession in the Nepal Himalayas* New Delhi: Vikas Publishing House 1976.

Hobsbawm, Eric and Terence Ranger, eds., *The Invention of Tradition* Cambridge: Cambridge University Press 1983.

Hodges, Jill and Athar Hussain "'La Police Des Familles' A Review Article" *Ideology and Consciousness* 5:87-124, 1979

Karmay, Samten "A General Introduction to the History and Doctrines of Bon" *The MTB Offprints Series No. 3*, (Memoires of the Research Dept. of the Toyo Bunko, no. 33) 1975.

Karmay, Samten "The Rdzogs-chen in its Earliest Text: A Manuscript from Tun-huang" In B. Aziz and M. Kapstein, eds., *Soundings in Tibetan Civilization* New Delhi: Manohar, 1985.

Karmay, Samten "L'Ame et Le Turquoise: Un Rituel Tibetain" *L'Ethnographie* 83(100/101):97-130, 1987.

Kuhn, Thomas *The Structure of Scientific Revolutions* Chicago: University of Chicago Press 1970.

Lalou, Marcelle "Rituel Bon-po Des Funerailles Royales" *Journal Asiatique* 240(3):339-62 1952.

Latour, Bruno "Visualization and Cognition: Thinking with Eyes and Hands" *Knowledge and Society: Studies in the Sociology of Culture Past and Present* 6:1-40, 1986.

Latour, Bruno and Steven Woolgar *Laboratory Life: The Social* Construction of Scientific Facts Princeton: Princeton University Press 1986 (1979).

Lessing, F. D. "Calling The Soul: A Lamaist Ritual" Walter Fischel, ed., *Semitic and Oriental Studies* Berkeley: UC Press, 1951.

Lock, Margaret and Nancy Scheper-Hughes "The Mindful Body: A Prolegomenon to Future Work in Medical Anthropology" *Med. Anthro. Quarterly* 1(1):6-41, 1987.

Macdonald, A. W. "Religion in Tibet At The Time of Srong-Bstan Sgam-Po" *Bibliotheca Orientalis Hungarica* 29(2):129-140, 1984.

Macdonald, A.W. *Essays on the Ethnology of Nepal and South Asia Vols. I & II.* Kathmandu: Ratna Pustak Bhandar Publishers 1983, 1987.

Mani, Lata "Contentious Traditions: The Debate on SATI in Colonial India" *Cultural Critique* 7:119-156, 1987.

Mauss, Marcell *The Gift* London: Cohen & West 1937.

McHugh, Ernestine "Concepts of the Person Among the Gurungs of Nepal" *American Anthropologist* 16(1):75-86, 1989.

Meyer, Fernand *gSo-Ba Rig-Pa: Le System Medical Tibetain* Paris: Centre National des Reserches Sociales 1988.

Mullings, Leith *Therapy, Ideology and Social Change: Mental Healing in Urban Ghana* Berkeley: UC Press 1984.

Mumford, Stan Royal *Himalayan Dialogue: Tibetan Lamas and Gurung Shamans in Nepal* Madison: Univ. of Wisconsin Press 1989.

Obeyesekere, Gananath "Theodicity, Sin and Salvation in a Sociology of Buddhism" In E.R.Leach, ed., *Dialectic in Practical Religion* Cambridge: Cambridge University Press 1968.

O'Neill, John *The Five Bodies: The Human Shape of Modern Society* Ithaca: Cornell University Press 1985.

O'Neill, John "Sociological Nemesis: Parsons and Foucault on the Therapeutic Disciplines" In Mark Wardell and Stephen Turner, eds., *Sociological Theory in Transition* Boston: Allen and Unwin 1986.

Ortner, Sherry *High Religion: A Cultural and Political History of Sherpa Buddhism* Princeton: Princeton University Press 1989.

Ortner, Sherry *Sherpas Through Their Rituals* Cambridge: Cambridge University Press 1978a.

Ornter, Sherry "The Decline of Sherpa Shamanism: On the Role of Meaning in History" Manuscript. Department of Anthropology, University of Michigan 1978b.

Parry, Jonathan "The Gift, The Indian Gift and the 'Indian Gift'" *MAN* 21 (3):253-73, 1986.

Parsons, Talcott "Definitions of Health and Illness in Light of American Values and Social Structures" In G. Jaco, ed. *Patients, Physicians and Illness* New York: The Free Press 1951.

Paul, Robert "Some Observations on Sherpa Shamanism" In J. Hitchcock and R. Jones, eds., *Spirit Possession in the Nepal Himalayas* New Delhi: Vikas pp.141-52, 1976.

Paul, Robert "Dumje: Paradox and Resolution in Sherpa Ritual Symbolism" American Ethnologist 6(2):274-304, 1979.

Rabinow, Paul "From Sociobiology to Biosociality: Artificiality and Enlightenment" Fragments for a History of the Human Body, Zone Publications, volume 6, 1991.

Rabinow, Paul *French Modern/Norms and Forms of the Social Environment* Cambridge: MIT Press 1989.

Rahul, Ram *The Government and Politic of Tibet* New Delhi: Vikas Publishing 1969.

Richardson, Hugh "Early Burial Grounds in Tibet and Decorative Art of the 8th and 9th Centuries" *Central Asiatic Journal* 8(2):73-92, 1963.

Richardson, Hugh "Tibetan Inscriptions at Zva-hi Lha-khang, Parts I & II" *J. Royal Asiatic Society* October 1952 pp. 143-54 and April 1953 pp.1-11.

Richardson, Hugh "Three Ancient Inscriptions from Tibet" *J. Royal Asiatic Society* 15(1):45-65, 1949.

Rinpoche, Rechung *Tibetan Medicine* Berkeley: UC Press 1973.

Rona-Tas, Andras "Social Terms in the List of Grants of the Tibetan Tun-Huang Chronicle" *Acta Orientalia Hungarica* 5(3):249-270, 1955.

Samuel, Geoffrey "Tibet as a Stateless Society and Some Islamic Parallels" *J. of Asian Studies* 41(2):215-29, 1982.

Samuel, Geoffrey "Early Buddhism in Tibet: Some Anthropological Perspectives" In B. Aziz and M. Kapstein, eds., *Soundings in Tibetan Civilization* New Delhi: Monahar 1985.

Samuel, Geoffrey *Mind, Body and Culture: Anthropology and the Biological Interface* Cambridge: Cambridge University Press 1990.

Snellgrove, David *The Nine Ways of Bon: Excerpts from the gZi-brjid* London: 1967.

Snellgrove, David *Indo-Tibetan Buddhism* London: Serinda Publications 1987.

Snellgrove, David and Hugh Richardson *A Cultural History of Tibet* New York: Frederick A. Praeger 1968.

Stein, Sir Aurel "L'Habitat, Le Monde et Le Corps Humain en Extreme-Orient et en Haute Asie" *Journal Asiatique* 245(1):37-74, 1957a.

Stein, Sir Aurel "Le Linga Des Danses Masquees Lamaiques et La Theorie Des Ames" *Sino-Indian Studies* 5(parts 3&4):200-234, 1957b.

Stein, Sir Aurel *Tibetan Civilization* Stanford: Stanford University Press 1972 (1962).

Tatz, Mark *Buddhism and Healing: Demieville's Article 'Byo' from Hobogirin* New York: University Press of America 1985.

Tatz, Mark "T'ang Dynasty Influences on the Early Spread of Buddhism in Tibet" *The Tibet Journal* 3(2):3-32, 1978.

Taussig, Michael *Shamanism, Colonialism and The Wildman: A Study in Terror and Healing* Chicago: Univ. of Chicago Press 1987.

Tucci, Guiseppe "The Secret Characters of the Kings of Ancient Tibet" *East and West* 6(3):197-205, 1955.

Tucci, Guiseppe *The Religions of Tibet* Translated by Geoffrey Samuel, London: Routledge and Kegan Paul, 1970.

Turner, Bryan *Medical Power and Social Knowledge* London: Sage 1987.

Turner, Victor "Betwixt and Between: The Liminal Period in Rights of Passage" In J. Helm, ed., *Symposium on New Approaches to the Study of Religion* Seattle: Proceedings of the American Ethnological Society 1964.

Turner, Victor *Drums of Affliction: A Study of Religious Processes Among the Ndembu of Zambia* Oxford: Clarendon Press 1968.

Weber, Max (translated and edited by Hans H. Gerth) *The Religion of China* The Free Press 1951.

Weber, Max (translated and edited by Hans H. Gerth and Don Martindale) *The Religion of India: The Sociology of Hinduism and Buddhism* The Free Press 1958.

Yang, Mayfair Mei-Hui "The Gift Economy and State Power in China" *Society for Comparative Study of Society and History* 31:25-54, 1989.

Zola, Irving K. "Medicine as and Institution of Social Control" In B. and J. Ehrenreich, eds., *The Cultural Crisis of Modern Medicine* New York: Monthly Review 1978.

Malay Medicine, Malay Person

Carol Laderman

Medical anthropologists have often disagreed as to whether an "emic" or an "etic" approach can prove most fruitful for the analysis of their material. Each route has its perils: the "emic" approach may cast the studied population in the role of the Other, whose beliefs and practices have little relation to those of the West, while the "etic" approach tends to narrow the field of vision, attempting to fit the data into a Procrustean bed of Western manufacture.

Since this book is devoted to ethnomedicine, I think it most appropriate to follow the "emic" route in my discussion of traditional Malay medicine. I will try to avoid its pitfalls by concentrating upon the landscape of indigenous concepts but noting as well the signposts for cross-cultural comparisons as they appear on the road.

After drawing a picture of Malay ethnomedicine and concepts of the self, I will argue that an understanding of their bases must necessarily call into question some recent Western theories concerning non-Western peoples' beliefs, feelings, and practices.

"USUAL" ILLNESSES

While linguists have long discarded the notion that it is possible to understand non-Indo-European languages by referring to Indo-European syntactical and grammatical rules, some medical anthropologists have found it useful to analyze non-Western medical systems in reference to Western categories, dividing disease etiologies into "natural" and "supernatural" categories, or assuming a human duality of mind and body, either or both of which can produce or be affected by illness. These are the underpinnings of secular Western belief; our own "emic" view of the world, which does not necessarily correspond to categories employed by non-Western peoples.

Rural east coast Malays, for example, do not divide their illnesses into those that are "natural" and others that are "supernatural," but, rather, speak of "usual" (biasa) and "unusual" (luar biasa) illnesses.[1] The distinction is based on incidence and not on suspected etiology. Illnesses may sometimes combine the features of biasa and luar biasa, calling for a combination of treatments. There is no emphasis on the "unnaturalness" of the spirit world and its manifestations. Furthermore, Malays conceive of humanity as being more complex than a simple mind-body dichotomy

CAROL LADERMAN is Professor and Chairperson in the Department of Anthropology at City College—CUNY, New York, NY 10031. She has done fieldwork primarily in Malaysia and has published on issues dealing with childbirth, nutrition, traditional medical systems, and ethnopsychiatry.

or duality. The Malay person includes other forces that must be taken into account in an explanation of health and illness.

"Usual" health problems may be attributed to a number of causes, either singly or in conjunction: accidents, poor personal or communal hygiene, a bad diet (whether due to poverty, bad habits, or other causes), too many intestinal worms (a small number is considered normal), changes in the weather that upset the body's internal balance, overwork, and worry, among others. A specialist known as a *mudin* treats broken bones and sprains. Obstetric and perinatal problems are the province of the *bidan* (midwife). Masseurs and masseuses are in demand for muscular aches and abdominal pain. Other "usual" problems are treated by patients and their families, often with the aid of a *bomoh*, an indigenous healer whose services are sought after by villagers for both "usual" and "unusual" problems, in spite of the increasing availability of cosmopolitan medicine and in the face of objections from the Islamic hierarchy.

The work of the *bomoh* is not confined to curative medicine. The *bomoh*'s duties as a healer extend from clinical (private treatment of sickness) to preventive medicine (public rites for warding off impending disaster). Their public performances include *tolak bala* (averting evil), done to ward off an impending epidemic or other calamity; *buka hutan* (opening the jungle), intended to protect the well-being of farmers who will be working on land after it is claimed from the jungle for agriculture; and, until recent times, *puja pantai* (invocations at the seashore), a yearly celebration featuring offerings to the sea spirits.[2]

Besides the protective measures they employ for the health and safety of the community, *bomoh* advise individuals who intend to build new houses, attempt to bring back errant husbands by magical means, send their familiar spirits to urge undesirable tenants to vacate clients' houses, try to increase a fisherman's chances of getting a good catch or a prospective driver's chances of getting a license, and help clients abrogate their contracts with the spirit world. But, although their range of expertise is vast (I have mentioned merely a few examples), the *bomoh*'s practice is primarily that of healer.

The majority of illnesses treated by *bomoh* are those that Malays call "usual." Ordinary fevers, respiratory ailments or digestive upsets are believed to result from a humoral imbalance, either to the hot or the cold polarity (for further information regarding the Malay humoral system, see Laderman 1981, 1983, 1991). They are treated with herbal remedies, dietary adjustments, and thermal treatments such as steam inhalation and cold compresses, calculated to restore the patient's body to its normal state. Muscular aches are believed to be caused by lumps of phlegm (the cold humor) blocking the flow of blood (the hot humor). They are treated by massage, which breaks up the clots of phlegm and allows the hot blood to flow unobstructed through the muscle.

"Usual" diseases are classified by criteria that interpret empirical evidence in the light of humoral reasoning. These include:

1. External heat: conditions such as fever or boils that are hot to the touch.
2. Internal heat: illnesses that make the patient experience hot or burning sensations, such as sore throat or heartburn.
3. Visible signs: hemorrhages are evidence that the hot element has boiled over; clotted phlegm indicates that the cold element has become colder.
4. Deficiency or excess of a humor deduced from internal evidence: *kurang darah* (literally, "not enough

blood," roughly equivalent to anemia) is cold since its sufferers' supply of the hot humor is insufficient; *darah tinggi* (literally, "high blood," roughly equivalent to hypertension) is hot since an excess of blood is presumed to have gone to the head (considered by Malays to be normally hotter than the rest of the body), thereby overheating it.

5. Pulse reading: A fast pulse denotes heat, since its speed is owing to the rate at which blood travels through the veins; a slow pulse is a sign that inner cold has thickened the blood and made it sluggish.

6. Illness symptoms reminiscent of normal reactions to thermal temperatures: The chills and shudders that accompany malaria, reminiscent of a healthy person's reaction to cold weather, cause this illness to be termed "cold fever" (*demam sejuk*).

7. Behavioral considerations: Some forms of madness are thought to occur as a result of the brain's overheating, causing violent and angry behavior. Such behavior is called *panas* (literally, "hot"). Madness can result from too much thought (such as excessive amounts of studying), or violent emotions. Prescribing hot medicines for hot conditions can also lead to madness when their combined heat reaches the brain.

8. Response to treatments: If illnesses respond to treatments already classified as hot or cold, this indicates that these illnesses have the opposite humoral quality, i.e., asthma is cold since it responds to steam inhalation; heatstroke is hot since it responds to cold water.

9. In reference to age. Malays follow medieval Islamic medical theory in attributing a greater degree of cold to the aged. Since rheumatism is most often found in old people, it is classified as cold.

While Malays do not classify pregnancy and childbirth as illness, they (in common with adherents to humoral theory in other cultures) believe that childbirth with its concomitant blood loss precipitates a woman into an abnormally cold state. They attempt to redress this problem by encouraging women in the puerperium to eat "hot" foods and avoid "cold" foods. Treatments such as sleeping over a low fire (so-called "mother-roasting"), bathing with warm water, and tying warming sashes about the waists of new mothers are also used to bring their bodies back to normal humoral balance.

Although, as we have seen, it is possible to codify the workings of humoral thought and use these codes as general guidelines, it is a basic tenet of humoral systems both ancient and contemporary that each person must be considered as a separate case, since bodily humors do not exist in the same proportions in everyone. This explains, for example, why some Malays whose bodies are "hotter" than ordinary will classify foods as "cool" or even "lukewarm" which the majority of their neighbors rank as "very cold." Their classification of both these foods and their own humoral condition rests partially on the fact that they can eat their fill of these usually problematic foods with impunity. Conversely, a person who is congenitally "colder" than usual can ingest the "very hot" herbs that produce diarrhea in most people without experiencing ill effects.

Should everyday health problems not respond to the usual treatments, or should an illness appear to be unusual in kind or in its course, a suspicion may arise that the sufferer's problems are due, at least in part, to the attacks of spirits, sent by an illwisher or acting on their own initiative. The illness is then reclassified as "unusual." A whole, healthy person normally has little to fear from *hantu* (disembodied spirits), but, should an imbalance occur, whether humoral or in relation to one's component parts, the integrity of the person is breached. His "gates" no longer protect the "fortress within," but have opened to allow the incursions of disembodied spirits.

THE MALAY PERSON

The person, in the Malay view, is composed of more than a mind that thinks, a body that decays after death, and a soul that lives on in Heaven or in Hell.

Inner Winds (*angin*) that will determine the child's individual personality, drives and talents are already present at birth.[3] Their presence, type and quality can be deduced from the behavior of their possessor, but they are palpable neither to observers nor to their owner, except during trance, when they are felt as actual presences: high winds blowing within the possessor's breast.

Human beings, like all God's creatures, must inhale the Breath of Life (*nyawa*)[4] at birth, if they are to live. The *nyawa*, containing the elements of air and fire, animates the watery, earthy body; without it the body must die. It drives the blood in its course; its effects are felt within the body and its presence is obvious to observers when it emerges as breath, just as the presence of a breeze, though itself invisible, is signalled by the rustling of leaves and the feeling it produces as it blows on the skin.

Semangat (Spirit of Life) is not limited to animals. It permeates the universe, dwelling in man, beast, plant, and rock (cf. Endicott 1970). The universe teems with life: the life of a fire is swift and soon burns out; a rock's life is slow, long, and dreamlike. *Semangat* strengthens its dwelling place, whether the human body or a stalk of rice, and maintains its health and integrity. However, it is extremely sensitive and can be depleted: it can even flee, startled or frightened, from its receptacle. The vulnerability of the *semangat* governs the conduct of the traditional Malay rice harvest (whose performance has become increasingly rare as modern technology supplants the handiwork of traditional methods of rice production). Modern methods may be more efficient, but they are not calculated to spare the feelings of the Rice Spirit (*semangat padi*). To a traditional Malay, the field of rice is like a pregnant woman, and the harvest is equivalent to the birth of a child. It is inaugurated by the taking of the Rice Baby, a stalk of rice swaddled like a human child after being cut from its plant with a small, curved blade concealed in the hand, so as not to frighten the Rice Spirit by its brutal appearance. The harvested rice crop is stored in a special bin with a coconut, coconut oil, limes, *beluru* root (used for shampoo), bananas, sugar cane, water, and a comb, all for the use of the Rice Spirit, personified as a timid young woman (see also Firth 1974: 192–195). Since she is easily frightened, the rice must be brought back to the storeroom and left there in silence for three days.

Semangat in humans is similarly timid and must be cherished and protected. It can be summoned by spells such as thwarted lovers may use to regain their beloved. It can be called by a *bomoh*, using the same sound Malays use to call their chickens[5] (*kurrr*), to assist a woman in childbirth. Where the *semangat* goes, the body must follow, and so the loved one is drawn to her lover, and the baby is encouraged to make its way into the world.

The timidity of *semangat* makes it prone to leap and fly at the approach of a frightening object or the sound of an unexpected noise. The effect of the startle reaction is most serious in people who are already in a vulnerable condition, such as pregnant women whose fear may be communicated to their unborn children, resulting in infantile abnormalities.

Although most people live secure within the "gates" of their individuality, some people's boundaries are riddled with tiny openings, more like a permeable membrane than a wall. At times, such people find their thoughts becoming confused, their actions less than voluntary. The extraordinary permeability of some individuals was offered to me by many Malays, both professional healers and laypeople, as the explanation of *latah*, a condition in which being startled by a loud noise or an unexpected event triggers a spate of obscene language or imitative behavior. This startle reaction in turn increases the permeability of the membrane, allowing the thoughts of others to mix with those of the *latah* victim's own and govern his or her actions (cf. Lutz 1985 on similar beliefs among the Ifaluk). It can also open the way to spirit attacks.

A short prayer (*doa*) or spell (*jampi*), recited by the patient, a family member, or a *bomoh* frequently accompanies treatments even of "usual" illnesses, both to add to their effectiveness and to strengthen the patient's "gate" against incursions from the spirit world. Shamans, by the very nature of their profession, must have the means of strengthening their bodily defenses, particularly when going into trance. They mobilize their inner resources, personified as the Four Sultans, the Four Heroes, the Four Guardians, and the Four Nobles, to "guard from above and become a shelter; guard from below and become a foundation; guard from before and become a crown; guard from behind and become a palisade." They call upon their familiar spirits (*penggawa*) to "guard the inner fortress closely; guard and strengthen the outer gates."[6] Shamans who omit these basic precautions may put their lives in jeopardy. Pak Long warned his apprentices never to forget the fate of Pak Dollah, a *bomoh* who had lived in a nearby *kampung*. He neglected to summon his *penggawa* at the proper time during a seance. A powerful *jin* (genie), sensing that his "gates" were ajar, entered his body and squeezed his heart until he died.

The natural barrier between spirit and mortal usually ensures an adult protection from spirit attacks. Children are more vulnerable, since their *semangat* has not yet "hardened" (cf. Massard 1988). Illness, overwork, and fright cause breaks in the barrier, allowing the spirits to come into contact with the unprotected body. Spirit attacks are particularly dangerous to those already weakened by "usual" problems. A divination will often reveal that the patient was startled and fell just prior to attack from the spirits (see Kapferer 1983: 50 for similar beliefs in Sri Lanka).[7] *Hantu*, sent by an enemy, may fail to penetrate a strong man's "gates," and, in their anger and frustration, attack his more vulnerable wife or children instead.

These disembodied spirits are composed of only air and fire, and lack the earth and water of which our own bodies are made. Their attacks can range in force from merely greeting the victim to striking him, but most often consist of blowing on the victim's back, thus increasing the elements of fire and air and upsetting his humoral balance.

Divinations employed to discover the cause of these illnesses often follow a humoral model. The most popular method uses rice popped by dry heat. The shaman places handfuls of popped rice on a pillow and counts out the grains in pairs, two each for earth, air, fire and water. If the count ends on earth, it might point to a cold illness, or one caused by the earth spirits. If it falls on fire, it might signify that the patient has incurred someone's hot wrath, whether human or spirit, or it might simply mean that the condition was hot. Should the count end on air, the diagnosis points to a problem with the patient's Inner Winds.

Since illnesses can be attributed to a variety of causes, operating in conjunction, treatments often combine the seemingly pragmatic, such as medications and massage, with the seemingly symbolic, such as spells and prayers. In the case of "unusual" illnesses, it may be considered wise to treat the ravages of the body with medication and diet after the afflictions of the soul have been eased. For "usual" illnesses, treatment includes an incantation to add to the healer's efficacy and to guard against the possibility of spirit attack upon an already vulnerable patient.

Malay incantations invariably include Koranic sentences and other appeals to Allah, his Prophet, and his saints. Belief in the dangers of *badi*, that hot, impersonal, destructive spiritual force emanating from the corpses of jungle animals and human beings, however, makes no appeal to Islam for the authentication of its power. *Badi* holds particular danger for the unborn, working indirectly through their parents. To avoid its risks, prospective fathers are advised to forego hunting for the duration of their wives' pregnancies, and mothers-to-be are warned against visits of condolence to homes of the yet-unburied dead (Laderman 1983).

TREATMENT OF "UNUSUAL" ILLNESSES

Herbal treatments and dietary changes alone cannot alleviate the symptoms of illness due to spirit attack. Excess fire and air must be removed and earth and water increased. *Bomoh* counteract the spirits' hot breath with their own, made "cool" by an incantation. After blowing on the patients' backs, the shaman often advises that they bathe in cold water made still cooler by the addition of lime juice and the chanting of a cooling spell. Earth and water are further increased by applying *tepung tawar*, neutralizing rice paste, to the patient's forehead. Destructive spiritual influences may be swept away from the patient's body with leafy branches. If the *semangat* has been lost, measures must be taken to entice it back to the body, using sweet-smelling incense and the sweet words of the *bomoh*'s incantation.

Bomoh are usually well acquainted with the life circumstances of their patients, and ask them telling questions to aid in the diagnosis. They take the pulse and assess the patient's physical and emotional state. If the cause of an illness is still not apparent to the *bomoh*, a divination may provide the answer.

The divination used by Pak Su Weng, when he was called by my assistant, Yusof, to treat me for a mysterious ailment, reminded me of tea-leaf readings offered in Gypsy tea rooms in New York City. I had been ill with a raging fever for three weeks, two of which I spent in the General Hospital in Kuala Trengganu, and was extremely weak when I returned to Merchang. After testing me for 11 other diseases, my doctors discovered I had mononucleosis. They had not suspected it sooner because mononucleosis appears to be rare in Malaysia. No wonder it seemed like an "unusual" illness to Yusof and Pak Su Weng.

Before the divination, Pak Su felt the pulse at my fingers, wrist, inside my elbow, at my shoulders, ears, and finally my toes. Had I been a man, he would also have felt the pulse in my chest, but he was afraid that if he did so it would make my husband angry. *Bomoh* feel the pulse in many places, he said, because the pulse can travel. If the ears and fingers are cold, the fever has lodged in the body but not in the head. If the toes are warm and the fingers are cold, the fever is going down. If the fingers are warm and the toes cold, the fever is traveling up. In my case, the coldness of my fingers, toes and ears showed that the heat was buried within, making me weak and taking away my appetite. The doctors at the hospital were not able to find this internal fever, he said, since it cannot be measured with a thermometer.

Pak Su asked Yusof to chew a betel quid and spit into a cup. His saliva, bright red and frothy from the betel quid, formed patterns in the cup. Pak Su pointed to a winding bubbly line in the saliva. This, he said, was the path I travelled when I visited Kg. Durian Pahit, the furthest inland of Merchang's hamlets, recently claimed from the jungle. The *hantu* there, living at the jungle's edge, are more hostile toward people than spirits who dwell in the village. Not only had I been working long hours and was tired and thus more vulnerable, I had also neglected to take elementary precautions when I went to Durian Pahit, he said. In the future, I must be sure to keep my fists together when traveling to such places, to make a protective "fence" for my body, and I must ask permission of the *hantu* before intruding on their land.

The *hantu* responsible for my sickness was the *Hantu Bisu* (Mute Spirit), who was beside himself with envy at meeting up with a person who spoke so much and in so many languages. The hot breath that he blew on my back caused heat to travel through my body, causing fever, and later settling in my throat, causing swellings. It was lucky that the *hantu* in question was a comparatively weak spirit, said Pak Su. A really powerful one could have caused my whole body to swell up, and killed me instantaneously.

After he divined the cause of my illness, Pak Su cut the red saliva with a sharp knife, destroying the picture he had seen in the cup and breaking the *hantu*'s power over me. He dipped a *sirih* leaf (one of the components of the betel quid) into the liquid. Using the leaf as a brush, he painted two lines on my forehead in the form of a cross, representing the four cardinal directions. He made red circles around my ears, on my shoulders, elbows, wrists, knees and lastly on my ankles. This would cause the *hantu*'s heat to leave my body, exiting by way of my toes. Then he sat behind me and recited a *jampi*, periodically blowing his supernaturally cooled breath on my back, to counteract the *hantu*'s hot breath.

The *bomoh* still had to deal with the problems remaining after the *hantu*'s influence had left. I was very weak and needed medicine to strengthen me. He prescribed two kinds of *akar kayu* to be taken internally (the literal meaning of *akar kayu* is "woody roots," but it is used as the generic name for all herbal medicines). Both were made of humorally cold ingredients, which would help to rid me of any vestiges of noxious heat. They would act like vitamin pills, said Pak Su, and give me back my strength and my appetite.

Before being discharged from the hospital, I had complained of a fiery spot on my shoulder. The doctor shrugged his own shoulders—there was nothing visibly wrong, and nothing he could do about it. Pak Su Weng made a cooling lotion to apply to the fiery place, by rubbing a mixture of ingredients on the inside of his medicine bowl. In all, the ingredients comprised elements of the animal, vegetable and mineral kingdoms, some (like the stone from Bukit Bintang, a hill noted for spirit activity; and the camel's kneebone, associated with the Prophet Muhammad) undoubtedly receiving efficacy from their associations with holy or magical persons; others (such as *isi teras kait hijau* [*Zizyphus elegans*]) having been noted by researchers (e.g., Burkill 1966: 2347) for their use in treating fevers. Pak Su combined the scrapings with water and poured the lotion into a bottle. I patted some on my shoulder. After the first application, the fiery feeling was noticeably diminished; after the next, it disappeared.

Before he left, Pak Su asked my husband to fill a large pail with the water from the well in our backyard, and to pick three limes (*limau nipis*) from the tree that grew in front of our house. He recited a *jampi*, made two cuts in each lime, tracing the four cardinal directions, and squeezed their juice into the water, throwing the fruit in as well. He advised me to bathe in the cold water, made still cooler by the addition of the lime juice and the chanting of a cooling spell, to cool down my inner fever. The treatment was complete; both the symptoms and their underlying cause had been dealt with.

I gradually recovered from my illness, and my treatment was considered a success due both to Pak Su's skill and the harmony that existed between us. A *bomoh*'s treatments, no matter how skillful, may not help if his relationship to his patient is not harmonious (*sesuai*). Internal and external harmony are the keys to good health and a peaceful life, in the view of rural Malays. Traditional healers and midwives attempt to bring their patients into greater harmony with their own inner being and with the outer world. A mother-to-be who is not in harmony with her unborn child risks spontaneous abortion. Should the child survive, this lack of harmony may cause him to be sickly and develop badly, unless he is adopted (usually informally) and raised in a household more compatible with the child's nature. Even the lack of harmony between a child's individual nature and his name may seriously affect his well-being. Because of this, many children have two names: a school name, given to them at birth, which appears on their birth certificate, and a home name, given as a prophylaxis during childhood ailments.

Adults can also suffer from the effects of disharmony, particularly during illnesses, following the birth of a child, and after circumcision. During these times of vulnerability, they will avoid eating foods considered *bisa*, meaning "intensifier of internal disharmony." Many of these foods have been objectively demonstrated to be toxic, particularly to vulnerable people (see Laderman 1983: 62–72).

If one *bomoh*'s ministrations do not work, patients may seek another, more harmonious practitioner, or they may look to biomedicine for a cure. Should the patient still not improve, it may be necessary to hold a spirit-raising seance.

MAIN PETERI

Bomoh can be found today in every part of Malaysia (including the capital, Kuala Lumpur), but the spirit-raising seance seems to have disappeared from, or become rare in, most Malaysian states. In Kelantan, however, and in its neighboring state, Trengganu, to which Kelantanese have migrated in large numbers, the seance is still thriving.

During twenty-one months of research in Kelantan, in the late 1960s, Kessler attended ninety-eight performances (1977: 302). I attended a similar number in Trengganu, during 1975–77, and, again, in 1982. They occurred irregularly: occasionally weeks went by with no performance, but often performances were held almost every night.

The east coast seance known as *Main Peteri* is often a measure of last resort, not undertaken lightly. It involves a substantial expenditure, since the patient's family must hold a feast for the shaman's entourage before the seance begins, pay a fee to each performer, and distribute refreshments to the audience of friends, neighbors and relatives who have come to offer moral support and to be entertained, when the night's proceedings have come to an end. At a minimum, the performers include the *Tok 'teri*, a *bomoh* who acts as shaman; the *Tok Minduk*, a *bomoh* who plays the spike fiddle and acts as interlocutor; a drummer; and a player of the floor gongs (often merely overturned pots). Larger scale *Main Peteri* can include several *tok 'teri* and *minduk*, players of gongs, large drums, and other percussion instruments, and a *serunai* (a variety of oboe) player. They usually attract a large audience, even now when villagers have the choice of watching programs such as "Kojak" and "The Six Million Dollar Man" on television, since the *Main Peteri* is a drama whose elements of comedy, tragedy, melodrama, surprise, music, song and dance are played out before the onlookers' eyes with a force of reality and truth that rivals the spell of other entertainments.

Before the *Main Peteri* can proceed, the patient's problem must be diagnosed by means of divination. A divination that points to any combination of earth, fire or water often points to *hantu* or *jin* as causal factors. These spirits may have been bribed by an enemy of the patient, or they may be acting on their own volition, angered, perhaps, by the trampling of their invisible abodes or a shower of urine on their invisible heads.

On the whole, a healthy whole person has little to fear from the *hantu*. *Hantu*, I was told, are much like dogs. Left to their own devices, they will rarely attack. Unlike dogs, however, they are invisible. One therefore runs the risk of inadvertently disturbing and offending them, thus arousing their wrath. They are never truly vicious, however, unless they are harbored by people who use them to harm others. Occasionally, too, they may turn feral if their human "master" has abrogated an agreement without their consent, or if he has neglected them, or died, leaving them unfed and uncared for.

Although they are our older brothers, God did not grant them the power of reason (*akal*) that makes us truly human. Lacking reason, they behave like simpletons or children, easily flattered, cowed by threats, and easily caught out in their lies by clever *bomoh*, whose insulting remarks make their human audience roar with laughter but elude the spirits' understanding. When, for example, a *jin* appears during a seance, announcing that his name is the Jin With the Lookalike Face (*Anak Jin Serupa Muka*), and the *minduk* answers, "Oh, you are the Jin With the Asshole Face" (*Anak Jin Sejubor Muka*), the spirit completely ignores the insult, rushing ahead with his speech.

If an illness shows signs of spirit-connected etiology, the suspected spirits must be brought to the seance by the officiating shaman's own familiar spirits (*penggawa*). The *minduk* flatters, coaxes, promises them offerings, and occasionally insults and threatens them, to induce them to restore the patient to health. Their victim's humoral balance has been put awry by the spirits' airy heat. To complete the healing task, they must remove their unbalancing presence: "clear every stifling vapor from the body and soul" of the patient. The *minduk* exhorts them to return to their origins and restore, as well, the balance of the universe, whose integrity is threatened by their encroaching upon humanity.

Complications can arise when the patient's birth-sibling joins the disembodied *hantu*'s attack. The birth-sibling, the afterbirth that accompanies the birth of each human child, is the mirror image of the *hantu*. Both are incomplete: the spirits lack the earthy and watery elements of which the body is made, while the birth-sibling never receives the airy and fiery Breath of Life that animates its human sibling when the baby takes its first breath. Semi-human, the birth-sibling deserves a decent burial. The midwife washes the placenta in water into which limes have been squeezed, as carefully as if she were laying out a corpse. Then she wraps it in a white winding sheet and lays it in a half coconut shell coffin. The father buries it beneath a coconut palm, "the sky for its cover, the earth for its pillow." The birth-sibling is not a malevolent force, but, like all siblings, it may experience the pangs of sibling rivalry. Although they "traveled down the same path" (the mother's birth canal), they are unequal heirs. The human child received all the love and property of the parents, and the birth-sibling only a half coconut shell and a scrap of cloth. The afterbirth, although it resents its unequal treatment at the hands of its parents, is not an implacable enemy of its human sibling. In fact, it and the blood of parturition are referred to as "black caretaker of the soul, yellow[8] caretaker of the spirit" (*hitam gembala roh, kuning gembala semangat*) in the *Main Peteri*.

In order to effect a cure, the good will of the siblings, both spirit and afterbirth, must be obtained by offering them fair words and property. Spirits are satisfied with symbolic reality, offered to them in place of material reality; extracting the essence of food without damaging it for future consumption by creatures with bodies (animals, if not humans), and accepting statuettes of animals and models of kitchen utensils in lieu of the real objects.

When the shaman counts out the grains of popped rice arranged in three piles during the divination, if the count in any pile ends on air (*angin*), it points to a diagnosis that the patient's problem was not caused solely by external entities, either disembodied *hantu* or the birth-brother. It lies as well within the patient's own personality.

ANGIN: THE INNER WINDS

Conditions treated by the Malay *bomoh* who specializes in shamanic healing (the *tok 'teri*) are rarely attributed solely to spirit attacks. The majority are referred to as neither "usual" nor "unusual," but as *sakit berangin*, or sickness due to a problem with the Inner Winds.

The Inner Winds, as understood by east coast Malays, are close to Western concepts of temperament, both in the medieval sense of the four temperaments and as artistic temperament. They are the airy component of the four humors: the traits, talents and desires we inherit from our ancestors, "down the family line through all generations, turning up now here, now there," as the *minduk* sings in the *Main Peteri*.

People may be heir to several different Inner Winds; their endowment can range from mild breezes to hurricane-strength. Possessors of strong Winds will often be respected for their talent and skill; indeed, acquiring many skills depends upon a combination of hard work and appropriate Inner Winds. Everyone who hopes to be successful in any of the specialized roles that Malay village society provides (most of which are, or were, connected with rituals) must not only study diligently. He or she must also have the *angin* specific to that role. No amount of study can substitute for *angin*.

The Inner Winds do not merely guide their possessors into professional activities, they shape the basic personality. Those who have inherited the Wind of the young Demigod (*Angin Dewa Muda*) crave life's luxuries, both material and psychic, needing love and admiration as much as dainty foods and handsome clothes. From a Western viewpoint, such people are dependent and narcissistic. Heirs to the Wind of the Weretiger (*Angin Hala*) are quick to anger and heedless of its consequences, unable or unwilling to control their anger and hostility.

People with gentle Winds run little risk of *sakit berangin*. Strong winds will not harm their possessors if they are able to be expressed in ways that satisfy the individual and enrich the community. If they cannot, their *angin* is trapped inside them, where it accumulates, unbalancing the humors, and causing disharmony within the person. The symptoms of *sakit berangin* include backaches, headaches, digestive problems, dizziness, asthma, depression, anxiety; in short, a wide range of what we call psychosomatic and affective disorders. Asthma in particular represents a graphic example of repressed *angin*—Wind that is locked within, choking its possessor.

The Inner Winds of a patient in the *Main Peteri* who has been diagnosed as suffering from *sakit berangin* must be allowed to express themselves, to be released from the confines of their corporeal prison, enabling the sufferer's mind and body to return to a healthy balance. This is accomplished within the context of the *Main Peteri*: After the offending disembodied spirits have been brought to the seance and exorcised, the patient afflicted with *sakit berangin* is put into trance by means of appropriate music and the story of the *angin*'s archetype, as recited by the shaman. When the correct musical or literary cue is reached, the patient achieves trance, aided, as well, by the percussive sounds of the musicians and the rhythmic beating of the shaman's hands on the floor near the patient's body.[9]

In shamanic ceremonies whose primary aim is to remove demonic influence from human sufferers, the patient's trance is "the peak moment [at which] the object of the demonic enters into direct communion with the subject" (Kapferer 1983: 195). For the Malay patient, trance does not occur during the exorcistic parts of the *Main Peteri*. The communication achieved by trancing patients is not with the demonic, but with their own inner nature.

While in trance, patients are encouraged to act out the repressed portions of their personalities until their hearts are content and their *angin* refreshed. Entranced patients may sing and dance, call upon familiar spirits, perform the stylized moves and stances of *silat* (the Malay art of self-defense), or roar and pounce like a tiger. The relaxation experienced by patients after coming out of trance is profound. Headaches and backaches have disappeared, and asthma sufferers find they can once more breathe freely.[10]

Patients feel a separation between themselves and their physical bodies during trance. They are in a state Malays call "not remembering" (*tak ingat*). While remaining conscious of the music, the smell of incense, and the faces of the people in the room, they feel they are floating somewhere above the body that they know is seated on the floor. Patients "forget" themselves so far as to exhibit behavior that would be socially unacceptable under other circumstances, but "remember" themselves enough to be cognizant of their surroundings during trance, and to recall their actions when the trance has ended.

The trance, in allowing the Inner Winds to blow freely, removes their unhealthy accumulation, returning the patient to a state of balance and harmony. The outside air, in the form of breath (*nyawa*), can flow unobstructed through the lungs, within the blood stream, and out again normally. The correction of imbalance strengthens the patient's "gate," protecting the *semangat* within (see Laderman 1991).

CONCLUSIONS

The Malay emphasis on *angin* as a determinant of individual personality structure casts doubt upon Hsu's contention (1985: 24–55) that "the concept of personality is an expression of the Western ideal of individualism" which does not correspond to concepts in other cultures.[11] Perhaps the concept of individual personality is not tied to Western ideals, but, rather, is most salient in cultures without strong lineage or other corporate ties.

Although symptoms of *sakit berangin* bear a great similarity to complaints reported by Kleinman's depressed Chinese informants (Kleinman 1980), the idiom is quite different. Malay theories concerning *angin* do not aim at somaticizing the experience, but, rather, locate the problem within the patient's personality. This emphasis differentiates Malay perceptions, as well, from Japanese cognition about depression as reported by Marsella (1977): external metaphors—clouds, rain, mist—are employed by Japanese, in contrast to the Malay internal metaphor of the Inner Wind.

Marsella believes that "depression has far less crushing implications for the sense of self [in non-Western people] because the language/thinking process permits the experience to be coded and communicated in either somatic terms or in impersonal external referent terms" (1985: 302). He also assumes that folk healing focusses "more on relations (with other people, or with supernatural entities) than with processes internal to the individual" (Marsella 1984: 88). Malay ethnomedicine and conceptions of the self are exceptions that test the rule.

Although some aspects of Malay traditional medicine focus on external relations (as do certain aspects of Western medicine, e.g., public health and epidemiology), others do not. Depression for Malays who, like Westerners, refer to their inner states in personalized terms, is both psychologized and somaticized as it is in the West. It is common knowledge that depression in Westerners, particularly the aged, is often expressed by patients in physical terms and so misdiagnosed by physicians. The Malay humoral system with its focus on individual physiological processes, and the concept of *sakit berangin*, based on individual personality problems coded and communicated by Malays in personal internal referent terms, should give pause to those who might be tempted to view non-Western societies *en masse* as the Other.

ACKNOWLEDGMENTS

Research upon which this article is based was supported by the N.I.M.H., S.S.R.C., N.E.H., John Simon Guggenheim Memorial Foundation, Rockefeller Foundation, and Fordham University, to all of which I am sincerely grateful.

NOTES

1. My remarks derive from fieldwork in the states of Trengganu and Kelantan. Variations in belief and behavior undoubtedly exist in other Malaysian states.
2. In a publication of the Trengganu Office of Religious Affairs (Haji Mahmud Salim 1976), many of the *bomoh*'s practices are cited as dangerous deviations from Islam. They are said to "treat sick people by means of worshipping spirits and devils, and to throw away trays of propitiatory food offerings." Their public performances are listed as examples of the kinds of superstition that must be rooted out. *Puja pantai*, in particular, is not only anathema; its performance, if revealed, can lead to a stiff fine and prison sentence.
3. For an extended discussion of the Inner Winds, see Laderman (1988, 1991).
4. *Nyawa*, the Breath of Life, is related to the Greek *pneuma*, both conceptually and etymologically.
5. Cuisinier (1951: 204) writes that the conception of the soul or spirit in the form of a bird is a common belief throughout the Malay Archipelago. The *semangat* or *roh* is often personified as a bird in the *Main Peteri*. Malay identification of the *semangat* with the chicken (the bird most in evidence in their lives) is shown by the use of the chicken in circumcision feasts, rituals to release a new mother from the postpartum period (Laderman 1983: 205–209) and in the frequent representations of chickens at wedding parties. Skeat (1972 [1990]: 587) notes that *bomoh* of his day called the soul by the sound used to call fowl.
6. Similar metaphors can be found in other cultures, such as *babana* in the Solomon Islands, a term that describes building a barrier, conceptualized as making one "hard" and hence less vulnerable to penetration by dangerous forces such as spirits or malevolent human stares (White 1985: 334).
7. It is interesting to compare this formulation with Western psychoanalytic theory. Freud believed that hysteria begins with a violent emotional shock (fright, anxiety, shame or physical pain). "In traumatic neuroses the operative cause of the illness is not the trifling physical injury but the effect of fright—the psychical trauma" (Freud and Breuer 1895: 40).
8. Yellow as well as red symbolizes blood in Malay magic.
9. Percussive music has been considered an important means of achieving transition to an altered state (e.g., Neher 1962; Needham 1967). The most effective rhythm appears to be four to seven beats per second, exactly the optimum frequency for pain relief through electrically stimulated acupuncture. This rhythm matches the EEG frequency of theta waves, produced by the brain most strongly during periods of deep meditation. It is also the rhythm of the drum beat at the height of the music that accompanies the trance in the *Main Peteri*.
10. The cathartic effects of abreaction in the healing of psychological trauma and psychosomatic pain have been attested to by many studies. Dramatic relief of asthma, in particular, has been observed following catharsis (French 1939; Doust and Leigh 1953; Weiner 1977): "The motor expressions of emotion, i.e., weeping, laughing, the acting out of anger . . . proved to reduce symptoms and remove the oxygen deprivation which characterized these patients" (Doust and Leigh 1953: 304).
11. For recent discussion of "the self" in various cultures, see Marsella, DeVos, and Hsu (1985); Shweder and LeVine (1984); White and Kirkpatrick (1985); Marsella and White (1984).

REFERENCES CITED

Burkill, I. H.
   1966   A Dictionary of the Economic Products of the Malay Peninsula. Kuala Lumpur: Ministry of Agriculture and Cooperatives.
Cuisinier, J.
   1951   Sumangat: l'Âme et son Culte en Indochine et en Indonesie. Paris: Gallimard.
Doust, J. W. L., and D. Leigh
   1953   Studies on the Physiology of Awareness: The Interrelations of Emotions, Life Situations, and Anoxemia in Patients with Bronchial Asthma. Psychosomatic Medicine 15: 292–311.
Endicott, K. M.
   1970   An Analysis of Malay Magic. London: Oxford University Press.

Firth, R.
1974   Faith and Skepticism in Kelantanese Village Magic. *In* Kelantan: Religion, Society and Politics in a Malay State. W. R. Roff, ed. Kuala Lumpur: Oxford University Press.
French, T. M.
1939   Psychogenic Factors in Asthma. American Journal of Psychiatry 96: 89.
Freud, S., and J. Breuer
1895   Studies on Hysteria. (reprinted 1966) New York: Avon Books.
Hsu, F. L. K.
1985   The Self in Cross-cultural Perspective. *In* Culture and Self: Asian and Western Perspectives. A. J. Marsella, G. DeVos, and F. L. K. Hsu, eds. New York: Tavistock Publications.
Kapferer, B.
1983   A Celebration of Demons: Exorcism and the Aesthetics of Healing in Sri Lanka. Bloomington: Indiana University Press.
Kessler, C. S.
1977   Conflict and Sovereignty in Spirit Seances. *In* Case Studies in Spirit Possession. V. Crapanzano, and V. Garrison, eds. New York: John Wiley and Sons.
Kleinman, A.
1980   Patients and Healers in the Context of Culture. Berkeley: University of California Press.
Laderman, C.
1981   Symbolic and Empirical Reality: A New Approach to the Analysis of Food Avoidances. American Ethnologist 9(3): 468–493. Special issue on Symbolism and Cognition.
1983   Wives and Midwives: Childbirth and Nutrition in Rural Malaysia. Berkeley: University of California Press.
1988   Wayward Winds: Malay Shamanism and Theory of Personality. *In* Techniques of Healing in Southeast Asia, a special issue of Social Science and Medicine. C. Laderman, and P. Van Esterik, eds. 27(8): 799–810.
1991   Taming the Wind of Desire: Psychology, Medicine and Aesthetics in Malay Shamanistic Performance. Berkeley: University of California Press.
Lutz, C.
1985   Ethnopsychology Compared to What? Explaining Behavior and Consciousness Among the Ifaluk. *In* Person, Self, and Experience: Exploring Pacific Ethnopsychologies. G. M. White, and J. Kirkpatrick, eds. Berkeley: University of California Press.
Mahmud Salim bin Haji Mhd. (Haji)
1975   *Al Imam* (The Faithful). Trengganu Office of Religious Affairs.
Marsella, A.
1977   Depressive Experience and Disorder Across Cultures. Handbook of Cross-Cultural Psychology, Vol. 5: Culture and Psychopathology. H. Triandis and J. Draguns, eds. Boston: Allyn and Bacon.
1984   Culture and Mental Health: An Overview. *In* Cultural Conceptions of Mental Health and Therapy. A. J. Marsella, and G. M. White, eds. Dordrecht: D. Reidel.
1985   Culture, Self, and Mental Disorder. *In* Culture and Self: Asian and Western Perspectives. A. Marsella, G. DeVos, and F. L. K. Hsu, eds. New York: Tavistock Publications.
Marsella, A., G. DeVos, and F. L. K. Hsu, eds.
1985   Culture and Self: Asian and Western Perspectives. New York: Tavistock.
Marsella, A., and G. M. White, eds.
1984   Cultural Conceptions of Mental Health and Therapy. Dordrecht: D. Reidel.
Massard, J.
1988   Doctoring by Go-between: Aspects of Health Care for Malay Children. Social Science and Medicine 27(8): 789–798.
Needham, R.
1967   Percussion and Transition. Man II: 606–614.
Neher, A.
1962   A Physiological Explanation of Unusual Behavior in Ceremonies Involving Drums. Human Biology 34: 151–161.
Shweder, R. A., and R. A. LeVine, eds.
1984   Culture Theory: Essays on Mind, Self, and Emotion. New York: Cambridge University Press.

Siti Hasmah
  1975   The Role of Traditional Birth Attendants in Family Health. Paper presented at a Workshop for the Instruction and Practice of Midwifery, Kuala Lumpur.
Skeat, W. W.
  1972 [1900]   Malay Magic: Being an Introduction to the Folklore and Popular Religion of the Malay Peninsula. New York: Benjamin Blom.
Weiner, H.
  1977   Psychobiology and Human Disease. New York: Elsevier.
White, G. M.
  1985   Premises and Purposes in a Solomon Islands Ethnopsychology. *In* Person, Self, and Experience: Exploring Pacific Ethnopsychologies. G. M. White and J. Kirkpatrick, eds. Berkeley: University of California Press.
White, G. M., and J. Kirkpatrick, eds.
  1985   Person, Self, and Experience: Exploring Pacific Ethnopsychologies. Berkeley: University of California Press.

An Ayurvedic Theory of Cancer

Margaret Trawick

Ayurveda is a healing system widely practiced throughout South Asia. It is founded upon a set of Sanskrit texts composed two thousand years ago which describe in detail a theory of humoral balance within the body. The name Ayurveda means "that which has been seen to be true about long life."

In 1975 in southern Tamil Nadu, an aged practitioner of Ayurveda conducted for the author's benefit a series of lectures about cancer, in which he propounded his own idiosyncratic theory regarding the nature of this disease. The doctor's lectures were a linguistic and topical pastiche, melding Indian and Western biologies, psychologies, and sociologies. The lectures were fascinating for they demonstrated many lines of kinship between ideas expressed in the ancient Sanskrit texts and ideas afloat still in the modern world. But for all their richness Mahadeva Iyer's lectures were seemingly unfocused, and his motives for developing them were unclear to the author. Only when the author was able to see these lectures, not as cultural artifacts, but as messages addressed from one historically situated personality to another, did the reason for the doctor's conveyance of them to her become clear.

Mahadeva Iyer was past eighty when I met him, and I was twenty-five.[1] He was a widely respected, wealthy, and erudite doctor; I was a student without money or reputation. He was a South Indian Brahman patriarch; I was a casteless American girl. He was the head of a large and distinguished family. I had only my unemployed husband and my baby. I thought my presence could only be a disruptive annoyance to such a man. Yet when I asked Mahadeva Iyer if I could stay in his village and observe his practice of the venerable medical system called Ayurveda, he welcomed me hospitably and enthusiastically. At the time, and often later, I wondered why.

In his old age, Mahadeva Iyer had become deaf and immobile. He would sit all day on the couch on his front porch, waiting for visitors. When someone arrived, his eyes would light up and he would talk incessantly. It was hard to get him to stop talking once he had started, as though in the few months remaining before his body failed completely he felt an urgent need to pour the contents of his mind into other vessels, or to heal with his spoken thoughts the disorders that daily ever more darkly menaced his world.

Some people said he was senile. They accused him of running aimlessly off at the mouth. But to me it was more like a reckless brilliance, a sometimes humorous, sometimes bitter, cutting clarity that the words he poured in the direction of his visitors displayed.

MARGARET TRAWICK *is Associate Professor in the Department of Anthropology at Hobart and William Smith Colleges, Geneva, NY 14456. Her research interests are in the areas of ethnopoetics, spirit possession, and the anthropology of emotion, and she has done extensive fieldwork in South India.*

Mahadeva Iyer was fluent in several languages—Tamil, Malayalam, Sanskrit, English. Like many educated Indians, he would rapidly switch back and forth from one language to another while he talked. It seemed almost impossible for him to stick to any one language for very long. He knew enough to follow each language's rules as he spoke it, but for some reason he chose not to. His speech was peppered with ungrammatical idiosyncrasies. He liked changes and surprises.[2]

I asked him once, as a "native healer," to tell me something about the growth of plants. (Ayurvedic doctors make extensive use of medicinal plants. A plant's stage of growth has much to do with its healing properties.) I had told him I wanted him to speak to me in Tamil. So in Tamil he commenced his discourse about seeds falling to the ground, trees growing, certain trees flourishing and shading out other trees, certain weeds stealing nourishment from cultivated plants. Then he switched to English[3]:

Whichever plant, whichever tree is victorious, that is called 'survival of the fittest'. Just like man who holds money ignoring all others' convenience and necessities, he absorbs all the money and keeps it for himself. Apart from this there is nature to keep a balance among all his children. But even in these circumstances some plants and trees grow very high, very happy and very big, and become an abode for birds and other animals to stay, but no one can escape the target of man who is supposed to be the highest being with intelligence. Not only man but all things have got a power given by God to produce a thing and grow it to a maximum condition and then cut it into pieces and make it into furniture and other utensils. Man digs out gold from earth with much difficulty, and he takes out the gold from the mines a very great distance from the earth's surface and he purifies the gold and makes it into pieces and again he builds a concrete building below the surface and keeps it quite safe guarded by soldiers with loaded guns. Even then the gold seeks a very nice protected place under the ground.

No one can destroy a thing nor keep a thing in the same stage but he must follow the principle of God.

Why was he telling me this? No matter what I or anyone else asked Mahadeva Iyer, his thoughts seemed always to drift toward certain topics, taking his sentences with them. One topic he often returned to in this way concerned the harm done when one being becomes "overgrown" or "overnourished" at the expense of other beings, or when one being consumes the substances belonging to other beings, so that they weaken while it grows strong.

In Ayurvedic thought, any disease-process might be described in such terms. The body is considered to be composed of many substances. All of them are necessary, but any of them may give rise to sickness if it becomes "angry" or "overwrought" or "overflows its proper channels." Health is a matter of keeping all substances in balance, so that no substance becomes "excessive" while others become "deficient."[4] Mahadeva Iyer tended always—or at least while I was present—to blame physical excess for the various ills he observed. Deficiency was not such a serious problem in his scheme of things. He considered the overall reduction of bodily substance to be a moral and physical virtue. In his view the most praiseworthy yogis, for instance, were ones who had learned to live only on light and air, so that they were nearly transparent. He regarded vegetarianism as desirable because "a person should not grow his own body at the expense of the bodies of others." The substances Mahadeva Iyer regarded as most likely to become excessive in the body were "dirty" or "impure" (tuśippu) ones, such as feces. When these became "arrogant" and got out of hand—when, for instance, a person was constipated and feces accumulated inside him—then trouble began. No substance should be allowed to accumulate in one place indefinitely; everything should be kept moving and changing in its proper order. This was "the principle of God."

Cancer fascinated Mahadeva Iyer, as it did many Indian physicians I met, and he lectured to me often about it. One interesting thing about cancer in the context of Indian medicine is that cancer receives scant attention in the traditional Indian medical texts, but modern Indian doctors devote considerable thought to it, at least in part because the Western biomedical description of this disease happens to fit very well the Ayurvedic paradigm of all diseases. In Ayurveda there are no absolute evils: no microorganisms which should be eliminated from the face of the earth, no poisons which should never enter the body, no processes which should be stopped completely. The very same processes and substances which are necessary for life are also responsible for illness and death. Only when things get out of order, when one being becomes too big, crowding out other beings, when one substance invades the channels made for other substances, when the growth of one tissue proceeds unchecked, then the entire system to which the arrogant being or substance belongs falters, and may die.

Cancer for Mahadeva Iyer, like cancer for us Americans, had strong moral and metaphorical significance. A cancerous tumor in the body was like a fetus in the womb, a kind of "foreign body" that grew large at the expense of its host, that had in the normal order of things to be expelled, and that had a life and a will of its own. The original sin shared by all creatures was that they lived for a long twenty months as parasites upon their mother, "drinking her blood for ten months in the womb and then drinking her blood in the form of milk for another ten months after they are born." Only at one's own peril did one fail to acknowledge this inherent pollution within each living creature, this unrepayable debt to the Mother:

[In mixed Tamil and Sanskrit] All the animals in the world are born in a female womb. This is mother of yoga, transcendent power, birth-giver of the world. Therefore if he does any evil to a woman, he will be destroyed, there will be no mercy upon him, he will be ruined. If he sees a woman, he must think of her as Mother, and he must worship her and obtain her blessings. Only such people become long-lived. . . .

Those who at the very beginning, by experience, discovered and brought food and medicine were members of the family of women. Men made it an occupation and made it into a way to earn an income.

Mahadeva Iyer explained to me that cancer might begin in the mother's womb, as unexpelled excrement in the fetus, or as a "fault" (*kuṟai*) transmitted to the fetus from either of its parents. The very process of embryogenesis, he emphasized, following the classical Ayurvedic description of tissue-formation, gives rise to different kinds of dirt, which collect in different parts of the body. These different kinds of dirt, especially the dirt collecting in the sexual organs, may become "angry," he said. Then after birth such collected dirt may become manifest as various diseases of childhood, especially rashes and sores (*karappāṉ*). Such sores, in turn, may become places where cancerous fluid (*cūlai nīr*, "stabbing water") will collect. The collection of *cūlai nīr* in a single location results in a hard, painful boil or tumor (*nīr kaṭṭu*, "bound water"), which grows increasingly large. To surgically remove the boil or tumor will effect only a local cure; it will not eliminate the underlying cause of the cancer:

[In Tamil] In the fetus, the flaws of the mother and the father, the condition of the organs, mind, intelligence, these all take form. When a portion of the food [eaten by the mother] joins with the fetus, [that portion becomes] its muscles, nerves, and blood. The different kinds of dirt (*aṟukkukaḷ*) [produced by this process] wander in the body, travel with the blood, and are deposited in the body. For these impurities to be excreted, they undergo certain divisions. That is, the dirt in the eyes, the dirt in the ears, the dirt in the nose, the dirt congealing on the teeth, the dirt lodged in man's reproductive organs (*ñānēntiriyaṅkal*)—the anger created by these, every day as age increases, starting with birth [gives rise to] blood deficiency, scabies, scabs, wounds and sores. These scabies become great sores and become like cancer, cancerous. With this cancer, bound water arises, the poison increases, large scabs appear, and they become sores that will not heal . . . . In the body, the property of growing correctly decreases and the property of cancer growing increases. By way of the sore, the fluids in the body ooze out. It begins to grow through the ulcer. Therefore, if you cut out the cancerous sore, or perform an operation, or char it with fire, you will not heal it. You will level only the property of its' becoming a sore.

The substance that Mahadeva Iyer referred to as *cūlai nīr* was in his opinion the root of cancer. One of its special properties was its tendency to collect and form hard spots on the body.

In the body, *cūlai nīr* arises. This *cūlai nīr* comes from certain poisons and bad foods. As time passes, these poisonous waters and this sharpness mingle with the body and here and there harden and become bound water, and scabs, and sores that will not heal. These sores become cancer as time passes.

The hardness of a boil or cancerous tumor was an important matter in Mahadeva Iyer's overall scheme of knowledge, for in his view hardness and hardening processes were tantamount to the destruction, or more accurately, the obstruction, of the flow of life. Much of his therapeutic practice, therefore, consisted in fostering softness and fluidity in the bodily substances of his patients. The use of purgatives and oil massages, two of the most common therapeutic measures in Ayurveda, he explained in terms of softening and fluidification. The process of aging was, as he described it, primarily a process of hardening and stiffening—hardening of the arteries, hardening of the nerves, stiffening of the joints. Vegetarian foods were to be consumed because they were "soft;" non-vegetarian foods were "hard" and the bodies as well as the hearts of those who ate such foods were likewise hard. "Hard" people were precisely those who were cruel enough to live at the cost of the lives of others.[5] In Mahadeva Iyer's view, hardness accompanied excessive accumulation of substance in one place, the appropriation of substances to oneself that rightfully belonged elsewhere, and so it was inseparable from such emotional qualities as arrogance, cruelty, and anger. *Cūlai nīr* embodied in a material form all of these characteristics. The word *cūlai* is related to *cūlam* which means trident or impaling stake.

At the same time, *cūlai nīr* is associated with sexual fluids, or more precisely, with sexual poisons and sexual disease. A *cūlai kaḍḍi* is a venereal sore or swelling. White discharge from the vagina or the urethra is sometimes called *cūlai nīr*. Mahadeva Iyer associated *cūlai nīr* with congenital syphilis.

The *cūlai nīr* which arises in the body is the cause of many diseases. For little children, there is a "red disease" (*civappu rōkam*) that comes from the blood of the mother and father. When children are born with this disease, blood-colored boils arise on the chest. Then they arise in many places on the body. They arise on the neck, in the armpits, on the genital organ, on the arms and legs. They break and become bloody. This *cūlai nīr* is the cause of many kinds of torment—it is the cause of shortage of breath, liver disease, and many other kinds of diseases.

Mahadeva Iyer also believed that *cūlai nīr* was a transformed version of the fluid he called *muppū*, the liquid expelled from the womb with the infant at parturition. This liquid was intensely toxic and polluting, and yet also was capable of yielding an elixir of immortality, which could cure (among other things) cancer, if one knew the proper alchemical processes to which it should be subjected. If one consumed this elixir, one would live forever unchanging, with a body as hard as diamond. The formula for this medicine, however, was known only to *siddhars*, anti-social magical yogis who cared nothing for others, but lived only for themselves.[6]

Mahadeva Iyer said that cancer might also begin as a "wound" on the "margins" of some organ. If it was not healed, the wound itself would become an "organ" and would grow, producing "particles of pollution" (*tuśippu anukkal*) which would spread throughout the bloodstream, setting up new colonies at various places throughout the body, crowding out previously existing organs, drawing energy from them, and poisoning the host:

[In Tamil] What is called cancer we know on the outside when in some organ's edge or in the place where it secretes water it is injured and that injury does not heal but grows and in many forms joins with the flesh, and comes and is embedded in the body's waste waters and in its blood and comes to light by way of that wound and every day grows bigger and those wounds grow like a separate organ. The other things in the body make room for these bad pieces of flesh to grow. They make food. The character of these polluting foods is that the processed substance from the intestines will be defective. To make these defective secretions be gone, if you join certain food preparations or medicines with those secretions and feed them to the body, it gives the body the power to destroy all the rest, all the remaining substances, those secretions which are joined with that food, except for the substances with true life essences. . . . Many kinds of light are also able to make cancer not be there, and cure it. However, from that healed wound, not stopping there, those secretions alight somewhere else and create a new cancer. Therefore you must heal the patient by removing those polluting particles which spread the particles of cancer.

Mahadeva Iyer referred also to the cancerous "particles of pollution" as "unnecessary matter" and as "foreign substances" (*tēvaiyillātavai, vēṇḍātavai, vērupaḍḍa porutkal*). These foreign substances might be expelled by the body itself, by means of "clean blood cells" which would "beat the drums of war," "band together for war," and "drive out the foreign substances in their midst." Cancer could also be cured, with difficulty, by means of medicine. However, no one medicine by itself could work against cancer. Rather, a number of medicines had to be employed, and in such a way that they would work cooperatively together.

One plant is not enough; each works in its own department. [He lists a series of herbs.] These herbs must be made into medicines and used for cancer from the beginning stage-by-stage. By means of a single medicine, every cancer cannot be cured.

Moreover, whatever medicines are used against cancer, they should be "light medicines." If one strong medicine is used,

even if those wounds are healed, in some other place the qualities in the body will change and cause a permanent evil (*stīnamāna keḍai*). For this, after the disease comes, treatment is performed and it is healed, somewhere else another will naturally occur. If you do not obstruct wounds and defects, and the body acquires the capacity to heal them and heals them, it is very good. . . .

The growth of cancer could be abetted by a person's consuming "excessive" or "needless" substances. These substances could be "reduced" or "destroyed" by "pure" substances, especially, by pure breath (*prāna*, as it is called in yogic parlance) or "oxygen."

[In English] Cancer is an inherent disorder that has been doing mischief for much time and has developed into a disastrous disease, the cause of which has not yet been well traced or treated. The unnecessary matter in the body has been reduced or destroyed by oxygen that is carried throughout the body by cells. This has been introduced into the system by breathing pure oxygen from the atmosphere and by taking iron preparations, a compound of which is included in the blood cell to carry it everywhere in the body and is able to reduce any extra growth or poisonous matter or foreign matter in the body. If proper oxygen through iron is taken, it will destroy the foreign matter other than the living cells. So a natural way of inculcating is to be found out according to the living body to neutralize and to eliminate from the very cell to the circulatory function. One sort of preparation is not at all particularly sufficient to deal with this disease. . . . *Muppū* [the medicinal salt MI says is formed from the fluid expelled from the womb at parturition] will stay in the body for a long time and react with unnecessary substance—the necessary substance will withstand the reaction—and the question is how to find out the proper compound according to the individual body which has developed this grave disease.

[In Tamil] There must be something which is able to create in the body the power to take to the blood cells the substances that they need, to push out the needless substances, and to make the harmful things which arise as wastes go out of the ducts created in the body. If these paths in the body grow tired or if they start to do strange work, that pollution will be bound in the body. For polluting substances to go out, from the mouth to the place where things go out [i.e., from mouth to anus], it must move without stopping, doing its work correctly. Man for many reasons does not eat the needed foods and does not eat at regular times. For this reason the necessity of cleaning the intestine and other organs at particular times is an important matter . . .

Mahadeva Iyer's sentences were rambling, as the reader can see, but he was careful in his choice of words. The habit of translating continually from one language to another in his mind affected his use of words considerably. When he referred in English to cancerous tissue as "extra growth," "poisonous matter," "foreign matter," "unnecessary matter" and when he referred in Tamil to cancer-promoting processes as "polluting" (*tuśitta*) or "strange" (*vērupaḍḍa*) or "unwanted" (*tēvaiyillāta*), he used terms that had for him, as a South Indian Brahman, strong moral and social resonances. When he called cancer a "disorder" (English) which happened when certain parts of the body did "strange work" or "different work" (Tamil—*vērupaḍḍa vēlai*), he used the same words that he used when he lamented the disorder in the social world around him, the kind of disorder he thought must occur when different types (*jāti*) of people fail to follow their own dharmas and instead follow the dharmas of others, when castes are mixed and pollution spreads.

Mahadeva Iyer took from the Sanskrit Ayurvedic texts the habit of referring to substances in the body as though these substances had wills and feelings of their own—they could be "angry" or "arrogant" or "hungry" or "tired" or "calm" or "happy." The use of such terminology was not just metaphorical. Certain processes in the body were gods who should be worshipped and to whom sacrifices should be made—embryogenesis and digestion were the most important of these: there was a god in the stomach as well as one in the womb.[7] Other processes were mainly demonic—cancer was one such; it had literally (in MI's words) "a life of its own." Its demonic quality was revealed in the way it behaved, always changing form. A healer might suppress it in one place but then it would pop up somewhere else in an even more virulent guise. The most effective way to handle it was to treat it gently, and let it depart in a natural way.

Beside this cancer, many diseases become started which turn into ulcer and cancer. A child is born and immediately all over its body red-colored obstructions (*taḍuppu*) arise. Those change into sores. Those become sores that will not heal. Even when harsh treatments are performed to heal this disease it heals only in its own time. It heals and then in one or two days it becomes the disease called asthma. If the asthma too heals it affects the liver and becomes a liver disease. It turns into hard spots on the liver and liver cancer. When the body grows thin, because of bad blood, diabetes arises and from that, too, sores that will not cool and boils that will not heal arise. Knee diseases and rheumatic swellings and the like arise.[8] For this *cūlai nīr* that arises in the body some herbal medicines were discovered by the Siddhars . . .

The disease cancer, in Mahadeva Iyer's view, could not be considered separately from the patient who suffered from the disease. Like a baby inside its mother, the body of the disease was merged with the body of its host, and similarly the mind of the disease pervaded the mind of the person in whom it was embedded. The demonically changing will of cancer made itself known through the changing will of the patient, just as in Ayurvedic theory the cravings of a pregnant woman are only reflexes of her indwelling baby's desires:

Before that cancer comes, in the body and in the organ of the mind changes arise and cause the body to weaken. Decrease in the weight and energy of the body; in any matter, thinking in a strange way; while doing some deed, becoming weak of one's own accord; feeling great worry over needless, trivial things; body and mind becoming dispirited; lying down and worrying without sleep coming . . . as time goes by a state arises which is similar to that caused by impure bile (*tuśitta pitta*).

The Ayurvedic body, the body that Mahadeva Iyer knew, was a microcosm in an ancient and non-metaphorical sense. It was a world composed of many living beings with many different wills. This world, this body, could be in a state of harmony, or it could be in a state of conflict, or it could be in a state of imperialist global domination. We will return to this latter point presently.

The fetus-tumor-demon analogy, which we sometimes come across also in modern Western writing, formed an important part of the substrate of Mahadeva Iyer's thinking about cancer. This I believe is one reason for his frequent drawing of seemingly unmotivated connections between intrauterine events and cancer. But this paradoxical analogy was not one that Mahadeva Iyer dreamed up on his own, nor one that he got from his readings of English literature or English-language medical texts. It has deep roots in Ayurvedic tradition. The old texts make much of the fact that the presence of a fetus is destructive of the body of the mother, drawing nourishment and life energy away from her. Caraka says a fetus "eats its mother's flesh and drinks her blood" just as a demon is said to do. Thus, like a demon, a fetus must be exorcised. Only after the fetus is expelled can the mother's body return to something like a state of equilibrium again, the texts say. Of course it is natural anyway for the fetus to be ejected in due time from the body of the mother. Like a demon, it is drawn to the sexual parts and sexual fluids, and so, like a demon, it is polluting. It is for these reasons that the baby in the womb, the very aim and pinnacle of the mother's life, is classified by the Ayurvedic texts as a form of excrement.[9]

So striking is this paradox that one major Indian philosophical system regarded it as the fundamental principle behind the organization of the cosmos. This philosophical system, called *Sāṃkhya*, was chosen by the early Ayurvedic writers as their cosmology of choice.[10] It grounds the empirical realities described by Ayurvedic writers in an overall teleology, and gives Ayurveda a moral and religious dimension which otherwise it might seem to lack. Besides being a cosmology, *Sāṃkhya* is also a theory of the relation between the observer and the observed. Here I hope I will be forgiven for digressing through a description of it, for I believe it may shed some light on the purpose behind Mahadeva Iyer's discourses on cancer to me.

In the beginning, says the philosophical text *Sāṃkhya-kārikā*, there are two principles, called *Puruṣa* and *Prakṛti*. *Puruṣa* in Sanskrit means "man," or sometimes, "husband." *Prakṛti* is best glossed as "nature," or "matter," or literally, "she out of whom it is made." *Puruṣa*, therefore is a masculine kind of being, and *Prakṛti* is feminine. These two also have other qualities. *Puruṣa* is roughly equivalent to what we think of as being the soul. *Prakṛti* is roughly the body. *Puruṣa* is indivisible, atomic, and non-productive. He is not able to give birth to things. *Prakṛti* is divisible and productive. She is able to give birth. Both *Puruṣa* and *Prakṛti* are eternal. *Puruṣa* is also called the observer. *Prakṛti* is what he observes. In one metaphor, *Prakṛti* is a dancing girl, and *Puruṣa* is the king sitting immobile on his throne before whom she dances. Hereafter, we will refer to *Prakṛti* and *Puruṣa* respectively as Nature and the Spirit of Man.

Before time begins, Nature is unmanifest, i.e., nobody sees or observes her, and she is in a state of equilibrium, at peace and unchanging. Then the Spirit of Man impregnates her with his essence. So, Nature becomes pregnant by the Spirit of Man. Pregnant by and pregnant with him—he now is a helpless baby inside her. She, having become pregnant, enters a state of disequilibrium, she starts going through changes, and she becomes manifest. The Spirit of Man, impregnating her, knows her and so she becomes manifest, she becomes perceived by him. This living entity, Nature impregnated with the observing Spirit of Man, thrown into disharmony by this pregnancy, proceeds to evolve the ever-changing forms of living matter out of herself, and so becomes the world that we know—the entire universe, and also our own living body. (Bear in mind that we know the world only through our body. Thus, it is difficult to draw the line between the world that we know and the body through which we know it.)

The Spirit of Man in this schema is not active but totally passive. There is only one thing in the world that he really does. He observes. Being imprisoned inside of Nature, he thinks that he is a part of Nature, or even that he *is* Nature, he confuses himself with her, and believes that what is happening to her is happening to him, but his confusion is precisely that. In reality, he is not her, he is just inside her, watching the changes that she goes through. His presence causes her to change, and he may think that he is in control of those changes, but actually he is not. Nature evolves according to her own laws, and the Spirit of Man has no control over these laws at all.

This state, of the Spirit of Man being imprisoned in Nature and Nature being in disequilibrium and going through change after change, characterizes every living organism. It is the fundamental condition of embodied life, and it is inherently painful. But it is a good and necessary state, because only through involvement in the Body can the Spirit know itself. Only through involvement in Nature can Man know himself. Though Man is the knower, Nature alone holds the key to his knowledge. This key is called *manas*, "mind," or *cit*, the fluid of consciousness. The mind is a material object or substance, part of the material body, part of Nature. It is the instrument through which the observer sees the world, and it is also the mirror in which the observer may observe himself. When, at the end of Nature's evolution, at the end of the evolution of the body, the Spirit of Man sees himself in this mirror, then he and she separate, the body and the one who experiences the body separate. The Spirit becomes liberated, and Nature is left in peace, alone in harmony with herself again. The matter of the body becomes again undifferentiated, and the Spirit once again becomes free.

In the practice of Ayurveda, what the doctor has to deal with is what is called the patient's *prakṛti*, the peculiar constitution of that particular patient's body, that patient's physical nature. There is much discussion in the Ayurvedic texts of the different kinds of physical nature that individuals may have. When the patient is sick, the patient's nature is in some kind of disequilibrium. In actuality, the disequilibrium that is called illness is a smaller disturbance within the larger disturbance that is life itself. This larger disturbance must be allowed to work itself through to the end of its natural course if the patient is to achieve long life and the goal of life, which is self-understanding. The smaller disturbance, illness, blocks this process, and it must be dissolved, the illness must be healed, if long life is to happen.

The doctor, in dealing with a sick patient, has two goals. One is to help restore equilibrium within the nature of the patient, to heal the patient. The other is to acquire knowledge of his own. In the therapeutic situation, therefore, the doctor becomes the observer, the nature of the patient becomes the observed. During the course of treatment, we might say that a kind of temporary new organism is formed, composed of doctor as knower and patient as known, and during this time the two become inseparable. "Research," or action upon the system of the doctor's knowledge, and "treatment," or action upon the body of the patient, likewise are inseparable. This is not a consciously adopted principle of Ayurveda, but it is the way that the doctors I knew proceeded, as a matter of course. Watching a course of treatment or a dialogue between Ayurvedic doctor and patient, one sees a very rapidly changing feedback system, during which (as in the evolution of Indian personalities, perhaps), consistency over time, "sticking to one's convictions," as it were, does not appear to be a moral imperative.[11] In Mahadeva Iyer's practice, both diagnosis and treatment varied from moment to moment as new knowledge came in. The doctor did not necessarily wait until he had all the information he could get before forming a diagnosis. Tentative diagnoses were rapidly formed and rapidly replaced by others. An experimental attitude prevailed.

Just as diagnosis and treatment of a disease may vary from moment to moment in Ayurveda, so may the disease itself. Like a theory regarding disease, disease itself is not an isolated entity that may be considered independently of the ever-evolving, fluid system to which it belongs. It is a disturbance in the pattern of the system as a whole. In Ayurveda, therefore, it is axiomatic that one cannot treat an isolated part of the body. Treatment virtually always entails regulation of diet, bathing and sleeping habits, et cetera. And when symptoms of an illness abate, it is generally not said that the disease is gone, rather it is said that the disease has "changed" (*māriyirukku*). When a doctor prescribes a medicine, he must always ask himself what overall changes in the system of the body will result. Often these changes will be surprising.

In Ayurvedic understanding, the evolution of knowledge is a physical process, part and parcel with the evolution of the material world.[12] Precise parallels between the growth of the world, the growth of the body, and the growth of knowledge are outlined in the old texts. One of these parallels consists in the systemic, ever-evolving character of them all.

For the Ayurvedic physician, as I have tried to suggest, the body is an integrated system. A change in one part inevitably brings about changes in other parts. To alter a disease means to adjust the overall system of the body, which ultimately includes the patient's own knowledge of and theories about his disease, as well as the patient's diet and living habits, the prevailing weather, political conditions, and all the rest of what we call "context."

In just the same way (though less self-consciously in Ayurveda), knowledge is treated as a total system. Each part is dependent upon each other part. Since the system itself is always changing, a single assertion cannot be categorically demonstrated or denied. An isolated theory cannot be proved or disproved. A theory can only be true for the moment, while the system as a whole maintains a particular configuration. As the system as a whole evolves, isolated statements gain truth or falsehood.

Our own civilization is not without similar ideas. The Ayurvedic view of knowledge corresponds in some ways to a hypothesis advanced by some of our own physicists and philosophers (Duhem, Heisenberg, Quine, Lakatos) to the effect that an isolated theory can never be categorically verified or falsified.[13] A challenge to a particular theory entails a challenge to the entire system of knowledge of which it is a part. The total system of knowledge includes so-called empirical observation. Theory and observation cannot be treated as independent "variables." If an observation contradicts a theory, this does not mean that the theory has been falsified. The presence of a contradiction between observation and theory calls the whole system of knowledge into question, including the observation itself. Virtually any assertion may be verified, or falsified, if appropriate adjustments to the overall system are made. The overall system (like the system of the body) ultimately includes weather, politics, et cetera. As "theory" and "observation" are part of the same overall, dynamic system, so are observer and observed. A change in one effects a change in the other.

Our own much loved and much maligned "Sapir-Whorf hypothesis" may be considered only a special case (or perhaps a generalization) of this principle. The organization of language (a people's system of observation, the substrate of the body of theories determining how they are to observe what) cannot be separated from the organization of the world in which the people who speak that language live. Meaning is not a question of correspondences between isolated words or statements and isolated events or objects in the world. The meaning of a word or statement is dependent upon the total language/world system of which that word or statement is a part. So a statement which makes perfect sense and is truthful in one language, may appear absurd and false when translated as accurately as possible into some other language. (The strange appearance of the soliloquies of Mahadeva Iyer, a man living all the time in many disparate languages, demonstrates this reality.)

So-called postmodernist and reflexivist anthropology may also be seen as continuations of this tradition, a tradition so old that people in India share its roots with us. We are being told now, as though it were some new discovery, that the anthropologist as observer is not and cannot be a separate entity from the informant as observed. In the encounter between them, their two personalities become part of a single system. *All* of us on this planet are part of a single system. To think and act as though the life of one is not dependent on the lives of all the rest leads to big trouble.

And now we return to Mahadeva Iyer's lectures to me on the topic of cancer. We return also to the question of why this man bothered to convey his knowledge and his theories to such a person as me. I never asked him about cancer. I did not have cancer. None of the patients who visited him while I was in his village had cancer. Unasked, he dictated these lessons to me, and at his bidding I wrote them down, word by word. Why was I made to do this?

A few points are obvious. First, though I was female, young, and casteless, I was also from America, and for my Indian friends this latter property of mine probably overshadowed all the rest. I was the only Western student Mahadeva Iyer had ever had. I was the only chance for him to make his voice heard here. What I published was very important to him. Through me he could say whatever he had to say to Americans.

Second, as we defined our situation, I, the Western scholar seeking knowledge of India, was the observer; Mahadeva Iyer together with the world in which he lived was the observed. I was also, however politely I was treated, a polluting foreign substance in his household.

Third, cancer as it is understood in India is a Western disease, in several senses:

(a) It has been defined as a single disease entity by Western biomedical researchers and its etiology is described in Western biomedical terms. The Indian medical tradition has no independent description of the causes and mechanisms of cancer.

(b) In India, cancer is a disease of the urban upper and middle classes, which means that only Westerners and moderately Westernized people are commonly known to get it. (How many of the rural poor actually develop cancer, and how many die of it, are two great unknowns.) Moreover, cancer is associated with unchecked consumption of the kinds of expensive poisons Westerners are thought to favor, most notably cigarettes and hard liquor.

(c) Cancer is also a Western disease in that it is a widely used metaphor for the activities of Western governments and Western-owned companies in the Third World.

Certainly this metaphor was not unknown to Mahadeva Iyer. Exogenous capital enterprise did have some rather cancerous effects in the region where he lived. For instance, near his village there was a sizeable mountain that for centuries had lain covered with hardwood such as jacktrees and teak. Mahadeva would go to this forest to gather medicinal plants. In the 1960s, a foreign company acquired rights to the mountain, the forest on it was clear-cut, and the entire mountainside was planted in rubber. The people who had lived on the mountainside and practiced a combination of foraging and subsistence cultivation there now earned their living by tapping the rubber trees and selling the rubber to the company. The income they earned in this way was several times greater than their previous income from gathering firewood off the ground and selling it in the towns, but they now had to buy most of their food. They still had some money leftover after food was bought, however. This was reputedly spent in the government-owned liquor stores. I learned this story from Mahadeva Iyer and his son.

After the mountain was planted in rubber, medicinal plants stopped growing there and Mahadeva Iyer stopped visiting the mountain. He said it grieved him beyond bearing to go there and see the changes that had occurred. Was this not an example of one being arrogating too much of the substance of others to its own growth? "Some plants and trees grow very high, very happy and very big, and become an abode for birds and other animals to stay, but no one can escape the target of man who is supposed to be the highest being with intelligence." So Mahadeva Iyer had told me. Might he have been thinking of the rubber company when he said these words?

These days, I cannot read Mahadeva Iyer's lectures to me on cancer without believing that his real intention (or one of his intentions, anyway) was to deliver a series of covert sermons on the relationship between countries like mine and countries like his, in hopes that I might someday convey these sermons to people here, as I am doing now. Certainly his lectures were not morally neutral, and many of the statements he made in them could only be interpreted as comments on social events. For instance, Mahadeva Iyer's portrayal of the systemic damage that results from "injury" on the "margins" of some local system, the migration of dislodged particles from the "wounded" place and their disruptive settlement elsewhere applied not only to physiological but also to international processes taking place in his time. His idea that the body itself must acquire the power to carry all the needed materials to all the places within itself, and to gently but firmly expel foreign elements, "down to the very cell," sounded very much like a message calling for local self-government and grass-roots mobilization, not unlike Gandhi's message to the colonized India of some decades ago.

His talk of "pure cells beating the drums of war to drive out polluting foreign substances" sounded more like a Bose or a Tilak. It is not unlikely that as a young man, Mahadeva Iyer had been moved by the messages both of the Gandhians and of the militant nationalists, who shared the goal of making India strong and self-sufficient and of ending foreign rule. Now, the British colonists were decades gone, but colonialism lived on in India, demon-like, in changed forms. For instance, there was myself, the anthropologist. I had arrived in India with no intention of becoming an integral, contributing part of it, but planned only to collect a kind of symbolic capital, the intellectual wealth of Mahadeva Iyer and others, to carry back home and use for my own profit. (I borrow the rhetoric of the Indian government here.) In a way I was just like the foreign rubber company, accumulating materials for myself without limit and without thought of the needs of others. The only thing that redeemed me was the fact that I as a lone individual was relatively ineffectual, powerless, and harmless.

Mahadeva Iyer seemed to be telling me in many different ways that no one substance, person, law, theory, or way of life should ever dominate others: there should be no "survival of the fittest." He valued women because, as he saw them (rightly or wrongly), their way was *not* to dominate; if men were the consumers, women were the consumed. His notion that women invented healing and men made it into a "business for profit" was typical of his thought on this topic. Just as power and capital should not be allowed to accumulate in one place, just as no one person should rule the show, so no one treatment was sufficient to heal all cancers, and no one language was sufficient to convey all messages. His was a radically pluralistic world-view, and I think he hoped to communicate the necessity of such pluralism to me, to us, before he died. I think in this way he was trying to make his contribution toward the healing of the world.

The last time I saw Mahadeva Iyer was in 1980. He could not sit up unassisted and he no longer recognized the people around him, but the look on his face as he greeted me, trustingly, uncomprehendingly, was still cordial and kind as before. I cannot say he was at peace. As I left his bedside and returned to the front of the house I heard an anguished howl ring through the hall. He was calling for his mother, long, long dead. His wife told me such cries burst from him every few hours now, night and day.

When he passed away that year his middle-aged sons showed terrible grief in their eyes, which clearly was not feigned. What they had lost in their father was sacred to them and they knew it would never return and could never be replaced. I felt the burden on myself to make Mahadeva Iyer's name known in the Western world. I felt his family's disappointment in me that I had only heard a small part of his teachings, and would never be able to publish more than a small part of what I had heard, fragments of his thought lodged in my professional papers, like so many tissues under a microscope.

NOTES

1. The research on which this paper is based was carried out in Kanyakumari District, Tamil Nadu, India during the years 1975–76 under a grant from the Social Science Research Council. I am grateful to Nick Dirks and Vincent Crapanzano for their comments on an earlier version.
2. Turner, Boon, Geertz, Rosaldo and others have discussed cross-cultural commentary and other forms of cultural pastiche—mixed media, languages, artistic genres, etc.—as an important matter for anthropologists at the turn of the twenty-first century to consider and indeed to celebrate. Indian medicine is a prime example of the power and efficacy of mixed-media presentations. See for instance Nichter's (1980) description of "medicine masala" in South India; Zimmerman's (1987) description of "overdetermination" (or, I would say, multi-perspectivalism) in early Ayurvedic texts; and my own (1987) discussion of the scientific value of mixed paradigms and openness to paradox in Mahadeva Iyer's world view.
3. Code-switching among multi-lingual speakers is a complex process, widely discussed by socio-linguists (see especially Gumperz 1971, 1972, 1982; Labov 1973). Among South Indian Brahmans, at least three functions for code-switching can be discerned, which might be labelled the conceptual (Sapir-Whorfian), the micro-political (Foucaultian), and the poetic-ludic (Jakobson-Turnerian). Many acts of code-switching entails all three agendas; each to a certain extent implicates the others.

   Conceptual code-switching occurs when a speaker switches from language A to language B in order to discuss topics or ideas that are more characteristic of discourses in language B than of discourses in language A. So Mahadeva Iyer switched to English when he spoke of Spencerian philosophy or germ theory, to Sanskrit when he recited the names of the divine Cosmic Mother, and to Tamil when he discussed particular local events or local theories of disease causation.

   Micro-political code-switching occurs when a speaker desires to communicate to his interlocutors a message concerning his and their relative ranks on the power/knowledge continuum (or to avoid communicating such a message, as the case may be). Mahadeva Iyer would sometimes recite a verse in Sanskrit and then translate it into Tamil for his listeners (very few South Indians, even Brahmans, are fluent in Sanskrit). In this way he reminded his listeners that he had access to a prestigious body of knowledge that was beyond their ken. At the same time, he would emphasize and frame the message—set it off as distinct from the surrounding speech, and draw attention to it—by repeating it in two different languages. South Indian Brahmans often use English in a collusive fashion (cf. Goffman 1981) to distinguish between those among their interlocutors who are educated enough to know the prestigious foreign language, hence are solidary with the speaker, and those who do not know English, hence are excluded from full participation in the conversation. (Interestingly, American urban blacks often use code-switching for similar collusive purposes.) Mahadeva Iyer avoided this kind of code-switching when he spoke with unschooled local laborers, sticking to the local vernacular and deliberately not using "high" literate Tamil, as though to avoid exacerbating the vast status differential that already separated him from the villagers upon whose goodwill his regional reputation largely depended.

Poetic-ludic code-switching is done for playful and aesthetic purposes, i.e., for fun. The "focus on the message" that Jakobson considered the poetic function of language is here playing with the message as though it were a toy, putting it together in different ways to see how it will come out. Indian children learning English in school exercise their poetic-ludic skills when they compose mixed-language poems, much to the dismay of those parents for whom poetry is an object of reverence, not a plaything. Mahadeva Iyer's daughter-in-law coined mixed-language words like *unsāhikkable* (from English "unbearable" mated with Tamil *"sāhikkātu"* which means "it will not bear") for my entertainment. Mahadeva Iyer himself seemed to enjoy switching languages largely because of the element of comic surprise such changes entailed. His parodic reframings of Hindu and Western dogma were often keyed by a change in language, as in his discussion of the doctrine of "survival of the fittest." In a conversation with a woman patient he said

[In Tamil] Even all of God's [switch to English] reincarnations [back to Tamil] were born in the bellies of women . . . Jesus Christ and all the demons had to serve this jail term. You cannot deny the Gita [a sacred Hindu text]. All the work can be given to women. [English] Fifty percent of the jobs can be given to women. [Tamil] If you give all the [English] economic matters [Tamil] to them there would be no danger in that. [English] Wife must be given equal power in the administration. [Tamil] Great souls and sages and lights of the house, women give milk to children.

The playfully iconoclastic character of Mahadeva Iyer's use of mixed-language discourse is evident here (for more examples see Trawick 1987).

Many other functions of code-switching could be listed. But there is an overall "metafunction" that I wish to stress in this paper. The very employment of multi-lingual discourse, this mixed-language stew so characteristic of the speech of Mahadeva Iyer and others like him, regardless of the particular functions served by particular acts of code-switching, bespeaks a non-totalizing, even anti-totalizing, vision of truth. It is impossible even to imagine Mahadeva Iyer speaking in one language only, for the very reason that an irreducible pluralism was essential to his genius.

4. See for example Susruta vol. 1, pp. 130–135, 194–235; Susruta vol. II, pp. 190–215; Caraka ch. 1, sec. 9, verses 4, 43; Caraka ch. III; Caraka ch. V.

5. For detailed descriptions see Trawick (Egnor) 1978, 1983.

6. The fundamental values of Siddha yogis and the medical system they founded contrasted with the values of Ayurveda. Siddha yogis sought to obtain physical immortality by hardening the body and arresting life processes, while Ayurvedic practitioners encourage longevity by softening the body and promoting life processes. See Trawick (Egnor) 1983.

7. See Trawick (Egnor) 1978, 1987, for descriptions from Tamil and Sanskrit medical literature of the gods in the heart, the stomach, and the womb. See Caraka ch. I, sec. XII for hymns of praise to each of the three humors in the body (wind, bile, and phlegm), laudatory descriptions of their activities, and attribution of godhood to them. Verse 8 of this section concludes, *"Vata* [wind] alone is god." See also Caraka ch. I, sec. XXX, for a laudatory description of the heart; Susruta vol II, p. 134, for a laudatory description of the spirit in the womb. Often in Caraka and Susruta there occur debates concerning the relative greatness of various processes or objects in the body. The question generally asked is, To which of these processes or objects should hegemony rightfully be attributed? These debates are reminiscent of religious debates that take place in India concerning the relative greatness of various gods.

8. Cf. this description by a village laborer of a demon he came across one midnight in an orchard:

I went all by myself. I just had a flashlight and a stick. Then a demon . . . you know what it did? . . . some people say your mind itself is the demon. A brave man will say, "What's all this stuff about demons?" They say all that. Well, I am not afraid of anything. I will go anywhere I want, fear-lessly. . . . Well, when I went, there was a small . . . like the kind people raise inside their house, you see, a cat. It ran in front of me and I saw it and thought, "What is this? It looks like a cat." So I watched it, and as I watched it, it changed into a dog. And as soon as it changed into a dog, it changed into a cow. A peacock-colored cow. Then from a peacock-colored cow it became a Mohini [a seductive female demon]. And I thought, "What is this? First it came as a cat, then as a dog, then as that weird cow, now she is a woman weeping." Then fear came to me. . . . Even though I am a brave person, it had changed into so many forms even I was afraid. . . . Then it went, that Mohini went into a thorn bush. . . . She went and sat down. Look! That Mohini was nowhere to be seen! . . . The following dawn, the fear hit me. I could not sleep. I was sitting up, wide awake. . . . The other workers, too, said, "Yes, boy, there is a Mohini there." "It's just your mind," the other older people said. But from that time on I have refused to go on that path.

Just like cancer, demons are associated not only with changes of form but with changes of heart, with loss of mental steadfastness, and above all with fear. When a demon attacks a person, it will instill fear in the person's heart (*payamuruttum*), and when a person dies of demon-affliction, the person is said to have died of fear.

9. Susruta vol I, p. 127; vol. II, p. 148; Caraka ch. IV, sec. IV, verse 22; ch. IV, sec. VIII, verses 38–49.
10. Trawick (Egnor) 1974. See Gaudapada (1887) for exegesis of *Sāṃkhya* cosmology.
11. Cf. Daniel 1984, Shweder 1987. Richard Fox in preparing his forthcoming biography on Mohandas Gandhi has commented that Gandhi, not being subject to Western popular psychology, never saw his personality as fixed from childhood, and consequently felt free to change it throughout his life (Fox, personal communication).
12. See chapter I of Caraka, outlining the evolution of Ayurvedic knowledge. "There was no time when either the stream of life or the stream of intelligence did not flow." Caraka ch. I, sec. XXX, verse 27.
13. Lakatos (1970), Feyerabend (1982).

REFERENCES CITED

Boon, J.
    1984   Folly, Bali and Anthropology, or Satire Across Cultures. *In* Text, Play and Story, M. Bruner, ed. Pp. 156–177. Washington, D.C.: American Ethnological Society.
Caraka
    1949   Caraka Samhita. Shree Gulabkunverba Ayurvedic Society (ed. and trans.). Jamnagar, India.
Daniel, E. V.
    1984   Fluid Signs: Being a Person the Tamil Way. Berkeley: University of California Press.
Feyerabend, P.
    1982   Science in a Free Society. London: Verso.
Gaudapada
    1887   The Sāmkhya-Karika of Iswara Krishna with the Commentary of Gaudapada. H. T. Colebrooke, trans. Bombay: Tookaram Tatya.
Geertz, C.
    1983   Blurred Genres: The Refiguration of Social Thought. *In* Local Knowledge: Further Essays in Interpretive Anthropology. Pp. 19–35. New York: Basic Books.
Goffman, E.
    1981   Forms of Talk. Philadelphia: University of Pennsylvania Press.
Gumperz, J. J.
    1971   Dialect Differences and Social Stratification in a North Indian Village. *In* Language and Social Groups. J. J. Gumperz, ed. Stanford: Stanford University Press.
    1972   Communication in Multilingual Societies. *In* Cognitive Anthropology. S. Tyler, ed. New York: Holt, Rinehart and Winston.
    1982   Discourse Strategies. Cambridge: Cambridge University Press.
Labov, W.
    1973   Language in the Inner City. Philadelphia: University of Pennsylvania Press.
Lakatos, I.
    1970   Falsification and the Methodology of Scientific Research Programs. *In* Criticism and the Growth of Knowledge, I. Lakatos and A. Musgrave, eds. Pp. 60–90. Cambridge: Cambridge University Press.
Nichter, M.
    1980   The Layperson's Perception of Medicine as Perspective into the Utilization of Multiple Therapy Systems in the Indian Context. Social Science and Medicine 14B: 225–234.
Rosaldo, R.
    1989   Culture and Truth: The Remaking of Social Analysis. Boston: Beacon Press.

Shweder, R.
  1987   Determinations of Meaning: Discourse and Moral Socialization. *In* Moral Development through Social Interaction. W. M. Kertines and J. L. Gerwitz, eds. Pp. 197–244. New York: Wiley.
Susruta
  1907   Susruta Samhita. K. K. L. Bhishagratna, ed. and trans. Calcutta, India.
Trawick (Egnor), M.
  1974   Principles of Continuity in Three Indian Sciences. Master's thesis. University of Chicago, Department of Anthropology.
  1978   The Sacred Spell and Other Conceptions of Life in Tamil Culture. Ph.D. dissertation. University of Chicago, Department of Anthropology.
  1983   Death and Nurturance in Indian Systems of Healing. Social Science and Medicine 17(4): 935–945.
  1987   The Ayurvedic Physician as Scientist. Social Science and Medicine 24(12): 1031–1050.
Turner, V.
  1985   The Anthropology of Performance. *In* On the Edge of the Bush: Anthropology as Experience. Pp. 177–204. Tucson, AZ: University of Arizona Press.
Zimmerman, F.
  1987   The Jungle and the Aroma of Meats. Berkeley: University of California Press.

Ethnomedicine: Diverse Trends,
Common Linkages

COMMENTARY

In this commentary I will highlight major points raised in the collection of essays which comprise this volume, offer constructive criticism, and use individual essays as a platform from which to suggest directions for future ethnomedical research. I will discuss the ten essays in four sets. In the first set, Anderson as well as Weller, Reubush and Klein call for more empirical studies of ethnomedicine which draw upon epidemiological approaches to the study of treatment efficacy and illness prevalence. Next, Glass-Coffin, Brodwin, and Nuckolls discuss identity construction through narrative and discursive practices in cultures pervaded by multiple ideologies, healing traditions, and moral frameworks. In such contexts, scripts of illness and healing are carefully constructed and the instantiation of inference plays an important role in negotiating an illness identity. Essays by Sobo, Taylor, and Adams illustrate different approaches to the anthropology of the body as this site of investigation both informs and is informed by studies of ethnomedicine. Considered is the complementarity between notions of ethnophysiology and health in the physical body and exchange relations maintaining health in the social body; conflict between capitalist and precapitalist social relations manifest in health concerns; the manner in which emergent forms of healing reflect tensions and transformations in society; and medico-religious practice as an instrument of productive power. Essays by Laderman and Trawick illustrate the relevance of ethnomedical studies to the anthropology of self and consider the role of illness discourse as moral commentary on metamedical states of affairs. Several of the essays contribute in substantive ways to multiple themes.

Toward the Empirical Study of Ethnomedical Phenomena

The first set of articles advocates greater empirical rigor in the study of ethnomedicine inclusive of the application of epidemiological approaches to the study of treatment response and illness identification. Anderson's essay is discussed at greatest length for two reasons. First, it advances a type of research advocated by two recent reviews of ethnomedicine which call for biocultural studies (Browner, Ortiz de Montellano and Rubel 1988; Rubel and Hass 1990). Second, it deals with one of the most controversial topics in ethnomedicine, therapeutic efficacy.

Like Browner et al. (1988), Anderson argues for cross cultural comparisons of ethnomedical results based on etic measures of "species wide" physiologic response. Toward this end, he discusses methods employed within biomedicine to establish clinical efficacy in relation to measures of intended post-treatment change.[1] His paper focuses on how it is that we can validate that a treatment is efficacious as distinct from questions of how, why or for whom the treatment is more or less efficacious.

Let me dispense with four criticisms of the essay and then proceed to discuss why I think issues raised by Anderson are important. I will then use the article as a backdrop against which to discuss the contextual study of treatment efficacy in a manner which looks beyond disease entities and technical fixes. Anderson's argument for the etic assessment of traditional treatments of disease is overly simplistic for the following reasons. First, studying treatment response to isolated diseases is immensely difficult in the real world where a complex of health problems are coexperienced by most of the worlds' population and treated by traditional practitioners. Second, just as the classical model of epidemiology (host-pathogen-environment) is too narrow in targeting pathogens as the exclusive cause of disease (Audy and Dunn 1974, Dunn and Janes 1986, Turshen 1977), so a focus on medicines is too narrow for studying treatment response.[2] Third, treatments are often people as well as illness/symptom specific. It is important to appreciate that treatments are often tailored to individuals and that:

Nonmedical healing is empirical in the sense that it is often based on systematic observation and interpretation of symptoms, suffering, cause, effect and response to treatment. It is this empirical basis that establishes the ground for comparative study of healing systems (Csordas and Kleinman 1990:13).

Fourth, Anderson minimizes the importance of patient satisfaction and perceptions of efficacy.[3] The following question may be posed: If the pathophysiology of a disease is treated but a patient is not satisfied such that a sick role is sustained, is the treatment outcome positive? Kleinman's (1986) study of neurasthenia in China illustrates that even when a "biomedically appropriate" intervention for a pathological state is undertaken, this does not necessarily mean it will prove effective in context. Two questions relevant for ethnomedicine arise: a) what social and cultural factors influence patient and practitioner expectations of treatment and perceptions of efficacy and b) to what extent do these perceptions influence the experience of illness and treatment response over time inclusive of life change? While the first question demands meaning centered research, the second requires both meaning centered and biocultural investigation.

While I am critical of relying upon biomedical measures of treatment efficacy, I found Anderson's essay important for two reasons. First it constitutes a reaction to the loose way in which many anthropologists have made claims about therapeutic efficacy. These claims are often based on anecdotal data or equations of symbolic healing with placebo response, carthesis, an unspecified psychotherapeutic effect, or endorphins. As the old Yiddish proverb states, "For example is not proof." More systematic data collection is called for in ethnomedicine. On the other hand, we must beware of mystification in the form of research designs and tests of statistical significance which appear to be objective and definitive. While appearing objective, they may constitute the quantification of subjective judgements masquerading as fact (Ratcliffe 1983). Empiricism posits sets of procedures for the validation of experiments which appear to be rather straightforward, yet conceal implicit assumptions (Bajaj 1990). As Whitehead once noted, we must seek simplicity (in design), yet mistrust it! We must beware of misinterpreting statistics which test hypotheses as yielding proof as distinct from probable association which may be explained by other or better explanations.

The second reason Anderson's essay is important is that it reviews for us a number of research designs which may prove useful in ethnomedical research if used judiciously. Critically assessed are research designs for testing curative efficacy ranging from the case report ('the weakest') to designs using comparison groups in retrospective or cross-sectional studies, prospective cohort studies, and the most "convincing" of all studies, a randomized control design where a placebo is used in double blinding. Attention is focused on the details of technique.

It is important for anthropologists to be aware of alternative research designs as well as to consider the strength of using multiple designs.[4] Research designs must be carefully selected in accord with the type of research questions being asked. It must be recognized that methods are not ideologically neutral, they produce particular types of data that privilege particular types of research questions. What I find dangerous is the rank ordering of research designs and focusing on technique to the extent that research questions become overly structured and predictable.

Within the field of epidemiology there has been concern expressed of late about a preoccupation with technique leading to a missing of the forest for the trees. A narrowing of research to the measurement of relations between exposure and effect, treatment and response, has superseded the investigation of effect distribution and determinants (Susser 1989). As Vandernbroucke (1989) has argued in a recent article on clinical epidemiology, the dogmatic application of a hierarchy of methodologies in scientific research can prove counterproductive and misrepresentative of the path of real progress in medicine. Observational studies, not just gold standard double blind studies, lie behind breakthroughs in research on treatment effect. As Moerman (1983a) has demonstrated in an insightful review of double blind trials of cimetidine (an ulcer medication), what appears to be a gold standard may be fools gold if not weighed carefully.[5]

Randomized control trials and designs, which call for blinding or withdrawal of an intervention mid-treatment following a measurement of difference, are rarely feasible for operational as well as ethical reasons in ethnomedical field studies. Recognizing this, Anderson discusses the need to identify other methods for establishing efficacy which are practical.[6] His call to develop methods which enable the systematic study of treatment response needs to be considered by those who reject his central project of etic assessment of treatment outcome. Indeed, his call for systematic study of treatment response needs to be expanded beyond intended effects to reported side effects, diagnosis, and prognosis. Anthropologists might, for example, consider the application of methods of systematic data collection being experimented with in pharmaceutical behavior studies. Confederate studies employ mock patients presenting predetermined sets of symptoms to examine over the counter medicine sales of pharmacists and shopkeepers in third world contexts. This method might be employed to document the sensitivity and specificity of indigenous diagnostic procedures, the continuity of treatment patterns and the propensity to medicalize life problems.[7]

The research format presented by Anderson which I found most noteworthy entails the development of better designed longitudinal observational studies and case series. Predictability of treatment outcome is ascertained on the basis of systematic sampling, follow-up studies to account for short-term placebo response, and checks on relapse. I would support Anderson's call for both more carefully designed observational studies and longitudinal studies which provide follow up on initial responses to treatment procedures. If for no other reason, data from such studies may contribute to ethnomedical studies of treatment expectations, adherence, and self regulation as well as perceptions of treatment compatibility and impact over time.

It is Anderson's emphasis on the time dimension of treatment which I think is important to highlight. As Csordas and Kleinman (1990) have noted, therapeutic process, not just discrete events, needs to be the center of attention. Individual acts of treatment or diagnosis (which may in and of themselves constitute treatment) may produce marked short term impacts. Let me illustrate this by a biocultural phenomena known as "white coat hypertension." Among a significant number of people it has been observed that a visit to a doctor or clinic can provoke a rise in blood pressure leading to misdiagnosis (Floras et al. 1981). Initially, researchers argued that this response indicated that, among such people, elevated blood pressure constituted a generalized response to life stress. Studies of the phenomena, however, have not necessarily found this to be true (Lerman et al. 1989; White et al. 1989). Evidence suggests that more than 20% of patients currently diagnosed as mildly hypertensive in the clinic have normal blood pressure at home (Laughlin et al. 1980; Pickering et al. 1988). The very act of consulting a practitioner, being tested or diagnosed, or receiving treatment affects one's physical status.[8]

In the real world, claims of efficacy are subjective, provisional, and based upon contingencies which often involve social relational concerns.[9] In field contexts: a) illnesses are often defined in terms of illness scenarios and not just features; b) coexisting illnesses (and biomedically defined diseases) are common and interpreted in relation to one another; c) episodes of illness are viewed as conditions; d) somatic expressions constitute an important idiom of distress; and e) illness narratives are negotiated and influence symptom presentation as well as treatment evaluation. Self-report statements relating to efficacy are complex and often metamedical. In the face of this complexity Anderson argues that patients' interpretations of outcome satisfaction constitute a very limited measure of success, noise which should somehow be screened out. I disagree. This complexity is central to ethnomedicine and the study of treatment response.

I would argue that ethnomedical studies of therapeutic efficacy entail investigation of both curative and healing efficacy, as well as the social relations of illness discourse and symptom reporting. Curative efficacy is generally defined as the extent to which a specific treatment measurably reduces, reverses, or prevents a set of physiological parameters in a specified context. Healing, which may or may not entail curing, involves the perception of positive qualitative change in the condition of the afflicted from the vantage of the afflicted and/or concerned others. I would question the extent to which curative efficacy can be neatly separated from symbolic aspects of a treatment (healing efficacy) inclusive of placebo response and what Michael de Montaigne (1958) has described as symptom expectation.

Instrumental and symbolic efficacy merge, are coextensive, and interactive. Even a double blind experiment must attend to more than the uniform administration of two or more indistinguishable substances or procedures. The explanation that accompanies the agent must be uniformally culture-specific to the subjects' prevailing system. "It must be rational-scientific or mystical such that it is matched and syntonic with the systemic conceptualizations of subjects" (Adler and Hammett 1973; Bajaj 1990; Medawar 1967). One can no more study a medication's physical capacity to cure without a consideration of healing efficacy, than study healing efficacy on the basis of psychological representations at the mental level without a consideration of treatment performance as it influences self transformation (Atkinson 1987; Devisch 1983; Laderman 1988).[10]

As Etkin (1988a,b) has noted, assessments of physiologic response of even a single herb requires the researcher to take account of the context in which the herb is used and the way in which it is administered. Context includes subtle changes in health-related behavior (eg. diet, bathing) which mark the act of treatment and influence expectations as well as bodily state. It is necessary to test the combined efficacy of a contextualized treatment recognizing that there is a range of both biological and symbolic response to any treatment.

This raises a point related to the testing of traditional medical treatment among a study population where samples have been selected on the basis of etic criteria such as a biomedical disease category. Studies of treatment efficacy employing a standard intervention which derive samples by etic criteria do not test actual treatment procedures.[11] Within the South Asian cultures in which I have studied ethnomedicine, skilled practitioners tailor medicine content, dosage and mix to the patient.[12] Emic assessment of a patient's constitution and life context are considered inclusive of age, humoral proclivity, strength, digestive capacity, normal diet, and work routine. Medicine compatibility based upon past experience (self report and practitioner observations) is also considered.

My point is that running case-control trials of single fixed traditional remedies might be useful for pharmaceutical companies searching for raw sources of essential compounds having clinical efficacy in the lab. These trials are not, however, valid tests of a treatment's efficacy in real life contexts. In fact, as Lock has vividly described in Japan (1984, 1990), an empirical approach to isolating the essential ingredients of traditional medicines can prove to have harmful effects. What needs to be studied are treatments, not entities per se. Treatments entail the tailoring of medicines in a context where individual response to treatment regimes are affected by symbolic aspects of treatment and diagnosis, concurrent illnesses, states of malnutrition, dietary behavior, etc.

Much of traditional medicine is illness process, not disease entity based. This point was raised by an ayurvedic practitioner with whom I studied in South India in the mid 1970s. I asked the practitioner for permission to run a trial of his renowned "diabetes" medication on a sample of patients. My intention was to track these patients with blood sugar tests, and then to have him discontinue medication eight weeks after treatment was initiated (mid treatment course) for one week to see if their blood sugar levels returned to a pretreatment baseline.

He found my notion of such a trial to be ill conceived. While he was quite willing to have patients test their blood during treatment (to provide him additional data upon which to taper his treatment), he found it wrongheaded to reason that after suspending treatment the body would return to the state it has been before, complete with the original disease. This assumed that the same set of conditions that caused the illness persisted, that the medicine alone was affecting symptoms, and that a disease entity persisted as a definitive form. He emphasized that "diabetes" was a symptom complex associated with a range of dietary disorders, that medications were adapted for each patient's changing humoral status, and that his treatments altered a patient's humoral status by normalizing the digestive process, not by ridding the body of an abstract disease entity. If treatment were suspended, vitiation of the bodily humors might take several forms resulting in any number of symptoms sets, not necessarily those symptoms I associated with diabetes. While I wanted to test the action of an herbal medication on a disease, his treatment was process based. An assessment of the latter would require far more than a monitoring of sugar in the urine or blood! As Trawick has noted in this volume:

Just as diagnosis and treatment of a disease may vary from moment to moment in Ayurveda, so may the disease itself. Disease itself is not an isolated entity, it is a disturbance in the pattern of the system as a whole. And when symptoms of an illness abate, it is generally not said that the illness is gone, rather it is said that the disease has changed.

Do studies such as those advocated by Anderson belong to the field of ethnomedicine? I would argue that biomedical measures of treatment outcome are useful data for assessing therapeutic response, but constitute no gold standard against which to evaluate treatment efficacy. I would further argue that studies of treatment response are ethnomedical when they contextualize treatment-related behavior and consider the interface between expectation and reported response. Such studies may be juxtaposed to more limited ethnopharmacological research by the provision of details on 1) treatment preparation, dosage, and administration; 2) for whom and when treatments are and are not administered; 3) expectations of and criteria for judging treatment; and 4) cultural interpretation of physiological response inclusive of those signs and symptoms paid credence and ignored. Without such details, all that is tested are extractions and abstractions. Left unaccounted for are synergistic or antagonistic actions of mixes of medicines, physiologic states affecting absorption, shifts of meaning and expectations which affect treatment response.

In the next paper in this volume, Weller, Reubush and Klein provide us with an epidemiological description of the folk illness *empacho* in Guatemala. Among those anthropologists most active in developing methods for systematic data collection in ethnomedicine, Weller is best known for her experimentation with empirical methods enabling hypothesis testing within structured domains (Weller 1984), and cultural consensus analysis as a means of judging "cultural competency" between and among informants (Romney, Weller, and Batchelder 1986).[13] As noted by Garro (1988) in her commentary following the Browner et al. article (cited above), Weller's work on the cognitive organization of illness domains constitutes an alternative to bioscience in assessing equivalences across cultures.

In the present essay, Weller, Reubush, and Klein place emphasis on establishing the prevalence of folk illnesses and those at risk to them prior to an evaluation of patterns of health care seeking. Their attempt to estimate the illness burden of *empacho* by age and gender in Guatemala follows in the tradition of the Rubel et al. (1985) study of *susto* among the Zapotec and Mestizo of Mexico. A study of self-reported predisposition to *empacho* leads them to an investigation of distinguishing characteristics of *empacho* in contrast to other forms of gastrointestinal and non-GI tract related illness. A central question is posed: "Are there a set of signs, symptoms, and treatment choices which differentiates *empacho* from other illnesses?"

This question is germane whether it is directed toward folk illnesses, popular ill-nesses labeled with biomedical terms, or the study of biomedically defined dis-eases as they are recognized in cultural contexts (Nichter 1989, 1991).

Weller and her colleagues find that *empacho* does have a significantly different profile than other gastrointestinal illnesses on the basis of five variables, but they conclude that the model of *empacho* generated by discriminate analysis is better at predicting the absence of *empacho* than its presence. I find their research approach of practical utility in field conditions in which the anthropologist wishes to gener-ate a consensus profile of an illness and estimate illness prevalence. Additionally, such a study could yield information on whether the representation of an illness by healers constitutes a consensus of experts and differs from that of the lay popula-tion raising questions about the distribution of health knowledge, mystification, etc.[14] A limitation of the approach is that it does not address social relational factors associated with illness labeling (Crandon 1983). These factors are less feature-based and more processual in nature. It is here that feature checklist models of ill-ness give way to illness scenarios and taskonomic considerations (Nichter 1989).

For example, there is (hypothetically) the possibility that *empacho* might consti-tute a more popular and culturally available idiom of distress for males than fe-males if the latter have a wider range of distress communication options open to them. While I have no idea if this is the case in Guatemala, an illness I investigated in South India having similar characteristics led me to consider this possibility.

The illness category *gulma* in South Kanara shared many characteristics with other GI problems, but was distinguished in illness scenarios by the suspicion that a person was being physically poisoned (*kayi vesha*) by someone having access to their food (source of sustenance). As in *empacho*, most cases of *gulma* which were reported to me were by men. Also similar, only a proportion of those self-diagnos-ing their problem as *gulma* consulted traditional practitioners. Five households were observed in which a *gulma* case was reported. In each case, the treatment ac-tion taken was discussed among significant others in such a way that discourse in-dexed sensitive scripts about the illness which were not articulated directly. In three cases, *gulma* was inferred from and instantiated by consultations with special-ists who validated suspicions of sorcery. In two other cases, *gulma* was discussed in terms of ineffective home remedies which "should work" if the problem was a sim-ple digestive disorder.[15]

My point is not to suggest that *empacho* is like *gulma*, but to raise a research ques-tion which can only be addressed by data of a different order than that offered to us by Weller, Reubush, and Klein in this essay. Such data will not be generated by a search for a consensus prototype of *empacho* and the charting of illness episodes which share attributes with it, for the latter may only be incidental or part of a for-mulaic description. The data required are more image schema and illness scenario based, taking into account the manner in which the latter influence symptom recog-nition and reporting. What is required is information about the meaning of *empacho* to the local population inclusive of causality, notions of responsibility, social re-sponse to the afflicted, and *empacho* related discourse. Also needed is a sense of how the timing of an illness in a person's life affects its meaning. An illness is not just a variation away from a cultural model of health, but a marked life event often accompanied by a new set of norms or a new approach to one's lifeworld (Canguil-hem 1978).

Weller, Reubush, and Klein report that the treatment for *empacho* is the same as for other GI track disorders and that individuals labeling their illness as *empacho* are equally likely to consult a traditional healer as engage non-traditional therapy within a community where most illness is self-treated. Of all illnesses treated by healers, however, *empacho* cases are clearly the most common. An important methodological lesson provided by Weller, Reubush, and Klein is that practitioner-clientele data should always be cross checked against household-based prevalence and health care seeking data before illness-specific patterns of curative resort are assumed to exist (Durkin-Longley 1984; Nichter 1990).

Four general comments may be made pertaining to ethnomedicine and attempts to enhance methodologic rigor while avoiding rigormortis (Nations 1987). First, as anthropologists we must be aware of reified constructions and straw man representations of "positivism" and the "scientific method" which are abbreviated and based upon formal, mechanistic images of how science proceeds (Carrithers 1990). As Roscoe (1991) has skillfully argued, while positivist conceptions of "objective facts" may be misconstrued, the process of collecting, scrutinizing and interpretating data followed by those engaged in scientific inquiry shares much in common with interpretative studies. Interpretive studies, on the other hand, are often more empirical in practice than hermeneutic theory would advocate. Polemic fostered by the construction of a "positivist other" results in antagonists talking past one another and the sort of analytical reification which invites postmodern inquiry (Roscoe 1991:20). It is time that commonalities, not just differences, be recognized in more empirical and interpretive approaches to the study of ethnomedical phenomena.

A second point is that methodologic rigor in anthropological studies of ethnomedicine could benefit from serious attention being paid to triangulation procedures which enhance the trustworthiness of ethnographic accounts. This has broadly been called for in the social sciences by the "naturalistic inquiry" school (Lincoln and Guba 1985) as well as those advocating postpositivist critical multiplism (Cook 1985; Shadish 1989).16 Trustworthiness is established by employing multiple theoretical approaches when establishing the scope of data inquiry, methods of data collection, and sampling frames. This enables a comparison of data sets generated by different methods and the opportunity to question the extent to which data have been influenced by or constitute an artifact of a collection procedure (Meyers 1977; Trend 1978; Stone and Campbell 1984).

To the methods concerns raised by the "naturalistic inquiry" school should be added concerns addressed by Young (1981) in his discussion of the production of knowledge. Young draws our attention to the speaker's motivation, awareness of audience, the interactive character of discourse, and the representation of self through language use. Discourse analysis (Gumperz 1982), with its attention to voice (points of view given expression through context bound utterances), provides ways of studying shifts in knowledge production.17 This has important implications for ethnomedical studies of illness narratives, the negotiation of illness identities, and the practice of eclectic medicine.

A third point is that while anthropologists may make effective use of quantitative tools such as those found within epidemiology, they must recognize the limitations of such tools. Above all else, anthropologists must take care not to desocialize or reify isolated variables. To do so is to place run the risk of displacing historical and political economic factors underlying the incidence, diagnosis, labeling and social relations of illness (Young 1982).[18]

Fourth, there is just as great a need to study the logic (s) underlying folk epidemiologies of illness in the context of social change as there is a need to incorporate the problem solving framework of biomedical epidemiology within ethnomedicine.[19] Studies by Farmer (1990) on changing interpretations of AIDS among Haitians, and Nichter (1987a) on changing interpretations of Kyasanur Forest Disease among South Indians, illustrate how causal schemata are generated in response to social and political economic change as well as the tenacity of an illness and failure to control it. Likewise, studies by Comaroff in southern Africa (1985) and Taylor in Rwanda (this volume), illustrate how forms of healing are emergent in the context of social transformation.

Illness Narratives, Moral Discourse and Negotiated Scripts

The next set of papers are concerned with the way in which affliction and the experience of suffering are framed by discourse and healing is mediated through narrative.[20] Glass-Coffin's essay considers the role of discourse in identity management through an analysis of misfortunes associated with *Dano* in Peru. *Dano*, a form of magical aggression, is perpetrated by members of one's social network who are envious or jealous. Dano manifests in a variety of forms including domestic mishaps, interpersonal discord, business losses, and illness which does not respond to treatment. Extending Bourdieu's (1977, 1982) notion of "symbolic capital" to self esteem, Glass-Coffin engages in an analysis of the "symbolic economy of discourse" as this informs patterns of behavior related to identity construction, the meaning of *dano*, and the role of traditional medicine in treating *dano* through repair of threatened identity.

The researcher grounds the reader in a highly competitive if not dysfunctional environment where she is implored not to trust anyone or disclose personal vulnerability. In a context of petty mercantilism (redistributive economics), diminishing material wealth, inflation, and economic instability, individuals compete for honor and self-esteem through manipulating the symbolic capital (self worth) of others through gossip. This practice, it is suggested, substitutes for positive control over one's own identity and constitutes a "verbal mode of *dano*" undermining the identity of others.". A common script in *dano* narratives concerns those close to you who are envious and inflict injury upon you through gossip as well as contracting the services of a sorcerer (*brujo*).

Central to Glass-Coffin's analysis is the tension between the social relations of an unstable market economy where profit begets envy, and the social ideals of close family ties, cooperation, and reciprocity. The day-to-day dynamics of survival in this redistributive market economy clash with idealized precapitalist values, resulting in competing directives.[21] Dependency on others for one's sense of person as well as economic survival limits options for overtly expressing the hostilities towards others which are endemic in the marketplace. Given this situation Peruvians suspect the hidden agendas of others during social transactions while tightly monitoring their own public identity.[22] Glass-Coffin discusses how this state of affairs leads to superficial presentations of self and one's emotional state in public as well as child socialization practices designed to teach children to trust no one and that there is "no love without interest."

The focus of her essay is identity management. This appears to be a delicate balance achieved through stories crafted by an individual about herself which engage understatement, and stories told about one by others which either serve to reconfirm or point out discrepancies between their life context and self presentation. Caught between competing values, ideal role expectations and the pressing weight of resource constraints, Peruvians remain ever vigilant in their exchange of words.

Described is an economically and psychologically tense situation in which a concept of "limited good" is pervasive, denoting a zero sum mentality where one person's gain is another's loss.[23] What is not discussed is the extent to which "leveling mechanisms" (gossip, *dano*) might constitute resistance against the social relations fostered by capitalism.

Glass-Coffins' study joins that of Price (1987), Lewin (1979), and Early (1982) in calling attention to the importance of illness stories in establishing personal identity as well as constructing coherent scripts about misfortune which open avenues for conflict mediation.[24] In describing the power of discourse to wound as well as heal, she encourages us to look at discourse in terms of relations of power and agendas of human intent (Ricoeur 1971) that "systematically forms the objects of which they speak" (Foucault 1972:49).

Glass-Coffin argues that just as discourse in the form of gossip can cause a breakdown in one's identity and social welfare, healing rituals can restore one's sense of identity. This is accomplished through the creation of a narrative environment in which an illness scenario is suggested that displaces responsibility for role failure away from the sufferer and at the same time provides an explanation for illness or mishaps. One might also argue that a causal script which projects responsibility for misfortune onto an "other" in the form of sorcery attribution serves as a projective mechanism for unexpressed hostility.

The case study of a woman diagnosed as having *dano* is provided inclusive of her health care seeking behavior, evaluation of treatment and follow up data on how the overall conditions of her life have changed post treatment. The woman's life has not substantially improved, but she is satisfied with her treatment and holds the hope that additional healing ceremonies would help her if she could afford them. Glass-Coffin describes how a combination of factors contributed to the woman's healing experience aside from the illness narrative per se. Through the curandero's singing the patient's personal experience is linked to the culturally mythic in a way which is emotionally compelling. Whether or not this provided her "a language in which to express her pain" or merely a safe space in which to ventilate her feelings is hard to ascertain. What is notable is the "beauty of the song" and the interest displayed by the healer which the afflicted describes as having a "cleansing effect." Through crying, a display of vulnerability, the patient is emotionally unbound just as through narration she is symbolically unbound from holding spirits negatively influencing her life.

Glass-Coffin provides us with a brief symbolic analysis of the healing ceremony attended by the afflicted women. At the core of this ritual is a movement of the afflicted from the domain of life governed by the relations of competitive- redistributive exchange to the domain of life conducive to growth and productive activity. The spirit of the afflicted comes to symbolically rest in the garden of the healer where she is nurtured and "accounted for." Juxtaposed to Glass-Coffin's description of mistrust in the study population at large, this ceremony strikes the reader as providing refuge.

Glass-Coffin's description of the poor caught between social obligations and personal needs, scarcity, and ideals of hospitality, is becoming increasingly familiar in the ethnographic literature of societies in transition. In a context of competing ideologies and discourses, it is important to consider the range of social institutions which have emerged to both mediate conflict and articulate resistance as well as distress. What would make the present account more complete would be additional information about other culturally sanctioned responses to insecurity and ways in which the "productive" is articulated and nurtured. Are there positive emotional ties which transcend superficiality in the climate of mistrust described which serve to buffer feelings of vulnerability? What systems of social support exist in the context of competition? Are there ways other than *dano* attribution to articulate distress associated with a state of real or perceived identity aggression? Do other healing modalities exist associated with the church? What factors influence affiliation with coexisting modes of healing?[25]

Future research into *dano* might go beyond a single case study and pay credence to research questions raised by scholars in the first set of essays. It would be useful to know something about the prevalence of *dano* (by age, gender, class) as well as the frequency of *dano*-related discourse. Followed up as a longitudinal study, the case of Mari might reveal how the experience of *dano* influences perceptions of the afflicted in her extended social network as well as her perception of self over time.[26] Is the narrative which the sufferer of *dano* constructs always accepted by others or is its credibility challenged by those who engage different scripts in moral discourse? Who participates in identifying and instantiating scripts of misfortune associated with *dano* other than the Brujo?

Brodwin's essay complements the research of Glass-Coffin in the sense that it also focuses on the negotiation of identity in the context of healing. Only in this case, it is the identity of the healer which is the subject of inquiry. Brodwin investigates medical pluralism in the context of a larger study of how religious discourse frames the meaning of affliction in Haiti. The negotiation of an illness identity in rural Haiti involves negotiating between competing moral worlds. A single episode of illness can generate several moral discourses, and these are met by competing ideologies advanced by different healing specialists. Brodwin is attentive to the moral discourse generated in response to sickness in a context of competing ideologies represented by different healing modalities. In Haiti, these modalities are associated with ancestor and spirit worship (Voodoun), conventional Catholicism, and fundamentalist Pentecostalism.

Distinct forms of healing coexist in Haiti, each having its own focus, discourse about Satan and the spirits, and perception of human responsibility (Brodwin 1990). Voodoun proposes a sociocentric reading of affliction. Satan is an amoral vehicle which one uses to "send sickness" upon the intended victim. To treat such a "sent" sickness—the result of human malice—the Voodoun specialist ritually invokes protective powers which surround the victim and ward off future attack. Within formal Catholicism, Satan is an autonomous non-human enemy and the body is the site of a cosmological battle between the forces of good and evil. Pentecostalism advances a counter-discourse with Satan embracing all who are not converts. Within the context of sickness, suffering constitutes a sign of sin with responsibility laid upon not only the afflicted but all those who invite Satan into the lives of the afflicted through "non Christian" healing modalities which play into the devil's hands.

Brodwin describes a religious landscape in which therapeutic pluralism is the source of considerable tension. Healing practices and the sources of healing powers are not neutral, but associated with moral stances. Discourse about the moral status of the afflicted and their household are structured around not only the form of the illness experienced (e.g. its onset, severity, and duration), but the type of treatment engaged and the public identity of the healer(s) consulted. While in normal circumstances several healing modalities may be resorted to and deemed complementary in some general way, the actions of therapy management groups are open to challenge by neighbors who choose to use the occasion of individual suffering as a platform for metamedical debate about God, morality, and self.[27]

It is in this context that the life histories of healers which Brodwin presents take on importance as scripts establishing their moral status. The two healers which Brodwin describes draw upon plural discourses of popular religion and innovative interpretations of ethnopsychology to establish their therapeutic practice as morally correct. Notably, they derive their identity largely through juxtaposing their practice to that of houngan who come to represent the powers of darkness by making a covenant with the devil. Public repudiation of the antithesis of Christian virtues is a discursive strategy which establishes one as a good Catholic. Brodwin illustrates the variety of scripts which may be rendered to establish a healer's morality while at the same time establishing the legitimacy of their calling through stories which entail reference to the powers which inhabit their lifeworld. A key element of these stories, well illustrated by the case of Mme. Beaumont, is the agency of the healer. While a moral healer may be assisted by spirits or angels, she does not request their assistance, which would infer serving their wishes.

Brodwin's research stands in marked contrast to studies of health care seeking behavior which divide up health care arenas into separate categories of secular and religious healers, assume a rational man stance to decision making, and privilege illness attributes and enabling factors. Attention is called to both the complexity of healing traditions and the dynamics of constructing an identity as a healer, and another set of predisposing variables influencing health care seeking and the framing of discourse about affliction. In calling attention to competing moral worlds, Brodwin's study of healing in Haiti, like Adam's study of medico- religious traditions in Tibet, demonstrates the mutual contribution of studies of ethnomedicine and popular religion.

Nuckolls develops a cognitive anthropological approach to the study of possession-mediumship which draws upon theories of knowledge, schema, and script-processing to describe causal thinking and inference. In an extension of a previous paper (Nuckolls 1991), the author raises a fundamental question for ethnomedical studies: in the context of healing, what is the process by which clients and practitioners construct an explanatory account which is satisfying to both? This question has been addressed by other scholars of ethnomedicine in South Asia who have studied the ways in which astrologers and ayurvedic practitioners negotiate narratives of illness and misfortune (Nichter 1981b; Pugh 1983). Nuckolls charts new territory by rigorously exploring both the manner in which episodically organized knowledge structures frame causal explanations for misfortune, and how explanatory adequacy is negotiated through the voicing and instantiation of inferences. This adds a new dimension to the study of diagnosis as an attempt to establish a consensus for purposes of action (Fabrega 1975). It also calls attention to how illness narratives are socially constructed as interactionally accomplished events (Labov 1972).

Similar to Lakoff (1987), Nuckolls argues that a repertoire of culturally derived knowledge structures are organized around stereotypical event sequences (schemata, scripts) which generate inferences that resonate with life experience. Moving beyond Lakoff's discussion of idealized cognitive models, Nuckolls explores propositional schema.28 Examined are diagnostic scripts in the divination procedures emerging from social scenarios. Such scripts index paradoxes and ambivalence embedded in the kinship system of the Jalari caste. The politics of generational succession in Jalari extended households entails competing demands and motivations for maintaining/enhancing social relations with agnates and affines. This produces a problematic situation wherein enhancement of relations with one group leads to a weakening of social relations with the other. Misfortune is divined in relation to established causal scripts which index diminished relations in these social domains.

The linking of divination in its various forms to structurally induced ambivalence as it relates to kinship relations is not new. What is impressive about Nuckoll's account is the open ended and dynamic process in which participants in a series of possession-mediumship events try out, evaluate, and tailor scripts of misfortune as strategies of redressing precipitating causes. While "efficient causes" are identified and temporarily mediated in a fairly straightforward manner, "precipitating causes" need to be instantiated in convincing ways to different audiences concordant with the gravity of the situation and the magnitude of change required. Left unaccounted for, however, is the role played by marked and unmarked notions (scripts) of ultimate causality associated with the stars, karma, fate, etc. (Nichter 1987a). Scripts may be chosen not only for the meaning they convey, but in the "subjunctive mode" (Barthes 1987, Bruner 1986) as a means of leaving causality indeterminate or ambiguous (Last 1981; Nichter 1989).

Nuckolls' description of how Jalaris engage different types of specialists engaged in the identification of precipitating causes of misfortune is a valuable contribution to both the literature on the health care seeking process and the mobilization of therapy management groups. Jalaris need to work out tentatively formed causal hypotheses inclusive of their social ramifications and to test inferences in a convincing manner so as to marshall support for changes needed to redress conditions underlying problems. They have recourse to two sets of specialists. With the first they can openly engage in rigorous argument in the course of identifying and synthesizing relevant scenarios. The second set of specialists engage in a more dispassionate validation of inferences publicly. Subtle reasons why and when clients choose to utilize different divination specialists emerge.29

Reading Nuckolls' account led me to review my own data on health care seeking in coastal northern Karnataka among a multicaste sample of informant households. The data suggest distinctive practitioner utilization patterns among castes having similar household composition, economic and educational status, and morbidity profiles (Nichter 1990a). Notably, fishing caste households (in comparison to agriculturalists) reported the greatest number of modal consultations to exorcists, diviners, and oracles. Nuckolls' paper suggests new avenues of research to account for these intercaste differences which complement considerations of household dynamics, idioms of distress and responses to uncertainty.

Another issue raised in Nuckoll's paper is worth highlighting as it has general relevance to the study of ethnomedicine. It entails a unit of analysis issue noted by several ethnographers, but often neglected in surveys which simplistically try to identify illness or age specific patterns of curative resort. An illness experienced by one person is often interpreted as a sign of a problem in a larger social body. This has been a recurrent theme in my own ethnomedical research on maternal and child health problems. Commonly, an illness which occurs in a more vulnerable member of a social group will be associated with other misfortunes of the land, crops, domestic animals, etc. which have affected the group. The illness constitutes a trouble symptomatic of vulnerability in a social domain which remains to be specified. In the present study, Nuckolls identifies the "principle of indirect attack" as central to illness scripts which place pressure on decision makers to act because of the shame associated with causing the innocent to suffer undeserved pain. As Nuckolls notes: "The ill or suffering person is always a moral hostage to somebody else." This dynamic will need to be assessed in relation to emergent as well as residual causal scenarios which link morbidity/mortality to broader uncertainties and social ambivalence in a changing world.

The studies by Glass-Coffin, Brodwin, and Nuckolls, as well as Taylor and Adams invite us to examine the afflicted body as a site where ideologies are contested and mediated through medico-religious discourse, techniques, and institutions which have moral implications. Times of sickness and vulnerability may either constitute occasions when the resources available in one's lifeworld are marshalled without much reflection, or times when the everyday meanings of life and the order of the world are reflected upon and juxtaposed. In either case, multiple interpretive frameworks enhance cultural resiliency by providing options, hope, reflection, choice, and autonomy. Illness histories are motivated inventions of the past responsive to the agenda of those living in the present. They are texts in need of study at several levels of analysis.

Ethnomedicine, the Anthropology of the Body, and Productive Power

Essays by Sobo, Taylor, and Adams involve social relations as they are articulated at the site of the body and through modes of healing which reproduce social values and/or mitigate tensions related to social transformation. In each of these essays the body is a bearer of meanings through performative memory (Connerton 1989). Sobo's essay investigates the embodiment of ideology in Jamaica and the homologous relationship between social and physical pathology. In the Jamaican lifeworld, health is engendered by timely and properly flowing resources which have known origins and specified destinations; bonds strengthened and reproduced by reciprocal exchange; and periodic purges of excess and all that is unincorporated. Ill health is fostered by all that which stagnates, becomes overripe, and causes decomposition, as well as unknown forces which interfere with the proper flow of resources through appropriate channels. Decay, over ripeness, and bad blood emerge as organizing metaphors extended to multiple dimensions of Jamaican life.

After providing us with a rather earthy description of Jamaican ethnophysiology, Sobo leads us to a consideration of the importance of menstrual blood in Jamaican culture. Menstrual blood is something more than a polluting substance associated with the lower status of women related to the inherent impurity of a biological process. Sobo's analysis demonstrates the need for contextualized studies of ethnophysiology which explore not only the complementarity between perceptions of the physical body and the social body, but tensions between gender relations as they are communicated through health concerns.

In order to explain the importance of menstrual blood as a source of a woman's power as well as a symbol of all that is toxic and dangerous, Sobo explores the way in which kinship relations are perceived as entailing the incorporation of bodily substances through the blood, breastmilk, and food. Bonds between kin in Jamaica are substantive. A woman's power to consubstantiate is linked to her power to initiate reciprocity through natural inclinations which compel kin to act altruistically. A moral economy is physically constituted, but also challenged.

A woman's power may be used in a socially sanctioned as well as a devious manner. Just as a mother may create a bond with her child in utero through her blood, a woman may "tie" another to her through the ingestion of her menstrual blood or other bodily secretions. Men must beware of being "tied" to others though an unknown sharing of potent bodily substances which once incorporated lead one's inclinations in directions out of their immediate control. The illicit "tying" of males to females outside of a social relationship associated with established claims of reciprocity and a negotiated sense of responsibility, constitutes an economic threat to the household production of health.

Central to Sobo's analysis is the juxtaposition of gender values and the way in which they are articulated around issues related to sexuality and health. Jamaican men value independence in a context of matrilocal residence where unstable "visiting unions" are common and often based upon "instrumental relations" in the context of poverty. Among men, frequent sex is deemed healthy as a means of "clearing the line" and removing semen before it stagnates. For women reciprocity in a context of economic insecurity is central to survival. Sexual exchange entails economic exchange and expectations of a negotiated measure of support.

A woman's health is less dependent on the physical act of sexuality than a man's and the processes of menstruation and childbirth are deemed healthy for her body, constituting means of cleaning and removing excess. Moreover, according to popular health culture, it is dangerous for a woman to engage in sex with multiple partners as this places her at risk to both experiencing a toxic reaction by absorbing semen which is incompatible, and having her genitals manipulated too often to accommodate the shape of her partners' genital organs. Health ideology, inclusive of a male fear of being poisoned by menstrual blood related to acts of illicit "tying," serves to delimit (in principle?) the range of male sexuality. This reinforces the flow of resources in the direction of healthy reciprocal exchange where clean food and "safe sex" are available.

Sobo's study also reveals the manner in which cultural models of ethnophysiology are extended to explain new health threats, in this case AIDS. Images of decaying semen deposited in body spaces not equipped to absorb or expel it are linked to the festering body extrusions associated with AIDS. Sobo is careful to point out that this is not the only emergent model of AIDS, but a viable schema well grounded in popular health culture. Ethnomedical studies contribute to a broader medical anthropology of AIDS in other ways as well. Sobo not only informs us about perceptions of deviant and healthy sexuality, but the social and economic importance of sexual exchange, gender ideology which fosters sexuality, and fears associated with sexual exchange with unknown partners. Taylor (1990) in his research on the meaning of sexual exchange in Rwanda has further noted why technical fixes to the AIDS problem (condoms) are not popular because of ethnophysiological perceptions of healthy bodily exchange related to core cultural values pertaining to social life and personhood. Utilizing a condom implies the blockage of a reciprocal flow of secretions in a society in which a person is neither an individual nor merely a member of a group, but a fractal person in a perpetual state of being produced through exchanges of gifts.

Taylor's present essay is an extension of an earlier article (1988) in which he examined cultural models of health and ethnophysiology in Rwanda as they articulate social values related to processes of production, exchange, and reproduction. Like Sobo, Taylor draws attention to an embodied ideology involving exchange relations, and like Glass-Coffin he points to conflicts between capitalist and precapitalist social orders in his analysis of ethnomedical phenomena.

Taylor's analysis of traditional and emergent healing traditions in Rwanda takes place in a context where modes of precolonial exchange based upon a principle of reciprocity coexist with modes of commodity exchange characteristic of a global market. Within traditional culture, the body of the king served as a conduit for the flow of celestial beneficence, and the bodies of his subjects were "open systems fully participating in the process of social exchange" (Tousignant and Maldonado 1989).[30] Properly regulated flow within physical bodies was necessary for the well being of the land to the extent that sources of deviated or blocked flow (e.g. nonmenstruating women, women failing to lactate) placed the kingdom at risk and were eliminated. In this cosmology, social identity was articulated through the idiom of food wherein a hierarchy of production and status was predicated upon a distancing of self from the toil of the earth and its hardness as a source of impurity. In a modernizing world, the value of flow has been superseded by the profit motive which favors an accumulation of hard capital and a new concept of liquid assets.

Taylor draws attention to etiology as ideology. Traditional healing centers around sorcery accusation and a hydraulic model of flow in the microcosm of the body as well as the macrocosm of the universe. The principle of reciprocity is embodied in the form of a health culture in which well being is promoted through fluid intake and exchange. Illness results from either blockage of one's internal flow or non-regulated, diminished, or excessive flow. Those accused of sorcery, like illnesses associated with sorcery, are linked to a breakdown in reciprocity required for the replenishment of physiological and social systems. Treatment places the body of the patient in a contiguous relationship with the elemental forces of nature such that flow is reestablished through the manipulation of natural symbols which analogically stand in relation to bodily processes.

Central to Taylor's essay is an emergent form of therapy based upon a confessing of sins. This therapy form reflects a coexisting ideology associated with a transition to capitalism, commodity exchange related values, and the rise of individualism. The confessional cult stands in opposition to and distances itself from practices which reproduce an ideology of reciprocity. According to the cult, illness is caused by fear, jealousy, and ultimately sin. Sin causes one's protecting saints to let down their guard, rendering one vulnerable. Within the cult, saints replace ancestors, the protectors of traditional values. As distinct from the ancestors, saints do not demand sacrifices as reciprocity for providing protection. Veneration of ancestors and belief in sorcery become sins according to the new cult. In sum, the cultural model constructed around the principle of reciprocity is undermined and collective fears associated with sorcery are replaced by a search within. The aim of therapy becomes to identify and expunge the blockage within the self, rather than the blockage within a larger social body.

The confessional cult leader described by Taylor is a culture broker who has mediated the dilemma between traditional gift values and market values and restructured the flow/blockage dialectic in favor of the market system. As a healer he has inverted the values upon which the Rwandan social hierarchy is based. In order to be successful, however, the cult must encompass pre-existing health concerns associated with a hydraulic model of ethnophysiology. Taylor points out that health concerns carried over from traditional health culture are accommodated within confessional healing. Notably, purgatives and sudorifics are used to cleanse the body in a process analogous to confession which "evacuates the soul." Hydraulic reasoning is appropriated.

What struck me as particularly interesting in Taylor's analysis was the type of people attracted to the confessional cult and what the cult tells us about social and economic transformation in Rwandan society. Participants in the cult are not described as the wealthy looking for an ideology which rationalizes their accumulation of wealth, but those caught in the middle of a double bind of gift logic (which would lead to their impoverishment) and commodity logic (which would lead to being accused of selfishness). Participants are the petit bourgeois, those "perceived as rich" as a result of having a secure position within the market economy yet having little disposable (fluid) income. Such people typically have a need to establish their status materially through the display of token commodities (commodity fetishism), yet do not have the herewithal signified by these commodities to share with relatives in their kinship network. Taylor describes patients from this group as asked to pass along wealth which they only appear to possess, leaving them guilt ridden and, over time, alienated.

At issue is both how successful the confessional cult may be in mediating guilt among patients by providing them a new identity and cultural model to justify their behavior and the cult's capacity to invalidate preestablished causal schema for illness. It is one thing to suggest that a form of healing acts as a conduit for an emergent ideology giving converts a new sense of self and establishing a therapeutic community which provides a sense of belonging and connectedness to those who are alienated. It is quite another thing to suggest that those who consult confessional cult priests substitute new scripts of misfortune for old ones as opposed to adding them to their causal repertoire in an eclectic fashion.

A key question is when and in what contexts different scripts for misfortune are deemed more relevant. Taylor touches on this issue in remarks he makes regarding the household as the last social sphere in which flow/blockage ideology persists, a sphere in which parental relatedness to children's illnesses remains relevant and market ideology does not govern interaction. Given the amount of morbidity and mortality associated with children, and the fact that children's illness is often related to the vulnerability of the household, it is important to examine change and continuity in the scripts used to explain both adult and children's illness.

It would also be important to assess the impact of biomedicine on popular health culture through the commodification of health, a process where wealth is exchanged for health as a commodity (Caplan 1989; Illich 1975; Nichter 1989). Future research is required on the relationship between confessional therapy with its emphasis on the morality of the individual, and commodified therapy which is amoral and fix-oriented. Another subject for future research is the extent to which rising competition for scarce resources (social as well as economic), the challenges of modern living, and new uncertainties (ranging in scope from AIDS to pesticides) lead members of the new social order to feel a need to protect themselves from representations of collective as well as individual anxieties. In Asia, numerous accounts are available of rises in the use of amulets, belief in sorcery, consultations to astrologers, etc., by avid participants in capitalism who simultaneously engage in meditation and consult practitioners who treat them for "psychosomatic" complaints with psychiatric medications.[31] Concordant with Appadurai's notion of regimes of value (1986), ideals of precapitalist and capitalist exchange may come to coexist, be mediated, or be allocated spheres of relevance in Rwandan society such that one's identity may be derived from both.[32]

Where they are co-present, it is important to investigate when sociocentric and egocentric healing traditions are maximized as means of relieving suffering.[33] This entails a consideration of practicalities, the social relations and moral implications of therapy choice, and conditions under which differences between therapy systems are blurred or accentuated. It also entails an examination of changes in the range of therapy options and how forms of therapy emerge and are altered in response to social and political economic transformation. This is a strength of Taylor's study. He poses the question: How can one accumulate wealth in present day Rwandan society without being considered someone who blocks the flow of gifts, i.e. is a witch? Resolution of this dilemma, he suggests, involves a shift of flow imagery from the social to the individual body and expunging "blockage" within the self rather than the group. An emergent sense of self distinct from one's social person is supported by therapeutic forms espousing confession (sin and guilt) rather than accusation (witches). This is indicative, claims Taylor, of a historical process wherein Rwanda is being incorporated in the world economy. Confessional therapies reflect and reinforce capitalist distinctions between matters of substance and contract— who one is versus what one does.

Consideration of emergent therapeutic forms in Rwanda leads Taylor to reflect on the writing of Foucault about social transformation in the West as it is related to the rise of individualism and subtle forms of state control exercised in conjunction with an altered perception of self and personal guilt propagated by such therapeutic forms as psychotherapy. This theme is further reflected upon by Adams in a discursive study of Tibetan history which attends to the way in which the afflicted body becomes the site of contested versions of social order. By focusing on medicoreligious traditions and their transformation, Adams provides insights into the ways different representations of self, body, and sickness are produced as instruments for state control.[34]

Adams examines the utility of Foucault's concept of biopower in the study of medicine as an agency of control, arguing that its more generic form "productive power" might be appropriate in non-European contexts. Biopower as described by Foucault is a tacit apparatus of state control emerging in post-monarchical Europe, related to the production of knowledge about the body as a site of subjectification. Internalized judgments about normalcy fostered by the medical sciences served to take the place of the state and supersede the church in regulating behavior. Control of the populace was achieved through anatamo-politics wherein measures of normality were established as representations of the truth and concepts of bodily refinement motivating self improvement. The body was increasingly exposed as an object of surveillance and discourse, the body coming to constitute a text in which corruption was made visible.[35] Biopower was thus bipolar, manifest both in forms of physical regulation and discourse about normalcy and personal transformation. It was productive in the sense that knowledge leading to self regulation and self discipline was "forever expanding."

Adams invites us to look at productive power in the Tibetan context wherein medico-religious forms came to exercise control through notions of unattached selfhood and an asocial body, the monastery as a repository of spiritual knowledge and power, and enlightenment as spiritual wealth. She argues that a local form of productive power was instrumental in creating a state-like society in what was once a stateless society of warring valley kingdoms in pre-Buddhist Tibet. While Foucault's discursive history of Europe is marked by breaks in the social order and corresponding shifts in discourse about the body, Adams lays emphasis on gradual change in Tibet marked by the Buddhist absorption and encompassment of pre-Buddhist representations of cosmology, self, and sickness. Generated were alternative discourses, healing traditions, and a flexible ideology which appealed to different segments of the populace in accord with their level of knowledge and embeddedness in social relations and productive relationships with the state.

Pre-Buddhist Tibet was organized around both kin-based and tributary modes of production linked through relations of reciprocal exchange. Beliefs in spirits and demons as well as shamanic healing traditions reproduced sociocentric values, encouraged communality and supported contingent social relations. In this environment Buddhism linked disparate groups by overriding if not shedding primary social alliance to the family. Emphasis was placed upon the transitory nature of social commitments and obligations. Self-identity was associated with a chain of reincarnations, not ancestors representing the lineage and demanding reciprocity in return for prosperity. Monasteries reaffirmed these self-identities and through receiving "true gifts" associated with merit, assisted the living to obtain a better incarnation in their next life. This ideology, supported by an elaborate ritual apparatus, a self discipline theology, and a loosely linked system of monasteries constituting a "clerical religion," colonized the Tibetan lifeworld and served to unite a widely dispersed populace (Samuel 1990). The state exercised its power through a "flexible apparatus" for the production of truths in the form of spiritual knowledge.

Adams points out that supporting Tibetan Buddhist ideology is a conception of an unbound individual self beneath the sociocentric web of one's own weaving and a body which is ultimately controllable by a disciplined sentient mind.[36] While this ideology emerged as the official discourse of the Tibetan state, it superseded, but did not supplant, residual ideologies. In order for Buddhism to flourish in Tibet it had to not only decenter popular knowledge and discourse about the body and sickness, but recenter both. To do this it had to be innovative and accommodate the shamanic within Tantric practices (absorbed by Lamanism) which ultimately deconstruct the forms of external demons locating them as forces within to be defeated (Aziz 1976). It also reconstructed social anatomies into natural bodily anatomies within Amchi medicine as a means of deconstructing spirits and establishing the non-social nature of sickness.

What I find compelling about this essay is the subtlety of Adams' argument and her ability to move between the historical record and her own fieldwork among the Sherpa. While focusing on productive power she is careful not to make grandiose claims about hegemony. She chooses instead to point to the incompleteness of Buddhist teachings as a counter-representation to a kinship-based social order and reveals the presence of alternative discourses and practices in Tibetan life. Described is the manner in which doctrinal emphasis on individualism penetrated the structure of the family unit rather than destroying it.

Reasons why the social self has not been subverted by Buddhism are offered both in this essay and another paper (Adams 1988), where Adams explores social formations associated with peasant production and the role of Shamans and Lamas in reinforcing communality at a time of capitalist penetration into Nepal. While she draws the reader's attention to three sets of healers who attend to three aspects of the Sherpa self (the social, physical, and mental), her ethnography reveals that irrespective of the central ideology to which a healing tradition subscribes, popular interpretation of healing practices subsumes messages within a context of communality. Adams' message about plurality and how the residual ideology of collectivism is sustained in the interstitial spaces of a dominant discourse on individualism is powerful.

Like that of Taylor, Adams' essay contributes to the interface between ethnomedicine and an anthropology of self which is situated historically. In both cases, knowledge about the body and self is a product of contestation. As in Glass-Coffin's essay, dual directives associated with coexisting concepts of self impact on both everyday behavior and notions of illness. In Tibet, sickness is perceived to result from multiple sources (humoral imbalances; social offenses to the living, dead, and deities; karma; etc.), with tensions recognized between the mental and physical as well as the individual and social self. In her discussion about sickness among women, Adams points out that illness may result from either over liking (too much attachment, associated with sociocentrism) or under liking (too little attachment associated with excessive independence). Revealed in this model of sickness is the tension between coexisting self ideals associated with collectivist and individualist ideologies.

An issue discussed in passing by Adams is worth highlighting as a reminder for those conducting ethnomedical studies. This entails the plural meanings of ritual performance associated with Buddhist teachings about the self which involve teaching by analogy. Ritual performances for the laity which involve extensive paraphernalia, images of demons, and a decentering of consciousness through the use of sound are attempts to appropriate symbols as a means of facilitating reflection on the transcendent nature of consciousness. The importance of this observation is that multiple agendas may be involved in any ritual performance as well as multiple interpretations of what is taking place.

Ethnomedicine, Agency and the Anthropology of Self

In the final two essays we move from an analysis of intransient self to a consideration of the ethnographer as object of discourse. Both essays, in distinct ways, address the issue of agency. Laderman's essay follows up on a series of issues raised in a previous article (Laderman 1988). In that article, she examined cultural models of personality in Malaysia as a means of questioning simplistic analysis of healing which juxtapose psychotherapy to shamanism. The former is typically characterized as internalistic while the latter is externalistic. Psychotherapy is a process wherein clients present individual myths to a therapist who facilitates a giving of language to that which is repressed. Shamanism is typically thought to produce remission without insight through projection and the imposition of social myths external to the patient's personality.

Laderman rejects this dichotomy and argues that some Malay spirit raising performances incorporate a theory of personality which is analogous to a Jungian approach to recognizing archetypes. Far from identifying sources of frustration with externalistic entities (ghosts and spirits), patients are freed to let inner winds (dispositions) basic to their personalities emerge from within. So doing helps them clarify problems and paradoxes. Such performances are not repressive, but are expressive means of confronting that which is inherent.[37] The afflicted act out repressed aspects of their personality, their inner winds blow free and they are refreshed. Rather than a cure in the sense of ridding oneself of an affliction, such performances facilitate healing by putting one in touch with his/her inner nature, thereby engendering balance.[38]

In the present essay, Laderman extends her analysis of the Malay concept of self, arguing against the limitations of a dichotomy between western and eastern constructs of egocentric/sociocentric selves. She emphasizes that despite Malay belief in spirits which articulate cultural values and vested power relations, Malay notions of self are closer to western notions of personality than kinship based models of person described as being predominant in Asia.

Laderman argues that Malays perceive of illness less as natural or supernatural and more as "usual", "unusual" or associated with inner winds, their determinations having more to do with "incidence than suspected etiology". Healing rituals coexist which attend to both externalistic and internalistic causes of illness (Young 1976). Rituals centered on external spirit/ghosts entail scripts which index and modify tensions within the social structure. Other rituals recognize one's personal disposition which resists being subdued by the exigencies of their life world. Individual resistance is recognized as inherent within a world where social status and pedigree constrain one's public behavior.

Two issues struck me while reading Laderman's essay. First, I could not help but wonder how socioeconomic and political changes have influenced the popularity and transformation of the healing traditions described inclusive of those which are sociocentric (spirit) and individual (inner wind) centered.[39] Second, discussion about the range of interpretations of inner winds within Malay culture is absent. Do all people consider these winds to be inherent personality constructs one is born with? Or do some people perceive them to be personality problems associated with social relations or external forces which invade or overwhelm people thereby becoming established within the body? How does this affect the "social aesthetics"(Brenneis 1987) by which members of a local audience evaluate the coherence and effectiveness of possession performances?

It might be worth attempting a deconstructionist analysis of the play of winds Laderman so vividly describes.[40] Lynch (1990), in his discussion of emotions as interpretations, points out that emotions have no single authoritative meaning and take on meaning in a play of difference. Following Derrida, he draws attention to multiple and provisional interpretations of texts caught up in a play of difference with other texts. Does this approach have relevance to a study of possession? My own experiences interviewing kin, neighbors, and onlookers attending a variety of possession rituals in South India suggest that it does. Interviews revealed a variety of interpretations of the meaning of a particular possession event related to both the representations of the spirit forms embodied and the life narrative of the possessed. As Adams has described of Sherpas and Brodwin of Haitians, concurrent medicoreligious traditions influence multi-level interpretations about what is taking place. The genre of Malay ritual theater may well involve a play of differences where form is given to psychosocial feelings as an idiom of distress, inherent aspects of the self are acknowledged and instantiated, catharsis experienced by some, insight by others, and the enactment of resistance by still others.

Laderman's research on *sakit berangin*, illnesses interpreted as signs of a blocked disposition, documents Malay recognition of individual variation in temperament and the propensity to refer to inner states in "personalized terms." Recognized is a spirit which lies outside relations and practices of power, a spirit which actively constitutes the self as much as social roles, conventions, and cultivated dispositions. While considerable anthropological analysis has focused on habitus (Bourdieu 1977; Maus 1935) and biopower (Foucault 1980), Laderman draws attention to agency in the form of an active spirit (inner winds) flowing within the body, a spirit which "may range from a mild breeze to hurricane force."

Essays by Adams and Laderman prompted me to reflect on indigenous constructs of self and personality as they relate to cultural models of disposition and "constitution" articulated by healing systems.[41] Discursive as well as comparative study of such constructs which attend to both issues of agency and productive power is called for within ethnomedicine.[42]

Three additional contributions of Laderman's essay may be highlighted. First, attention is directed to the study of vulnerability.[43] Laderman's analysis of *Semangat* (spirit of life) places emphasis on the felt need to protect one's spirit from shock, and to guard it like an inner fortress from external forces of disruption. Images of the self as permeable are common in Asia and beyond (e.g. LittleJohn 1963). They underlie much preventive and promotive health behavior interlinking internalistic and externalistic causes of illness as well as territories of self. Such perceptions influence, among other things, emotional response to misfortune (e.g. Kapferer 1983; Rhodes 1983; Wikan 1989).

Second, Laderman calls attention to a cultural recognition that a state of non-fulfillment leaves one vulnerable to illness. This theme is prominent in ethnographies of tribal groups in Northern Malaysia such as the Semai (Robarchek 1977) and Chewong (Howell 1981). These ethnographies describe vulnerability to illness as associated with frustrated desires which make desire a dangerous state. Laderman identifies a new dimension of non-fulfillment related to notions of self and constitution. Third, she identifies harmony between patient and practitioner as an important individualistic dimension of traditional healing.[44] This dimension is commonly overlooked by sociocentric analysis of healing which places emphasis on how one labeled deviant is reintegrated into his/her social group (Nichter and Nordstrom 1989).

Trawick's study of a sole ayurvedic practitioner's unsolicited discourse on cancer differs from the other papers presented although it shares with Taylor's paper an attentiveness to the metamedical aspects of healing discourse as commentary on transformations in the social order. It represents an important new trend in ethnomedicine addressing some of the reflexive concerns of the postmodern movement without leading the reader into a hall of mirrors. Trawick attends to the voice and intentions of her teacher, Mahadeva Iyer, reporting on both the referential and indexical dimensions of his lectures to her as student as well as representative of an "other" he wishes to address. In this sense she provides us a collaborative ethnography.

Mahadeva Iyer's use of medical discourse for social commentary was strikingly familiar to me. Indeed, both the form and content of Mahadeva Iyer's lectures complemented discourse I routinely received in a different region of South India from two Brahman ayurvedic practitioners. Living with these practitioners for extended periods of time in the 1970s, I found that they routinely engaged in metacommunication extending ayurvedic schema in their discussions of a full range of life problems. One of these practitioners was renown for his wit and ability to explain problems in terms of philosophical principles brought down to earth in the form of analogies to humors and illness states. He would often be invited to join a group which had been convened to settle temple disputes in neighboring villages. In this capacity, he would assist the community in their consultations with an astrologer by both posing questions and interpreting divinations in terms of an ayurvedic framework. The latter was made explicit to the audience through the use of Sanskrit verse (*sloka*) followed by cultural common sense posed in terms of body humors and the ecological principles upon which they are based. Like Mahadeva Iyer, he shifted between frames of reference from the medico-religious to the micropolitical and poetic-ludic. My reason for noting this is to suggest that Mahadeva Iyer's discourse on cancer needs to be appreciated in terms of a more general style of reasoning which is deeply rooted in Brahmanic culture and ayurvedic tradition.

Mahadeva Iyer does more than employ analogical reasoning in his discourse on cancer as commentary on modernization. Cancer is not merely cloaked in metaphor in the sense described by Sontag (1977), although cancer is used throughout South Asia as a metaphor for the invasive activities of western capitalism and the ill effects of a western lifestyle.[45] Mahadeva Iyer's efforts to extend the ayurvedic paradigm arise out of a deep sense of moral order, a desire to heal a breach of meaning placing the world at risk. His sense of moral order strikes me as that acknowledged by Toulman (1982) in his discussion of the need for a moral cosmology in science.

The core of Mahadeva's discourse revolves around two sets of coextensive scripts, one for explaining disequilibrium in the universe and the other disease within the body. The first is inspired by Samkhya philosophy and addresses the relationship between spirit and matter. The second set extends an ayurvedic model of disease based upon the principles of humoral balance, appropriate nourishment, removal of impurities, and unobstructed flow within the body. Cancer is associated with a state of overnourishment, overgrowness, and accumulation leading to stagnation. Mahadeva's discourse moves between references to the body, ecology, and the ways of the universe proceeding much like Bateson's (1972) efforts to foster stage three learning through layers of multiple comparison. Trawick provides not only a detailed description of Mahadeva's application of an ayurvedic model to explain cancer, but an analysis of the multidimensionality of his communication style and efforts to instantiate his world view inclusive of code switching.[46]

Implicitly challenged by Mahadeva is a survival of the fittest mentality.[47] The moral of the lectures is that when one being (tissue, individual, nation) becomes too big at the expense of others or blocks normal channels of flow/exchange, the entire system becomes diseased and may perish. Foreign bodies must beware that they do not grow so large at the expense of the host that they cause the latter to die, in turn sealing their own fate. Health is to be fostered through appropriate practices of consumption which engender softness and fluidity. In content, these practices appear to be similar to those described by Taylor as incorporated in traditional Rwandan health culture. However, in the case of ayurveda, health requires veneration not of external gods (who are honored by sacrifice), but of internal gods constituting universal processes within the body (e.g. digestion).[48]

In the end, Mahadeva's lectures provide us with a native philosopher's warning about encroachment, commentary on the events of the times, and an attempt to construct a pluralistic philosophy which encompasses the "other." Like Charaka, the formulator of ayurveda, Mahadeva encompasses rather than rejects the other, despite occasional references which allude to militant nationalism. He speaks of encroachment as a process existing on multiple planes, from world systems capitalism to forest conservation to a Brahman warning against a mixing of caste dharma.[49] For Mahadeva, cancer is not a metaphor or an isolated disease entity. Rather, it is a sign of a larger disequilibrium which the ayurvedic practitioner observes and contextualizes through a process of diagnosis and inference.

Trawick's reflexive examination of her own presence on the process of Mahadeva's narration and production of knowledge is notable. She leaves us with a powerful message. Arriving in the field to gather symbolic capital in the form of field notes which will bring profit to herself, she gains consciousness not only of her potential role in colonialism, but the way in which she is being used by the "other." Trawick becomes cognizant of not only what her informants have to say about a life world she is observing pen in hand, but also what they have to say to her as witness, representative, and conduit of voices which call out to be heard.

CONCLUSION

The essays in this volume were chosen to illustrate the range of research activities engaged in as ethnomedical inquiry. They exemplify diverse trends in the study of ethnomedicine, a diversity which leads us into the 1990s with new research questions, levels of analysis, and issues related to methodology and the production of knowledge. No one paradigm dominates ethnomedicine and a fair amount of pyrrhonic skepticism leads those engaged in ethnomedicine to consider alternative theoretical perspectives.[50] Insights from critical theory to postmodernism, epidemiology to hermeneutics, cultural knowledge to the anthropology of self and the emotions have influenced the researchers whose work is represented in this volume. Linkages between diverse research approaches are possible in an intellectual environment sensitive to the limitations of theoretical closure and responsive to the multidimensionality of human experience. No set of issues makes this clearer than those addressed by ethnomedicine.

NOTES

1. The issues discussed in Anderson's essay are also relevant to the study of side effects, a subject largely overlooked in medical anthropology. How are side effects determined? Looking at the United States, side effects are sometimes ascertained on the basis of clinical evidence, but often on the basis of self report by a sample of people receiving payments for participation in drug self-report trials. To what extent is gender, age, class, lifestyle and culture taken into account when assessing self report data?

2. Just as social and cultural factors play a role in placing a population at risk and effecting pathogen transmission, such factors influence the experience of suffering, pain, and treatment response.

3. Anderson's agenda for establishing treatment efficacy fails to recognize that for a significant number of illnesses, signs and symptoms are not clearly visible nor testable by simple diagnostic procedures. Moreover, individuals often have multiple health problems in the third world contexts in which I have worked, not to speak of nutritional deficiencies, parasite loads, etc. The clinical approach Anderson advocates compartmentalizes disease and requires a fair amount of experimental control.

4. Anderson might want to consider the use of multiple methods to test his own claim that questionnaires "reduce the likelihood of unconscious bias." On the use of multiple methods see my comments at the end of Section One of the Commentary regarding triangulation and increasing the trustworthiness of data.

5. Moerman (1983b) points out in his critique of double blind studies that they are based on several assumptions which are not tested. Stein (1985) lists these as follows 1) placebo effects are constant; 2) there is a difference in kind between placebo healing (thought to be psychologic) and pharmacologic healing (physiologic); 3) placebo and pharmacologic healing are concurrent and additive rather than interactive; and 4) randomizing treatment and blinding participants eliminates concurrent states of cure— even though practitioners are never randomized, only blinded.

6. A design not explicitly discussed by Anderson, but which might prove useful in studying treatment interventions is the lagged control design. In lagged control studies, half a population is given a treatment at one point in time and the other half form a control group. After a period of time, the second group is given the same treatment as group one and in the same way. Secular changes are noted. To increase the kind of rigor Anderson is calling for, consensus analysis (Romney, Weller and Batchelder 1986; Weller 1984) could be conducted wherein ratings of efficacy by illness attribute could be considered by group and across groups.

7. To the best of my knowledge this type of study has rarely been employed in ethnomedical studies. In the West, controversy was generated when a researcher posed as a patient in a psychiatric clinic (Rosenhan 1973).

8. This is in addition to what Moerman (1983b) has described as the metaphoric meaning of a treatment as it affects placebo response, and Devisch's (1983) description of efficacy in terms of the conciliation of existential paradoxes during the drama of treatment.

9. Wynne (1989) has provided an interesting case study illustrating how a clinical trial may impose an order and a limit on a respondent's experience skewing outcome data.

10. Alder and Hammett (1973), in a constructive yet critical article on double blind studies, emphasize that whether an agent is given in individual or group settings may have a significant impact on outcome.

11. One could argue that samples selected for case control studies of traditional therapies should be chosen on the basis of emic (e.g. humoral) criteria.

12. Standard ayurvedic formula, for example, are mixed and customized to the patient whose bodily signs are read by the skilled practitioner. Depending on the body's response, a practitioner might decide that the body is not yet ready to respond to the treatment offered and insist that the patient take a course of blood purifying or digestion enhancing medications. He might also change the "vehicle medication" offered to the patient as the carrier of the instrumental medication.

13. Weller has been active in the testing of nominal data generators inclusive of free lists, true-false questions, triads, pile sorts, paired comparisons, etc. For a review of other anthropologists who have employed these methods, see Bernard, et al. (1986). Nominal data generators are presently being used in research which employs multi-dimensional scaling, correspondence, and cluster analysis.

14. For intracultural variation in popular and expert systems of medical knowledge, see Garro (1986) as well as Linde (1987) on explanatory systems in oral life stories.

15. As Linde (1981) has noted, a narrative is often built around deviation from the expected. What is elaborated as well as downplayed or omitted in a narrative provides clues of cultural models which are largely taken for granted (Quinn and Holland 1981). What is said, as well as what is not said, and what is elaborated when telling an illness narrative in particular contexts is important data for the anthropologist studying ethnomedicine.

16. Adherents of critical multiplism call for the simultaneous testing of multiple hypothesis generated by different theoretical perspectives. Supporters of this position would claim that to falsify a single hypothesis generated by one theory is to engage in weak inference. Favored is multivariate approaches to data analysis.

17. Two different approaches to the study of voices are found in the works of Goffman (1974) and Bakhtin (1968, 1984).

18. Morsy's (1978) study of the relative contribution of gender, class, and power on the incidence of a cultural representation of distress in Egypt illustrates the necessity of contextualizing variables and looking beyond simple associations.

19. In need of study are ways in which traditional medical systems frame their own perceptions of risk, factors influencing illness distribution and transmission, and so forth. Sperber (1984) suggests that an agenda for the social sciences is the epidemiological study of representations (e.g. of illness) paying credence to dispositions, susceptibilities, and why some representations are more contagious than others at particular times. Sperber's essay, while thought provoking, needs to be read critically especially in relation to his concept of representations as having psychological properties. More broadly called for is an epidemiology of ideological practice sensitive to those social processes which serve to legitimate illness/disease identities.

20. My use of the term narrative here is general and not defined in relation to the structure of narrative described by Labov (1972). It encompasses stories of affliction and suffering which may be framed in several ways at one point in time, or over time through the use of proreferences.

21. In economies that are market dominated, but not market organized, there is an incomplete integration of peasants into capitalist economy and these people are caught between the exigencies of two sets of social relations (Greenberg 1981; Meillassoux 1981; Nash 1979; Taussig 1980; Wolf 1966). In such contexts, capitalist penetration has not entailed the destruction of local modes of productions and contingent patterns of social relations, as much as offered counter directives. It could be argued that this characterization applies to much of rural Peru. Glass-Coffin provides us a vivid description of the redistributive economics of a north coastal city. State level mercantilism is "endemic" and most economic activities are practiced outside of the law. Given migration patterns into Peruvian cities, I can not help but wonder to what extent various segments of the urban population are fully integrated into capitalist economy and how various stages of integration correlate with such phenomena as *dano*. Are social ties with rural kin maintained when one migrates to the city, how do social relations with kin change over time, are the values of cooperation described in other Andean ethnographies (e.g. Brush 1977) valorized? If so how does this relate to issues of identity associated with *dano* narratives?

22. As reported elsewhere in Central and South America, displays of hostility are hidden and strategies are employed to deflect attention away from one's shortcomings (O'Nell 1981).

23. This model was first proposed by Foster (1965). Other anthropologists have pointed out that Foster's model smacks of cultural idealism (Greenberg 1989; Gregory 1975; Taussig 1980). Depictions of peasants living in towns which constitute isolated moral universes have overlooked linkages between local communities and larger systems as well as the social relations entailed in adapting to changing socioeconomic conditions associated with scarcity (Smith 1977). Glass-Coffin's essay is sensitive to the latter issue.

24. The social relations and narrative structure of illness stories are important areas for future research. Kleinman (1989) has called attention to the empathetic witness role played by those who listen to illness stories enabling informants to tell (retell) stories of self which foster coherence and reduce suffering. Work by Riesmann (1990) has drawn attention to structural features of life narratives and the role they serve in the meaning process.

25. I have no idea whether other healing modalities exist, but as a general principle analysis of idioms of distress and coexisting therapy systems need to pay credence to deconstructionist concerns about the interplay between coexisting texts (Nichter 1981a).

26. In the story of Mari presented, did others really accept that her husband's behavior was entirely a result of *dano* associated with the jealousy of her mother-in-law ? Just how successful was Mari's new narrative (following her healing ceremony) in countering gossip? While the healing ceremony of Don Enrique provided Mari an illness narrative which reduced her personal suffering, did it result in a change in her social relations? Also in need of examination are local perceptions of risk to *dano*? Is risk only associated with external factors such as the jealousy of another, or is it also associated with personal proclivity in the form of strength and weakness? Studies of sorcery, witchcraft, possession states, etc., need to pay more attention to ethnotheories of emotion as they influence perceptions of strength and weakness.

27. Like Taylor, Brodwin points to the moral dimensions of medical pluralism at a time when emergent religious forms and transformations in established forms are taking place in the context of social change. The growth of religious groups is often linked to healing activities which give new meaning to sickness. The expansion of the Pentecostal movement in Haiti has directly been associated with conversions which occur at the time of illness (Conway 1978). Challenges to conventional healing modalities constitutes a conversion strategy. Conversion becomes a healing modality open to individuals as well as families.

28. Lakoff (1987) has argued that we organize our knowledge through idealized cognitive models which constitute prototype complexes as products of organization. Multiple structuring principles exist from propositional formats and image schema to metaphoric and metonymic mappings. Quinn and Holland (1987) reserve the term "model" for the entire prototypical event sequence which constitutes a "cultural model." A propositional— or image— schema is then a reconceptualization of all or part of a cultural model for some specific cognitive purpose.

29. Nuckolls' essay raises issues beyond those associated with the content of illness narratives. The interactional process (e.g. turn taking, interruption patterns) and structure of different forms of divination/diagnosis (as genre) needs to be studied in terms of power relations and instantiation.

30. On the "open force field" nature of the conception of self in traditional Africa, see Beattie (1980).

31. This is somewhat analogous to Buddhists accepting a paradigm of theodicy while being enmeshed in a world where disease may be cured and demons chased away (Tambiah 1977).

32. Appadurai (1986:15,57) has drawn attention to range and variability in the sharing of assumptions associated with exchange situations. Degrees of value coherence may be highly variable from situation to situation. Mediation between "regimes of value" needs to be explored. For example, wealth derived from capitalist transactions may be transformed through ritual activities. Deities (ancestors, etc.) once offered such wealth may uphold precapitalist principles of reciprocity by returning wealth with interest in the form of blessings of increased prosperity in its multiple forms (Greenberg 1991; Parry and Bloch 1989; Taussig 1980). Health and fertility, in addition to short term prosperity, constitute "proof" that such forms of mediation work.

33. Taylor might want to examine the frequency with which various types of households in North and South Rwanda employ different therapy options by illness, age, and gender. He might also want to establish the extent to which the practice and discourse of the healer he describes is representative of an emergent ideology within Rwanda.

34. Distinct from anthropological studies of medical systems which end by describing them as epiphenomena of political economic conditions, Adams calls attention to medical systems as productive of truths and raises the questions: how, for whom, and by whom did they achieve their dominance?

35. Examples of how the body came to be seen as a text in which corruption was made visible are provided by Gillman (1985, 1986).

36. Control of the body by the sentient mind persists as a theme in Tibetan Buddhism despite Buddhism's ultimate attempt to overcome subject-object dualism.

37. One wonders whether specific forms of spirit possession do not serve a variety of purposes for different participants. In Kessler's (1977) examination of Main Putri performance in Kelantan Malaysia, about half of eighty odd performances were linked to people having strained or ambiguous social positions (1977:302). Most of these cases involved women, supporting Lewis' (1971) social stress/political powerlessness theory of possession. Laderman's study urges us ask what other factors are associated with the ritual performance. To address this question adequately requires longitudinal data which provide insights into the pre-and post-ritual social relations of participants and concerned others. Both contexts of disequilibrium and articulations of "inherent qualities of self" need to be addressed.

38. Main Purti rituals are structured to enable one's personality to be celebrated. In South India, I suspect that sociocentric and egocentric aspects of self merge in possession rituals where a person chooses and identifies with the form of a possessing spirit. This choice may be unconsciously influenced by either the content of a story script or resonance with attributes of the spirit form. For example, when I first studied membership and spirit form selection in the Siri cult of South Kanara, I attempted to examine the congruence between cult member's personal narratives and the story scripts of multiple spirit forms. While there appeared to be an overlap of life and spirit scripts in some cases, in others attraction to the spirit form struck me as resonant with the personality irrespective of the life narrative the member. See Claus (1975) for a description of the Siri cult.

39. This is not to say that Laderman is not concerned with how socioeconomic and political change has effected Malaysian healing traditions (Laderman 1981). For a broader perspective of spirit possession in Malaysia one might read in addition to Laderman the work of Aihwa Ong. Ong (1983, 1987) has investigated spirit possession in Malaysia as a form of resistance to capitalist discipline by women factory workers. Ong suggests that spirit possession constitutes what Scott (1985) has termed a "weapon of the weak." Described is possession as resistance and indirect retaliation. She notes, however, that a cultural belief that women are vulnerable to spirit possession operates as a sanction against self and group assertion. Biopower in the form of discourse on occupational safety is further extended by factory administrators such that women workers who are possessed more than twice are dismissed. Ong's study raises questions about the social availability and decentering of genres of self assertion and protest which involve possession. On this issue also see Constantinides (1982).

40. I am by no means suggesting that Laderman abandon her research on expressions of autonomy and agency, or insight derived through ritual performance. Derrida's deconstructionist approach, while useful to the study of possession, has its own limitations. As Sangren (1990a) has noted, Derrida leans toward poststructualist idealism in his arguments against a metaphysics of presence wherein the human subject could be a source of creative productive power. This is important for studies of spirit possession in the postmodern world. Such studies need to explore the extent to which resistance is related to a subjectivity which is external to power. As Sangren (1990b) notes, it is here that Foucault's arguments about "local context," "centers of discourse," and "technologies of power" fail to resolve the problem of agency and resistance. In Foucault's writing, nothing appears to be "external" to power's discourses. The body is passive, actuated, and transformed by social practices always linked up to the organization of power (Dreyfus and Rabinow 1982). At issue is whether or not, or to what extent, spirit and body exist separate from if not prior to their signification by means of discursive practice.

41. I do not mean to infer that the study of such constructs will yield consistent self representations which exist in culture. Along with fellow South Asianists Ewing (1990) and McHugh (1989), I would support a characterization of multiple inconsistent self representations which are emergent and context dependant. While a cultural model of constitution reveals much about ideology, no single model of self is adequate to describe how selves are experienced or represented in any culture. What cultural models of constitution may help us understand is "a universal semiotic process by

which people manage inconsistency" (Ewing 1990:253). Laderman's study of inner winds illustrates how continuity is maintained in the context of inconsistent person-self representations.

42. Laderman draws attention to agency in her study of inner winds as innate dispositions. Theories of disposition and physiomorphism can also be used as a means of state control. An example of body constitution knowledge as productive power is provided by Gilman's (1986) study of the iconography of prostitution in late nineteenth-century art and medicine as well as Schwartz's (1986) brief history of American ideas of somatotype during this period. These "truths" were employed in the American legal system by expert witnesses such as Lambroso who argued that criminal tendencies were hereditary and could be detected on the basis of skull characteristics. His gaze was not directed at the skull alone. Inspection of the feet revealed those women most apt to be prostitutes. Both criminals and prostitutes were held to be more "primitive" members of the species (Gould 1981). Kretschmer (1925) adapted Jung's notion of archetypes to somatypes arguing that different kinds of unconscious minds might be correlated to sets of physical traits.

43. Massard (1988) complements Laderman's study of vulnerability among Malay adults with a study of vulnerability among children. His study addresses the role notions of vulnerability play in child socialization. Highlighted are ontological lessons learned through illness.

44. See also Tan's (1989) discussion of *Hiyang* in the Philippines and MacCauley's (1984) study of healing in Bali.

45. In the west, cancer has been associated with defective modernization and over-civilization as well as the failure of technology to master nature (Patterson 1987; Sontag 1977). In India, cancer is often associated with adulteration (e.g., food, chemicals). Cancer also constitutes a sign of an age marked by corruption and moral disintegration (Chattoo 1990) and the moral condition of an inner self visible on the skin (Parry 1989).

46. Hesterman (1978) and Parry (1985) note that in India those who recite the Veda (reproduce truth) often do so as a means of deriving authority to make pronouncements about conduct in everyday life. Knowledge of the text and the ability to recite it provides one with power and authority, although the content of the Veda has little to say about the "dharma" of everyday life. In contrast to Goody's (1977) notion that oral traditions restrict spontaneity, Parry argues that they are malleable to the requirements of daily life. Code switching (from local languages to Sanskritic Verse) legitimates the power of inference.

47. A survival of the fittest ideology underscores the moral discourse of the American health movement of the 1980's. See, for example, Stein (1982), Gillick (1984), and Nichter and Nichter (1991).

48. My own teacher of ayurveda was quite explicit in his view that "gods" and rituals associated with them constituted a repository of wisdom about universal truths. These could be deciphered (decoded) as science by those knowledgeable of ayurvedic principles. Offerings to gods reproduced knowledge which was embodied by participants.

49. Mahadeva Iyer's discourse on cancer and the order of the universe is highly Brahmanic and stands in stark contrast to Trawick's (1988) work on voices of protest and outrage which penetrate the songs of the oppressed low castes. While Mahadeva engages in code switching (invoking Sanskritic verse) in part to legitimate his claims, defiance of social codes is employed by low caste women in songs about death which portray their fragmented world. Trawick has described these women as lifting their voices if not their fists to their injustice and to rise above defilement to embrace a sense of wholeness. Solace is achieved through the genre of song by these women, just as solace is achieved by Mahadeva through his lectures. In both cases, the presence of Trawick as representative of an "other" influences the production of knowledge.

50. Pyrrhonic skepticism may be characterized as the position that one is not convinced of the absolute validity of any propositions or theories, while remaining open to the possibility of being convinced momentarily. This stance gives all points of view serious attention, but suggests that all theories overstate claims in order to attract attention. See Park (1985) for a more complete discussion.

REFERENCES CITED

Adams, Vincanne
   1988   Modes of Production and Medicine: An Examination of the Theory in Light of Sherpa Medical Traditionalism. Social Science and Medicine 27(5):505–513.

Adler, Herbert M. and Van Buren O. Hammett
  1973   The Doctor–Patient Relationship Revisited: An Analysis of the Placebo Effect. Annals of Internal Medicine 78:595–598.
Appadurai, Arjun
  1986   Commodities and the Politics of Value. *In* The Social Life of Things. Arjun Appadurai, ed. Cambridge University Press: Cambridge.
Atkinson, Jane Monnig
  1987   The Effectiveness of Shamans in an Indonesian Ritual. American Anthropologist 89:342–355.
Audy, J. and F. Dunn
  1964   Health and Disease. In Human Ecology. F. Sargent (ed) Boston: Houghton Mifflin.
Aziz, Barbara
  1976   Reincarnation Reconsidered—or the Reincarnate Lama as Shaman. *In* Spirit Possession in the Nepal Himalayas. John Hitchcock and Rex Jones (eds.). Warminster: Aris and Phillips.
Bajaj, Jatinder
  1990   Francis Bacon, the First Philosopher of Modern Science: A Non–Western View. In Ashis Nandy (ed) Science. Hegemony and Violence. Bombay: New Delhi. Pp. 3–67.
Bakhtin, Mikhail
  1968   Rabelais and His World. Helene Iswalsky, trans. Cambridge, MA: MIT Press.
  1984   Problems of Dostvevsky's Poetics. Caryl Emerson, ed. and trans. Minneapolis: University of Minnesota Press.
Barthes, Roland
  1987   The Rustle of Language. *In* The Rustle of Language, Translated by Richard Howard. Berkeley: University of California Press.
Bateson, Gregory
  1972   Steps to an Ecology of the Mind. New York: Ballantine Books.
Beattie, John
  1980   Review Article: Representations of the Self in Traditional Africa. Africa 59(3):313–320.
Bernard, R., Pelto, P., Johnson, A., Werner, J., Ember, C.,
Boster, J., Kosakoff, A. and A. Romney
  1986   The Construction of Primary Data in Cultural Anthropology. Current Anthropology 27(4):382–396.
Bourdieu, Pierre
  1977   Outline for a Theory of Practice. Cambridge: Cambridge University Press.
  1982   The Economics of Linguistic Exchange. Social Science Information 16: 645–668.
Brenneis, Donald
  1987   Performing Passions: Aesthetics and Politics in an Occasionally Equalitarian Community. American Ethnologist 14: 236–50.
Brodwin, Paul
  1990   The Body Possessed: Somatic Metaphors and Religious Classification. Paper presented at the Annual Meetings of the American Ethnological Association, Atlanta, Georgia.
Browner, C., B. Ortiz de Montellano, and A. Rubel
  1988   A Methodology for Cross–Cultural Ethnomedical Research. Current Anthropology 29:681–702.
Bruner, Jerome
  1986   Actual Minds, Possible Worlds. Cambridge: Harvard University Press.
Brush, Stephen
  1977   Mountain, Field, and Family: the Economy and Human Ecology of an Andean Valley. Philadelphia: University of Pennsylvania Press.
Caplan, Ronald
  1989   The Commodification of American Health Care. Social Science and Medicine 28(11):1139–1148.
Carrithers, M.
  1990   Is Anthropology Art or Science. Current Anthropology 31:263–272.
Chattoo, Sangeata
  1990   A Sociological Study of Certain Aspects of Disease and Death: A Case Study of Muslims in Kashmir. Ph.D. thesis, University of Delhi, Dept. of Sociology.

Claus, Peter
  1975   The Siri Myth and Ritual. Ethnology 14:47–58.
Comaroff, Jean
  1985   Body of Power, Spirit of Resistance. Chicago: University of Chicago Press.
Canguilhem, G.
  1978   On the Normal and the Pathological. Trans. Carolyn R. Fawcett. Dorcrecht: Reidel Press.
Connerton, Paul
  1989   How Societies Remember. Cambridge: Cambridge University Press.
Constantinides, Pamela
  1982   Women's Spirit Possession and Urban Adaptation. In Women United, Women Divided.
          Patricia Caplan and Janet Bujra, eds. Pp. 185–205. Bloomington: Indiana University Press.
Conway, Frederick
  1978   Pentacostalism in the Context of Haitian Religion and Health Practice. Ph.D. Dissertation,
          American University, Washington D.C.
Cook, T.
  1985   Postpositivist Critical Multiplism. *In* Social Science and Social Policy. R.L. Shotland and M.M.
          Mark, eds. Beverly Hills: Sage, 21–62.
Crandon, Libby
  1983   Why Susto? Ethnologist 12(3):153–167.
Csordas, Thomas and Arthur Kleinman
  1990   The Therapeutic Process. In Thomas Johnson and Carolyn Sargent (ed) Medical Anthropol-
          ogy: Contemporary Theory and Method. New York: Praeger. Pp. 11–25.
de Montaigne, M.
  1958   On the Power of the Imagination. *In* Essays. Hammondsworth, UK: Penguin. Pp. 36–48.
Devisch, Renaat
  1983   Beyond a Structural Approach to Therapeutic Efficacy. *In* The Future of Structuralism. Jarich
          Oosten and Arie de Ruijter eds. Göttingen: Ed. Herodot.
Dreyfus, Hubert and Paul Rabinow
  1982   Michel Foucault: Beyond Structuralism and Hermeneutics. Chicago: University of Chicago
          Press.
Dunn, F. and C.R. Janes
  1986   Introduction: Medical Anthropology and Epidemiology. In Anthropology and Epidemiology.
          Craig Janes et. al (eds.) Dordrecht: Reidel Pub. Pp. 3–34.
Durkin–Longley, M.
  1984   Multiple Therapeutic Use in Urban Nepal. Social Science and Medicine 19(8):866–872.
Early, F.
  1982   The Logic of Well Being: Therapeutic Narrative in Cairo, Egypt. Social Science and Medicine
          16:1491–97.
Etkin, Nina
  1988a   Ethnopharmacology: Biobehavioral Approaches in the Anthropological Study of Indigenous
          Medicines. Annual Review of Anthropology 17:23–42.
  1988b   Cultural Constructions of Efficacy. *In* The Context of Medicines in Developing Countries. S.
          van der Geest and S. Whyte, ed. Holland: Kluwer.
Ewing, Katherine
  1990   The Illusion of Wholeness: Culture, Self, and the Experience of Inconsistency. Ethos
          18(3):251–278.
Fabrega, Horatio, Jr.
  1974   Disease and Social Behavior: An Interdisciplinary Perspective. Cambridge: MIT Press.
  1975   Illness and Shamanistic Curing in Zinancantan: An Ethnomedical Analysis. Cambridge, MA:
          MIT Press.
  1975   The Need for an Ethnomedical Science. Science 189: 969–75.
Farmer, Paul
  1990   Sending Sickness: Sorcery, Politics, and Changing Concepts of AIDS in Rural Haiti. Medical
          Anthropology Quarterly, 4(1):6–27.
Floras, J., M. Hassan, P. Seyer, et al.
  1981   Cuff and Ambulatory Blood Pressure in Subjects with Essential Hypertension. Lancet
          2:107–109.

Foster, George
   1965   Peasant Society and the Image of Limited Good. American Anthropologist 67: 293–315.
Foster, George and Barbara Gallatin Andersen
   1978   Medical Anthropology. New York: Wiley.
Foucault, M.
   1972   The Archeology of Knowledge and the Discourse of Language. New York: Pantheon.
   1980   Power/Knowledge. Colin Gordon (ed) New York: Pantheon.
Garro, Linda
   1986   Intracultural Variation in Folk Medical Knowledge: A Comparison Between Curers and Non
           Curers. American Anthropologist 88:351–370.
   1988   Commentary. C. Browner, B. Ortiz de Montellano and A. Rubel. A Methodology for Cross–
           Cultural Ethnomedical Research. Current Anthropology 29:705–706.
Gillick, M.R.
   1984   Health Promotion, Jogging and the Pursuit of the Moral Life. Journal of Health Politics, Policy
           and Law 9:369–387.
Gilman, Sander
   1985   Difference and Pathology: Stereotypes of Sexuality, Race, and Madness. Ithaca: Cornell Uni-
           versity Press.
   1986   Black Bodies, White Bodies: Towards an Iconography of Female Sexuality in Late Nineteenth
           Century Art, Medicine and Literature. In "Race", Writing, and Difference. Henry Lewis Gates,
           ed. Chicago: University of Chicago Press.
Goffman, Irving
   1974   Frame Analysis. New York: Harper and Row.
Goody, Jack
   1977   The Domestification of the Savage Mind. Cambridge: Cambridge University Press.
Gould, S. J.
   1981   The Mismeasure of Man. New York: W. W. Norton Co.
Greenberg, James
   1981   Santiago's Sword: Chatino Peasant Religion and Economics. Berkeley: University of Califor-
           nia Press.
   1989   Blood Ties: Life and Violence in Rural Mexico. University of Arizona Press.
   1991   Capital, Ritual and Boundaries of the Closed Cooperate Community. Unpublished manu-
           script.
Gregory, J.
   1975   Image of Limited Good, or Expectation of Reciprocity. Current Anthropology 16(1):73–92.
Gumperz, John
   1982   Discourse Strategies. Cambridge: Cambridge University Press.
Heesterman, J.
   1978   Veda and Dharma. In The Concept of Duty in South Asia. W.D. O'Flaherty and J. D. Derrett
           (eds) New Dehli: Vikas Pub.
Howell, S.
   1981   Rules not Words. In Indigenous Psychologies: The Anthropology of Self. Andrew Lock, ed. Pp.
           133–144. London: Academic Press.
Illich, Ivan
   1975   Medical Nemessis. London: Marion Bayars.
Kapferer, Bruce
1983   A Celebration of Demons. Bloomington: Indiana University Press.
Kessler, C.
   1977   Conflict and Sovereignty in Kelantanese Malay Spirit Seances. In Case Studies in Spirit Posses-
           sion. Vincent Crapanzano and Vivian Garrison, eds. Pp. 295–331., New York: John Wiley.
Kleinman, Arthur
   1986   Social Origins of Distress and Disease: Depression Neurasthenia and Pain in Modern China.
           New Haven: Yale University Press.
   1989   The Illness Narratives. Suffering Healing and the Human Condition. New York: Basic Books.
Kretschmer, E.
   1925   Physique and Character. London: Harcourt, Brace and Company.

Labov, W.
1972   Sociolinguistic Patterns. Philadelphia: University of Pennsylvania Press.

Laderman, Carol
1981   The Politics of Healing in Malaysia. Studies in Third World Societies 16: 143–158.
1988   Wayward Winds: Malay Archetypes, and Theory of Personality in the Context of Shamanism. Social Science and Medicine 27(8):799–810.

Lakoff, George
1987   Women, Fire and Dangerous Things. Berkeley: University of California Press.

Last, Murray
1981   The Importance of Knowing About Not Knowing. Social Science and Medicine 15b:387–392.

Laughlin, K., D. Sherrard, and L. Fisher
1980   Comparison of Clinic and Home Blood Pressure Levels in Essential Hypertension and Variables Associated with Clinic–home Differences. J. Chron. Dis. 33:197–206.

Lerman, C., D. Brody, T. Hui, C. Lazaro, et al.
1989   The White Coat Hypertension Response: Prevalence and Predictors. Journal of General Internal Medicine.

Lewin, Ellen
1979   The Nobility of Suffering: Illness and Misfortune Among Latin American Immigrant Women. Anthropology Quarterly 52(3):152–158.

Lewis, I. M.
1971   Ecstatic Religion: An Anthropological Study of Spirit Possession and Shamanism. Harmondsworth: Penquin Books.

Lincoln, Y. and E. Guba
1985   Naturalistic Inquiry. Newbury Park: Sage.

Linde, Charlotte
1987   Explanatory Systems in Oral Life Stories. *In* Dorothy Holland and Naomi Quinn (eds.) Cultural Models in Language and Thought. New York: Cambridge University Press.

LittleJohn, James
1963   Temne Space. Anthropological Quarterly 36(1):1–17.

Lock, Margret
1984   Licorice in Leviathan: The Medicalization of Care for the Japanese Elderly. Culture, Medicine and Psychiatry 8:121–139.
1990   Rationalization of Japanese Herbal Medication: The Hegemony of Orchestrated Pluralism. Human Organization 49(1):41–47.

Lynch, Owen
1990   The Social Construction of Emotion in India. In Owen Lynch (ed) Divine Passions. Berkeley: University of California Press. Pp. 3–34.

Massard, Josiane
1988   Doctoring by Go–Between: Aspects of Health Care for Malay Children. Social Science and Medicine 37(8):789–797.

Maus, M.
1935 [1973]Techniques of the Body. Economy and Society. 2(1):70–88.

McCauley, Ann
1984   Healing as a Sign of Power and Status in Bali. Social Science and Medicine 18(2):167–172.

McHugh, Ernestine L.
1989   Concepts of the Person Among the Gurung of Nepal. American Ethnologist 16(1):75–86.

Medawar, P. B.
1967   The Art of the Soluble. London: Methven.

Meillassoux, Claude
1981   Maidens, Meal and Money. New York: Cambridge University Press.

Meyers, Vincent
1977   Toward a Syntheses of Ethnographic and Survey Methods. Human Organization 36(3):244–251.

Moerman, Daniel
1983a General Medical Effectiveness and Human Biology: Placebo Effects in the Treatment of Ulcer Disease. Medical Anthropology Quarterly 14(4):3,13–16.

1983b Physiology and Symbols: The Anthropological Implications of the Placebo Effect. *In* The Anthropology of Medicine: From Culture to Method. L. Romanucci–Ross, D. Moerman and L. Tandreci, eds. New York: Berlin.

Morsy, Sohier
1978   Sex Roles, Power and Illness in an Egyptian Village. American Ethnologist 5:137–150.

Nash, June
1979   We Eat the Mines and the Mines Eat Us: Dependency and Exploitation in Bolivian Tin Mines. New York: Columbia University Press.

Nations, Marilyn
1987   Epidemiological Research on Infectious Disease: Quantitative Rigor or Rigormortis? Insights from Ethnomedicine in Anthropology Epidemiology. *In* Anthropology and Epidemiology, C. R. Janes, R. Stall, and S. M. Gifford, eds. Dordrecht, The Netherlands: Kluwer Press.

Nichter, Mark
1981a Idioms of Distress: Alternatives in the Expression of Psychosocial Distress. Culture, Medicine and Psychiatry 5:379–408.
1981b Negotiation of the Illness Experience: The Influence of Ayurvedic Therapy on the Psychosocial Dimensions of Illness. Culture, Medicine and Psychiatry 5:5–24.
1987a Kyasanur Forest Disease: An Ethnography of a Disease of Development. Medical Anthropology Quarterly 1(4):406–423.
1987b Cultural Dimensions of Hot–Cold and Sema in Sri Lankan Health Culture. Social Science and Medicine 25(4):377–387.
1989   Anthropology and International Health: South Asian Case Studies. Dordrecht, Netherlands: Kluwer Press.
1990b Diarrhea and Dysentery: Using Social Science Research to Improve the Quality of Epidemiological Studies, Interventions and Evaluations of Impact. Reviews of Infectious Diseases, forthcoming.

Nichter, Mark, and Mimi Nichter
1991   Hype and Weight. Medical Anthropology.

Nichter, M. and C. Nordstrom
1989   The Question of Medicine Answering: The Social Relations of Healing in Sri Lanka. Culture, Medicine and Psychiatry 13:367–390.

Nuckolls, Charles
1991   Culture and Causal Thinking: Diagnosis and Prediction in Jalari Culture. Ethos (In Press).

O'Nell, C.
1981   Hostility Management and the Control of Aggression in a Zapotic Community. Aggressive Behavior 7:351–366.

Ong, A.
1983   Global Industries and Malay Peasants in Peninsular Malaysia. *In* Women, Men, and the International Division of Labor. June Nash and Maria Patricia Fernandez–Kelly, eds. Albany, NY: State University of New York Press.
1987   Spirits of Resistance and Capitalist Discipline: Factory Women in Malaysia. Albany: State University of New York Press.

Park, Thomas K.
1985   Pyrrhonism in Anthropological and Historical Research. History in Africa 12:225–252.

Parry, Jonathan
1985   The Brahmanical Tradition and the Technology of the Intellect. *In* Reason and Morality. Joanna Overing, ed. Pp. 200–225. New York: Tavistock Press.
1989   The End of the Body. *In* Fragments for a History of the Human Body. Michael Feher, ed. New York: Zone Publishing.

Parry J. and M. Bloch
1989   Introduction: Money and the Morality of Exchange. *In* Money and the Morality of Exchange. Jonathan Parry and Maurice Block, eds. Cambridge: Cambridge University Press.

Patterson, J.
1987   Dread Diseases: Cancer and Modern American Culture. Cambridge: Harvard University Press.

Pickering, T. G., G. D. James, C. Boddie, et al.
1988   How Common is White Coat Hypertension? JAMA 259:225–228.

Price, Laurie
    1987   Ecuadorian Illness Stories: Cultural Knowledge in Natural Discourse. *In* Cultural Models in
            Language and Thought. D. Holland and N. Quinn, eds. New York: Cambridge University
            Press.
Pugh, Judy F.
    1983   Astrological Counseling in Contemporary India. Culture, Medicine and Psychiatry 7:279–299.
Quinn, Naomi, and Dorothy Holland
    1987   Culture and Cognition. *In* Cultural Models in Language and Thought. D. Holland and N.
            Quinn, eds. Pp. 3–40. Cambridge: Cambridge University Press.
Ratcliffe, John W.
    1983   Notions of Validity in Qualitative Research Methodology. Knowledge: Creation, Diffusion,
            Utilization 5(2):147–167.
Rhodes, Lorna
    1983   Laughter and Suffering: Sinhalese Interpretations of the Use of Ritual Humor. Social Science
            and Medicine 17(14):979–984.
Ricoeur, Paul
    1971   The Model of the Text: Meaningful Action Considered as Text. Social Research 38 (3). Pp.
            528–562.
Robarchek, C.
    1977   Frustration, Aggression and the Non–Violent Semai. American Ethnologist 4:762–79.
Rorty, R.
    1989   Contingency, Irony, and Solidarity. Cambridge: Cambridge University Press.
Roscoe, P.
    1991   The Perils of "Positivism": A Critique of the Image of "Positivism" in Cultural Anthropology.
            Unpublished manuscript.
Riesmann, C. K.
    1990   The Strategic Use of Narrative in the Presentation of Self and Illness: A Research Note. Social
            Science and Medicine 30(11):1195–1200.
Romney, A., S. Weller and W. Batchelder
    1986   Culture as Consensus: A Theory of Culture and Informant Accuracy. American Anthropolo-
            gist 88:313–338.
Rosenhan, D. L.
    1973   On Being Sane in Insane Places. Science 179:250–258.
Rozin, P. and C. Nemeroff
    1990   The Laws of Sympathetic Magic. *In* Cultural Psychology. J. Steyler, R. Shueder and G. Herdt
            eds. Cambridge: Cambridge University Press.
Rubel, Arthur and Hass, Michael
    1990   Ethnomedicine. *In* Thomas Johnson and Carolyn Sargent (eds) Medical Anthropology: Con-
            temporary Theory and Method. New York: Prager Publications.
Rubel, A, C. O'Nell, and R. Collado
    1985   The Folk Illness Called *Susto*. *In* The Culture–Bound Syndromes. Ronald C. Simons and
            Charles C. Hughes, eds. Pp. 333–350. Holland: D. Reidel Publishing Company.
Samuel, Geoffery
    1990   Mind, Body and Culture. Cambridge: Cambridge University Press.
Sangren, P.
    1990a   Post–structuralist and Interpretist Approaches to Subjectivity and Personhood: A Critique.
            Paper presented at the Annual Meeting of the American Anthropological Association, New
            Orleans, Nov. 27.
    1990b   The Vicissitudes of "Power": Implications for the Anthropological Study of Chinese Society.
            Paper presented at the Annual Meeting of the American Anthropological Association, New
            Orleans, Nov. 27.
Schwartz, Hillel
    1986   Never Satisfied: A Cultural History of Diets, Fantasies and Fat. New York: Free Press.
Scott, James
    1985   Weapons of the Weak. Yale University Press: New Haven.

Shadish, W.
　1989　Critical Multiplism: A Research Strategy and its Attendant Tactics. *In* Health Services Research Methodology: A Focus on AIDS. Sechrest, Freeman and Mully, eds. Washington D.C.: NC HSR.
Smith, W.
　1977　The Fiesta System and Economic Change. New York: Columbia University Press.
Sontag, Susan
　1977　Illness as Metaphor. Farrar Straus and Giroux.
Sperber, Dan
　1984　Anthropology and Psychology: Towards an Epidemiology of Representations. MAN (n.s.)20:73–89.
Stein, Howard
　1982　New Darwinism and Survival Through Fitness in Reagan's America. Journal of Psychohistory 19(2):163–187.
　1985　Abstracts and Comment on General Medical Effectiveness and Human Biology: Placebo Effects in the Treatment of Ulcer Disease, by D. E. Moerman. Continuing Education for the Family Physician 20(2):171–172.
Stone, Linda, and J. Gabriel Campbell
　1984　The Use and Misuse of Surveys in International Development: An Experiment from Nepal. Human Organization 43(1):27–37.
Strathern, M.
　1979　The Self in Self–Decoration. Oceania 44(4):241–57.
Susser, Mervyn
　1989　Epidemiology Today: 'A Thought–Tormented World.' International Journal of Epidemiology 18(3):481–488.
Tambiah, Stanley
　1977　The Cosmological and Performative Significance of a Thai Cult of Healing through Meditation. Culture, Medicine and Psychiatry 1:97–132.
Tan, Michael
　1989　Traditional or Transitional Medical Systems? Pharmacotherapy as a Case for Analysis. Social Science and Medicine 29(3):301–307.
Taussig, Michael
　1980　The Devil and Commodity Fetishism in South America. Chapel Hill, North Carolina: University of North Carolina Press.
Taylor, Christopher C.
　1988　The Concept of Flow in Rwandan Popular Medicine. Social Science and Medicine 27(12):1343–1348.
　1990　Condoms and Cosmology: The 'Fractal' Person and Sexual Risk in Rwanda. Social Science and Medicine 31(9):1023–1028.
Toulman, Steven
　1982　The Return to Cosmology. Berkeley: University of California Press.
Tousignant, Michel and Mario Maldonado
　1989　Sadness, Depression and Social Reciprocity in Highland Ecuador. Social Science and Medicine 28(9):899–904.
Trawick, Margaret
　1988　Spirits and Voices in Tamil Songs. American Ethnologist 15(2):193–215.
Trend, M. G.
　1978　On the Reconciliation of Qualitative and Quantitative Analysis: A Case Study. Human Organization 37(4):345–354.
Turshen, M.
　1977　The Political Ecology of Disease. The Reviews of Radical Political Economics 90 (1): 45–60.
Vandernbroucke, J. P.
　1989　On the New Clinical Fashion in Epidemiology. Epidemiology Information 102:191–198.
Weller, Susan
　1984　Consistency and Consensus Among Informants: Disease Concepts in a Rural Mexican Town. American Anthropologist 86:966–975.

White, W. B., P. Schulman, E. McCabe, et al.
   1989   Average Daily Blood Pressure Not Office Blood Pressure, Determines Cardiac Function in Patients with Hypertension. JAMA 261:873–877.
Wikan, Unni
   1989   Managing the Heart to Brighten Face and Soul: Emotions in Balinese Morality and Health Care. American Ethnologist 16(2):294–311.
Wolf, Eric
   1966   Peasants. Englewood Cliffs, New Jersey: Prentice Hall.
Wynne, Anna
   1989   Is It Any Good? The Evaluation of Therapy by Participants in a Clinical Trial. Social Science and Medicine 29(11):1289–1297.
Young, Allan
   1976   Internalizing and Externalizing Medical Belief Systems: An Ethiopian Example. Social Science Medicine 10:147.
   1981   When Rational Men Fall Sick: An Inquiry into Some Assumptions Made by Anthropologists. Culture, Medicine and Psychiatry 5(4):317–335.
   1982   The Anthropologies of Illness and Sickness. Annual Review of Anthropology 11:257–285.